LAND AND THE NATIONAL QUESTION
IN IRELAND
1858–82

D1326296

Paul Bew

Land and the National Question in Ireland 1858-82

Gill and Macmillan

First published 1978 by
Gill and Macmillan Ltd
15/17 Eden Quay
Dublin 1
with associated companies in
London, New York, Delhi, Hong Kong,
Johannesburg, Lagos, Melbourne,
Singapore, Tokyo

0 7171 0820 1

Printed in Great Britain by
Bristol Typesetting Co. Ltd, Barton Manor, St Philips, Bristol

To Dr Mary Bew

Contents

Contents, continued

Contents, continued

Maps

Acknowledgments

My interest in the subject-matter of this book was first aroused by Dr E. R. Norman in his 'Home Rule Debate' special subject lectures at Cambridge in the academic year 1970–71. Dr Norman was also the supervisor of my doctoral thesis on the land war. I would like to thank him for his help and encouragement.

I have gained much from general discussion of the issues of Irish history with Greta Jones, Peter Gibbon and Henry Patterson. Professor Anthony Morris gave some very useful technical advice. I also owe a great deal—as the notes to the text make clear—to the recent advances in Irish historical scholarship and to all those associated with it.

The Northern Ireland Department of Education awarded the major state scholarship which enabled me to carry out my research at Cambridge, and Pembroke College, Cambridge, gave me all the assistance necessary for research of this kind.

For permission to consult materials in their care I am grateful to the Directors of the National Library of Ireland; the State Paper Office, Dublin Castle; the Bodleian Library, Oxford; the Public Record Office, London; the British Museum, London; the Linenhall Library, Belfast; the New York Public Library. I am particularly grateful to the staff at the British Museum newspaper library at Colindale.

I would also like to add my personal thanks to Colm Croker for the care he has taken with the manuscript.

Paul Bew
Belfast
March 1977

Chronology

THE LAND WAR, 1879–82

1877–79
Poor harvests; decreasing demand for
agricultural produce; prices falling

1879

6 or 13 April	Parnell, Devoy and Davitt meet in Dublin to discuss 'New Departure'
20 April	Tenant demonstration at Irishtown, Co. Mayo
1 June	Second meeting of Parnell, Devoy and Davitt
8 June	Parnell addresses meeting at Westport
14 August	Richmond Commission appointed
16 August	National Land League of Mayo founded at Castlebar
21 October	Irish National Land League founded, with Parnell as president
19 November	Davitt, Daly, Killen and Brennan prosecuted (proceedings dropped, March 1880)

1880

January–March	Parnell and Dillon on tour in America
11 March	Parnell founds Irish National Land League of the United States
March–April	General election: Gladstone and Liberals in power
29 April	National conference on the land question
30 April	Forster appointed Chief Secretary
17 May	Parnell elected chairman of the Irish Parliamentary Party
29 July	Bessborough Commission appointed
4 August	Compensation for Disturbance (Ireland) Bill defeated in House of Lords
19 September	Parnell advocates policy of social ostracism in speech at Ennis
September–November	The Captain Boycott affair
2 November	Parnell and leaders of Land League prosecuted (jury fails to agree, 25 January 1881)

1881

4 January	Report of Bessborough Commission
14 January	Preliminary report of Richmond Commission
31 January	Ladies' Land League founded
2 March	Protection of Person and Property (Ireland) Act
21 March	Peace Preservation (Ireland) Act
22 August	Land Law (Ireland) Act, with provision for fair rent, fixity of tenure and free sale, and for the establishment of the Land Commission
15–18 September	National convention of Land League: decision to assess the act by test cases
13 October	Parnell arrested
18 October	'No rent' manifesto issued by Parnell and other imprisoned leaders
20 October	Land League suppressed
16 December	First Special Resident Magistrates appointed

1882

2 May	The 'Kilmainham Treaty': Parnell and other leaders released
2 May	Forster resigns
6 May	The Phoenix Park murders
12 July	Prevention of Crime (Ireland) Act
18 August	Arrears of Rent (Ireland) Act
17 October	Irish National League founded

Preface

The broad outlines of 'the Irish question' have been clearly established. Historically, the Irish experience has been of foreign conquest, poverty and oppression. The most obvious and significant feature of social life was the existence of a mainly Protestant landlord class extracting rent from a mainly Catholic peasantry. In the second half of the nineteenth century Ireland was the scene of intense conflict between these two groups and their supporters.

Before the 1850s there had been a number of protest movements. These organisations, with their relatively narrow and limited objectives of middle-class leaders, stopped short of rejecting any accommodation with Britain. The structure, policy and leadership of these earlier protest movements was radically challenged by the founding, in 1858, of the Irish Republican Brotherhood. The leaders of the IRB, otherwise known as the 'Fenians' (a name which properly belongs to the American wing of the movement), overtly rejected anything short of the establishment by force of arms of an independent Irish republic. On social policy they developed a radical rhetoric. The Fenian press constantly emphasised the IRB's special links with urban artisans and mechanics, rural smaller peasantry and agricultural labourers. Not only did they divide 'the people' along the lines of opposition between Protestant landlord and Catholic tenant; but also they emphasised the divisions between the urban and rural Catholic bourgeoisie (particularly the large graziers) and the popular democratic base of the Irish revolution. The Fenian movement, therefore, had to concern itself with a relationship that in this century has played a particularly important role in world history—the connection between national and social liberation. The efforts of the Fenian movement to grapple with this problem are presented in this book.

Without reference to the ideas of agrarian justice that developed in Ireland after the Great Famine, the characteristic views of the Fenian movement are inexplicable. This book's first chapter is concerned to understand what was meant by 'tenant right'. The emphasis of the peasantry's case against landlordism changed over a period. It cannot be treated as the manifestation of a single theme. The spectrum of notions that made up the Irish peasantry's case cannot be reduced to a unitary principle, whether it be insecurity of tenure or a sense of racial dispossession.

Spokesmen for the peasantry devised and broadcast a social criticism that was concerned with the whole pattern of post-famine Irish development. There was widely based hostility to the tendency towards consolidation and the increased emphasis on pasture as opposed to tillage. This transition to pasture was resisted on the grounds that it encouraged emigration and was not an economic success. These claims, supported by a mixture of justificatory notions, constituted the tenantry's moral case against consolidation. These ideas included resentment against the historical fact of confiscation; tenants' lack of security of tenure; the insufficient rewards for tenants whose efforts had enhanced—indeed, largely created—the land's value; opposition to absentee landlords; and frustration at the lack of any prospect of alternative employment for the Irish peasant in Ireland. Not singularly in isolation, but together, these elements constitute the world-view or ideology of radical Irish agrarian agitation in the late nineteenth century.

The landlords in turn replied. For them the transition to pasture, even if it meant increasing emigration and consolidation, made economic common sense. The role of Irish agriculture was to supply the British market, regardless of broader social and national considerations. The emigrant boat to America offered more hope than the tiny bog farm in Connaught. The landlords also participated in the debate on the standard of living in the late nineteenth century. They argued that a comparison of rent levels and prices for agricultural produce revealed that farmers in post-famine Ireland had enjoyed a substantial rise in their standard of living. The landlords claimed also that they had made a much more substantial contribution to investment in Irish agriculture than was generally recognised. The validity of these claims and counterclaims is assessed in Chapter 1. What is revealed beyond question, however, is that an acute division of interests existed in the countryside.

It is within the context of this division of interests that various movements which challenged landlord power grew up in Ireland. There was the legal Tenant League of the 1850s and the agrarian terrorism of the Ribbon societies. The IRB presented itself as the one organisation capable of transcending the limitations of these prior tendencies. It attempted to mobilise the resentment felt in Ireland about what was seen as the country's deplorable social condition behind the policy of armed insurrection. For this reason 1858, the date of the foundation of the Irish Republican Brotherhood, has been chosen as the starting-date for this study.

The object of this work is to analyse the nature of the land war and its bearing on the national struggle in Ireland from 1858, when the Irish Republican Brotherhood was founded, to 1882, when the 'Kilmainham Treaty' signalled the end of the Land League crisis. The relationship of the social question and independence question in this period was a complex one which changed radically. This book is not therefore a chronological history of Ireland in the period.

The IRB's attempt at insurrection in 1867 failed. Despite severe divisions, the movement's members continued to play a significant role in Irish political life. In certain areas where economic and social pressures were particularly strong they made a commitment to the less ambitious practice—as compared with armed insurrection —of agrarian struggle against landlords. Certain others began to take a more sympathetic attitude to the constitutional politics of the Home Rule movement which was led in the 1870s by Isaac Butt. Finally, after many setbacks in that decade, and with Irish-Americans taking the lead, the majority of the Fenians formally reorientated their position. They moved cautiously towards an alliance with the young Charles Stewart Parnell, who had attracted their favourable attention by his displays of militancy in the British parliament.

This new-found spirit of co-operation between a majority of the revolutionaries and at least some of the constitutionalists was a marked feature of the land war which broke out in 1879. The basis of this alliance is fully discussed in Chapter 3. The land war was a stormy period, and it has been difficult for historians to discover the truth of all the claims made by participants. What were the precise objectives of the neo-Fenian leadership who were so important in the Land League? What, on the other hand, were Parnell's precise objectives? What did he have in common with the Fenians, and where did they part company? These questions receive close attention in Chapter 3. The key to this inquiry is to examine the relationship between the land question and the national question as it existed in 1879–82 and to unravel the various interpretations of the different groups. This enterprise produces some unexpected results.

For three years Ireland was shaken by a tremendous social crisis. Tenants refused to pay rents at the old levels. The landlords attempted by every possible means to obtain the rent they were legally due; the tenants resisted intransigently. In its account of the land war this book is concerned to demonstrate the ways in which that struggle was carried on. At the time, both parties to the dispute actively promoted their own version of the events. Land League spokesmen emphasised the solidarity of the people which expressed itself in such well-known practices as the boycott of 'land-grabbers' (and of the unlet land of evicted tenants) and mass resistance to process-servers. Spokesmen for the landlords emphasised violence and intimidation both as directed against themselves and as the means of maintaining an artificial unity among their opponents. Both these accounts have passed into modern history books. They point to two significant aspects of the land war: the degree of popular unity attained at the time by the Irish peasantry; and the part played by violence in helping to preserve that unity. Some historians have felt that to understand the land war it is sufficient to reconcile these two accounts to find the correct 'balance'. The argument of this book is very different. The *dominant* forms of class struggle were different varieties of highly legalistic strategies: the tenants remained within the law and used every possible legal loophole to resist the landlord's claims. This book presents not only a more realistic (if less 'dramatic') account of the land war, but also emphasises the existence of a considerable degree of peasant disunity within the overall anti-landlord unity of the Land League framework.

The core of this book is concerned with the process of conflict that marked Ireland in the period 1879–82 and, of course, with the efforts made by the British government to deal with the situation. In the spring of 1882 the 'Kilmainham Treaty' arrangement between Parnell and Gladstone marked the end of a struggle that had left both sides temporarily exhausted. The high hopes for political and social revolution of some of the Land League's founders had not been achieved.

In an acute passage James Connolly later summed up both the Land League's success and failure from the radical nationalist point of view:

> We believe profoundly that a close study of the events of that time would immensely benefit the militant Socialists of all countries. It would help to demonstrate how the union of the forces of social discontent with the forces of political agitation converted the latter from a mere sterile parliamentarianism, impotent for good, into a virile force transforming the whole social system, and bringing a political revolution within the grasp of the agitators.[1]

But Connolly sadly concluded that the Land League had left untouched the social misery of the 'subject class' in Ireland.

Nevertheless, the Irish scene had changed. In 1860 the tendency to amend the land law of Ireland in favour of the landlord culminated in the Land Act of 1860 (Deasy's Act), which proceeded on the assumption that land is the exclusive property of the landlord[*] and that the tenant's interest is nothing more than that of a person who has agreed to pay a certain remuneration for the use of the soil for a limited period. The assumptions of Irish land law were shortly to change radically. The Land Acts between 1870 and 1903 involved a transfer of the greater part of Ireland from the landlord to the peasant class. This was in effect an agrarian revolution. The crucial moment in this process was the Land League struggle of 1879–82. The Land League was a genuinely novel political form. It combined three elements: open agrarian agitation, parliamentary action, and revolutionary conspiracy. This mass movement compelled a reluctant British government to produce a far-reaching measure of land reform. It transformed the Irish political scene by placing at the very forefront a new variety of militant constitutional nationalism—'Parnellism'. It weakened Britain's moral hold on Ireland. In conjunction with other very important factors, it even played a role in the remodelling of British Liberal and Conservative politics in the 1880s. It is hoped that the present study will be of value in enabling the roots of these developments to be more clearly understood.

1

From the Famine to the Land War

> Within the last twenty-two years under the benevolent
> English government and the wise statesmanship of Lord
> Beaconsfield, Mr Lowther and the rest of those who
> preceded them . . . Scotland has increased her livestock
> by about 900,000 head, and remember that we are
> always told that though Ireland is not rich in men and
> crops, she is rich in cattle. But I would rather see the
> country moderately rich in men and women and happy
> families than in any number of cattle. But we are not
> even rich in cattle. We have gained no compensation
> for the expatriation of three millions of our people
> beyond the seas. . . . Besides there has been a decrease
> in the number of sheep in our country. But we will
> beat England in resources again.
>
> MITCHELL HENRY, speech at Ballinasloe
> (*Western News*, 29 Nov. 1879)

1. *Prologue*

Writing in 1856 in the *Oxford Essays* of that year, William
O'Connor Morris was inclined to take an optimistic view of the
Irish situation.[1] The years 1845–51 had taken the lives through
hunger and disease of at least 800,000 people; in particular, the
small farmers and labourers were decimated, and a further one
million had emigrated.[2] But five years later the situation seemed
to be greatly improved. The immediate situation of the post-famine
adjustment seemed to justify a certain satisfaction. Bank deposits,
a useful indicator of agrarian income, rose from £8 million in 1845
to £16 million in 1859.[3] Cattle numbers increased steadily between
1847 and 1859. Even tillage decreased only by 4 per cent in the
1851–59 period.[4]

But the 'bright hopes' which Morris held 'in common with most
other persons'[5] were to be disappointed. An immediate cause of
this disappointment was the depression of 1859–63, when both
tillage and livestock declined together. One product of this depression was a vigorous debate about the nature and success of the
post-famine adjustment in Irish agriculture. It involved many sides
of Irish opinion, including, on the one hand, the statistician Dr W.
Neilson Hancock and, on the other, the Irish Republican Brotherhood. Hancock acknowledged the sharpness of the 1859–63 depression, 'resulting from inclement seasons',[6] but he laid great emphasis

upon the advances made before 1859.[7] He expressed basic confidence about the post-famine adjustment: the years 1855–59 had seen 'a remarkable increase in the prosperity of the country',[8] and he was critical of his opponents' use of statistics, for example on crop yields.[9] The IRB, on the other hand, took a sharply pessimistic view of the whole pattern of post-famine development and identified itself with Hancock's critics in the Statistical Society. In their view the problem was not a mere temporary setback: it resulted from the 'flocks and herds' doctrine, which, despite all emigration, constantly aggravated the problem of rural unemployment.[10] The economic and social situation called the relationship with Britain into question. Thus from the very beginning of this debate it was possible to deduce its fundamental political implications.

In order to gain a deeper understanding of this problem it is necessary to turn first of all to an examination of post-famine trends in Irish agriculture and then to the contrasting views held by the spokesmen of the landlord and tenant classes about these trends.

2. *Patterns of Adjustment: The Distinctiveness of the West*
The period from the famine to the outbreak of the land war was characterised in the greater part of Ireland by a transition from tillage to pasture[11] combined with a steady consolidation of holdings[12] and a considerable fall in population. Between 1841 and 1871 the total number of cattle in Ireland grew from 1·8 million to 4·0 million, while the population fell from 8·2 million to 5·4 million, so that the ratio of cattle to people rose from 22 per 100 to 74 per 100 in the course of thirty years.[13] The Catholic Church, which greatly increased its influence in the later half of the century— attendance figures rose from a probable 40 per cent before the famine to 90 per cent in the 1890s[14]—fully reinforced the value system of this late-marrying rural society.[15]

The landlords and their allies saw this process as the purest rationality—the more obvious effect of the rise in cattle prices— and often forced farmers to keep the land for grazing purposes only. Irish banks tended to share this assumption. James Balfe, the nationalist publicist, alleged, in fact, that they made it a stringent rule in all their agreements with grazing farmers when lending them money on the collateral security of their leases, that they kept the land for cattle-fattening only, regardless of whether it paid them or not.[16] Of course, grazing was often a profitable activity in this period. But it was also, according to a widespread prejudice, a 'gentleman's life' which required little real agricultural craft, merely an ability to take advantage of a favourable rise in the price of livestock. The comment of the *Irish Farmer's Gazette*'s editor is typical:

> He [the grazier] is not much bothered during summer with his occupation, his herd taking all the trouble; and, as there is nothing which demands his attention during the winter, he has plenty of time at command for hunting and other amusements. These are considerations which have a certain amount of weight with some people.[17]

In a lengthy study in 1872 he cited Spenser, Arthur Young and Robert Thompson, author of the *Survey of Meath,* in support of this view.[18]

The only real opposition to these general trends was in the province of Connaught, South Kerry and the west coast of Co. Donegal.

Connaught appeared to be integrated with the rest of the country through its role in the Irish agricultural division of labour. The breeding, rearing and fattening of cattle was divided fairly systematically among the eastern, western and southern provinces. Munster contributed the main proportion of the store cattle, though fattening was also carried out in the rich grazing lands of Limerick and Tipperary; Connaught reared a large share of the cattle, while Leinster concentrated mainly on fattening the animals—cattle and sheep—from both provinces. But the demographic trends of Connaught were markedly different from those of most of Leinster and Munster. In the immediate post-famine decades the population fell more sharply in the eastern and midland counties than in the poorer western ones. In the West the rate of natural increase of population was more rapid than in the rest of the country. On the other hand, although the western counties were poorer, emigration from them was no greater than from the more eastern counties.[19] Connaught had been devastated by the famine more than any other part of Ireland. Holdings in the 1–5 acre category fell from 100,254 in 1841 to 18,463 in 1851.[20] After 1852, however, the situation stabilised. It is not too much to speak of a survival of the pre-famine economy—with all its implications for potato-based, early-marrying peasantry merely surviving on minute holdings—in the West. Why did such social conditions continue to survive?

It is necessary to turn to Allan Pollock, a Scottish landlord based in Co. Galway,[21] for the beginnings of an analysis. Pollock explained to Sir George Campbell, chief commissioner of the central provinces of India, 'that we had a peculiarly favourable opportunity [of consolidation] during the years subsequent to the famine, but that he would not dream of attempting the same thing again. It would now be totally impossible to get rid of the small tenants.'[22] The account of Pollock's efforts to clear part of his estate in 1854–57, when he faced pressure exercised through direct violence (the burning of his house), clerical denunciation, resistance in the law courts, and even became the subject of a parliamentary debate, illustrates the point.[23] The smallholders of the West after the immediate famine crisis kept a firm grip on their holdings—'they seem to cling with unreasoning fatuity to so narrow a destiny',[24] as one landlord spokesman, James Frost, saw it. In some areas the number of holdings of under fifteen acres actually increased.[25] Although other trends have been detected,[26] this was nevertheless a very significant fact.

From the small farmers' point of view the situation was acceptable largely because of a heavy reliance on the potato sector. East Galway was the only part of Connaught with a potato share of tillage as low as 35 per cent; even 35 per cent was well above East Ulster and all of Leinster and the eastern third of Munster.[27] Seasonal migration to sell labour power at the English harvest (involving of necessity 17·3 per cent Mayo males)[28] and the cash loyalty of children who had emigrated also helped.

There was also a somewhat more ambiguous factor. Shopkeepers, particularly after the increased security given to the tenantry by the good seasons which followed the 1870 Land Act, allowed substantial credit. A contemporary observer noted that 'Gombeen men have multiplied. A wholesale stationer informs me that he prints the forms and makes up and sells five times the number of bill books he did ten years ago.'[29] At the very most, the action of the shopkeepers could only conceal or stave off a crisis—often, of course, they aggravated it. The preliminary report of the Richmond Commission, when it eventually appeared in January 1881, contained some useful information on this topic gathered by the assistant commissioners, Thomas Baldwin and C. Robertson. One gombeen man who showed his books to Baldwin and Robertson was charging 43 per cent on his advances, which often consisted of goods supplied from his own shop and at his own prices.[30] The Cork butter market charged the small farmers of South Kerry anything from 6 to 20 per cent interest.[31] The problem was outlined before the Richmond Commission by C. H. Hemphill, QC:

Q. (THE PRESIDENT) The butter merchant combines the two functions of butter merchant and money lender?
A. He does; and I found that to be the case especially in Kenmare. The course seems to have been to send the butter to Cork

to these merchants. The farmer might want money to pay his little debts, or to pay his landlord and he used to give a bill to the butter merchant, at three months, say, which was constantly renewed; and the butter merchant used to charge a discount of 10% upon that. Besides which the farmer was completely in the power of the butter merchant as to the price of the butter.[32]

It is no surprise to find that the stronger farmers of North Kerry responded to this situation by setting up a butter market in Listowel; in that way, of course, the farmers of this district had the advantage of being able themselves to bring the butter into the market.[33] But for the smaller farmers there was often no way to avoid the trap of rural usury.[34]

A further factor was the complicity of many of the landlords in the Western situation, perhaps to a greater extent than has been generally realised. The land in the West was often poor and unsuited for grazing, and tenants were prepared to work or reclaim land which tenants in other parts of the country with higher expectations might have ignored. Finally, the relevant comparison for many landlords must have been the level of rent which it was possible to extract from the small tenant as opposed to the large-scale capitalist farmer.

The evidence rather surprisingly suggests that the small farmer ? held his land at a higher rental per acre of good land than the capitalist farmer. The president of the Richmond Commission publicly expressed his surprise when he encountered a case where a Scottish capitalist farmer paid substantially less per acre than the poor cottiers he had replaced—25 to 30 per cent less.[35] Several witnesses before the Bessborough Commission in 1881 indicated that the average rent on smallholdings, many of them consisting partly of bog and unreclaimed land, was in the region of £1 per acre in Mayo and Donegal.[36] Yet a tenant of Lord Lucan's, Simson, a substantial Scottish farmer of Cloonagashel and Gallowshill, took over 2,200 prime acres at £1 an acre after a clearance of 300 families in the famine years and held the land at this rate until 1880.[37]

Simson employed a hundred labourers, and although only some thirty-five or forty were labourers in the 'English' sense (that is, completely separated from the land), the others—sons of nearby small farmers—were always at his command, and there can be no doubt about the extensive and professional scale of operation.[38] Yet in 1880 even Simson came to the conclusion that he could no longer pay his rent, and he successfully fought a legal battle against

Lord Lucan for substantial compensation for improvements.[39] It is no surprise therefore to find James Daly, the editor of the *Connaught Telegraph* and a local tenant leader, concluding:

> If Mr Simson, a first-class farmer of undoubted ability, as an agricultural and stock manager with ample capital and the most modern and most improved machinery at his disposal cannot, or to put it in a milder sense is afraid to, or has refused to farm at £1 per acre 2,200 acres of the primest lands for agricultural purposes in Mayo, how is it that other landlords will have the assurance to charge considerably over, in many instances double, treble, the amount per acre for their lands which are no better than snipe-walks in comparison to the lands which are the subject of this dispute?[40]

Despite the fact that certain landlords (for example, and for rather different reasons, Lord Leitrim and Lord Lucan) intensely disliked the situation, there was a tacit acceptance of it by many members of the landlord class. This was so even though in some cases (as in Sir Roger Palmer's large Mayo estate) they had to pay the whole —as opposed to half—the poor rate of tenants valued at under £4 per annum.[41] The alternative was to allow substantial tenants, who had a strong bargaining position because of their relative scarcity, to hold the best land at a cheap rate.

For a complex of reasons, then, the West tended to be less affected by the full operation of some major trends in post-famine Irish agriculture. In this context Michael Davitt offered a reconstruction of the 'untutored view of the Celtic cottier and tenant of Mayo'. The county of Mayo had suffered more from the manifold evils of the landlord system than any other Irish county. It had lost more of its population, had experienced more 'clearances', possessed a greater number of people on the borderline of starvation, and contained more paupers in proportion to the population. In a period of thirty years its inhabited dwellings had decreased by over 25,000, and yet there had been no corresponding improvement in the conditions of the enormously reduced numbers of landworkers who remained. The explanation was that cattle and not labour were placed on the lands from which the cultivators had been evicted since 1849, while the diminished population were crowded in upon the poorer soils of the county. This, however, was only half the evil. The reclaimed bog-land, or mountain-side onto which the people who could not emigrate were compelled to migrate was, according to Davitt, rack-rented in defiance of all economic or equitable principles. Without the labour which alone reclaimed such soil and kept it in a state of cultivation, it could not produce

Principal Landowners in Ireland, 1880

Source: F. Dun, *Landlords and Tenants in Ireland* (1881)

a shilling of rent per acre. Rent for such land was regarded as sheer robbery sanctioned by law. Davitt concluded: 'Every movement against landlordism found its readiest recruits in the part of Ireland that of her thirty-two counties had perhaps the bitterest experience of . . . wrongs and privations.'[42]

3. *Landlord and Tenant Spokesmen: A Conflict of Analysis*

While there was general agreement about the nature of developments in post-famine Irish agriculture, landlord and tenant spokesmen had very different responses to its dominant tendencies: transition to pasture, consolidation, high emigration, and low rate of population increase. The landlords embraced one particular tradition in political economy. Market forces, they argued, should in no way be tampered with and in the fullness of time Ireland would experience a landlordist transition to a large-scale capitalist agricultural system. Nassau Senior allowed expression to this view in a classic formulation:

> No friend of Ireland can wish the war to be prolonged [between the landlords and tenants], still less that it should end by the victory of the tenants. The sooner it is over, the sooner Ireland becomes a grazing population with the comparatively thin population a grazing country requires the better for all classes.[43]

The market—in deciding the primacy of pasture or fixing the rent for land—was the supreme arbiter. The most articulate spokesmen of the class espoused this view and, combining it with a vulgar social Darwinism, looked to emigration as the only remedy for the ills of the small farmers. Naturally many, probably the majority, of landlords baulked at the large-scale depopulation required to make Ireland a land of capitalist agriculture and merely wanted to collect their rents in peace. The recommendation of the 'three Fs' (fair rent, fixity of tenure and free sale) by the Bessborough Commission in 1881 was widely reckoned to have transformed the Irish landlords into mere rent-chargers, but the report itself claimed that it was in the majority of cases simply suggesting a legal recognition of an established social reality. The implication must be that the Irish landlord was frequently a mere rent-charger long before the 1881 Land Act.

From the point of view of the English model of agriculture, such men were acquiescent in a criminally inefficient system. From the point of view of the Irish model of a peasant proprietary, they were socially useless and parasitic. Hence the importance of a minority of combative landlordist spokesmen, men like Bence Jones, G. F. Trench, King-Harman, Pollock and Lord Cloncurry.

For it was these men who fought the ideological battle on behalf of Irish landlordism. Bence Jones's essays collected in his *The Life's Work in Ireland of a Landlord who Tried to Do his Duty* (1880) were a particularly important contribution in this respect. But the review of one of these essays contained in a *Freeman's Journal* editorial is of particular relevance:

> Admitting, however, the truth of Mr Bence Jones' account of his own estate, we must feel that he does not look outside it when he says the only progress in farming in Ireland is due to the example set by landlords and Scotch bailiffs. Is he aware that in every part of Ireland there are numerous and extensive districts where neither landlord, agent nor bailiff (in the sense of agriculturist) are ever seen, except for the purposes of rent collection?[44]

It became an apparent battle between those who believed (citing rainfall, temperature and prices) that Ireland was fit only for large pastoral farms and those who held what the *Freeman's Journal* itself called—in a comment on Lord Cloncurry's position—'teleological' views, holding that the object of a country was to support the population thereon in comfort and happiness and not simply to provide sustenance for the shipbuilders of the Clyde and the miners of Lancashire. Was the soil of Ireland for supporting the largest number in a sufficiency of comfort, or was it to provide a very much smaller number with a great and unnecessary abundance?[45]

It is important to note that the advocates of the tenantry's case argued that the typical landlord policy implied not only a smaller population and larger exports but also a fall in the gross produce of the soil. Not only was tillage on the retreat, but the transition to pasture had been marked by what was to many an unimpressive rise, or even a fall, in livestock numbers.[46] This seemed to echo Marx's claim in *Capital* (1867):

> The depopulation has thrown much of the land out of the culti-vation, has greatly diminished the produce of the soil and, in spite of the greater area devoted to cattle-breeding, has brought about in some of its branches an absolute diminution, in others an advance scarcely worthy of mention and constantly interrupted by retrogressions.[47]

Nationalists were keen to attack the effects of this process. Parnell argued that the absence of draining, fertilisation and the laying down of new grass seeds was a product of the grazier's speculative mentality which had rendered much of the grazing land unfit.[48] He cited the *Gardener's Chronicle* as stating that 4 million acres of Irish pasture was unfit for the purpose.[49] John Callanan, the editor of the *Western News*, commented on the grazing region near Ballinasloe that 'Half the land is covered with rushes. Whenever rushes are seen they are a clear indication that drainage is required.' But the graziers were unwilling to lay out any money for drainage or to give employment to labourers.[50] In this context it may be worth noting that it had long been an axiom of the advocates of fixity of tenure that the Irish farmers had hesitated to sink their capital in the land, merely spreading it on the land (in the form of cattle) and thus avoiding the risk of loss of investment.[51]

There was a general insistence on the hard economic basis of this critique. 'To put it as plain as possible,' said Andrew Kettle, secretary of the Central Tenants' Defence Association, 'if an acre of land under the exclusive pasture system will make so much meat, I believe, with the exception of a limited number of acres in Ireland particularly adapted for pasture, that more meat could be raised under the same quantity of land under a good mixed system.'[52] In a work published in 1870 John Murphy argued that there was a particularly good case for the extension of root crops on the basis of 1860s figures: 'Here we have a decrease of 66,388 acres in the area under root crops since 1851; and yet, by turnip culture our production of meat in many districts might be almost doubled.'[53] 'I have today looked over the official returns of Ireland for some years past,' wrote James Balfe, 'and I find that . . . one million acres of middling good wheat at twelve barrels to the acre would be worth twelve million pounds . . . just as much as the whole twelve million acres of grassland producing cattle, sheep and butter.'[54] While Balfe's passion for wheat would have been regarded as wrongheaded by many nationalists, there was a widespread feeling that the transition to pasture had been less than a success.

The view that the 'pure grazing system' had failed even within its own terms was shared not only by the nationalists (although the nationalists were not surprisingly rather 'blind' to the existence of allies)[55] but by politically neutral and even Unionist commentators. The *Times* correspondents had analysed the crisis in 1861, 1870 and early 1880 in this spirit. The *Times* correspondent John Algernon Clarke wrote in 1861: 'The lighter soils embracing . . . two-thirds of the area of cultivation, would produce more meat and store animals, besides the corn, dairy produce and wool, if farmed as a mixture of grass and tillage instead of being purely grazed.' He added: 'The addition of four million acres to the labour-needing area would provide work for about 660,000 men, representing in terms of numbers probably two and a half million inhabitants.'[56] In 1870 O'Connor Morris recanted his earlier optimism, admitting that he had 'been rather under the impression that the changes effected since 1846–48 were greater than they actually were, that the progress of the nation had been more decisive and the process of consolidation had been attended with better economic results, that the small farm system was not so deep-rooted in the social frame of the country as it now is.'[57] The English Liberal MP Lyon Playfair supported this general point in his paper 'On the Declining Production of Human Food in Ireland'.[58]

Professor Baldwin, the Richmond Commission's assistant commissioner and chief inspector of the government agricultural schools and model farms in Ireland, was also a strong critic of the evolution of the grazing system. In his report for the Richmond Commission the grasslands were described as being in a still worse condition than the tillage lands, not producing one-third of the amount of nutritious herbage they could have done if properly drained and placed in a system of rotation tillage before being laid down to grass.[59] He was an advocate of a 'good mixed system'[60] and a system of internal migration. Perhaps most significantly, the strongly anti-Parnellite group of writers connected with the *Irish Farmer's Gazette* supported this analysis with great vigour in almost every issue. The classic exposition of their case by R. O. Pringle, the editor of the *Irish Farmer's Gazette,* appeared in the *Journal of the Royal Agricultural Society of England* in 1872 in an article entitled 'A Review of Irish Agriculture'.[61] Like John Murphy, he drew strong attention to the lack of attention devoted to cattle-feeding crops. The decrease in the amount of root food produced in Ireland from 1866 to 1870, he argued, represented the loss of the winter keep of 577,370 head of cattle (approximately one-seventh of the total) as compared with the years 1851–55.[62] Pringle outlined the essentials of this position in a clear passage:

> We have seen that the farmers whose holdings do not exceed 50 acres in extent are possessed of stock at over £17½ millions sterling. In the case of the larger class of landholders, the value of their livestock is very little over 18 millions sterling, although the extent of their possession is more than 8¾ millions of acres irrespective of bog and waste against a little over 7 million acres held by the smaller class of occupants. Hence it is evident that the occupation of large holdings, when such are kept chiefly or wholly as grazing land, is not a system calculated to develop the food-producing resources of the country, inasmuch as it produces or maintains a smaller proportion of stock than we find maintained where cultivation, even though in many respects defective, is the predominating feature.[63]

But there was a difference of emphasis between the nationalist and non-nationalist commentators. Support for the mixed system, in Pringle's view, did not rule out acceptance of the fact that in many areas of Ireland emigration and consolidation were the only answers. Baldwin, in particular, believed that subdivision and lawlessness in the West went hand in hand. On the other hand, although the 'realities' were privately accepted, no nationalist politician in the period could afford to advocate publicly a scheme of consolidation coupled with emigration for the West. It would have appeared to take the pressure off the landlords.

The fact that the two groups had differing priorities was illustrated clearly by the Simson case of 1880. It was a symbol to both the *Irish Farmer's Gazette* and the nationalists. Simson's system of mixed tillage farming—800 of his 2,200 acres were under tillage— was applauded by Pringle in the technical journal of farming at some length.[64] The economists of the *Irish Farmer's Gazette* were undoubtedly annoyed that Lord Lucan had failed to offer Simson better terms.[65] But ultimately what they regretted was the loss of a competent and inspiring example of farming from the Irish countryside. The nationalists drew a more dramatic lesson. James Daly, the editor of the *Connaught Telegraph*, saw the collapse of Simson as a sign that foreign competition would bring about a redistribution of the large farms of Ireland among the middle and small farmers of Ireland. He requested Lord Lucan to divide his estate into twenty-five- and fifty-acre residential holdings, implying that he could thereby increase his rental by 25 per cent as against that paid by Simson.[66]

Daly's demand recalled the advice of Matthew Harris to the Shaw Lefevre Committee during a discussion of the failure of large tillage farms in the West. In his view there was a stark choice between a system of small tillage and large grass farms.[67] The *Irish Farmer's Gazette* cadre did not support Daly's demands. For political reasons they were not prepared to support the Western agrarian militants' call for 'redistribution' of the land. They also felt that there was a point at which a justifiable desire to see a better mixed system in Irish agriculture shaded off into obscurantist dreams—which had their roots in nationalist social aspirations —of a return to the high population and supposedly sturdy peasant 'community' of pre-famine Ireland.[68] To many outside its ranks it seemed that the Land League's project was to have Ireland dominated by a 'petite culture'[69] rather than a system of scientific farming.

4. *The Moral Critique*

It was very obviously the case that in the background to the economic and social views of the Land League leaders there lay nationalist value-judgments. The massive emigration had after all brought very little tangible advantage. It was Karl Marx who noted that 'The production of relative surplus population has more than kept pace with the absolute depopulation.'[70] Marx also pointed out that the English attitude implied that Ireland's 'true destiny' was to be an English sheep-walk and cattle pasture;[71] and this was something that even the most moderate nationalists were determined to oppose. For such men it was *a priori* good that depopulation be prevented by increasing the demand for labour; that tradesmen and not simply the grazier and the landlord should benefit from agricultural production; that the grazing system, which was not farming in the proper sense, should be ended; and that farms in general should be medium-sized. The argument was, as Andrew Kettle phrased it monotonously before the Richmond Commission, explicitly from 'a state point of view . . . national point of view . . . public point of view . . . community point of view'.[72]

These nationalist value-judgments were buttressed, it must be added, by a series of assumptions concerning the moral superiority of the Irish tenantry's case. Before the first of the great Irish Land Acts—that of 1870—it was widely claimed that the Irish tenantry lacked security of tenure. In the strong sense the argument about insecurity of tenure is clearly not viable. It is impossible to argue that either eviction or rent-raising was of such a level as to prevent widespread economic progress. It is more reasonable to state that there were sufficient cases of hardship as to create a significant degree of peasant discontent. Dr Brodie, the Poor Law inspector, in a fairly typical report of this date, claimed there were enough cases of loss of value of improvements to cause discontent.[73] As O'Connor Morris shrewdly noted, cases where landlords precipitately raised rents on improvements were rare— yet so were the peasant outrages which struck terror into the hearts of thousands and influenced the administration of hundreds of estates. Why did not the same principle apply to landlord transgressions?[74] The insecurity of tenure argument enjoyed a particular prominence in 1870—a fact which was due both to the limited nature of the legislative possibilities and the agrarian movement of the time. While in this specific form it has a certain credibility— the campaign about it was really a means of focusing critically on an image of the landlord's potential power[75]—it should not be thought to constitute the sole basis of the Irish peasantry's argument. Eleven years later Parnell omitted it altogether from his exposition of the *differentia specifica* of the Irish land question in Birmingham in April 1881. These were, he argued, firstly, the historical fact of confiscation which had separated the majority of the Irish people from ownership of the soil; secondly, most of the present value of the land had been created by the tenants; thirdly, large numbers of Irish landlords were absentees; fourthly, there was an absence of alternative industries.[76]

The history of the confiscations was undeniably a theme of Land League orators—although it was very much subordinate to the themes of local grievance and proofs of the need for rent reduction. It was perhaps significant that the Mayo activist John Walsh (not to be confused with the better-known Land Leaguer Joseph B. Walsh) was speaking in Co. Tipperary—where he probably lacked local knowledge—when he resorted to historical arguments:

> What right had my lord this or that to come to them and to demand rent? Let them only ask by what title did he hold the land? They would find that in the majority of cases they held from a title under Oliver Cromwell (*groans*) or some other military title. Did they believe that any man who held over a title from Oliver Cromwell, who came to the country and butchered their fathers and mothers because they were Irish—did they believe that any man holding land by that title had a just title to the land?[77]

Walsh went on to give his theme of historical confiscation an interesting additional slant:

> Somebody had spoken that day of communists. He would ask who were the real communists—the Land League or the landlords? The latter took property which did not belong to them, which was confiscated under Oliver Cromwell, Queen Bess and the broken treaty of Limerick (*cheers*).

But it is worth noting that the Land League did not exempt from its campaigns those landlords whose claims to ownership did not originate with the conquest of the sixteenth and seventeenth centuries. J. S. Mill's view that before the conquest the Irish people knew nothing of absolute property in land—the chieftain being little more than the 'managing member'[78] of the association—was widely accepted. Parnell had claimed 'that confiscation was the result not only of the confiscation of the titles of the original great lords who acted as chiefs over the Irish people, but of the titles of the occupiers of the soil who formerly held the land in joint ownership with the chieftains'.[79] Mill went so far as to suggest that the Irish people were motivated in their struggle for the land by a folk memory of this happy period.[80] The Duke of Argyll complained bitterly to Gladstone shortly before his resignation from the cabinet of 'the nonsense . . . that ancient Irish tenures were more favourable to the tenants or cultivators than the English system. . . . The cultivators were at the mercy of the chiefs—who could and indeed did remove men and levied arbitrary evictions.'[81] But Mill's views still enjoyed wide support, including that of Gladstone.[82] It is hardly surprising to find Davitt, whose family had been evicted in the Mayo clearances, inserting Mill's thesis in the protocols of the Land League of Mayo.[83] Nor is it a surprise to find Healy giving the confiscation theme prominence in his major pamphlet of the land war, *Why There Is an Irish Land Question and an Irish Land League.*[84]

Historians have disagreed about how much importance to ascribe to this sentiment. N. D. Palmer, writing in 1940, followed Mill very closely, but more recent writers have detected a different emphasis. T. N. Brown has written: 'Not the folk memory of a collectivist golden age but fears inherited from the past mixed with hopes for better days seem to have motivated the tenant farmers of Ireland.'[85] Joseph Lee has developed the point: 'The Land League not merely articulated, but largely created, that aspiration [for peasant proprietorship], legitimised it with an immaculate pedigree by which tenants acquired retrospective private shares in a mythical Gaelic garden of Eden, and pushed it through to within sight of ultimate victory.' In this cogently argued view the League pioneered on a mass basis a technique destined to become indispensable in nationalist agitation, 'the appeal to spurious historical rights'.[86]

E. D. Steele, however, has ignored this trend and has made 'the sentiment of being dispossessed as a race' the core of his thesis. Tenant right (by no means limited to Ulster) was a manifestation of this sentiment. In consequence Steele has written of Irish land reform movements, including the Land League: 'The third F [freedom to sell the tenant right] was the one that really mattered; the other two were intended to secure its legalisation from being defeated by arbitrary eviction or increase of rent.'[87] But, as Professor Lee has pointed out, 'It is disconcerting, after the clinical rigour of this analysis, to find Gray defining tenant right as "fair rent" and Maguire defining it as "fixity of tenure". Dr Steele would reply that these demands were important, but only because they maintained the market value inherent in "free sale". There is certainly some truth in that, but the confusion of contemporary spokesmen suggests that the subjective essence of tenant right may have varied from place to place, depending partly, perhaps, on the extent of the local land market. Free sale was largely irrelevant to the small farmers in many areas of the West. They appear to have been more anxious to cling to their holdings at any cost than to secure a "free sale" of their interest, even where tenant right existed.'[88] In fact the Land League's attitude towards free sale was

B

profoundly ambiguous. The reason is not hard to find. An agent on a large Western property reported to Dr Brodie, the Poor Law inspector: 'I think the [free sale] custom is gaining ground for the purpose of enlarging farms; landlords permit it.'[89] Leaders like Dillon felt that the right of free sale constituted a bribe to peasants not to keep a firm grip on their holdings.[90]

The argument concerning the tenants' right to compensation for their own improvements was in many ways decisive. There is evidence to support the view that the majority of Irish tenants carried out the bulk of their own improvements. An Irish Land Committee survey suggested that the landlord had been the sole improver on 11·01 per cent of the area, the tenant on 26·62 per cent and both combined on 62·3 per cent. The tenant's superior record as a sole improver establishes the strong probability that where both landlord and tenant carried out the task jointly most of the burden fell on the tenant. In fact landlord expenditure on improvement in the period 1850–75 did not exceed £7 or £8 million—perhaps 3 per cent of gross rents received over these years.[91] The comment of the Conservative *Irish Times* on the statistics collected by a landlord body which covered only one-third of Irish land is also worth noting: 'Owing to the regrettable omission in the replies of so many landlords it must be admitted that the statistics collected by the Land Committee have lost much of their value in some most important respects.'[92]

Some recent valuable historical research by Cormac Ó Gráda has demonstrated that the *Irish Times* was right to have instinctive doubts about the accuracy of the landlords' figures. The Irish Land Committee's document implied a total landlord expenditure on improvements of some £15–£20 million since 1840. However, since one landlord spokesman, Colonel Tottenham, admitted that the greater part of the money spent by landlords on their estates was money borrowed from the Board of Works, and since it is known from Board of Works figures that this sum did not exceed £4 million in that period, the Land Committee's document was not an accurate representation of the facts.[93]

Within the improving tenantry there was one particular section —the 'reclamation' tenantry—which were of particular importance in the propaganda struggle. Many tenants, including some of those who had been cleared at the time of the famine, had been obliged to reclaim waste or bogland or to farm what was effectively barren mountain-side. In a major article of 1884 Davitt claimed (though without offering any hard evidence) 'that there are probably near 200,000 holdings of this description in Ireland'.[94] This fact above all conditioned his attitude towards purchase proposals.

In the late 1870s, even before the land war proper began, the Buckley libel case had shown how exposed the landlord might be in such a case. A Fenian, Sarsfield Casey, had polemicised against rent-raising and other unpopular practices in the treatment of tenants on the Buckley estate in the Galtees. Patten S. Bridge, the agent of the estate, proceeded against Casey for defamation of character. Isaac Butt, the counsel for the defendant, examined several tenants, whose stories of hardship, of unremitting toil, of the carrying of lime and manure on the backs of men and boys up the steep mountain-side to fertilise land which had paid little or no rent before the advent of Mr Buckley, created such a feeling against the landlord system that the jury disagreed, the result being equivalent to an acquittal.[95]

In this context Walter M. Stickney, a Yorkshire land agent and a friend of James Hack Tuke, gave a typical response:

No wonder Englishmen do not understand the demand for fixity of tenure in Ireland. I have no hesitation in saying that the tenant's outlay throughout the district I was in yesterday [Spiddal and Carraroe, Co. Galway] in building the cabin, fencing the land, and clearing the stones exceed many times the value of the fee simple before such outlay.[96]

The view was that the tenant by his own labour had created an unusually obvious interest for himself in the land. Marx saw this as an added provocation, but a real one:

What he [the Irish tenant] pays to the landlord in the form of rent frequently absorbs not merely a part of his profit, that is, his own surplus labour (to which he is entitled as possessor of his own instruments of labour), but also a part of his normal wage which he would otherwise receive for the same amount of labour. Besides, the landlord, who does nothing at all for the improvement of the land, also expropriates his small capital, which the tenant for the most part incorporates in the land through his own labour. This is precisely what a usurer would do under similar circumstances, with just this difference: that the usurer would at least risk his capital on the operation.[97]

Even those well outside Marx's political circle were impressed. It was the justice of the case of the reclamation tenantry, combined with the realisation that they could not hope to achieve proper compensation for improvements under the terms of the 1870 Land Act, which finally broke down Assistant Commissioner Baldwin's resistance to further land reform.[98]

The case against absenteeism was accepted on all sides and was particularly popular in England. Probably one-quarter of the total rental of Ireland went to landlords who habitually lived outside the country.[99] Barry O'Brien went so far as to write in 1880 that the Anglo-Irish landlord was 'in the main, an absentee today'.[100] But as Parnell admitted before an Irish audience at Beaufort, Co. Kerry,

> Undoubtedly the principle of expropriating absentee landlords and the London Companies, corporations drawing vast revenues from Ireland but returning nothing, is correct, but at the same time I cannot help saying that many of the absentee landlords and some of the London Companies own the lowest-rented estates in Ireland and I should prefer to see a measure of compulsory expropriation first sanctioned in the case of rack-renting landlords.[101]

The emphasis on the absence of alternative opportunities in industry for the Irish tenant was also of great significance. It was an important factor in counteracting the landlordist cry of freedom of contract: freedom of contract, it was claimed, was non-existent in Ireland. Anna Parnell commented:

> English statesmen almost invariably allude to the fact that whereas an English landlord cannot find a tenant for a vacant farm, an Irish landlord has no lack of applicants eager for the privilege of paying his rent as a proof that Irish tenants are in a better position than English tenants. They might as well say that because shipwrecked men will fight for a bare plank tossing on the cold water, more fiercely than they will ever fight for a comfortable armchair in a warm room, a man is therefore better off clinging to a bare plank in a storm at sea than if he were sitting in his armchair at home.[102]

This issue has crucial implications for the case regarding the tenant's right to his own improvements. The landlords argued that as the tenants were not forced to take the land and that as the landlord himself might have used it for a different purpose, he was entitled to have the increased value or at least a share created by the tenant's improvements.

It was on precisely this point that Gladstone's efforts to meet the land agitation by a mere modification of the 1870 Land Act broke down.[103] W. E. Forster, the Chief Secretary of Ireland, on 27 December 1880 refused to accept this position. He pointed out that Baron Dowse (of the Bessborough Commission's majority tendency) had argued that a tenant should not be evicted from his holding, except for non-payment of rent, waste, subletting or subdividing. Gladstone, on the other hand, proposed merely to fine the landlord for evicting by compelling him to give the tenant seven times the rent. Forster was certain that such a plan would not be acceptable to the tenants. But the Chief Secretary's concluding comment is all-important:

To my mind the Irish tenant has, from history, and especially from the fact that he has as a rule given the land what facilities for cultivation it possesses, a right, if not to joint ownership, at any rate to continuous occupation, and if he has such right, then also he has the right to enjoy such occupation on 'liveable' terms, that is, at a rent not exorbitant; nor do I think, he has lost this right, because, owing to his inability to find any other mode of living, *he has no freedom of contract* [my italics].[104]

This was the case 'in justice' for the Irish tenantry. In this form it does not raise the problem of rent levels. Nor does it deal with changes in the condition of the tenantry (for better or for worse) in the period since the famine. The landlords believed that it was in these areas that their case was strongest.

5. *Rent Levels and Living Standards*

The vexed question of the fairness of the Land League policy of urging the tenantry to accept no higher rent than Griffith's valuation has to be analysed in this context. The landlords and their allies totally opposed the conception that the government valuation (1852–68) made by Sir Richard Griffith was a standard for a fair rent in 1880, and a mass of writing was produced on both sides on this subject. In June 1880 the Irish Land Committee produced a pamphlet which expressed the landlord view in its essentials.[105] Griffith's valuation, it was pointed out, had as its object not to lay down a standard for rent but rather to provide a basis for taxation. The valuation, far from being an accurate reflection of the rent at the time it was made, was some 25 or 30 per cent below the full value of the land. Since that date, of course, there had been a major rise in the prices of agricultural products. As the pamphlet put it,

But the prices of 1852 did not long continue. In the very next year they began to rise, and ever since the prices of cereals have been higher than the scale of the Act of 1846, and the prices of meat higher than those laid down in the Act of 1852, and in some cases enormously higher. The valuation meanwhile has remained unchanged; so that the excess of rent, which Sir R. Griffith estimated at 33%, might now be safely set down as a very much higher rate.[106]

In support of this view, Mrs Bramston Smith, Griffith's daughter, wrote to *The Times* in November to claim that her father had always stated that he had valued the land at 25–30 per cent below the letting value. She referred her readers to Ball Greene, her father's successor at the Valuation Office, for confirmation.[107]

In fact Ball Greene, who was no ally of the tenantry, was at approximately the same time preparing a memorandum for the cabinet on the subject. He admitted—as did most nationalists—that the valuation had been carried out for taxation purposes, but he regarded it as a reasonable indicator of the value of the land at the time it was taken.[108] Ball Greene did not offer any explanation of the source of the contrary view expressed by the Land Committee pamphlet and by Mrs Bramston Smith, but the nationalists felt that it was, in fact, possible to do so. For what had Griffith meant when he said that one-third should be added to the amount of the general valuation to give the full rent value of the land under ordinary proprietors? Obviously here the whole point at issue depended upon the meaning of the words 'full rent'. Fortunately for the cause of the tenants, the author's own interpretation was on record:

> In regard to the difference between the valuation of the land adopted by me under the Act and the actual letting value, I have to observe that our valuation is about 25% under the full or rack-rent value.[109]

He added that the rack-rents prevailed 'over more than ¾ of the arable area of Ireland'. It seems, therefore, reasonable in this light to suggest that Griffith's valuation represented the fair letting value of the land when it was carried out.[110]

The advocates of the tenantry were keen to strengthen their case even further. In 1852, when the valuation was begun, the tenant's claim to his property, at all events to the improvements effected by him, was ignored, wrote William J. Walsh, President of Maynooth. But (he over-optimistically went on to claim), as the act of 1870 had since declared, the property thus valued was the property of two distinct owners.[111]

But the landlords still had one major argument in the rise in agricultural prices. Following Ball Greene and other evidence, one historian has calculated that 'The Griffith valuation was a fairly accurate reflection of real rental values in 1848–52, but already by the mid-1860s it was perhaps as much as 15 per cent below real values, and by the late 1860s as much as 20 per cent below. Around 1870 it was perhaps between 20 and 25 below value, and from 1875–80 somewhere between 25 and 30 per cent.'[112] These figures are still remarkable. After all, an Irish Land Committee questionnaire—which admittedly covered only one-third of Irish lands—showed that on 70 per cent of the area covered, excluding grazing lettings for one year or less, rents were less than 20 per cent above Griffith's valuation, and only 14 per cent of the area returned rents more than 30 per cent above it.[113] Since the valuation, however, Ball Greene had argued in his cabinet memo that cereals had risen 20 to 30 per cent in price, while the produce of the grasslands had enjoyed increases varying from 50 to 83 per cent.

These figures appear to constitute dramatic evidence of the generosity of the landlord class for, far from raising rents, they appeared to have gained little from the rise in agricultural prices. But there was another side to the debate. It is worth noting the analysis offered by Karl Marx of post-famine trends in Irish agriculture:

> Nevertheless, with the fall in numbers, rents and farmers' profits rose, although the latter not as steadily as the former. The reason for this is easily comprehensible. On the one hand, with the throwing of small holdings into large ones, and the change of arable into pasture land, a larger part of the whole produce was transformed into surplus produce, the surplus produce increased although the total produce of which it formed a fraction decreased. On the other hand, the money value of this surplus produce increased yet more rapidly than its mass in consequence of the rise in the English market price of wheat etc. during the last twenty and especially during the last ten years.[114]

In fact a recent calculation by Cormac Ó Gráda[115] makes it difficult to argue the optimistic[116] case about post-famine readjustment in Irish agriculture and its effect upon living standards. The post-famine rental increase of 30 per cent by the mid-1870s[117] had led to a situation where the landlord share of total agricultural value added was greater in the early 1870s than in the early 1850s.[118]

Table 1: Rent and Agricultural Output in 1840–45, 1852–54 and 1869–71

Year	Output	Rent	Output (£m) (pre-famine prices)
1840–45	49·8	12·0 (15·0)	49·8
1852–54	51·1	8·5 (9·0)	39·9
1869–71	48·6	12·0	33·3

Source: C. Ó Gráda, 'Agricultural Head-Rents, Pre-Famine and Post-Famine', *Economic and Social Review* V, No. 3 (Apr. 1974), 390.

As Ó Gráda has concluded, 'All in all, however, our results make the "cheerful" version of post-famine adjustment somewhat more difficult to argue. While the famine undoubtedly succeeded in reducing substantially the size of the rural proletariat, it may well be the case that the standards experienced by those who survived did not markedly improve. In other words, while average incomes rose, this may have been largely due to the fact that the farming section of the rural population was proportionately more important in the post-famine period.'[119] Certainly the claim that 'the readjustment of the Irish agricultural economy after the famine must have seemed in 1876 very nearly a success story'[120] hardly squares with the evidence presented in this chapter.

But if a more accurate assessment of developments in post-famine agriculture is possible on the basis of these comments, it was not possible in the 'prosperity' of the 1870s to claim that conditions in the Irish countryside had been deteriorating steadily since the famine. In fact agrarian reformers did not as a rule make such a claim, although they were, of course, keen to stress the effects of the bad harvests of the late 1870s. Professor Baldwin's opinion, expressed before the Richmond Commission, would have been acceptable to many even on the left of the League. 'There has been', he said, 'the growth of a middle class which is perhaps the most satisfactory feature of modern farming . . . but the main wealth has been confined to them and has not gone to the small farmers. . . . The small farmers are in as bad a position as they were forty years ago.'[121] It provides a basis for a further elaboration of the discussion of rent levels. For the smaller tenants had a particular set of arguments which they were determined to publicise.

In fact the smaller men generally could point out that the rise in price of their specialist products had been small. In considering cereals Ball Greene admitted that it ought not to be forgotten that the costs of labour had increased very much since 1858 and that it would not be too much to assume that increase to be 50 per cent. Oats were the principal grain crops of the light tillage lands occupied in smallholdings by the poorer tenantry—taking up four times the area of wheat and barley combined. It seemed reasonable, therefore, to take that crop as a standard of fair letting value. At the time of the act of 1852 the value of one acre of oats was £3·78; there had been an increase of 16s which could hardly have been expected to cover adequately the increased cost of labour. 'The present valuation of these lands', Ball Greene concluded, 'would appear to be high enough and no addition could be put on it.'[122]

Further, the increases in prices for the best butter tell very little about the prices received in South Kerry by the small farmers who had not the capability to produce such butter. The price of butter in Cork was not a guide to the price of butter in Achill; and the price obtained for a pound of butter sold by a farmer's wife at Cahirciveen was often very far short of the price obtained for the same pound when it reached the hands of the butter factor in Cork.[123] The evidence in 1880 of C. H. Hemphill, who had considerable experience as a county court judge in Kerry, is significant:

> The price of butter according to that list which you gave was 63s 4d per cwt, was it not?—Yes.
> And in 1877 it was 121s 4d?—Yes; but that depends upon the quality. It has been proved over and over again before me up to 1878 that the farmer very seldom got more than £3 or £4 for his firkin.
> You mean when the price was 121s per cwt?—Yes, because it was not the first quality.
> Whose fault was that?—Of course, it was the fault of the butter.
> Or of the maker of the butter?—No, because you will have dairy farmers in Cork with 60 or 70 cows. I know one myself with 70 milch cows; he makes a firkin of butter today, and he sends, perhaps, five or six firkins away in a week. These poor farmers with a few acres of ground in these mountain runs will be three weeks between himself and his wife collecting his firkin of butter, and it will be a different flavour and a different colour. It is impossible to expect that to be first-class butter.[124]

Potatoes, as well as oats and butter, provided similar evidence. James Daly of the *Connaught Telegraph* summed up the case of the Connaught small tenantry when he wrote:

> Those who have a craze for quoting Griffith valuation as 30 per cent under the actual letting value of the land in Ireland have never taken into consideration that one acre of potatoes could when this valuation took place maintain a whole family, what ten acres in these uncertain seasons may accomplish.

The main point here was the huge fall in the value of the potato crop (from £12½ million in 1876 to £3½ million in 1879)[125]—although it is worth noting also that the high Mayo potato yields of the early 1850s, which were bound to affect the valuation in the county in 1857, were never again reached in the 1860s or 1870s.[126] The small tenants had had little success with either their cash crops or subsistence crops.

All classes in the farming community naturally emphasised the rise in the costs of production. This was particularly important in the tillage or labour-intensive sectors, for example the dairy industry. In Sir Richard Griffith's instructions the wages of a dairy-maid were estimated at £4 a year. In 1880 they were reckoned at from £12 a year and upwards.[127] Tillage farmers generally complained about the rise in the wages of the agricultural proletariat. But the larger cattle farmers had neither the problems of the substantial tillage farmers nor those of the 'small men'. Indeed, one argument of the advocates of the smaller tenantry was a direct result of this disparity and ran counter to the interests of the graziers in particular. Griffith's valuation, it was said, had been carried at a relatively early stage in the transition from tillage to pasture before the full direction and force of price trends was made known, and as a result tillage land tended to be overvalued while the best grazing land was undervalued.[128] At a crucial Irish Parliamentary Party meeting Parnell in substance accepted that the graziers had little to complain about.[129]

The evidence seems to suggest that the larger cattle farmers had enjoyed a substantial improvement in living conditions since the famine. Other substantial farmers must have made some gains, but they had more problems, owing to the rise in the costs of labour. It seems fair, however, to accept Baldwin's claim of 1880 that the smaller tenantry had not had a significant share in the material advances of the previous quarter of a century and more. It is likely that they shared to some extent in the exceptionally prosperous years of the mid-1870s, but beyond that their lot seems to have remained almost as hard as ever. In short, it was felt that the bulk of the Irish tenantry had some objective basis for their sense of grievance on the rent question.

6. Conclusion

The notion that a 'frustrated revolution in rising expectations' sparked off the land war in 1879 has enjoyed considerable acceptance in recent years.[130] It has seemed to offer an explanation very much superior to the older conventional view of the land war as the product of an intolerable, rapacious land system which finally cracked under the weight of a severe agricultural crisis in the late 1870s. The 'frustrated revolution in rising expectations' thesis enjoys almost the status of a new orthodoxy.

In fact, although it may make some sense to see the participation of a prosperous tenant farmer in, say, Co. Cork in the light of a desire to maintain impressive gains made over the previous quarter-century, no such impressive gains over such a period of time appear to have been made by the small Western tenantry who took the lead in the Land League.[131] The smallholders of the West probably did make some gains in the heyday of the 1870s, and they were very unlikely to take kindly to the idea that they should lose those gains on account of the bad seasons that ended the decade. In this limited sense only, the thesis of a frustrated revolution in rising expectations may be made to fit even the behaviour of the smaller peasantry.

It is also worth noting that a rise in expectations, or, to put it more generally, a dislocation between popular expectation and reality, may have other causes than merely a halt in a rise of the standard of living. Earl Spencer, who had considerable political experience in Ireland, underlined this when he wrote:

> The Irish peasantry still live in poor hovels often in the same room with animals, they have few modern comforts; and yet they are in close communication with those who live at ease in the cities and farms in the U.S. They are also imbued with all the advanced political notions of the American Republic and are sufficiently educated to read the latest political doctrines in the press which circulates among them. *Their social condition at home is a hundred years behind their state of political and mental culture* [my italics].[132]

From a different political perspective Davitt made a similar point when he noted that the two 'progressive tendencies' in Irish politics in the 1870s (the revolt of the obstructionists within Butt's Home Rule Party, and the revolt within separatism against pure militarism —both protests, he said, against stereotyped methods) had their roots in the growing interconnectedness between 'our people' in Ireland and their race in America. The Irish in America were steadily in the ascendant, both politically and socially. They were being inoculated, he claimed, with practical ideas and schooled in democratic thought and action. American party organisations were training them for active participation in public life; and in proportion as they lifted themselves up from the status of mere labourer to that of business pursuits and professional callings did they find the opportunities and means of taking an active part in the government of cities and states. These experiences and advantages reacted upon opinion in Ireland through the medium of visitors, letters and newspapers crossing the Atlantic, and in this manner they helped to cultivate the growth of more practical thought and purpose in all political movements at home.[133]

Dr Duggan, Bishop of Clonfert, suggested before the Richmond Commission in 1880 that increased knowledge of America (and England) was responsible for the decline in subdivision practices in the 1870s. He was one of those most keen to insist on the survival of the Celtic way of life, but he argued that in this respect it had broken down completely.[134]

Certainly in the 1870s the Western tendency towards early marriage on a pre-famine pattern tapered off and the figures for these areas grew closer to those of the rest of the country.[135] The pre-famine pattern persisted, however, with regard to the emigration rates, which failed to rise significantly. This unevenness of development only served to ensure that the West was unable to export its intense problems on the ships to America and England.

The 'frustrated revolution in rising expectations' thesis, therefore, has a certain role to play in explaining the outbreak of land war in 1879. However, it is necessary to avoid laying too much stress upon it. Apart from the doubts here raised about some aspects of the 'optimistic' versions of post-famine adjustment,[136] there are basically two other reasons for this view. In the first place, this chapter has stressed the wide-ranging nature of the tenantry's case: the critique of the transition to pasture which appeared to have failed, both by economic as well as national/social criteria. It has also stressed those sources of grievances which lay in the background: alleged insecurity of tenure; the role (however inflated) of resentment over confiscation; absenteeism; the tenantry's (particularly the reclamation tenantry's) apparent lack of reward for improvements; and finally, the absence of real freedom of contract. When it is remembered that these factors must have been given all the more force in the popular mind by memories of the famine, then it can be seen that the problem of the consciousness of the peasantry cannot be reduced simply to the pangs arising out of a halt in a steady rise in the standard of living. It is significant that these views (and the conditions which gave birth to them) were much more prevalent outside Ulster, and this may well help to account for Ulster's very much more restrained participation in the land war, despite the fact that the Ulster tenantry offer a clear case of frustrated rising expectations.[137]

But there is another and even deeper reason for modifying the role of this factor. For the problem of the consciousness of the peasantry in 1870 and the reasons why they were 'available' for an agrarian mass movement is, although important, not the only problem which faces a serious study of the Land League. For had the Land League failed to produce ways of conducting the peasantry's struggle against the landlords effectively, the consciousness of the peasantry, no matter how militant, and no matter for what reason, would have been of little avail. The degree of the Land League's success as a peasant anti-landlord movement as compared with earlier post-famine agrarian movements, whether constitutional like the Tenant League of the 1850s or violent like the Ribbonmen who were most active in 1870, is very evident. Without a discussion of these prior forms of conflict, it is not possible to have a full grasp of the originality of the Land League and, therefore, of its true place in Irish history. As the Irish Republican Brotherhood claimed to offer a genuine alternative course for Ireland's dissatisfied rural inhabitants, it too has a place in the Land League's pre-history. The next chapter, therefore, attempts to deal with the development of these movements. The purpose of the chapter is to provide a basis for understanding the way in which the Land League marked a radical *rupture* with previous manifestations of agrarian discontent in Ireland.

2

Agrarian Movements before the Land League

> The Fenian ideology was simply nationalist: as such
> its aim was independence without any specific ideas
> about the social contents of the virtually established
> Irish republic.
>
> E. STRAUSS, *Irish Nationalism and British Democracy*
> (1951)

> For a secret society, they [the Fenians] went to little
> trouble to hide what they were about. They ran a news-
> paper, the *Irish People,* as a thinly disguised vehicle
> for their propaganda and trenchantly advocated peasant
> proprietorship.
>
> E. D. STEELE, *Irish Land and British Politics* (1974)

1. *The Tenant League and Ribbonism*

Shortly after the famine Ireland was the scene of a constitutional
movement for land reform. This movement was the Tenant League,
founded nationally in 1850; but a word of caution is required
regarding its origins.[1] The League was not a direct response to the
famine. In the South it represented instead the short-term reaction
of relatively prosperous grain farmers to a cyclical depression:
when agricultural prices rose in 1853 there was a subsequent loss
of tenant interest. In the North it represented the desire of tenants
to protect their apparently endangered tenant right. What it did not
represent was any basic sense of the injustice of the land system.
Reflecting its partial mobilisation, it put forward a partial critique.

It is, however, clear that open and legal agitation was not the
only form of peasant revolt in post-famine Ireland. The role of
terrorism has always caught the eye of interested observers. In the
police view it added necessary strength to the more open political
movement. It was always in the background in many regions, and
even at the most apparently promising moments, as in 1856, it
had a habit of expanding suddenly. O'Connor Morris had to admit
that 'It is not extinct . . . and compared with 1855, we fear, is
increasing.'[2]

Yet in one sense terrorism certainly lost impetus in the post-
famine period. From the early 1850s to the late 1870s there was a
definite lull by Irish standards. But this absolute decline in outrage
concealed a significant phenomenon. Agrarian outrages fell from

1,362 in 1850 to 232 in 1860. Yet the ratio of outrage to eviction rose steadily over these ten years.[3] The significance of this can be seen more clearly when it is considered in the context of other developments which help to reveal why the famine was such a turning-point in the history of Irish agrarian outrage.

Ribbonism was the term most frequently applied to agrarian crime both before and after the famine. However, the continuing use of the term masks two very important changes in its nature. In the pre-famine increase in outrages in Munster conflict between farmers and cottiers and labourers over conacre played a 'pivotal' role. But there was a marked decline in agrarian outrage during the famine: for as the potato failed and labourers and cottiers died or emigrated the demand for conacre for potatoes fell sharply.[4] The first post-famine outbreak of rural crime in Armagh, Louth and Monaghan revealed a new situation. Firstly, conacre no longer played such a central part. The struggles of the 1850s were no longer primarily the struggles of the agricultural labourers and cottiers. They were struggles of the tenant farmers who were 'much more comfortable'[5] than the inhabitants of the disturbed districts of Munster. The issue was explicitly the alleged high rentals of the area.[6]

The nature of the crime also changed. It was not simply that it no longer represented labourer–farmer conflict over conacre. It had changed in its organisational form also: it had lost the quality of *immediacy* which had characterised pre-famine outbursts. 'The peasant, if unable to procure a potato garden, has no hope of feeding his family and is driven to desperation,' Lieutenant-Colonel William Miller, Deputy Inspector-General of the Irish Constabulary, told the Devon Commission's inquiry into the Irish land system in 1845. The result was clear: 'The surrounding population . . . lend a willing hand to redress such evils by violent means.'[7] 'I think the conspiracies were got up by the tenants, or parties immediately concerned on the estates,' recalled H. J. Brownrigg, Inspector-General, of these same events seven years later before the select committee of 1852. For this reason he did not believe the Munster outrages were the products of secret societies in 'the same sense'[8] as those of the Armagh, Louth and Monaghan districts of 1850 and 1851. What we are dealing here with is no longer simply the last desperate lunge of the oppressed, as in the 1840s—though the justificatory image was to have a long life—but the more organised conspiracy of a *relatively* prosperous tenantry. In Brownrigg's view the Ribbon conspiracy of the 1850s proper had branches in Liverpool, Glasgow and Manchester and was co-ordinated by disloyal publicans. It had a movable headquarters in Dublin, Glas-

Table 2 : Ratio of Outrage to Eviction, 1853–80

Year	Outrages	Evictions	
		Tenants	Persons
1853	469	4,833	24,589
1854	334	2,156	10,794
1855	255	1,849	9,338
1856	287	1,108	5,114
1857	194	1,161	5,475
1858	235	957	4,643
1859	221	837	3,872
1860	232	636	2,985
1861	229	1,092	5,288
1862	363	1,136	5,617
1863	349	1,734	8,695
1864	304	1,924	9,201
1865	178	942	4,513
1866	87	795	3,571
1867	123	549	2,489
1868	160	637	3,002
1869	767	374	1,741
1870	1,329	548	2,616
1871	373	482	2,357
1872	256	526	2,476
1873	254	671	3,078
1874	213	726	3,571
1875	136	667	3,323
1876	212	553	2,550
1877	236	463	2,177
1878	301	980	4,679
1879	863	1,238	6,239
1880	2,590	2,110	10,657

Sources: *Return of Outrages reported to the Royal Irish Constabulary from 1844 to 1880*, 21–3, H. C. 1881 [C. 2756] LXXVII, 907–9; *Returns of Cases of Evictions in Ireland in Each Quarter of Each Year . . . for 1880*, 3, H. C. 1881 (2) LXXVII, 727.

gow, Manchester, Liverpool or Belfast.[9] Attacks, it appears, were frequently carried out by peasants brought from outside the district. It is not necessary to accept all of Brownrigg's characteristic opinions to see a qualitative change in the level of Ribbon organisation in the 1850s. Davitt later acknowledged: 'Ribbonmen have shown themselves to be . . . skilled in the methods of secret conspiracy.'[10]

This analysis must be borne in mind in any discussion of the effectivity of post-famine agrarian terrorism. This was, in fact, an area of disagreement between those interested observers of Ireland's troubles, Karl Marx and Friedrich Engels. Ribbonism's existence in the 1850s could be gathered from a number of repressive statutes: the Habeas Corpus Suspension Acts of 1849 and 1850, the Crime and Outrage Acts of 1853, 1854 and 1855.[11] Yet at the end of this decade Marx wrote dismissively that the peasants, 'despairing wretches . . . attempt feeble resistance by the formation of secret societies scattered over the land, powerless for effecting anything beyond demonstration of individual vengeance'.[12] Engels took a different line. He had the evidence of the 1860s before him when he wrote that agrarian crimes 'cannot be suppressed so long as they are the only effective remedy against the landlord. They help, that is why they continue and will continue in spite of all the coercive laws.'[13] But did they help? Was outrage a remedy for anything other than frustration?

The evidence seems to suggest that it was. In fact it appears that outrage frequently achieved the purpose of either preventing a rent increase or bringing about a rent reduction.[14] But this effectiveness—while it must be granted—was a limited one. The revolt always remained localised and spasmodic. An expansion of RIC activity, combined perhaps with a special commission—a kind of special assizes—was usually adequate to the task of stifling the conspiracy. Of all the agrarian storms between the famine and the Land League perhaps the most notorious were the 'Westmeath outrages'. Between January 1870 and February 1871 there were in that county some 173 agrarian crimes.[15] There was for a while very considerable alarm. But the holding of the select committee inquiry had a calming effect which was already noticeable in April.[16] In May the government decided to bring in its Westmeath Bill for the protection of life and property. Earl Kimberley claimed that the failure of milder forms of coercion left the government with no alternative but to have recourse to the arbitrary arrest of leaders in the troubled areas.[17] In July arrests were already being reported under the new act.[18] By the end of the year complete peace was restored.[19]

Engels, of course, was fully aware of these limitations, and his assessment of the 'agrarian trend' in Ireland seems fair. In his view such a form of resistance was a more or less inevitably recurring feature of Irish rural life; but he added: 'As regards its nature it is *local, isolated* and can never become a *general* form of political struggle.'[20]

But there was one movement which claimed that it transcended the limitations of both the Tenant League and the Ribbon type of struggle. That movement was Fenianism. It did not have the partial critique of the Tenant League: instead it thrust the famine and its implications into the centre of Irish political rhetoric. At the same time it was, in theory at least, capable of overcoming the localism implicit in Ribbonism. It is to the analysis of this movement and its attitude to rural conflict that we now turn.

2. *Fenianism and Agrarian Discontent*

The Fenian movement, the Irish Republican Brotherhood founded in 1858, had as its object the winning of Irish independence by armed rebellion. Marx commented in his notes for an undelivered speech on Ireland that Fenianism was a 'socialist lower-class movement'.[21] He later added 'socialistic . . . in a negative sense directed against the appropriation of the soil'.[22] In other words, despite its large number of urban adherents—only 10 per cent of those arrested in connection with the abortive rising of 1867 were farmers, farmers' sons or farm labourers[23]—Fenianism was an anti-landlord movement.

Fenianism was conditioned by the 1859–63 depression in a way which has yet to be sufficiently appreciated. Nevertheless, the Fenian attitude towards the social question in general, and the land question in particular, was of some complexity. Erich Strauss wrote with some disappointment of Fenianism's rather 'abstract and nebulous nationalism'[24] which played down the 'special'[25] interests of the oppressed classes.

Yet the Fenians proudly claimed to be based on the Irish 'democracy'. In an early discussion it was claimed that sections of the Irish aristocracy and Irish professional classes might come over to the nationalist side, but that this would happen only after it was clear that the IRB was winning a military victory. Although the Fenians would clearly have welcomed such a development, they did not regard the adhesion of the 'upper classes' as either essential or likely in the early stages of struggle.

What was striking, however, about this early article which appeared in the *Irish People* of 26 March 1864 was its complete omission of any mention of a significant section of Irish society who appeared to belong to the category of those who, in the Fenian phrase, had 'some share of the world's wealth' and cared nothing for Ireland. The group who had been 'overlooked' were the rural - bourgeoisie, in particular the graziers. A few months later, on 30 July 1864, there was, however, a substantial editorial devoted to the topic. Apologising for the failure to discuss the role of the graziers, the writer explained that it was partly because the Fenians expected little from them and partly because the Brotherhood had been 'communing' with better men, the 'hardy' honest sons of labour. The social pretensions of the graziers were regarded critically. They had much of the 'arrogant assumption' of gentility without any of its refinement: many of them were 'boors in broadcloth'. The writer tried to touch on a sore spot by noting (or supposing) the uneasy nature of the relationship between the graziers and the aristocracy. He claimed that 'even the smallest gentry' looked down upon the graziers, who were 'serfs of the haughty artistocrats who . . . look upon them as useful menials and nothing more'. Even the grazier farmers, it was added, could not find land · for all their sons. On these two counts they ought to come over to · the nationalist side.

But in the final analysis the Fenians did not attach any extraordinary significance to the adhesion of these men. The shopkeeper and the mechanic already realised that they depended more on the poor working farmer. Here, then, we have the Fenian attitude towards the problem of uniting the different Irish social classes in support of national independence: in theory they supported such a unity, but for all practical intents they relied on the 'sons of toil'. Everything basically depended on this group making a successful blow for national independence. It was the achievement of this object which would create as its effect the maximum possible national unity.

The same point—an insistence on the priority of military struggle —underlies the Fenian attitude on the land question. It is clear that the *Irish People* (the Fenian newspaper founded by James Stephens in 1863) argued in support of the demand for peasant proprietorship. But this, it was felt, could only be achieved following Irish independence. Recalling Father O'Shea's Tenant Protection Society set up in 1849, it noted:

> This movement had one thing to recommend it, it looked not at all to the foreign parliament. Father O'Shea's plan was to establish societies in every parish and to bind the people by a solemn pledge never to bid for land from which the tenantry had unjustly been evicted. Not to enter into the practicability of

this project, one object to its successful working was that men who had nothing in common with the people—'shoneens' in fact —would be enabled to get possession of the people's land upon easy terms. But in some instances, even these would shrink from the glare of *organised* public opinion and in many districts such men were not to be found at all. Such a project as this would be utterly useless *now*. But the 'flocks and herds' doctrine was not then so much the received religion of the Irish landlords and many persons believed that the Tenant Protection Societies might have saved many a struggling farmer from ruin.[26]

This passage is interesting in a number of ways. Here a project apparently similar to that later embodied in the Land League was—despite certain sympathetic comments—rejected. The word 'boycott' was, of course, not yet in use, but the concept was certainly in existence at this date. Apparently the 'flocks and herds' doctrine implied for the Fenian writer that the 'shoneen' was *'now'* able to seize the evicted tenants' land with impunity. There were, however, two lessons, one negative and one positive, to be drawn from this experience.

The negative lesson was the exposure of the snare of dishonest parliamentarians who had assisted in the eventual defeat of the Tenant League movement. The positive lesson lay in the clarified knowledge that it was useless for 'the people to waste their strength struggling for anything but the one thing'. The meaning of all this is clear. The Fenians were not prepared to join in any struggles of the peasantry which had as their object anything less than the goal of national independence. In the Irish Republic, to be sure, landlordism would be abolished and every man would own his own land. But until then the discontented among the peasantry were advised to prepare themselves for an armed uprising. In this sense Strauss was justified in speaking of an 'abstract and nebulous nationalism'. What made it abstract and nebulous for the mass of the peasantry was its refusal to make any commitment to an agrarian agitation *unless it was non-parliamentary*. Effectively this ruled out any Fenian participation in the struggle for reform *except on exclusively Fenian terms*. James Stephens later concluded:

It is true that in the columns of the *Irish People* several articles were written advocating peasant proprietorship; but national independence was certainly put forward as the point to be gained first.[27]

The Fenian attempt at rebellion failed to initiate a widespread peasant response. It is an irony that the peasants, according to many observers, were of the mind attributed by the Fenians to the professional classes and aristocracy: they waited for success in the attempt at rebellion before committing themselves. Despite the exaggerated fears of a section of the government, the peasantry did not throw their weight behind the Fenians.[28] But it should be noted as a significant minority trend that the Fenians in some parts of the country had made some progress with the peasantry's militant vanguard—Ribbonism.[29]

There appears to be a sharp separation of Ribbon and Fenian objectives. As O'Donovan Rossa, a leading Fenian put it, 'They were sectarian and defensive against the enemy; we were national and aggressive.'[30] In other words, Ribbonism was basically the protective movement of the Catholic peasantry locked in conflict with a largely Protestant landlord class, while Fenianism had the broader objective of smashing the power of the British state in Ireland. But despite this difference in emphasis, the two groups enjoyed a definite rapport in certain areas. The Fenian commitment to the abolition of landlordism had allowed at least some successful penetration of Ribbon lodges, particularly in parts of IRB organiser Ned Duffy's region—Connaught, Cavan, Longford and West-meath.[31] Before the unsuccessful rising of 1867 Ribbonism in this part of the country apparently diminished in the face of Fenianism.

After the failure of the rising a murky period opened. Fenianism was still an effective symbol of discontent with the British link, but the structure of that body began to lose its shape and coherence. The conclusion of the very full RIC analysis of 1870[32] was felt to be unavoidable. As the Inspector-General himself noted,

> There is at the present time in Ireland a more widespread, deeper and more openly avowed feeling of dissatisfaction towards the government of the country than heretofore. While at the same time there is no evidence of any general organisation or acknowledged leadership, such as existed in previous periods of this conspiracy.[33]

This semi-chaotic state of Fenianism allowed members a great deal more personal initiative. Many Fenians gravitated towards the Home Rule movement in the 1870s.[34] Others moved towards Ribbonism. 'Fenianism has become engrafted on Ribbonism . . . and that has altered its character very much,'[35] Morris Reade, a Resident Magistrate, told the Commons select committee on outrages in Meath and Westmeath. The evidence of local police reports tended to support this view. The Meath County Inspector stated categorically that Fenianism had merged gradually into Ribbonism.[36] His colleague in Westmeath was rather more cautious. He admitted the difficulty of obtaining accurate information on such a topic,[37] but he felt sure that Fenianism was reviving and was 'combined' with Ribbonism.[38] Later reports from the same counties provide rather more clear evidence of an overlap in Fenian and Ribbon membership.[39] This is certainly a very plausible development. A significant number of Fenians would hardly have been squeamish about striking a blow against landlordism. There was a fair-sized Fenian contingent in the area, an informer's report of late 1871 noting that the two counties had between them 3,509 men and 177 new rifles.[40] This was a significant level of organisation, though it was not as advanced as in Connaught. It has even been argued that the Fenians came to 'dominate' Ribbon lodges in the 1870s.[41] The very currency of the term 'Ribbon Fenianism' in the late 1870s would appear to imply that there is truth in such a view. Nevertheless, there are certain problems involved in such an interpretation.

What would it mean to speak of Fenian domination of Ribbon lodges? Fenianism was certainly not successful in imposing its strategies for the achievement of national independence on the Ribbon lodges. They remained concerned primarily with much narrower agrarian goals. Nor was it the case that the IRB, having failed in the exceptionally difficult task of insurrection, was in some sense turning to the 'soft' target of local landlords as the means of pursuing the same basic objective of national independence. There was, in short, no coherent Fenian plan to make the workings of Ribbonism favour Fenian ends.

Indeed, many strong Fenian areas (for example, Tipperary) had no real involvement in Ribbonism. It is a remarkable fact that the Conservative *Westmeath Guardian* was, at the height of agrarian outrage in that region, highly sceptical of any supposed necessary connection between Fenianism and Ribbonism.[42] The reason seems to be fairly clear. At this juncture economic and social causes rather than the Fenian movement played the prime role in triggering off the agrarian disturbance. The Meath and Westmeath outrages provide an excellent example. Here is the analysis offered by O'Connor Morris:

> A considerable and increasing number of landlords keep large tracts of pasture in their own hands and farm on their own account; the whole of the remaining good grass lands is in the possession of substantial farmers; and, as I have said, the poor peasantry are relegated to the inferior soils. *The result is the most marked contrast between agricultural wealth and poverty that I have met, as yet, in any part of Ireland* [my italics], and a corresponding division in the ranks of society. The rich gentle-

man and rich farmers in this country are, speaking generally, exceedingly rich; the peasantry and agricultural labourers are, as I have noticed, exceedingly poor and the line of separation between these classes is marked by harsh and grievous distinctions. To this circumstance, and also because evictions during the last twenty years have been very frequent over Meath, is, I am convinced, to be mainly ascribed the peculiar spirit of discontent which is too prevalent in the county.[43]

More generally, O'Connor Morris saw in both Meath and Westmeath the same trends: a transition to pasture accompanied by a decrease in population and by an increase in livestock somewhat smaller than might have been expected.[44] In other words, in 1870 this area presented the picture of an acute degree of social differentiation combined with those defects which nationalist and anti-nationalist analysts regarded as typical of the post-famine transition to pasture. The anti-grazier motif was explicitly noted in press reports.[45]

Of course, O'Connor Morris admitted that agrarian secret societies played a role in outrage. It seems highly probable that some of the area's Fenians were also involved. But the question remains: on what basis were these men participating? If, as seems likely, they acted out of a common regional sense of social injustice, it is difficult to speak of Fenianism dominating Ribbonism. Agrarianism, in other words, appears to have been successful in this period in imposing its more local and specific objectives on some members of the more ambitious but somewhat disorientated national movement.

This point may be seen more clearly in conjunction with developments in Connaught. Connaught before the 1867 rising appears to have been the least well organised province.[46] But a Dublin Castle report of 24 September 1871 noted a change in an important comment:

> You will observe that Connaught is the best organised of the three [*sic*] provinces and during the past three years the leaders of that province have done more in the way of arming than I believe the other three put together.[47]

A report of a few weeks later compared Connaught with Leinster and Ulster to some effect. On paper, according to this document, Leinster still had more IRB members, 21,121, as against the 15,030 of Connaught and the 11,147 of Ulster. But in perhaps the most important index of militancy—the stocking of new rifles—Connaught was a long way ahead. Each of the five Connaught counties

had over 150 new rifles, while eighteen out of the other twenty
counties listed (Munster was omitted) had under 78, save for Dublin
with 201 and Westmeath with 101.[48] While the absolute figures
listed here may well be open to question, there is little reason to
doubt the proportions involved in the regional comparison.

In fact the visible signs of discontent in Connaught so alarmed a
local worthy, Mr Neal Browne, that he had in early 1870 claimed
that an insurrection was close at hand. His letter on this subject
provoked a Dublin Castle inquiry which in turn provoked a serene
reply from Stritch, the RM. Stritch's report was an exemplary text
for the study of the relationships between Fenianism and agrarianism—and, indeed, for the nature of Connaught agrarianism itself.
He admitted a growing insecurity of life and property, but decried
the possibility of an insurrection:

> Those who fear that an insurrection is imminent must really con-
> found two things, which are perfectly distinct, dissimilar and in
> some respects, even antagonistic, viz Fenianism and Ribbonism.
> Fenianism as an organised conspiracy—had for its avowed object
> the separation of Ireland from England and the separation of an
> Irish Republic. This, its acknowledged object, Fenianism pro-
> posed to accomplish by an armed rebellion and revolution. With
> a widely different object in view, the agrarianism which now
> affects this country proposes to accomplish that object by very
> different means. A social and political movement—widespread,
> but not organised—agrarianism hopes to attain its object—a
> thorough change in the land laws of the country and a more
> general distribution of the land itself—not by insurrection, which
> it well knows would be hopeless, but by terrorism. The pro-
> gramme is fixity of tenure—valuation of rents—the breaking up
> of consolidated, territorial farms. These specific objects agrarian-
> ism . . . hopes to attain not by a general rising, not by an *open*
> rebellion, but by the *secret* commission by individuals or by small
> parties generally under cover of night—of isolated outrages and
> by threats calculated to create and keep a feeling that neither
> life nor property would be safe as long as the demands of
> agrarianism were not granted. The agrarianism of today is not
> like a general organised conspiracy and is much more unlikely to
> meditate insurrection. What Ribbonism, Molly Maguireism and
> Terry Altism did in the past, agrarianism with much less organ-
> isation is doing today. The very absence of a special designation
> shows—or goes to show—that the agrarianism which now disturbs
> the peace of the country is not an organised conspiracy.[49]

This report does not just constitute an essay in clarification of the distinction between Fenianism and Ribbonism—a mere elaboration of O'Donovan Rossa's dictum. It implies something very much more: the major expansion in the armed potential of Connaught Fenianism did not mean that an insurrection was imminent, but it did, on the other hand, imply an increase in agrarianism. Fenian personnel may well have dominated (in a certain sense) Ribbon lodges by the 1870s, but at the price, however, of an acceptance of the traditional methods and objectives of agrarian outrage. This process was necessarily an uneven one: even at the peak of the land war in 1880 and 1881 a significant section of Connaught Fenians withdrew their support from the Land League in order to preserve the integrity of the original ideal of armed insurrection, but there can be no doubt of the basic tendency involved. The ideology and practices of 'agrarianism' appeared to become more and more significant among Connaught Fenianism in the very early 1870s. There is evidence of the same process in the other counties of Ned Duffy's region, Cavan, Longford[50] and Westmeath. The trend was clearly discerned by the Cavan County Inspector: 'We consider Fenianism, Ribbonism and agrarianism—all parts of the same machinery and I may call intimidation their artillery.'[51]

As the 1870s progressed, however, there was a growth of stability and prosperity in most parts of rural Ireland. There was a marked drop in outrages. What the developments of 1870–71 did mean was that when the agricultural situation soured towards the end of the decade there was a pre-existing tradition in certain areas of Fenian involvement in agrarianism. There was therefore an audience—or at least the possibility of a receptive hearing—for Michael Davitt and a number of local leaders when they attempted to initiate a mass movement on the land question at Irishtown, Co. Mayo, on 20 April 1879.

3

Land and the 'New Departure', 1879

Mr Dillon related how his father used to describe to
him how the leaders of the New Departure measured
the success of their meetings—they counted the numbers
who came forward afterwards and indicated they had
given up Fenian methods in favour of the Parnellite
Party and the New Departure.

Irish Times, 29 Dec. 1973

In our judgment the object aimed at by Mr Davitt and
the founder members of the Land League with regard
to the revolutionary party was not to put an end to, or
restrain its actions, by merging it with the new movement but to point out to those holding Fenian opinions
that the two parties did not clash.

Report of the Special Commission, 1888,
32, H.C. 1890 [C.5891] XXVII, 512

1. Realignments

For the Fenian movement the 1870s was a decade of disappointment. It was true that in the Clan na Gael it had developed an
American revolutionary body and leadership—of which John Devoy
was the major figure—which had proved capable of successfully
mounting the rescue by the *Catalpa* of six Fenian prisoners in
Fremantle, Australia, in March 1876. But important though the
Catalpa rescue was as a propaganda coup, it did not achieve any of
the fundamental objectives of Clan na Gael. Dr William Carroll
reminded his fellow Clan leader John Devoy in the same month as
the *Catalpa* rescue that it was 'the general opinion of our American
friends, that while we are capable of brilliant, desperate, discon-
nected personal effort, there is no hope of our ever rising to the
level of successful revolutionists'.[1]

John Devoy had vigorously combated the organisational concept
held by the former IRB leader James Stephens—its paraphernalia
of government of exile, its absence of secrecy, its mystique of the
leader—and the low quality of its officers.[2] But he had failed to
combat the militarist essence of the Stephens position. The belief in
armed insurrection as the sole means of achieving Irish independence, preferably while England's attention was distracted by some
imperial difficulty, went unchallenged. The Clan hoped that England

would go to war with Russia in the 1875–78 period over the crumbling Turkish power in the Balkans. After the Berlin Congress of 1878, which eased this difficult situation, they pinned their hopes on British troubles in Afghanistan; in 1879 attention was focused on Zululand.

A document issued by the General Military Council of the Clan na Gael on 23 December 1877, albeit written by the British spy General Millen,[3] probably accurately reflected opinion within the organisation. It declared that if the opportunity for insurrection accorded by the Anglo-Russian conflict was missed, 'we would despair of doing anything in the present generation'.[4] In fact any hope of fighting was a vain one. Carroll reported to Devoy from Ireland on 19 January 1878: 'You will be sorry to learn that our dear friend [the IRB] is in even worse health than we were informed, for, with characteristic modesty, he had not written fully the extent of his sufferings.'[5]

By this time Irish Fenianism had split three ways. Fenianism lost heavily to the Home Rule movement in the 1870s;[6] a small section (perhaps 1,500) still supported Stephens's claim to be the leader;[7] while the majority still supported the IRB, which was linked into the 10,000-strong Clan na Gael. Carroll's Irish tour of 1878 certainly improved matters: in particular, he won over the Leinster members (who had been particularly inclined to accept the leadership of Stephens) to the Supreme Council. Nevertheless, the final position was not a happy one. The Supreme Council commanded the allegiance of about 24,000, compared with over 40,000 a few years before. The process of arming had also been neglected, and there was little hope of a successful uprising in the near future.[8]

But if an insurrectionary policy was being called into question, was there any alternative? Was it possible to construct a popular Irish alliance? The hostility (or indifference) of Fenianism's traditional 'core' social grouping, the 'urban lower classes',[9] towards the better-off farmers who dominated land reform politics in the 1870s appeared to rule this out. James Stephens was by no means personally disinterested in social and political questions, as his decision to join the International revealed. But he explained in 1886:

I did not think it possible at the time to inaugurate a land movement for, in the first place, Messrs Charles Gavan Duffy, John Francis Maguire and others had previously damned whatever chances it might have had by running it into a parliamentary rut and all but annihilating it there, and in the second, I did not believe that I could unite the people on the issue of the land as it was looked on . . . as the raving of a Bedlamite; and moreover, I found the labourers and mechanics would never join the tenantry shoulder to shoulder in the enterprise.[10]

This feeling of hostility was heightened by the relative prosperity and stability of the farmers since the troubles of 1870 and 1871 which had seen some rural Fenians participate in Ribbonism; and it allowed the romantic Kickham–O'Leary faction which dominated the leadership and policies of the IRB to take little or no note of Irish landlordism except to hope that the sons of the landlords would be converted to nationalism by reading Davis's poems or Meagher's speeches.[11] But, as Michael Davitt noted in an important comment, this 'absurd credulity'[12] did not extend to extreme circles in the United States. It was dropped, he felt, in the passage over the Atlantic by those who had to thank landlordism for being the cause of their exile.[13]

This resentment was supplemented by the rise of Irish-American social radicalism in the 1870s.[14] Patrick Ford's *Irish World*, with its opposition to monopoly in money and land, was a symptom of this new development. John Devoy insisted that when Davitt came to America he found the leading Clan na Gael cadres already well versed in the argument (first developed by Fintan Lalor) that the land question could be made the material for victory. Let the occupiers of the soil, Lalor had argued, refuse all further payment of rent to the 'present usurping proprietors, until the people, the true proprietors . . . have in national congress . . . decided what rents they are to pay and to whom'.[15] It is safe to say that by 1878 the insurrectionary tradition was being modified. There was undoubtedly a new openness in Irish-America on the land question.[16]

There was also a softening in attitude towards that militant section of the Home Rule Party which had been attempting a policy of 'obstruction' in parliament. In 1875 Joseph Biggar had initiated an experiment with 'obstruction'. He delayed passage of an Irish coercion bill by reading long extracts from parliamentary blue books. Although this behaviour outraged Butt, the Home Rule leader, who always felt that Home Rulers should respect the traditions of the House of Commons, Biggar was joined by Parnell and a handful of other colleagues in the session of 1877. This intervention was regarded with approval by even the most militant varieties of nationalist opinion. Nevertheless, it should be stressed that the development of the Fenians' attitude to constitutionalists was often an uneasy and halting process.

At a meeting in Brooklyn in 1878 John Devoy explained that a rebuff from the Russian ambassador in Washington—who refused to enter into a Fenian alliance, pointing out the relative absence of publicly expressed opposition to British rule in Ireland—had made a particularly strong impression upon him. But it had taken two years for this point to sink home. As late as September 1877 the Clan na Gael leadership still felt that Parnell, one of the leading obstructionists, should be pressed into the 'regular work' of advocating separatism.[17]

2. The 'New Departure': Parnell, Devoy and Davitt

At the beginning of 1878 Parnell, who had systematically flirted with Fenianism in public, managed in private to convince J. J. O'Kelly and Dr William Carroll of his adherence to the principle of absolute independence while avoiding any commitment to the Fenian movement as such. Both men wanted to believe Parnell anyway, fresh, as they were, from the débâcle of the failure of their attempt to persuade the Spanish government to accept a plan for seizing Gibraltar. By the time of a second meeting in March 1878, at which Parnell remained largely silent, the basis of the contact had altered. There was no longer any question of engaging Parnell in 'regular work'. Rather the question now was: how were the Fenians to help Parnell? This was the background when in October 1878 Parnell was re-elected president of the Home Rule Confederation of Great Britain with Fenian support and against Butt's wishes, and when Devoy, misjudging the importance of the moment and believing that a crisis had come, offered Parnell the 'New Departure' package. He offered Parnell the support of American nationalists on the following conditions:

(1) Abandonment of the federal demand and substitution of a general declaration in favour of self-government.

(2) Vigorous agitation of the land question on the basis of a peasant proprietary, while accepting concessions tending to abolish arbitrary eviction.

(3) Exclusion of all sectarian issues from the platform.

(4) Party members to vote together on all imperial and home questions, adopt an aggressive policy and energetically resist coercive legislation.

(5) Advocacy of all struggling nationalities in the British Empire or elsewhere.

Devoy backed this up with five 'rigged' interviews with prominent separatists in the New York *Herald* in support of the new policy. Throughout the article he several times repeated the suggestion, already expressed by Parnell,[18] that a majority of members of parliament secured by such an alliance should eventually meet as an Irish legislature, 'making that declaration a signal for a war of independence' if the country 'were otherwise ready'.[19] It should not be thought, therefore, that this advocacy by Devoy of 'going into politics' to win representation in local government and, more particularly, to agitate on the land question, involved any abandonment of revolutionary aims. In fact Devoy felt that a much sounder revolutionary strategy had been formulated.

At this point his gloss on the second plank of what became known as the New Departure proposals should be noted. 'It aimed', he wrote, 'at educating the people to a more radical land settlement [than the Buttite policy of the 'three Fs'] which could really only be effected by an independent Ireland.'[20] Devoy felt that as the British government would never accept the demand for peasant proprietorship, the struggle for that objective was inevitably also the struggle for political self-determination. It is important to understand his position on this matter.

A Clan na Gael resolution of September 1878 had expressed it perfectly by speaking of the 'abolition of landlordism which an Irish republic alone can effect'.[21] Devoy noted: 'It will be seen from this that the most extreme and violent Land League orator or writer never during the whole course of the subsequent agitation went one iota beyond the original key-note in New York but rather the reverse.'[22] In December 1878 Devoy completed his exposition of the New Departure with a reassurance that no abandonment of nationalist principle was intended, and disavowing any 'alliance' with constitutionalists. He called on the Fenians to enter political life to fight, in particular, for land reform, and by so doing end their isolation.

I shall be told that an English parliament will never do any of these things [he wrote]. Then, I say, these things must only wait until an Irish parliament can do them better, but in the meantime good work will have been done, sound principles will have been inculcated, and the country aroused and organised.[23]

The full political programme of the New Departure was never agreed upon, let alone implemented. The IRB Supreme Council, dominated by figures such as Kickham and O'Leary, rejected it at a meeting in Paris in January 1879, although individual members were left free to take part in open political activity, though not, of course, to enter parliament. More important, the economic crisis of Irish agriculture in 1879, combined with the beginning of an agrarian agitation in Mayo, reduced the relevance of hitherto existing political plans.

Devoy fully recognised the fact that the agrarian crisis had greatly changed the context of political manoeuvres. At a meeting in Dublin as early as 6 April 1879 Devoy recorded that Parnell was prepared to accept the policy of a new national public movement which the two men had discussed in March in Boulogne. But the movement for which Davitt wanted his aid 'was an agrarian one, instead of the one planned in the New Departure. . . . The changed situation required careful handling, and he [Parnell] could not possibly foresee that Davitt and his friends would be able to keep the Mayo men so well in hand as they afterwards demonstrated their ability to do so.'[24] Parnell, at this point, refused to undertake the work, although he showed the keenest interest in the situation.

But Devoy nevertheless claimed that he and Davitt, 'speaking for large bodies of Fenians', although not official representatives, reached an agreement with Parnell on 1 June 1879. The agreement, while utterly ignoring details, was clear, definite and precise as far as vital political principles were concerned. It had four main points:

(1) In the conduct of the public movement, as far as Parnell and Davitt were able to influence it, there should not be anything said or done to impair the vitality of the Fenian movement or to discredit its ideal of complete national independence to be secured by the eventual use of physical force.

(2) The demand for self-government should not for the present be publicly defined, but nothing short of a national parliament with power over all vital national interests and an executive responsible to it should be accepted.

(3) The settlement of the land question to be demanded should be the establishment of a peasant proprietary to be reached by compulsory purchase.

(4) The Irish members of parliament elected through the public movement should form an absolutely independent party, asking and accepting no places, salaried or honorary, under the British government, either for themselves, their constituents or anyone else.[25]

The full political meaning of this agreement, for Devoy at any rate, can only be deduced from his comment on this last plank:

Parnell was already acting on it and it was his own policy. Davitt was not bothering himself much at that time about what might be done in Parliament. His mind was filled with the work to be done on the soil of Ireland and among the Irish in America. He and I agreed to the plank as a necessity of the situation *but Davitt seemed to me at that time to be as strongly as I was myself in favour of a policy looking to an eventual withdrawal from parliament* [my italics].[26]

It is very clear, therefore, that the neo-Fenian leadership did not fall into an 'economism' of the land question as a result of first-hand experience of distress in Mayo. In other words, their policy did not involve a suppression of the challenge to British state power in Ireland in favour of immersion in the cause of improving Irish conditions. It was still felt that the land question was the 'material for victory' in the sense that the British parliament's certain refusal of the full Irish demand for land reform would create the condition for a possible withdrawal from the House of Commons. As early as 1868 J. S. Mill in *England and Ireland* had pointed out that the rule of Ireland rightfully belonged to those who by means consistent with justice were able to make the cultivators of the soil the owners of it.[27] The point was not lost on the Fenians: given their own conception of 'justice', they sought to win the 'rule of Ireland' by taking up agrarian politics. At this moment, at least, there was no suggestion that the political problem of Irish independence should be suppressed in favour of a mere agrarian agitation. The land question had expanded in importance—particularly for Davitt—but the land question had always had dominance within the elements of the New Departure scheme.

This policy was for Devoy admittedly something of a gamble. He insisted a year later that the 'demands of the Land League will not be granted by a Parliament of British landlords. Of course they won't.'[28] But he admitted that there was a danger that the movement would be sidetracked into mere social reformism. Devoy was prepared in a debate on this theme with John Boyle O'Reilly to speak of 'defects in the current Land League programme—or more correctly want of a programme' with regard to the national question.[29] There was also the danger that the British government might concede just enough to defuse the agitation. He was even prepared at least to consider the possibility that the land question would be settled 'moderately well',[30] and he acknowledged the view that this would make the farmers loyal to Britain. He regarded this idea, however, as the greatest slander on the Irish cause. 'I repudiate such advocacy of nationality and contend that its best allies will be found in a sturdy, well-fed, well-clad and comfortably housed agricultural population, giving employment to a correspondingly comfortable class in the towns.'[31] In other words, Devoy felt that the gamble was justifiable because, even in the event of a failure to win complete victory, a step forward, at least, would have been made in the building up of nationalist forces. The national revolution might elude his grasp, but at least a generation of peasant nationalists—or at any rate peasants with good reason to be grateful to nationalists—would be created.

His allies intended to use the newly acquired strength, the increased vigour, activity and organisational development among the people, for the purpose of enabling those very people gradually to win the power of settling the land question and all other questions that affected their daily lives.[32] It was with justice, then, that Devoy insisted in March 1882 that the movement was undertaken with a thorough belief that under British domination a complete solution of the land question was impossible, and that whatever strength should be gained by the Irish people from concessions should be used for sapping the foundations of British rule.[33] But he admitted that neither he nor his traditionalist Fenian opponents had any control over the future.[34]

This exposition of Devoy's political position is a necessary preliminary to a discussion of his claim that a definite agreement was reached at the meeting on 1 June. Both Davitt and Parnell later strongly denied it. Parnell's evidence before the Special Commission was designed to protect his image of the late 1880s as a constitutional politician; it is certainly misleading on certain points as to the nature of his relationship with 'extreme men' in the late 1870s. Nevertheless, it has been felt unlikely that Parnell would compromise himself by such a compact. There are, however, hints in *Devoy's Post-Bag* which suggest that such an agreement may have existed or, at least, that Parnell may have connived at creating the appearance that such an agreement existed.[35] But it is certain that Parnell did not accept the 'spirit' of the compact as outlined in Devoy's supplementary remarks, for he did not share the Clan na Gael's view of the relationship between the land and national question. Parnell's view on this relationship was to emerge with a rare (for him) and unambiguous clarity in the course of the agitation. It is therefore clear that any agreement on 1 June could not have had a substantial basis.

Davitt equally was determined in later years to protect his image as a compassionate Christian reformer, and there is no doubt that he both suppressed the extent of his Fenian commitments (he was involved, for example, in gun-running in the first hectic days of the League), while exaggerating his involvement in the land question by the claim that he had largely evolved the Land League plan during his jail sentence. In fact Davitt's interest in the land question was relatively undeveloped on his release, although under the stimulus of Irish-American radicalism combined with the depression in Ireland his position was soon altered.[36] There is little doubt from the surviving letters that Davitt at least was bound to an agreement as Devoy suggested.[37] 'Mr Davitt's idea was greater than the land question when he first organised the Land League,' said Devoy in

C

1881. 'He believed in separation and the Land League was only a stepping-stone to it.'[38] There is no doubt also that leading Clan na Gael cadres accepted the existence of this agreement, and this was to be of decisive importance.

3. The Central Tenants' Defence Association

Devoy claimed that at the meeting on 1 June Parnell accepted Davitt's invitation to attend the Westport meeting of 8 June, the second in the new agitation. But Parnell was not easy in his mind about the project. He knew, for example, about the extent of clerical opposition to it in Mayo (which was largely owing to the failure of Davitt and his allies to consult the nationalist Archbishop of Tuam about the land meetings), and Davitt later felt that this was a possible reason for his caution.[39] There is some evidence to suggest that Parnell sought the support of Archbishop MacHale[40] and also Archbishop Croke of Cashel at about this time. At the beginning of June 1881 Croke claimed that at the start of the agitation Parnell had begged him on his knees to have the priests join the movement, for without the priests it could not succeed, and with the priests it could not fail.[41]

He decided to seek advice and sought that of Andrew Kettle, the secretary of the Central Tenants' Defence Association and one of its more radical members, at a CTDA meeting in the European Hotel.[42]

Recent developments within the CTDA had seemed to imply that there was some sort of basis for an agrarian agitation. The CTDA represented many of the larger cattle farmers who had suffered heavy losses owing to the increase in foreign competition resulting from better methods of transportation. The *Times* of 6 April 1880 reported that in the previous three years the number of American cattle imported into Britain had increased by 80 per cent. In 1879, according to Baldwin and Robertson, the assistant commissioners of the Richmond Commission, many of the graziers sold their cattle for less than they had paid for them. 'In the opinion of moderate and competent judges,' another report claimed, '£15m. could not fully represent the depreciation of Irish stock during these years.'[43] This was not perceived as a temporary setback, for both nationalists[44] and Conservatives[45] insisted that the time was ripe for some expansion of tillage.

The CTDA constituency was quick to demand reform. In 1876 Isaac Butt's land bill had been framed in close association with these prosperous farmers. 'The bill is really and truly', Mitchell Henry said, 'the product of the large farmers of Ireland.'[46] In 1877 the general prosperity created the situation whereby Butt was able to exclude the large farmers from his bill to give it a greater chance of parliamentary success. In early 1879 there was strong pressure within the CTDA to include once again this category within the terms of Butt's bill. Mitchell Henry, who had just been elected to the leading place on the Home Rule council by the electors of the Home Rule League and who was easily the most energetic and serious Buttite, opposed this step. Henry was supported by the Western land reformers, Matthew Harris, William Kilroe and John Callanan, all of the Ballinasloe Tenants' Defence Association. The Ballinasloe TDA group felt that Henry had adopted their principle that tenants holding land valued at £50 or over should be excluded from the benefits which fixity of tenure would confer.[47] Harris went so far as to give the landlords a virtual invitation to oppose the claims of the graziers, 'for as far as public odium is concerned the graziers themselves are as unpopular as the worst class of landlords'.[48] However, Henry was placed under great pressure by the criticisms of Thomas Robertson of Athy, who held 211 Irish acres,[49] and of the *Freeman's Journal*[50] itself. At the national conference of the Home Rule League of 5 February shortly before his death Butt surrendered to the better-off farmers, while Mitchell Henry gave way to the significant extent of opposing the inclusion within the bill of non-residential holdings only.[51]

But the incident had revealed one very important fact: the stronger farmers felt the economic crisis so intensely that they were prepared to displace their traditional Buttite leadership if it did not give a strong enough lead in the struggle for land reform. It ruled out the possibility of any co-ordinated Buttite–CTDA alliance against the new movement. Henry never really regained their trust. By August 1880 he was trying to suppress his position of 1879, but he still found himself listed by the Kilkenny Tenants' Defence Association as one of those who advocated 'restricting tenant right to smallholdings'[52] and 'the narrow . . . policy of depriving the large producers and the backbone of the agricultural labourer's interest in Ireland'.[53] On the other hand, the ultra-radical opinions of Matthew Harris can hardly have inclined the CTDA constituency in a favourable way towards the new land movement in the West with which he was so obviously connected.

Parnell had not made the mistake of antagonising the CTDA. He had distanced himself from Mitchell Henry's analysis of the large farmers' trading on the misfortune of the small with the comment that he did not believe that the House of Commons had any sympathy with Irish farmers large or small. He believed their sympathy amounted to 'that quantity known as nothing'.[54] But on the other hand, the decision to associate actively in the Western agitation was still a difficult one. The success of the first land meeting at Irish-town on 20 April 1879 certainly indicated a significant degree of potential support. An estimated 7,000 people heard a semi-revolutionary speech from Thomas Brennan, a parliamentarian one from John O'Connor Power, and an economic and social treatise on the land question from John Ferguson.

Nevertheless, Parnell found that Kettle was worried by the Fenian connections of the new movement.[55] (It should be remembered that Kettle had attacked the 'obstruction' policy[56] and was a loyal supporter of Butt until the latter's death.)[57] However, gesturing to the new militancy of at least a section of the 'respectable' men, he advised the squire of Avondale to join the Westport platform.[58]

Parnell accepted Kettle's advice, but his immediate experience of the Mayo land agitation did not mark a definite full-hearted commitment. In fact after his Westport visit Parnell once again resolved to keep his distance. From his point of view there were a number of alarming features about the new movement.

4. *Radical Agrarianism: Connaught*

As Matthew Harris had noted, the Connaught movement had broken with the previous style of agitation. Its leaders no longer proceeded in the manner of the old agitators, 'praising English law and the English constitution' as something almost divine, while 'in another part and in the same breath denouncing Perfidious Albion as the cause of all our woes and, of course, winding up with a pitiful whine about the loyalty of the Irish, or a degrading sentiment that we were willing to sell our loyalty for some paltry measure of relief'.[59] (It is particularly remarkable that Land League orators never appealed to the British Liberal Party as against the Conservative government, despite the fact that the Conservative Chief Secretary of Ireland, James Lowther, was in certain moods almost a parody of a blimpish colonial administrator.) For a full understanding of the nature of this militancy it is necessary to look at the exact relationship between the economic crisis and political developments.

As early as March 1879 John Walsh of Balla, Co. Mayo, a commercial traveller with a privileged access to the views and accounts of the shopkeepers in the West, gave Davitt a grim account of the situation.[60] The May fairs brought no improvement; editorials in the Western press commented anxiously upon the deterioration of prices as against those of 1878.[61] In August William O'Brien, whom the *Freeman's Journal* had appointed as their special commissioner in the West, argued in one of his influential articles that there was a 'desperate partnership' between small farmers and shopkeepers.

Although it was estimated that over £200,000 was owing to the shopkeepers in Mayo in 1879, there was only a slight increase in the number of processes in civil bill courts—a tribute both to the mercy of the creditors and the hopelessness of legal pressure.[62] The ideological basis of this 'desperate partnership' was given a classic exposition by J. Ward, a small trader of Ballinasloe, at the Ballinasloe Royal Agricultural Society in October 1879:

> The trade of this town . . . has suffered the last twenty years and upwards . . . [from] the clearing of those vast tracts of land on every side until those who constitute the mainstay of our business became nearly all swept away. . . . Whatever little independence has been earned by the traders of Ballinasloe it is certainly not due to the patronage extended to them by many of the graziers who go and buy their goods elsewhere; and to some of them it would appear not fashionable to deal in Ballinasloe.[63]

O'Brien's report continued in the same pessimistic vein. The Meath graziers who used to flock to the Western fairs to obtain young stock had ceased to attend. He had heard of cases of small farmers driving cows to five successive fairs to meet bills in the bank and returning home with tears in their eyes, having been unable to get a single offer.

It was clear also that the demand for harvest labour in England was to slacken as part of the slump. In the Ballyhaunis area, for example, the majority of the cottier tenants expected to earn in a few weeks in England double their annual income in Ireland.[64] In 1878 £22,000 had been sent home through the Ballyhaunis post office—a sum which would have made some impression on the £50,000 owed to the local shopkeepers.[65] The total loss to the peasantry of Connaught from this cause alone was estimated at £250,000 for the year 1879.[66]

There was a heavy reliance on Indian meal. In Castlebar alone the credit in this single article amounted to £18,000.[67] Two Castlerea merchants had distributed over £40,000 worth of the meal.[68] But O'Brien admitted there was 'as yet no downright hunger among the farmers'.[69] A good harvest—if it came—would avert famine. There would be enough potatoes to last till March, although the problem of debt would still remain.[70] In the event, the harvest failed, as the poor weather had implied. But the fact remains that primary distress was not a dominant feature of the situation until the effects of failure of the potato crop were felt.

It was this situation—the definite expectation of distress rather than its reality—which an assorted group of agrarian radicals, Fenians and Home Rulers moved to exploit in early 1879. It is this

Western agrarian

fact which helps, in part, to explain the content of the speeches made between June and October. In this respect, Sir Henry James's analysis of the speeches is accurate:

> I can, of course, find organisation for the purpose of placing the tenant in a better position against his landlord, but when you come to the question of this social crisis, this distress . . . I do not find the speakers urging on an audience they were addressing that any steps should be taken to relieve distress, and in all that occurred in Dublin on the 21st October 1879 [the first Irish National Land League conference] the like silence occurred.[71]

The militants were able to adopt a 'manly' tone. The likelihood of the impending crisis gave a spur to the tenant farmers, while at the same time it was possible to avoid, in the early stages, demoralising appeals for relief—and also (and more importantly) the demoralising effects of the work of relief agencies.[72] A much stronger ideological tack was possible. The point can be taken further. The speeches of the period June–October 1879 do indeed insist that tenants band together and refuse to pay a rack-rent, that they stay united until they won a reasonable reduction, that they (in Parnell's phrase at Westport) 'keep a firm grip on their homesteads'.

But this aspect of the matter must be placed in the context of the most deliberate and prolonged rumination on New Departure themes. The first resolution at Westport on 8 June was in favour of 'self-government', the phrase behind which Devoy had suggested the Fenians and the Parnellites should unite. Davitt discussed it in precisely this context. The crowd, he said, knew his definition of self-government (as a Fenian), but he did not wish the meeting to pass the resolution in a spirit which was unacceptable to Parnell. Michael M. O'Sullivan, the future assistant secretary of the Land League, expressed himself less diplomatically:

> All I have to say is that you may continue the demand for Home Rule, for you will never get it peaceably, and keep your eye very steadily on the other (*great cheering*). Moral force is truly a great power; but it becomes greater when backed up by physical force—by the power of sword (*great applause*). Do you expect autonomy from your hereditary enemies by peaceful means? Do you expect tenant right from a parliament of landlords? (*cries of* NO NO) No, my friends, you must depend upon yourselves and yourselves only (*loud cheers*).

They were to combine and offer a fair rent; if that was not accepted, they were to pay none. If they followed his advice,

Before many years you'll own your own lands (*great cheering*).
A VOICE: Three cheers for the revolution.
O'SULLIVAN: The rulers of your own country. (*Cheers and cheers*)
And here a '98 pike was made to perform significant flourishes in the air.[73]

At Milltown, the next meeting of the agitation, Thomas Brennan
—a member of the 'triumvirate' who with Davitt and Egan controlled the League's affairs in its first year of existence—argued
that he 'believed it was only in an Irish Senate the right to ownership of the land would be recognised. . . . They would be able to
act in such a way that Mr Parnell and others should be able to shake
the dust of Westminster off their feet.'[74] Both of these speeches
coalesce on one fundamental point: they insist that the British
government will not grant peasant proprietorship and that therefore an agitation which keeps this as its main demand will inevitably involve a struggle to set up an Irish parliament.

There is, however, a difference of emphasis between these two
speeches. O'Sullivan was a close friend and political ally of Matthew
Harris, who was, according to Devoy, 'strongly of the opinion that
an agrarian agitation could be made a powerful revolutionary
weapon[75] but so far as I could judge from his talk he seemed to
think that the agitation should be entirely outside Parliament and
free from any control of the parliamentary party'.[76] Harris and
O'Sullivan were closer to traditional Fenianism. Harris, indeed, felt
that Devoy by excessively abrasive handling of the New Departure
had needlessly alienated this respected if inflexible tradition.[77] On
the day of his arrest in April 1881 Harris still spoke of the hope of
Ireland lying with the 'advanced national party',[78] though they
should not commit themselves to any one mode of action, while he
also threatened the leaders of the land agitation with a 'day of
reckoning'[79] if they were not loyal to the people. O'Sullivan, for his
part, had written in a letter to the press—which was refused by the
Freeman's Journal but published in Western nationalist journals—
that 'A final appeal to the sword . . . should not altogether be lost
sight of.'[80] In New York in the late spring of 1881, after his departure from Ireland and shortly after the arrest of Harris, he
reiterated the point: 'I would be untrue to my own convictions if
I did not tell you that the only hope for the nationality of Ireland
lies in the ring of the musket and the flash of the sabre.'[81]

A letter from O'Sullivan to Harris in January 1880 reveals that,
despite their influence, both men were in a subordinate position
within the Land League hierarchy: 'There is a little circle—Egan,

Davitt, Brennan and a few others in town—that work with themselves. No person knows what they are about, what they have in view. . . . I am not in the confidence of the ring.'[82] It would seem that O'Sullivan and Harris were felt to be close to the old style of Fenianism—O'Sullivan's speech is an illustration of this—while the 'triumvirate' of Davitt, Egan and Brennan, as Brennan's speech illustrated, looked more explicitly, although not dogmatically, to an eventual Parnellite withdrawal from parliament. Egan revealed the basis of his political action in a letter to Devoy of 17 February 1882:

> I always thought that you and Michael Davitt were completely in accord. His views are mine, therefore you and I should be pretty much of one mind. . . . We mean to win it [Home Rule] peacefully if we can but win it somehow.[83]

At any rate, as far as both tendencies of 'Ribbon Fenianism' (as hostile commentators called it) were concerned, the dominant tactical concern at this stage was to ensure that the demand for peasant proprietorship be kept to the fore, not simply out of agrarian radicalism, but because it was seen also as a means of winning Irish independence.

Devoy's comment on the tone of the agitation is suggestive:

> The strong nationalist tendency was, in fact, the most remarkable feature of the agitation. Davitt's scornful repudiation of Butt's Home Rule scheme and all other attempts at compromise on the national question evoked severe criticism from the Home Rule League. But without resolutions and speeches expressing such sentiments the nationalists of Mayo could not have attended the meetings; it was they who gathered the timid farmers and marshalled the crowds that gave these meetings their importance. Besides this, they were the expression of the deliberate conviction of the speakers.[84]

5. Agrarianism and Constitutionalism

Parnell clearly had his doubts about the whole project. He was not inspired by revolutionary daring. When Davitt in May 1878 had outlined the plan culminating in secession to him he had asked 'And what then?' in a spirit of obvious caution.[85] According to Devoy, Parnell was afraid that the Fenians harboured 'insurrectionary projects which might be sprung on the movement in some period of popular excitement'.[86] Devoy argued that, in fact, Davitt had no notions of a putsch of this kind and that he had firm control in the West. Nonetheless, militant Mayo speeches to the frequent audience accompaniment of 'We will have total separation' were hardly reassuring. But the deeper substance of Parnell's difference with the 'Ribbon Fenians' lay not simply in his greater caution or concern over foolish public gestures of militancy: it lay in the fact that Parnell's nationalism, though genuine, was the nationalism of the Anglo-Irish gentry. Parnell had a completely different world-view and a completely different assessment of the relationship between the land question and the national question.

It is signalled by an anecdote of F. H. O'Donnell's: 'He [Parnell] could be frankly cynical in the presence of a comrade he never deceived. "But you know, Parnell, that abolishing the landlords is not abolishing the English." "Our beloved countrymen say they think it will!" ' [87] This reply illustrated that while Parnell certainly did not share the views of his beloved countrymen, he did have a position on the relationship between the land question and the national question. He stated it in early 1879:

> Now as regards the land question, I have never spoken of the land question in the House of Commons. However, I do not believe that that question can be advanced by the speeches that many of the Irish members are in the habit of making. . . . I do not believe that the settlement of the land question would injure the cause of self-government. If you had the land question settled on a permanent basis, you would remove the great reason that now exists to prevent the large and influential class of Irish land-lords falling in with the demand for self-government (hear, hear). I don't believe in starving the Irish people to make it national. [88]

He made the same point when he followed O'Sullivan in speaking on the Westport platform:

> Perhaps I may be permitted to refer to the great question of self-government for Ireland. You will say perhaps that many men have said that this struggling for concessions in the House of Commons is a demoralising thing. Now I am as confident as I am of my own existence that if you had men of determination or some sort of courage and energy representing you, you could obtain concessions (hear, hear).
>
> We are not likely to get them of such importance and such amount as to run the risk of being demoralised. I have always noticed that the breaking down of barriers between different classes has increased their self-respect and increased the spirit of nationality among our people. I am convinced that nothing would more effectively promote the cause of self-government for Ireland than the breaking down of these barriers between different classes.

Parnell's view

Nothing would be more effective for that than the obtaining of a good land Bill—the planting of the people on the soil. If we had the farmers on the soil tomorrow, we would not be long getting an Irish parliament (*applause*).[89]

The perspective here is, of course, entirely different from that of either O'Sullivan or Brennan. Parnell had clearly insisted on the possibility of winning land reform and, eventually, peasant proprietorship through constitutional means. He was not afraid to say that Home Rule could similarly be won. The neo-Fenians, on the other hand, saw the British government's certain refusal of peasant proprietorship as the prop of a campaign for self-government. Parnell, in fact—and this is the crucial point—saw a good measure of land reform as the way to bring the landlords as individuals into the nationalist movement. This decisively important point was repeated during each phase of the campaign. In an interesting passage Kettle described Parnell's views as expressed in a discussion in early 1880.

We reviewed the whole social system that existed in Ireland. He [Parnell] regretted having to take men away from their business and put them into public positions for which they had no training or experience. He was always very hopeless about the older landlords ever throwing in their lot with the people in Ireland but he expected that the young men would if the land question was settled by purchase. I always held that it would be an insult to commonsense to imagine that England would ever delegate the governing powers of Ireland into the hands of such men as Parnell was gathering around him unless the English radicals overturned their classes and got on to a democratic line in England. He would either go on to abolish the classes in Ireland or fall back and press them into the work of their own country. But we always agreed that to nationalise landlord and mortgagees and men with capital in Ireland it would be essential to push the land question to a final settlement as soon as possible.[90]

Parnell had no greater admiration for his class than had John Devoy, who in a stinging speech claimed that the Anglo-Irish gentry were utterly barren of intellectual eminence of any kind.[91] The Home Rule leader told William O'Brien: 'The only good thing the Irish landlords have to show for themselves are their hounds and perhaps in the Roscommon country their horses.'[92] Parnell simply felt that given the endemic class conflict in rural Ireland and the social composition of nationalist support, Home Rule was too much of a risk for any British government to take. Even on the day of his arrest—a moment of maximum irritation—in October 1881 he had said:

> The great difficulty about giving Ireland the right of autonomy is the existence of the landlord class in the country. So long as it is a continual source of dispute between landlords and tenants, how much rent is to be paid by the tenants and received by the landlords, I do not see how it is possible from the point of view of the government that they would give us autonomy. I think the land question has to be settled. If the land question were settled every other question would, I think, settle itself.[93]

Parnell's allies (with the exception of William O'Brien and Kettle) appear to have been indifferent to the precise nature of his position. But only the wild 'Transatlantic' of the *Irish World* seems to have opposed it:

> 'Individual landlords are well fitted to take their place as leaders of the Irish nation.' Who are these landlords, Mr Parnell? Except yourself, I see not one in the crowd. There was once a great land-lord leader in King-Harman, another in Mitchell Henry, another in Mr Meldon, another in Mr Shaw. Where are they today in the battle for the land? They are discovered easily in the government lobby today where the land is refused to God's child.[94]

It is little wonder that Parnell had fears about his Fenian allies—though it may also be seen how his peculiar, almost idiosyncratic, brand of conservative nationalism accommodated an agrarian radicalism which created the possibility of an alliance in the first place.

For what other constitutional politician could Davitt turn to? P. J. Smyth, MP, an old Repealer, and F. H. O'Donnell, MP, were the only possible alternatives. They were, at any rate, the only two other candidates discussed in the Devoy–Davitt correspondence. In certain respects they had more to offer the Clan na Gael. Smyth, a ''48 man', had an impeccable political youth behind him. O'Donnell had been, at least in his own view, the brains behind the obstruction campaign. But neither of these men could believe in the Land League. In particular, they could not see it as the means to national liberation. Smyth saw clearly the desirability of granting at least the 'three Fs', but he did not think this had any substantive political implications. He did see that peasant proprietorship had political implications, but these were ones which he strongly disapproved of. For he thought that immediately to institutionalise peasant proprietorship in Ireland would require setting up a vast British administrative machinery in Dublin, which would further increase rather than decrease England's hold over Ireland. 'The British Government', he wrote, 'would be landlords direct over all the lands of Ireland.'[95] Smyth did not wish the landlord class destroyed. It was entirely contrary to the principles of his non-sectarian but gentlemanly nationalism. Smyth's position was simply that of high-minded nationalism. As he put it at the Cloneen meeting to protest against the Kilburry eviction in June 1880: 'Selfishness was not the foundation of national greatness. Never did a nation become pure and strong except by resting its cause on a pure and high ideal.'[96]

Parnell claimed in public to regard Smyth's views as confused. In a speech in Tipperary he argued that it would give the government very much more power over a country to allow it every nine or ten years to revalue the land of the tenant and fix the rent which was payable rather than fix the sum to be paid by the people to the government for a certain period of years, so that at the end of that time there should be nothing to pay.[97] But in private he acknowledged to Davitt that there was a risk incurred in fighting for a final settlement of the land question, rather than for an Irish parliament through which a settlement safe for the national cause could be insured.[98]

F. H. O'Donnell, in a work published in 1910, later claimed a position very similar to that of Smyth: 'If Mr Devoy, like Mr Davitt, was ready to acknowledge the British parliament's right to legislate for Ireland on the great and important questions of land and the introduction of peasant proprietary . . . Mr Devoy and Mr Davitt had turned champion of the Act of Union.'[99] O'Donnell continued by describing the Land League as a 'huge take-in which hit so sorely all sections of nationalists that in order to avoid being posted as fools they called Parnellism a miracle of intelligence and honesty'.[100] At the time, however, O'Donnell himself had shown some disposition to be taken in. He often denounced in strong terms the very landlord class whose virtues he was later to discover, and he went so far as to apply—unsuccessfully—in October 1880 to join the Land League.[101] But his recollection is correct in so far as it suggests that he did not see the connection between the land and the national question as seen by Devoy—although it was the enthusiasm for the British Empire as expressed in his 'imperial' speech which actually ruled him out of consideration.[102] Parnell was, in fact, the only available politician who saw a positive link between the two movements for independence and a settlement of the land question—albeit in a different light from that of his Fenian allies.

But given the existence of these deep-rooted differences, it need not be a matter for surprise that Parnell's Westport speech by no means signalled his complete adherence to the Mayo movement. Davitt wrote to Devoy on 23 August 1879: 'The Home Rulers are afraid of a movement independent of them and fight shy of the Mayo one. Parnell is afraid to lead it too—but wishes it success.'[103]

For the months of August and September 1879, at any rate, Parnell stayed clear of the Western land agitation, but he did have contact with Davitt on political ground. In his letter of 23 August Davitt also told Devoy: 'The Gray party is completely crushed by Parnell, and from the meeting in the Rotunda the other night Home Rule in future means Parnellism. This shows the greater need there is of influencing him to abandonment of the name.'[104] But even at this successful Parnellite meeting in the Rotunda on 21 August Parnell had said:

> If we find that we cannot get sufficient force of men [MPs] to carry out our ideas, it will be our duty to give up parliamentary agitation altogether. But when I give up parliamentary agitation I don't promise to take up any other agitation.[105]

Davitt's remark to Devoy is a clear reference to the latter's demand that a condition of the New Departure was the replacement of Butt's federal demand for Home Rule by the demand for self-government. Also on 23 August there appeared a letter by Davitt in the *Connaught Telegraph* declaring:

> We have heard a great deal lately about fallacies concerning Home Rule but in my humble opinion the greatest fallacy in connection with it is the assumption the people of Ireland ever cared a jot for the federal scheme of which Mr Butt was the author.[106]

A week later he sent an even more forceful letter. He made it clear that although he opposed the principle of Home Rule, he saw no need to make personal attacks on its adherents, and he wished his political opponents would show the same charity. He opposed Home Rule, he added, firstly because, even from a constitutional point of view, it aimed at surrendering privileges and prerogatives which would preclude the possession of that independent legislature enjoyed in Ireland before the Act of Union. He said nothing of any separatist reasons he might put forward for opposing Home Rule, for he was dealing with the whole subject within constitutional ground only. Secondly, the Home Rule programme distinctly declared that if it was applied to Ireland, there would be no change in the present land settlement of the country. In other words, landlordism would remain. Thirdly, the conference at which the Home

Rule programme was drawn up was not a convention of delegates elected by the Irish people but an assemblage of gentlemen selected on a fancy franchise system of giving a privilege to those who would be likely to exercise it in the manner desired by the donors. Fourthly, the Home Rule policy had failed both in Ireland and England. Independently of Parnell it enjoyed no support in Ireland. Of all the Home Rule members, Parnell had identified himself least with the federal idea in his speeches in or out of the House of Commons.[107] Davitt was clearly committed to persuading Parnell to abandon the name 'Home Rule' and, indeed, to removing the demand from the political scene. But it was not immediately clear how this was to be done. He and other Fenians seized on an initiative which had been taken by the Sullivanite section of the Home Rule League[108] (i.e. the grouping organised around the determined Home Rule journal, *The Nation*) of calling for a national convention. This was the way to influence Parnell against Home Rule, he wrote to Devoy:

> Nothing but a Convention can effect this and none but myself is competing with T. D. S. [Sullivan] and his party as to how this should be organised. I proposed—in the presence of Parnell, T. D. S. and others—that a committee of twelve composed of four of the Home Rule League, four P. J. Smythites and four nationalists should be appointed to define a national platform and public policy. P. J. agreed to this but T. D. S. saw at once that a coalition between the nationalists and the repealers would swamp the Home Rulers, so he said nothing, which, of course, meant dissent.[109]

In September 1879, at any rate, it seemed important to Davitt that some action should be taken on this point. Accordingly the Home Rule League met on 11 September in the Rotunda in Dublin under the wing of Parnell and the extreme left of the Home Rule movement. They decided to take immediate advantage of the repeal of the Convention Act. Forty self-constituted members of the League determined to convoke an important convention in Dublin to imitate and foreshadow the Irish parliament. It was to consist of 300 persons elected as delegates, and every Irishman residing in Ireland who contributed a shilling was to be entitled to nominate ten persons for election and to elect 300 of the total number nominated. The only Home Rulers who publicly protested and refused to have anything to do with the new movement were Mitchell Henry and William Shaw. Henry, in particular, pointed out that the Home Rule League was being invited to commit political suicide. This was no less than the truth for, as T. D.

Sullivan made clear at the September meeting, the convention was required specifically to fill the political vacuum created by the Home Rule League's inability to deal with the land question. The Home Rule League had been founded, he argued, to unify opinion on the question of Home Rule only, and it was not competent to deal with other matters.

Henry reaffirmed his firm adherence to the principles and programme of 1873, and his refusal to be led beyond them under any pretence led him to observe 'that the committee is specifically prohibited from adding any other members of the [Home Rule] League but is to incorporate those who always repudiated its principle as being too mild for their nationality, and the convention itself when assembled is to have the power of admitting gentlemen from the other side of the water who have not been elected as delegates at all'.[110] Privately, Henry wrote to O'Neill Daunt that the

> conference proposal was a trick to unite in one body all who are in favour of self-government. . . . The moment the [Home Rule] League lets go of its *special* federal programme and admits to its ranks all those who are in favour of *any kind* of independence for Ireland, that moment it will lose all its really solvent and stable men.[111]

Aside from this political opposition, the purely organisational difficulties were immense. It was originally suggested that the elections should be held on the basis of a one-shilling franchise to one vast constituency rather than by locality and that they be held in early 1880. By 14 November the one-shilling franchise idea was dropped in place of manhood suffrage; the elections to the convention were to be held by means of localities and public meetings; and 1882 was fixed upon as the 'centenary' year likely to be made memorable by the first meeting of the Irish Convention.

The convention project seems, however, to have played a role in forcing Parnell to move away from the federalist principle which he publicly supported as late as 27 September 1879 in a speech in Tipperary.[112] In fact by mid-October he was claiming to find the whole issue a doctrinal irrelevance:

> Whether they were to have the restoration of the Irish parliament of 1782, or whether they were to have a plan of federalism such as that which was formulated by Isaac Butt (*cheers*) or whether in the course of years and in the march of events the Irish nation should achieve for itself a complete separation from England (*loud cheers*) was a matter which must be left to the course of events for solution.[113]

But while it seems that Parnell was prepared to be militant in his statements of political nationalism, it appears that he was much less prepared to be so on the land question. 'He could not see his way', Davitt recalled, 'to take a step which might look like the abandonment of the tenant defence associations and the throwing over of their local leaders in Limerick, Tipperary, Cork and elsewhere for a new association which had its birth in extremist plans.'[114] He frankly admitted—recalling advice offered by Isaac Butt—that he did not like the idea of a widespread organisation in which the leadership would be responsible for the action of its wildest members. Davitt, however, felt that these objections were apparently more 'expedient' than 'determinate',[115] and although Parnell was not directly involved in the Mayo Land League project in August, Davitt was hopeful that Parnell would ultimately join his agrarian movement. For one important basis of Parnell's objection was being clearly overcome.

By mid-July the clergy felt that it was necessary to give way. There were eleven priests on the platform at Claremorris,[116] despite the failure of efforts to include resolutions for Catholic education and in favour of the temporal power of the pope (the Fenians argued that these would have infringed the non-sectarian spirit of the agrarian agitation).[117] Many of the clergy were naturally sympathetic to the agitation, while the more unsympathetic felt that it was unwise to allow such a movement to continue without a clerical presence of some kind. As the cautiously inclined John McEvilly, Bishop of Galway and Coadjutor of Tuam, wrote to Tobias Kirby at the Irish College in Rome,

> In order to meet this evil and knock the wind out of the sails of those unprincipled ringleaders, it has been deemed prudent for the priests to formulate the resolutions at meetings in the interest of order and religion, to keep the lead and keep the godless nobodies in their place.[118]

At the Claremorris meeting, as the speeches grew more militant, Canon Bourke denounced them and retired.[119] Nevertheless, at every agrarian meeting in Mayo after this date the clergy felt required to join with the neo-Fenians on the Land League platform. This was frequently a very rough ride for the churchmen. The language directed against them was often strong. Harris explicitly warned the clergy not to side with the graziers.[120] Archbishop MacHale was challenged by a demonstration on his doorstep in Tuam.[121] James Daly openly accused Canon Geoffrey McDermott, who shared his Sligo platform in November, of being a liar over the question of his alleged support for the conservative Home Ruler

Colonel King-Harman.[122] But it was clear that the clergy felt that they had to accept such provocations.

Parnell's position was also strengthened by an electoral victory on 2 August (by 83 to 77) for James Lysaght Finigan, his candidate in the Ennis by-election in Co. Clare. Although there was no direct significance in this as far as Davitt and the Mayo agrarian movement was concerned—Finigan would have lost if Davitt had campaigned for him in Ennis[123]—it was a victory for Parnell. 'I would have retired from public life if Ennis had been lost,' he went so far as to say, according to Barry O'Brien, 'for it would have satisfied me that the priests were supreme in Irish politics.'[124] The Ennis victory was followed by a sectarian interlude in which Edmund Dwyer Gray, MP, the owner of the *Freeman's Journal*, alleged that Parnell had described some of his moderate colleagues as 'Papist rats'. Archbishop Croke's intervention for peace in this dispute was effectively against Gray, and there is no evidence that the affair did Parnell any harm.

6. *The Establishment of the Land League*

Although this weakening of clerical opposition must have encouraged him, Parnell did not make a decisive move until he attended the conference in Dublin which set up the Irish National Land League on 21 October 1879. The conference was reasonably moderate in tone—only five members of the sixty-member executive committee it appointed had any connections with secret organisations.[125] Devoy noted: 'The body which called the League into existence was not very large and few of those present had any influence in the country. There were a few MPs, a few lawyers of no particular distinction, some Dublin shopkeepers, priests, editors and clerks and the men who up till then had conducted the struggle in the West.'[126] Against this relatively low-keyed background, Parnell was able to maintain his caution. He personally supported a motion in support of peasant proprietorship; this was, however, to be achieved through the utilisation of the Bright clauses of the 1870 Land Act which (although scarcely availed of) were intended to aid peasant ownership.[127] In fact the conference commitment to peasant proprietorship—as opposed to its commitment to a reduction in rents—was highly formal. But for the time being Davitt was satisfied with this compromise with what he later called 'timid land reformers'.[128] It was an indication of Parnell's uncertainty that he made a speech effectively in support of the 'three Fs' at Enniscorthy a few days later.[129]

It was only at the beginning of November that Parnell finally put his name to a Land League address which startled the moderate

Home Rule Party. This spoke of peasant proprietorship as the inevitable outcome of the present crisis.[130] For although neither the body which brought the Land League into existence nor the executive committee were dominated by Fenians, four of the seven chosen officers of the League were Fenians or ex-Fenians (Biggar, Egan, Brennan and Davitt), and it was these officers who had the duty of issuing political statements. The address came, it should be remembered, almost immediately on top of the 'Jacob's advertisement' incident in which some Irish-American militants had publicly promised in the press an outbreak of guerrilla warfare in the event of a repeat of the famine.[131] If that was not enough, it also came on top of a League meeting at Gurteen, the first in Co. Sligo, when Davitt, Daly and James Bryce Killen gave speeches which made their prosecution for seditious language inevitable. But for the moderate Home Rulers the most worrying problem was the political line of the new League. A *Freeman's Journal* editorial declared its disquiet about the omission of the 'three Fs' from the League's programme.[132] Parnell was for the first time clearly implicated in what the Gray party felt to be a strategy to use the land question for separatist purposes. He was forced to make his explanations; and this he did throughout November, particularly at the meeting of the Central Tenants' Defence Association on 17 November.

He argued that the Board of Works had £1 million at its disposal for the purchase of holdings under the Bright clauses. This money, perhaps supplemented by another similar grant from parliament, would be sufficient to prove the superiority of peasant proprietorship. Parliament would then be reasonably asked for another £20 million. The only real peculiarity of Parnell's scheme was that he regarded the present requirements of any prospective proprietor (a third or a quarter of the purchase money) as much too heavy. He suggested rather that the Board of Works should advance two-thirds of the purchase money, the repayment to be at the rate of 2 per cent per annum with interest at 3 per cent, and that the landlords should be paid the balance in the same manner. Except for the large landed companies this was to be entirely a permissive scheme. Would the landlords act in the best interests of their country? 'Even already, as the member for Meath expressed it at one of the recent land meetings, the market is falling.'[133] Parnell concluded by insisting that he wanted to work with the advocates of the 'three Fs'.

The point was confirmed when Parnell, just before his departure for America, presided at the merger of the Land League and the Central Tenants' Defence Association. This was on the effective basis, as Parnell's amended resolution put it, of a platform comprising the claim for an 'occupation ownership' (i.e. peasant proprietorship) and where that was not possible, a claim for the 'three Fs'. The *Freeman's Journal* jubilantly declared that the Land League had adopted 'as the true programme, fixity of tenure at fair rent and free sale'.[134] But its jubilation was cut short by an angry letter from Davitt declaring this to be 'very strange reasoning'. Davitt argued that the League admitted that the 'three Fs' would be a gain for the tenant farmers, but as it could not be the basis of a final settlement, he failed to see any danger to the peasant proprietorship solution in the intermediary advocates amalgamating with the more radical land reformers. He then moved on to somewhat more casuistical ground when he argued that if the fair-rent reformers were willing to accept 'occupation ownership' as the central plank of the land platform, on condition that fixity of tenure at fair rents was to be applied where peasant proprietorship was not 'feasible', then there was no change in the original programme of the Land League in consequence of the amalgamation with the CTDA, as no Leaguer had at any time made the practically impossible a part of its programme.

This play on the meaning of the word 'feasible' so as to imply that the Land League had made no compromise did not impress the *Freeman's Journal*. The editor replied tartly:

A moment's consideration will show that, no matter which be made the 'central plank', if fixity of tenure is to be obtained, it must be by a bill dealing by a single stroke with all holdings, while when the intention of seeking to compel is in terms disavowed, it is equally evident that peasant proprietorship must be a question of time.[135]

It was the case, therefore, that no matter what the form of language used, as a matter of obvious logic the demand for fixity of tenure occupied the first place in the League's programme. The point is that if fixity of tenure was delayed until the acquirement of property rights in the case of each particular holding was found to be not 'feasible', it could well be delayed for a century.

Mitchell Henry was less pleased. He saw the dissolution of the CTDA as part of the same thinking which had produced the convention idea—the aim being to have 'as President Parnell who Davitt told us at Swinford is, like him, in favour of the total abolition of landlords and landlordism, which really means, in the intention of Davitt and his friends, the abolition of the English entirely and of all kinds of English government, whether Imperial for Imperial affairs or otherwise'.[136] He felt that the subordination of the CTDA to the Land League was inevitable. Henry, who had talked with Davitt and Parnell in the autumn of 1879, felt he knew the essentials of the plot. Parnell had no real plan for abolishing landlordism and had shifted his ground over and over again during the autumn. ('I could tell you some conversations I had with him.')[137] Parnell, who was actuated by his hatred of England—not love of Ireland—and intense ambition, was 'completely in the hands of Davitt, although he does not see where Davitt is leading him'.[138]

There were, it may be seen, two possible ways of interpreting Parnell. The *Freeman* chose to give him the benefit of the doubt; at any rate, it was so sure of mass support for the 'three Fs' that it was prepared to accept Parnell's offer of an alliance as honestly intended. Henry, on the other hand, felt that Parnell had been so inconsistent, and his proposals so lacking in practicality, that it was clear that he had fallen under separatist influence.

7. Conclusion

In a well-known article published in 1949 Professor T. W. Moody demonstrated that 'the new departure of 1878 was one thing, [and] the Land League of 1879 . . . quite another'. Professor T. N. Brown has more recently elaborated this distinction in *Irish-American Nationalism, 1870–1890* (1966). In reviewing this body of work, Professor Moody has commented:

> The new departure was a plan for a change in Fenian methods but not in the essential aim of Fenianism, a plan for 'open' instead of secret action, in which a radical settlement of the land question figured as one of a series of subsidiary objectives; the Land League was an emergency organisation with exclusively agrarian purposes—the immediate defence of the tenant farmers threatened with mass eviction, and their eventual conversion into peasant proprietors. The new departure called for a 'combination' between revolutionary and constitutional nationalists on prescribed terms; the Land League was open to all, whether nationalists or not, and those who joined it were not committed to any political doctrine or aim. The new departure is inconceivable apart from the American setting in which it was formulated by its authors, Devoy and Davitt; the Land League was the outcome of the responses of Davitt and of Parnell to a wholly Irish and agrarian situation, and a land league of some kind is conceivable without any American background. The new departure was designed to break up the union of Ireland with Great Britain; the objectives of the Land League were attainable, and were eventually attained, within the structure of the United Kingdom. There were, of course, important connections between

the new departure and the Land League, but the relationship was not that between a plan and its execution. The new departure, strictly speaking, was never put into effect, because both the IRB and—almost certainly—Parnell rejected it, but Devoy behaved as though Parnell had accepted the alliance that he and Davitt offered and in consequence threw all his immense influence into winning Irish-American support for the Land League.[139]

This passage constitutes a remarkable attempt to differentiate the Land League from the New Departure: undoubtedly much confusion has resulted from the tendency to collapse these two initiatives into one movement. Nevertheless, this chapter has attempted a number of modifications of Professor Moody's view. The stress on the Land League as an emergency organisation arising out of a spontaneous reaction to the distress of 1879 has been modified in the light of the fact that the agitation pre-dated the onset of severe distress in 1879 by some months. It is perfectly true to say that the objectives of the Land League were attainable, and were eventually attained, within the structure of the United Kingdom. However, in 1879 hardly anyone of any political consequence on either side of the Irish Sea would have accepted this view. It is a consequence of the immense revolution achieved by the Land League that it later came to be so widely held. In 1879 the neo-Fenian leadership of the Land League certainly believed that the abolition of Irish landlordism and the creation of a peasant proprietary could be achieved only when the British link was broken. In other words, the connections between the New Departure and the Land League, which Professor Moody allows, cannot be reduced to the matter of Devoy's probably genuine belief that Parnell was committed to the original New Departure. It lay at the very heart of the radical Land League leadership's conception of the role of their movement—to smash landlordism, certainly, but, by so doing, also to smash the British link. A land league of some kind is conceivable without the New Departure background, but it would have been a very different movement—characterised by an entirely different relationship between leadership and followers—from that which is the subject of this book.

4

Land League *versus* Moderate Home Rulers

But where are those parts where over-population
exists? They are on the sides of the mountains, in the
morasses, the valleys, the bogs and the uncultivated
wastes; but in the fertile land Ireland is devoid of her
people who are scattered by the system of landlordism
all over the world. Why is Ireland over-populated in
these parts? Because the graziers will not farm the bogs
and waste, it is then of no use to the landlords except
to give it to those poor creatures who pay them an
exorbitant rent to enable them to wallow in their
licentious luxury.

PATRICK CROSSWELL, speech at Glenamaddy
(*Western News*, 22 May 1880)

We never told you we would face the police and
prevent evictions by armed force. On the contrary we
told you from the beginning that we could not do that
because we have not got the means and the armed men
and the discipline to do it, but we pointed out to you
that what ruined the tenantry of Ireland in the past
was that it was a paying thing for a landlord to evict. . . .
We said that the Land League could make sure that
eviction was not a paying but a losing game.

JOHN DILLON, speech at Loughrea, 17 March 1881
(*Report of the Special Commission, 1888*, 140,
H.C. 1890 [C.5891] XXVII, 617)

In order to understand why an agrarian rebellion could take place
at all in Ireland in 1879 it has been necessary to outline the deep
social division which divided the country between the landlords and
the tenants. The sharp debate involving the two sides has been discussed in Chapter 1. The argument ranged over such questions
as the consolidation of holdings; insecurity of tenure; absenteeism;
the special case of the 'reclamation' tenantry; and the issue of 'freedom of contract'. The tenantry opposed at every point the landlord
claims. The landlords in turn replied as strongly as they could.
This underlying hostility between landlords and tenants made it
likely that an agricultural setback would bring in its wake an
increase in dissatisfaction with the land system.

This was the background when in 1879 Michael Davitt and a
handful of neo-Fenian allies organised the first meetings of the
Land League in Connaught—the poorest and most economically

backward of Ireland's provinces. Davitt also persuaded Charles Stewart Parnell, who had been doing his best to rejuvenate the constitutionalist Home Rule wing of Irish nationalist politics, to throw his weight behind the agitation. But this work represented only the completion of preliminary tasks. There was much to be done if the Land League was to become a nation-wide mass movement of major importance.

It was clear that the struggle against the position of the moderate Home Rule Party now became one of prime importance for the Land League. The *Freeman's Journal* was the most significant voice of those large areas of constitutional nationalist opinion which were still sceptical of the new movement; somehow the *Freeman's Journal*, and by implication its constituency, had to be made to see the League's potential. Accordingly the Land League's efforts resolved themselves largely into a new and forceful challenge to the *Freeman's Journal* and its owner, Edmund Dwyer Gray; and during the first three months of 1880 Gray and his newspaper were forced by pressure exercised in various forms to extend at least a friendly toleration to the Land League.

A further precondition for success in combating moderate Home Rule opinion was an increase in the League's financial resources. It was with this end in view that Parnell and John Dillon undertook their fund-raising tour in America between January and March 1880.

1. *The American Tour*

The American tour posed two serious political problems for Parnell. How was he to reconcile appeals to the Clan na Gael and the *Irish World* with appeals to the broader sections of the American public, in particular the wealthy Irish-Americans whom Davitt wanted him to reach?[1] There was also the problem of moderate British and Irish public opinion. 'If he can hold his ground with the Clan na Gael and afterwards hold it in the House of Commons, he will win Home Rule,' an Irish Home Rule member told Barry O'Brien on the eve of Parnell's departure. O'Brien added that 'Parnell himself set out on his mission with a light heart. What the House of Commons would think or would not think gave him little trouble. He was not in the habit of forecasting the future to an extent which would interfere with the operations of the present.'[2]

But immediately upon his arrival in New York he faced a crisis of the most immediate and direct sort. At a time when so much was needed for relief the New York *Herald* publicly declared its opposition to the collection of funds to be used for political purposes in Ireland.[3] Perhaps more important in view of Parnell's intended constituency, Cardinal McCloskey of New York agreed with the *Herald*'s view. These remarks were directed at the Land League, which had issued an appeal at the beginning of November for money for political purposes only. In fact the Land League had very quickly modified its original intentions. Parnell, on the day of his departure from Ireland, was 'authorised' by Davitt to collect for relief purposes as well.[4]

Nevertheless, Parnell insisted in the course of an interview with James Ives of the New York *Herald* given on board ship that his primary purpose was still the collection of funds for political ends, among which he included the defraying of expenses of those young men thirsting for the chance to lecture the people on the political economy of the land question.[5] On his arrival in New York he said that the League would collect relief funds, although it had regarded it as the duty of the government to deal with distress, but that £5,000 was immediately required for the political purposes of the League.[6] That this was no less than the truth is clear from the desperate tone of Davitt's comments to John Ferguson at this time.[7] The next issue of the New York *Herald* carried McCloskey's appeal for support for a relief fund but opposition to a political collection.[8]

The scene was set for an important conflict. At the opening meeting of the tour at Madison Square Gardens Parnell declared that the League had had to modify its intentions by the fact that 'a terrible, far and wider spread famine than expected is imminent'.[9] But he insisted that this distress was the outgrowth of a land system badly in need of reform. While managing to maintain the essential point of the Land League position, Parnell was clearly feeling the pressure of hostile opinion.

At this point Parnell was greatly assisted by the New York *Herald*'s overconfidence. The *Herald* set up a relief fund and named a committee consisting of Colonel King-Harman, MP, a conservatively inclined Home Ruler, William Shaw, MP, Professor Baldwin, Cardinal McCloskey and Parnell himself to administer the fund. It had, however, failed to consult any of these men before proposing them for the committee. The plan backfired badly. The only two members in America whom the journal had named instantly declined to have anything to do with it. Even McCloskey clearly felt unable to collaborate in such an obvious attempt to embarrass Parnell. The *Herald* underwent a remarkable transformation in its attitude towards Parnell and became at least polite. Parnell had undoubtedly won the first round.[10]

But the ideological struggle had only just begun. New York public opinion was hardly well versed in the technicalities of the Irish land question. It seemed open to diametrically opposed arguments on either side. Lord Dunraven sent a letter to the New York

Herald insisting on the fundamentally contradictory nature of the Land League position:

> They assert that no landlord has an absolute title to the land, that is to say, even if he bought his land under the Encumbered Estates or from former proprietors and [yet] they commence an agitation for the avowed object of creating a number of landlords who are to have an absolute interest in the land.[11]

The *Irish World* claimed that Dunraven had made an effective intervention and urged Parnell to secure his defences by adopting a coherent land nationalisation stance. It claimed that every man had an inalienable right to the land: 'Ground to powder between the millstone of natural rights and the lower millstone of landlord titles, what will be left of Mr Parnell six months from now?'[12] Parnell's interview with Ives and Arthur Kavanagh's letter—the most salient of a collection of landlord apologetics which had appeared in the New York *Herald* of 3 January—were resurrected. The effect was to produce a very strong reaction in some circles which was to Parnell's disadvantage. Cardinal McCloskey again discountenanced political debate and disapproved of any steps being taken to forward that movement with money obtained in America so long as the question of distress was either disregarded or made a secondary question. Judge Daly, Chief Justice of the Common Pleas, Richard O'Gorman (whom Davitt had been especially keen to win over),[13] James Barbour, James Lynch, president of the Emigration Bank, Eugene Kelly, banker, William Watson, linen manufacturer, and some other prominent men of Irish connection and descent who had set about obtaining relief refused to have anything to do with Parnell and his movement. They started an Irish Relief Fund of their own and denied all connection with Irish political questions. Within a few days they had collected $7,000.[14]

Journalistic attacks on Parnell were renewed in a much stronger and more effective manner. Letters from individuals appearing in the press were even more hostile than the leaders to any plan which gave political questions primacy over the relief of distress.[15] But Parnell fought back to prevent the Irish Relief Fund committee absorbing all the pecuniary sympathy for the distress in Ireland. He realised that he had been putting his political designs too strongly, and he published an address to 'the People of America' which had a very different emphasis.[16] The address stated that, having become intimately connected during the past few months with the conditions in Ireland, Parnell and Dillon considered it their duty to 'lose not a moment in laying before the American people the state of affairs in Ireland'[17] and to receive and administer any funds which the people of America desired to contribute to the alleviation of the distress. A 'rough' calculation revealed that 250,000 of the peasantry would be without the means of obtaining food for the next three months. It was stressed that the Land League, alone among relief organisations, could offer an already existing local organisation in famine districts which would make no charge for its services. Staff expenses would thus be minimised. This address, it should be noted, nowhere mentioned the raising of money for political purposes. Nor was it explained why such an address had not been produced immediately upon arrival in New York. Parnell even went so far as to suggest that even the money personally collected by him after the first $25,000 would go to the relief fund also.

These concessions to New York sentiment were probably necessary. But they proved to be the last concession required of Parnell. Once he moved outside of New York he found himself in an entirely different climate. 'Yielding to the tone of the New York *Herald* and of Fifth Avenue opinion,' wrote the *Irish Times* special reporter, 'Mr Parnell had begun to relegate the reform part of his programme from the first to the second place of importance in his speeches. Beyond New York there is a different state of things. It is evident that American views are really centred upon the land reform as the object of chief importance.'[18] Parnell, in fact, was condemned by some Americans as conservative because his policy of peasant proprietorship was still permissive and not compulsory.

But while Parnell was surmounting his difficulties in America Edmund Dwyer Gray was meeting increasing problems in Dublin. Gray's position as Lord Mayor of Dublin was proving to be a major embarrassment. Gray had hoped to dissociate himself from the extreme men by refusing to support a motion before the Irish Party expressing solidarity with the struggle in the West unless it was made clear that he was opposed to violence.[19] But this did not satisfy the Lord Lieutenant, who refused his invitation to the Lord Mayor's banquet on the grounds that Gray had condoned lawlessness.[20] Up to this point Gray was very much the injured party in the eyes of nationalist Ireland, but he made the error of attending the Castle levée on the following day. John Callanan, who was by no means committed to the Land League, for he had cool relations with Harris and O'Sullivan,[21] was one provincial newspaper editor who was alienated by the Lord Mayor's behaviour:

A time was when Irishmen would not brook the insult so contemptuously flung in the face [of the Lord Mayor of Dublin] who a moment after bows and curtsies and clasps the hand which smote him. . . . Such a degree of flunkeyism we cannot comprehend.[22]

By 1 February Parnell and Dillon felt strong enough to attack the Lord Mayor's Mansion House Relief Committee in a joint statement. They demanded that the Lord Mayor should take the landlords off his committee: 'It is not to be expected that any man will continue to work for land reform when the daily bread of his wife and children depends on a committee of landlords.'[23] It was an obvious attempt to divert money into the League's funds. Parnell made no real attempt, for example, to substantiate his Springfield claim that only tenants who had paid their rent would receive assistance from the Mansion House funds.[24] There is no reason to suppose that such an attack weakened Gray in Ireland; but the fact that it had been made at all—it would certainly have been impossible at the beginning of January when Parnell himself was under such pressure—was significant. Shortly after the attack on the Mansion House Relief Fund, Dr William Carroll sent a message to Devoy from Parnell:

He wishes me to say to you that nobody is hurt yet and if he goes down it will be with his colours flying, of which latter catastrophe, however, he sees no signs and has no fears. . . . There is a healthy straightforward ring in the tone which pleases me.[25]

Representative Americans were now jostling to share Parnell's platform. In two months he visited sixty-two cities and spoke alongside state governors, congressmen, local representatives, judges and clergymen. He also made a major speech before the House of Representatives.

He managed to avoid provoking a major split in the ranks of American Fenianism by making every possible rhetorical allowance. At Cincinnati on 20 February he even went so far, according to the *Irish World,* as to speak of destroying the 'last link' which kept Ireland bound to England.[26] Parnell may, in fact, not have used this phrase, which did not appear in the Cincinnati press.[27] He later claimed before the Special Commission that the offending phrase was an invention of the *Irish World.*[28] At any rate, the important point in the context of any analysis of Irish-American politics at the time is the fact that the *Irish World* printed the phrase and that Parnell, hardly surprisingly, did not issue any denial. In his strong nationalistic utterances at Brookland, Cleveland and Cincinnati Parnell, according to his biographer Barry O'Brien, 'spoke the faith that was in him'.[29] Sir Henry James had a more cynical view. He pointed out that Parnell had made the great majority of his American speeches before the 'last link' speech at Cincinnati. However, by that stage he had collected only four remittances totalling £920 for political purposes as against £11,343 for relief. But of this small sum £731 had come from Chicago—the home of extremists like Alexander Sullivan and J. F. Finerty. In the four months following the Cincinnati speech the League received not only £54,982 for relief but also £10,400 for political purposes.[30] But whatever his motive, Parnell was on the whole well received by the rank and file of American Fenianism.

Dr Carroll, the Clan na Gael leader, who had been friendly to him in 1878, did, however, break with the organisation. There were three reasons for Carroll's resignation; the first two were relatively serious. He resented Parnell's and his entourage's manipulative interest in the Clan na Gael,[31] and he felt also, even before Parnell's arrival, that 'Good as the land question is, it should not cause us to lose our heads about it to the neglect of the only ultimate means to our end.'[32] Somehow this became mixed up with a rather less weighty cause of irritation—Parnell's refusal to have his meetings addressed by the eccentric Highlander Dr Murdoch, who was one of Carroll's obsessions.[33]

This points to the fact that despite their public success, neither Parnell nor his entourage handled their behind-the-scenes relations with the Clan na Gael leadership with any great skill. Parnell gave his approval to a provocative draft plan submitted by Healy for the constitution of the Irish National Land League of the United States. This plan proposed that branches be organised in every state, with each branch to be independent and responsible to the executive in Dublin; but Devoy and the Clan na Gael fought against this usurpation of their authority, and it was eventually agreed that the American League should have an American executive.[34] The decisive factor in the Clan na Gael leadership's acceptance of Parnell was their recollection of heavy failures in the 1870s; given a certain public display of nationalist feeling, he was assured of Devoy's support. As Davitt pointed out, association with 'the new departure mission' had given the Clan great prestige.[35]

Strangely enough, Parnell's most nationalistic speeches were largely ignored in the Irish press at home, receiving virtually no comment. Parnell's development of position on the agrarian question was, however, another matter; and here both the reporting and comment were lengthy and detailed. On 3 January 1880 the New York *Herald* had published letters from a group of Irish landlords in their own defence, the most important of these being from Arthur Kavanagh, MP for Carlow. He assumed that 'Mr

Parnell's proposed object in appealing to the American public for aid in money is to find means to establish a peasant proprietorship in this country [Ireland] by sweeping the present owners from the soil.' He argued that peasant proprietorship in Ireland would lead to an enormous increase in subdivision. The problem of Ireland was not bad landlordism but the prevalence of smallholdings: 'The real disadvantages which tell against the majority of tenant farmers as a class in Ireland are their poverty and smallness of holdings.' Rents were on the whole low, and landlord failure to invest was an effect of the fact that 'the Irish landlords as a class could never afford to build houses and homesteads on all the small holdings on their properties.' The only true solution to this was emigration. Kavanagh's letter in a certain sense pricked the balloon. It attracted a great deal of attention, and Parnell was compelled to reply to it in his first American speech. The fundamental problems of Irish agriculture had at last been raised.

Parnell resolved upon the tactic of using one landlordist spokesman's testimony against another.[36] He cited William Steuart Trench's *Realities of Irish Life* on the point that landlords had indeed raised rents on the improvements of their tenants. He argued that subdivision was produced by the letting system and that no injurious subdivision would take place if free sale in land was operating in Ireland. Parnell was, as he had made clear on his arrival in America, fully convinced that the normal laws of capitalist development in agriculture would apply to Ireland.[37]

The debate, of course, continued, and Parnell returned indirectly at least to Kavanagh's points on frequent occasions during the tour, particularly in the speech before the House of Representatives and in an article which appeared in the *North American Review* of April 1880. But one thing was already noticeable: the 'three Fs' had been quite forgotten. In a sense, Kavanagh's style of pleading his case before an American audience had the effect of forcing his adversary to radicalise his position. Kavanagh's assumption that Parnell's aim was to establish a peasant proprietary by 'sweeping the present owners from the soil' was to have significant repercussions. He went so far as to insist that Parnell and his friends knew perfectly well that a peasant proprietary could never be achieved by 'fair' means but only by an 'armed rebellion'. Parnell could afford to ignore this charge, but he did have to accept Kavanagh's premises on the land question—and as Kavanagh had made no mention of the fixity of tenure plan, there was no reason for Parnell to defend it in his reply. It is doubtful if Parnell wished to make an advocacy of the 'three Fs'—or if Irish-American audiences would have tolerated him if he had done so. Parnell might ignore almost too pointedly all the advice the land nationalisation advocates of the *Irish World* gave him. The *Irish World* pleaded unsuccessfully with him, for example, not to take up the themes of John Bright's recent Birmingham speech or of continental experiments in land tenure in his own speech before the House of Representatives.[38] Nevertheless, he could not fail to stand for a peasant proprietary before those men and women whom landlordism had 'banished' from Ireland. The net effect of all this was to lead to a suppression of the compromise programme of the amalgamated League which had been agreed upon in Ireland. Parnell's new analysis of the agrarian question took in the problem of the famine clearances, the transition from tillage to pasture, the overcrowding in the West, the underpopulation in the East, in one broad sweep.

2. Parnell's Exposition: 'The Irish Land Question'
This analysis was developed in speeches and then presented in its most conclusive form in the article entitled 'The Irish Land Question' in the *North American Review*.[39] It amounted effectively to a pledge to 'undo the work of the famine'.[40] The article, published under Parnell's name but apparently written by his sister Fanny, argued that the first effect of emigration since the famine had been the throwing out of cultivation of vast areas of land. The landlords had turned the farms into pasture and raised cattle and sheep for export to England. The money they received was spent, for the most part, outside the country. However, of late the system had been failing in its object: the number of cattle and sheep, as well as the crop acreage, had been falling. Ireland was, he argued, a damp country, and in many parts the soil held rain like a cup. When kept properly drained, there was no land in the wide world more fertile than the great uninhabited grazing plains of Ireland; but left as they were, 'undrained and unfertilised, unsown with new grass seed', they had become unfit for grazing. The proportion of waste land was therefore increasing instead of diminishing.[41]

The second effect of the emigration of 1848, Parnell continued, had been, strange to say, to increase the competition for land. Those of the peasantry who did not emigrate were driven to the bogs and barren hillsides. In the course of time the population naturally increased. With this increase came greater competition for land, but the fertile soil lands of the country were no longer open to competition. The cost of labour had risen in consequence of its scarcity. 'The prices of produce had risen in slightly higher proportion but rents of land had risen a hundred, two hundred and, in some cases, five hundred per cent.' The practical worthlessness of emigration had been demonstrated by the period 1848–50. 'Supposing there should be a bad harvest next autumn and that the result would be death or emigration of three million people. Would it benefit the two millions left behind?' Would it benefit the wages of labour with no industries to give employment to labour? Would it lower the rents of the tenants with still larger areas of land turned into sheep-walks? What was there to prevent the population rising again and the situation occurring in the future? Despite areas of overpopulation Ireland was as a whole immensely underpopulated, as could be demonstrated by comparison with countries where peasant proprietorship predominated.

Then in an important passage he commented:

It is, in fact, not an emigration from Ireland to America but a migration from the barren hills of Connaught to the fertile lands of Leinster and Munster that we want. The old cry in Cromwellian days 'To Hell or Connaught' has been virtually the cry ever since in Ireland. The landlords have been occupied without ceasing in driving the peasantry from the best to the worst parts of the country. One of our principal aims is to cause a return movement and this can only be produced by causing large quantities of grazing land, in the middle and eastern counties, to be thrown upon the market and by facilitating the purchase of it by the Western peasantry.

Parnell went on to flirt slightly with separatism, but it was his internal migration scheme which irritated the *Freeman's Journal*. Parnell's extreme nationalism was treated as an irrelevance:

Nor need we discuss Mr Parnell's assumption that if Ireland by a good land system were rendered prosperous, it would, like Jeshurum when he waxed fat, kick and insist upon complete autonomy and that the object of English statesmen in keeping the country poor and helpless is to keep it in subjection.[42]

But Parnell's new-found agrarian radicalism was another matter. It was not that Parnell's critique of the transition to the grazing system was unacceptable to middle-of-the-road nationalist opinion. Indeed, it was acceptable to all shades of moderate nationalist opinion, including even the staid columns of the Dwyer Gray press. When John Ferguson had presented such arguments in the *Weekly Freeman* in September 1879[43] he was highly praised by the editorial, which added that Ferguson's analysis of the depopulation associated with the decline in tillage and consequently the high demand for labour showed that 'This is indeed a question for the town as well as for the country, as the merchant as well as the farmer is at last beginning to discover.'[44] Andrew Kettle had argued the same analysis before the Richmond Commission—more important, perhaps, because of the fact that much of the moderate evidence before the commission agreed with Kettle. Professor Baldwin, who was clearly regarded by the commission as an outstanding expert on Irish agriculture, argued that what Ireland needed was a mixed system of farming.[45] But at this stage it meant very little that Parnell, Kettle, the *Freeman's Journal* and Professor Baldwin could all attack the effects of the grazing system. For the question was : what could be done about it?

While there was general agreement about the ills of the transition to pasture, there was an important disagreement, particularly between Parnell and the *Freeman's Journal,* about the cure. Later in the year, shortly after an exposition of an internal migration scheme by Parnell at Waterford, Mitchell Henry pressed Baldwin at the Richmond Commission to declare his exact relationship to the Parnell plan. Henry said that, as he understood it, the plan would involve not only an internal migration to Meath but also the replacement of the Meath grazing lands by tillage. Baldwin replied that he did not contemplate any interference with the fattening lands which were best suited for their present purpose. But rather he advocated dealing with waste and semi-waste land principally in the neighbourhood of the people who were to be migrated.[46]

Parnell and Kettle apparently went further. But there was a massive problem involved in doing so. As the *Freeman's Journal* editorial put it,

> Mr Parnell reiterates the statement which, we think, he more than once made in his public speeches in America that it is not emigration but migration which was required to relieve the over-population which he considers exists in certain portions of the West. . . . In one of his speeches, if we remember aright, he put [the argument of the article] in another form and said that the surplus population of Connaught should be transferred to the fertile plains of Meath and Tipperary. This no doubt would be desirable if we were parcelling out a new country, but how is it in practice to be effected; or whether the occupiers of the fertile lands in question, who are themselves mostly tenants expecting to benefit by the Bright clauses when amended, would not very strenuously resist any attempt of this kind is the question; and until Mr Parnell tells us how the process of transferring the cottier tenants of Connemara to the grazing lands of Meath is to be carried out we cannot express any confidence in such a proposal being practicable.[47]

The *Freeman's Journal* was determined to remain firmly in the 'three Fs' camp and to reject Parnell's utopian solutions.

This debate pinpointed the contradiction at the heart of the Land League position, for if the leadership went beyond rhetoric about unfair rents—as the arguments of men like Kavanagh and Lord Cloncurry forced them to do—they inevitably took up a position which appeared to be hostile to the interests of those Irish tenants who were not smallholders. Once it was acknowledged that the level of rent was not the only aspect of the West's social crisis, the agrarian agitators were forced to advocate some form of internal migration scheme. Once they did that, they apparently threatened the interests of the stronger farmers.

In this context it is revealing that Bishop Nulty of Meath, who was a relatively advanced land reformer, declared himself in an interview with James Redpath to be totally opposed to a migration from the West into Meath. He said that if the present great estates were divided, they would only give the agricultural population of Meath itself fifty acres each. In his view this was enough to support a family in comfort, but it was out of the question for Meath to be subjected to a new influx of population from outside the county. Any land-reform scheme which could not claim the support of a figure such as Nulty obviously had little chance of success.[48]

On the other hand, the moderates also had their problems. At the beginning of June 1880, for example, O'Connor Power gave an eloquent reply to the Malthusians in the House of Commons, but was forced to end somewhat lamely. For, despite his rhetorical criticisms of the grazing system, he reached a timid conclusion. He insisted that he did not mean to convey that the gains of one portion of the community should be periodically divided among the rest were less fortunate. He cordially repudiated a theory so fatal to individual exertion and individual aspiration. But it seemed clear to him that the effect of the land system in Ireland was to confiscate the capital created by individual industry and consequently to deprive this industry of the aid necessary to its continuance and successful development. Thus Power, whose very speech had argued that the level of rent was not the central issue in many parts of the West, ended up by advocating the 'three Fs'.[49] However much this demand might be in conformity with 'justice', it was not the transformation of agrarian social relationships which Power had implied as being necessary to deal with the problem. After all, the problem had been that many existing holdings were too small to support a family, even if rent were abolished. But the centre in Irish politics clearly felt that such a position, for all its contradictions, was the only possible one. It was certainly preferable

D

to the dangerously directed and hopeless project of Parnell's American analysis.

Naturally the landlords did not express agreement with Parnell. G. F. Trench's response is typical:

> There were in 1871 about 117,500 holdings of 5 acres and perhaps there are not less than 450,000 families, counting labourers and small tenants, dependent upon the land alone, who are but little removed from a precarious existence. For an evil like this, Mr Parnell's idea of making small farms on the grass-lands of Meath, or even reclaiming the land profitably reclaimable, would be wholly inadequate apart from all questions of morality and good policy.[50]

But the Conservative Dublin *Evening Mail* also argued that the *Freeman's Journal* had failed to put forward a reasonable alternative solution. For example, the *Freeman* supplemented its 'three Fs' demands with the suggestion that the lands of the London companies in Co. Londonderry should be made available for distribution among tenants. But this could only be done by expropriating the middlemen who let these lands on long lease; and if this was done, what landlord was secure?[51] These remarks are an index of the landlords' suspicions. They certainly tended to agree with the Land League that rents could not be fairly fixed by arbitration as Butt had proposed. No one on the landlord's side helped the *Freeman's Journal* by coming forward to declare its proposals a reasonable basis for compromise. There was far too much hostility to the 'three Fs' for that to happen. The Duke of Argyll expressed a common landlord view of the problem:

> The demand for what is called fair rents is a demand that prices shall be cheapened by Act of Parliament in favour of the particular individuals who now hold farms in Ireland. The demand for fixity of tenure is a demand that all other Irishmen shall be prohibited from dealing with owners for those coveted possessions. The demand for the right of free 'sale' for the present holders is a demand that no part of these parliamentary privileges shall be passed on to any farmers coming after them.[52]

Perhaps some landlords already accepted Trench's view:

> All public honesty and honour demand that if the state determine either to infringe upon the sanctity of existing contracts or to repudiate any part of the title conferred in its name upon the purchase, it shall at the same time offer to take the land off his hands.[53]

Reactions like these effectively isolated the *Freeman*'s position. As a result, Parnell was able to say that its proposals were just as impracticable as his own—indeed, perhaps more so—with this difference, that they were less desirable.

3. *Developments in the West*

Parnell's published analysis of the land question was, however, only one of the problems facing the moderate elements in Irish politics in early 1880. The real difficulty was that Parnell's speeches appeared to be given substance by events in Connaught. It had been clear from the start that the Connaught agitation had been conditioned by the famine clearances and the intense overcrowding on the land. In Connaught 82·7 per cent of the holdings were under 30 acres, at an average valuation of £5, while the comparable figure for Leinster was 64·1 per cent at an average valuation of £9, and for Munster it was 50·2 per cent at an average valuation of £8.[54]

But as well as this exceptionally large mass of small tenants, Connaught was also characterised by a relative absence of the medium-sized tenant. Although the number of agricultural holdings in Connaught (115,804) was greater than either Leinster (99,386) or Munster (105,335), the number of what were, very broadly speaking, the middle range of tenantry in the 30–100 acre category was very much less. The Connaught figure was 15,297 as against 25,331 for Leinster and 39,808 for Munster.[55] The weakness of this buffer group meant that antagonisms between the small farmers and the large 'ranchers' were in Connaught much more open and direct.

As William O'Brien later noted, 'That happy phrase: "The Land for the People" bore three different meanings for as many differing schools of agitators.' For Davitt it meant land nationalisation. O'Brien added:

For the mass of the Irish tenantry . . . it meant the conversion of the 450,000 rent-paying tenants into proprietors of their own holdings by state purchase; for the smallholders of the province of Connaught, among whom the agitation originated, it meant not merely the purchase of their existing holdings, which were too small and poor to support life, but the restoration to the people's use of the enormous tracts of rich grazing lands from which their fathers had been extirpated in the hideous 'clearances' of the Great Famine (and of this special problem there was no particular mention in the original programme of the Land League, nor was it, indeed, understood at for many years afterwards outside the cabins of the congested districts).[56]

In these circumstances, by the end of 1879 the local tenant leaders were able to act more exclusively as the ideologues of the small-holders. R. J. Lynch at a meeting in Castlerea called for the breaking up of the large holdings.[57] Patrick Egan at Leitrim raised the same perspective.[58] At Mayo Abbey a meeting was held to denounce land-grabbing by a grazier—the first of its kind. Joseph B. Walsh moved a resolution denouncing the grazing system and strongly recommending that any grass farm which became unoccupied be subdivided into residential agricultural holdings. The speeches of the speakers at this meeting were interrupted by cries of 'Divide them!'[59] At Rathnacreeva, near Balla, a meeting was called in January 1880 which was expected to demand that lands given up to the landlord by impoverished graziers should be striped into twenty-acre residential holdings. There was also a project to dig up the surface and thus prevent its use for grazing.[60]

'Particular interest', it was reported on this occasion, 'was mani-fested by the farming classes who hold from three to ten acres in the neighbourhood.'[61] At Kilcolman, a day after the announcement of the Rathnacreeva project, a League spokesman emphasised the same theme: 300 grass farms, the fat of all the lands in Mayo, were owned by sixteen individuals, he argued, who had spent nothing on improvement or cultivation. The tenants, he added, ought to receive £7 or £8 for reclaiming bog instead of paying rent for it.[62] Thomas Hastings, a prominent Fenian, seconded Davitt on a Mayo platform later that month: 'Let us declare today that we will work earnestly to possess this land but also those consoli-dated farms from which thousands of Irish homesteads had been cleared away at the sacrifice of thousands of Irish lives.'[63] He thought this end could only be achieved by Fenian means: 'Let not the coming of Ireland's day of destiny find you with bowed heads and folded arms. Be led not aside from the path by parlia-mentary agitation.' Even the clergy—whom Matt Harris had speci-fically warned not to side with the graziers[64]—joined in the denun-ciation of the strong farmers. The Rev. D. Mylotte backed up Hastings's words on the Port Royal platform by declaring that the small farmers had no prosperity in the last thirty years, while the graziers in some places held the land much cheaper than the poor who resided on the bogs and the mountains. At Ballindine in March 1880 Canon Bourke declared the purpose of the demonstra-tion to be a protest against consolidation.[65]

The rhetoric was given a cutting edge by the increase in distress. The local committee of the Mansion House Fund claimed in May 1880 that 232,759 persons were in distress in Munster, while in

Connaught out of a population of 911,339 some 421,750 were in extreme distress.[66]

Prices had slumped in late 1879. At Banagher fair in September 10,000 of the 12,000 sheep were driven away unsold. 'Those who have money to buy', the newspaper report commented, 'are holding out till the last till the poorer classes of farmers of Ireland are forced to yield. . . . The greatest loss is sustained by the small farmers who usually supply the . . . graziers with store stock.'[67] Although 29,800 sheep were sold at Ballinasloe fair which followed three weeks later, the prices obtained were even lower by 3s to 5s a head than Banagher. Judged by Ballinasloe standards, this represented a fall from 52s to 30s since the fair of October 1878. The small farmers, it appeared, felt that as the November rent came close they needed the ready money above all else.[68] Even so, some 14,200 sheep were unsold, whereas the usual figure was about 6,800.[69] Two-thirds of the cattle on offer enjoyed the same fate, cattle prices having shown a decline of £2·50 to £3 since the previous year.[70]

Although there was some improvement in prices in the fairs of early 1880, there was still clear evidence of crisis. The *Western News* reporter at Aughrim fair drew attention

> to the apparent scarcity of small farmer's stock. . . . In former years this very noted and old fair used to be crammed with what is commonly called 'poor man's stock', comprising one- and two-year-old cattle, sheep, lambs, etc. But in this year it was so poorly supplied with the latter class that there could have been a hurley or cricket match played in the Green with very little interference from the public, and it is a well known fact that what were commonly called 'May fairs' which were held in this part of the country during the past season were but little better than half supplied with small tenant stock compared with last season. The above is a matter of the greatest consideration as it goes to prove that the small farmers . . . whose crops failed last year, sold their stock during the harvest, winter and spring to pay the landlord his rent and to next purchase the common necessaries of life. So that they are now possessed of very little stock on their farms and none to sell.[71]

The emigration enumerators noted that in 1880 a total of 42,272 harvest labourers went to England, but the police who made their inquiries somewhat earlier found only 22,900 who thought themselves likely to go.[72] This discrepancy was popularly attributed to a unique uncertainty in the West about the prospects for harvest work in England in the oncoming season.[73] But in fact it is a persistent feature of the statistics which did not apply to just one year.[74] It would seem therefore that uncertainty about prospects (combined with suspicion of the police)[75] was an enduring facet of Connaught life.

It is often argued that the poor peasantry and the agricultural proletariat (as opposed to the more independent middle peasantry) rarely initiate militant action, partly because these classes are often enmeshed in relations of dependence with the dominant classes, the landlords and their allies. It should be noted, however, that no such relations of dependence existed as far as the smallholders of the West were concerned. It was not simply the case that the West was 'the stronghold of absenteeism'[76] or that five absentee proprietors, Viscount Dillon, the Earl of Arran, the Marquis of Sligo, Lord Lucan and Sir Roger Palmer, who between them held 36,900 acres in the area, from which they received £80,000–£100,000 per annum, contributed nothing to the relief funds[77] (Lord Clanricarde, who personally drew £30,000 a year, also had a bad record; indeed, 'in Mayo . . . nine owners hold upwards of 20,000 acres each, amongst them draw annually £100,000 from this poor Western county, and spend not one-tenth of their income on their estates').[78] Also of importance was the fact that absenteeism was regarded as merely an aggravated case of a more general parasitism. The landlord was seen as being simply irrelevant to the process of production.

All efforts to create these relationships of dependence were rigorously opposed by the League. Davitt wrote to Devoy on 6 February 1880:

> Every effort is now being made to turn the flank of the new firm, by those who are dispensing charity, and the greatest possible exertion and vigilance is required to prevent the work of the past year being undone through the demoralising influences of meal and money![79]

Davitt felt the demoralising effects of relief funds so deeply that he announced the ending of the famine crisis[80] rather too quickly for Dillon, who was raising funds in America at the time. Dillon wrote an angry letter to Parnell on the subject,[81] and Davitt was quick to make a public retraction.[82] The type of activity which worried Davitt is clear. When the Duchess of Marlborough, wife of the Lord Lieutenant, left Ireland on 21 April, following the Conservative election defeat, she issued a farewell address to the people of the West. The address, which expressed her continued solicitude for their welfare and emphasised the generous response which her appeals had met in England, was translated into Irish, and 10,000 copies were distributed to the recipients of relief.[83] But the success of such interventions in decreasing support for the Land League was slight. The crucial fact is that the agitation had begun before the relief work, giving the Land League a head start in the struggle to win over the peasantry.[84] The deepening social radicalism of the Fenian-led agitation in Connaught is undeniable. However, it must be set alongside another development which was to play a less dramatic but equally important part in the Irish land war.

4. *Resistance or Relief?: Self-help or Legal Action*

From the start the Land League faced major problems in the task of orchestrating class warfare in rural Ireland. Parnell's famous Westport injunction was to keep a firm grip on the homestead; but how precisely was this to be done? In the event of an eviction, of course, no tenant was to bid for the land thus unoccupied. The landlord would thus be faced with an empty holding and a loss of revenue. It is clear, however, that only the poorer section of the landlord class would be immediately deterred by such a prospect.

When the landlords recovered from the first shock of the agitation, when they had conceded reductions, as Davitt wrote to Devoy, 'through fear'[85]—what would happen? The conclusion of a recent valuable regional study of Galway should be noted: 'The prediction that following the isolation of particular land-grabbers the doom of landlordism was sealed proved false, since the landlords allowed their lands to remain unproductive and vacant rather than accept the League's demands for the reinstatement of evicted tenants. Furthermore, in spite of intimidation, boycotting and personal attacks on land-grabbers, the landlords frequently found people willing to take their property from which their fellow-tenants had been evicted.'[86]

The famous case of the Dempsey eviction in December 1879 was to illustrate very sharply the inadequacy of the Land League strategy when faced by a determined landlord. The first attempt to evict Dempsey was resisted by mass peasant opposition to the process-servers. The scene was so tense that it is likely that only Parnell's personal intervention prevented large-scale violence.[87] For his speech that day Thomas Brennan was sent for trial. The landlord, however, persisted, and on 10 December Dempsey was evicted without any trouble. The Land League was faced with a new and difficult problem. If Dempsey remained evicted over the Christmas period, this defeat would have a serious demoralising effect on the peasantry. The alternative was to pay out of the League's slender resources the sum of £33 16s 8d: £26 for Dempsey's rent and £7 16s 8d for the costs incurred by the process of resisting eviction thus far. This was in a sense an acknowledgment of defeat, putting money as it did into the landlord's pocket. However, it was felt to be the lesser of two evils, and on 24 December Dempsey received the £26 for the rent, while the costs were raised by local subscription.[88] The Dempsey case revealed two things: firstly, that publicity alone was not particularly effective—the case had attracted world-wide attention, but the eviction had gone ahead anyway; secondly, that spontaneous resistance by the peasantry alone was likely to have, at most, only a delaying effect.

It is true that at the beginning of January 1880 the 'Battle of Carraroe' was fought and won. This was the first successful attempt to prevent a process-serving by crowd resistance—or, at least, to delay it by three months by preventing it before the expiry of its legal time on 6 January. Davitt later reproduced his own newspaper account of the battle in an effort to give his 'younger readers some idea of the early struggles of the Land League movement'[89]:

> The force next marched to Mrs Mackle's and received such a warm reception that bayonets were freely used by the police in efforts to protect Fenton [the process-server]. Mrs Mackle succeeded in throwing a shovelful of burning turf upon Sub-Inspector Gibbons and thereby driving him from the house. A fierce fight now commenced, in which the constabulary used their bayonets, but not in any savage manner.
>
> This attack upon the women roused the men to action, and in a second the police were surrounded and attacked with stout blackthorns and stones and compelled to retire from the front of the house.
>
> They re-formed again on the road and fired a volley over the heads of the people, but this, instead of having the desired effect, only excited those the more who were thought to be intimidated, and they rushed upon the constabulary and drove them completely before them, pursuing the flying peelers and Fenton to the doors of the barracks.[90]

This remarkable account appeared to many both at the time and since to contain the essence of the Irish land war. The conflict between the poverty-stricken, mainly Irish-speaking tenants of Carraroe and the landlord's agents seems to contain all the necessary dramatic ingredients: the passion of the Celtic peasant, the demoralised police and, in the background, the demands of the landlord. It is all the more necessary, therefore, to insist that this account does not give us a typical picture of Land League methods —except perhaps for the very early part of 1880. On 9 January William O'Brien was already writing: 'I am thoroughly inclined to think that if the "battle" of Carraroe . . . [was] to be fought again . . . the results might be very different from what they were.'[91] The RIC had changed their tactics to very good effect. The blunder had been to move the police in a solid phalanx instead of breaking them into detached squads and so enabling them to repulse an attack on flank or rear without being obliged to weaken their front.[92]

Davitt, however, still seems to have believed that a policy of limited guerrilla warfare would meet the situation. He wrote to Devoy on 6 February that the people of the West were keen to have arms; he also claimed credit for personally prompting 'several of the successful attacks upon the opposition'.[93] Five days later J. J. O'Kelly wrote that he was distributing arms 'gratis' in the West: 'Kyle [Davitt] says the people will use them and one event of that nature would settle one important question. This is not to be understood as suggesting anything like general action which would be madness.'[94] But although in the West Riding of Galway alone 107 officers and 3,300 men were required to protect process-servers in the first months of 1880,[95] they were basically successful in their task. Davitt, although very proud of the Carraroe incident, later acknowledged that the Land League required new methods of struggle.[96]

It was by no means clear what this new method of struggle was to be. The original protocols of the Mayo and National Land Leagues had emphasised mainly propaganda warfare. The limitations of such activity had clearly been shown by this time. There had also, however, been mention of resisting 'by law actions of landlords or their agents who may propose doing them an injury', but no steps in this direction had been taken. For one thing, the Land League at this time simply did not have the money to finance such a move. There was also doubt about its inherent value anyway. In his interview with the New York *Herald* reporter, James Ives, Parnell explained: 'We do not propose to defend processes in the courts because the processes before the courts are farces and no substantial justice can be obtained in them and the money only goes into the hands of the lawyers.'[97] Parnell insisted that the money granted to the Land League for political purposes would be used only to help the evicted tenants and to defray the costs of those 'numbers of talented young men in Ireland who were able and would gladly undertake the task of educating the people with regard to the political economy of the land question'.[98] It was certainly the case that money was urgently needed for these purposes. There is ample evidence that Davitt and others were near financial breaking-point. But Parnell's good intentions not withstanding, it proved impossible to abstain from action in the law courts.

James J. Louden and Matthew Bodkin, two Connaught lawyers who were also active land reformers, decided to try out a manoeuvre in the courts.[99] There was no doubt that this was a popular decision with the peasantry of the West. Defence of the ejectments rather than succour to the evicted seemed much the best policy to them. 'Prevention is better than cure,' as James Daly put it in this context.[100] Louden confronted the surprised Mayo judges at the Westport and Castlebar land sessions with a novel interpretation of Section IX of the 1870 Land Act, which was designed, in his view, to ensure compensation for disturbance and improvements for that category of evicted tenants with a valuation of £15 or under. But in practice, for the ten years of its existence, the provision of this act had been understood to refer only to rent-paying tenants.

The number of tenants who had won a claim under Section IX of the Land Act for the years 1877, 1878 and 1879, according to Colonel Tottenham, citing a parliamentary return, had been nil.[101] But, as Davitt noted, the tenants had never been in a position to put the matter to the test.[102] Louden now attempted to see if this section of the act applied to all tenants who had been evicted on account of exorbitant rents. Bodkin developed a similar line of argument before a startled T. Rice Henn in the Galway land court.

In all these instances the judges were compelled to admit that this was a possible interpretation, and they ordered a stay of eviction while the matter was considered. It is not surprising the *Irish Times* reacted nervously.[103] More significant was the perceptible increase in support for the League. John Callanan, editor of the *Western News* and leading figure of the Ballinasloe Tenants' Defence Association, had been sharply critical of Parnell and the Land League in December 1879.[104] But, following the Clondergan case, Callanan actually moved the affiliation of the Ballinasloe Tenants' Defence Association to the Land League, citing the legal activity connected with the case in his speech.[105] The full extent of the strategy's success only became clear when Louden's case came up again in April 1880. The judge ruled that there was no legitimate case that tenants who had been paying an exorbitant rent had been disturbed, but he did feel that under the terms of the act they qualified for compensation for improvements.[106] He awarded sums of compensation which amounted to well over double the amount due—and was thus a very severe fine for the landlord. Bodkin had the same success. He managed to reduce the total rent of the Clondergan tenantry from £336 to £272, knocked 25 per cent off their arrears, and gained a promise from the landlord to borrow £300 from the Board of Works to invest in the land—the tenants agreeing to pay the interest.[107]

James Louden's summary of a year later is surely just:

> He had some experience of the working of the Land Act in the West and he found that where attorneys fought the battle of the tenant, even where they were being evicted for non payment of rent, that the amount received for disturbance or improvements or both were such that the landlords were forced ultimately to strike their colours and accept the terms which the tenants offered.[108]

Davitt later noted with some satisfaction that the effect was widespread and that by these means 'a great number of owners in the West' were induced to come to terms with their tenants.[109] In May 1880 at the Trenof Hall, New York, he described this legal battle as 'the shape' which the Land League struggle had now taken.[110] In a document on the Land League's achievements prepared a few weeks later for American consumption this activity in the law courts was given pride of place.[111] It was claimed that every case of eviction was investigated by the League to see if it offered the possibility of successful legal action. Parnell on his return from America had no alternative but to accept the *fait accompli*. At Irishtown—at a meeting to mark the first anniversary of the agitation—he publicly gave it his sanction with the words: 'We will protect you in the courts by fighting points of law.'[112]

The arrival of cash from America altered the League's relationship with the priests and people of Connaught.[113] The £10,000 spent on seed potatoes in January was a major propaganda coup in itself. The Land League's open policy was to avoid areas—Co. Clare was explicitly mentioned by Michael M. O'Sullivan[114]—where the other relief committees had been very active. Even so, it should be noted that T. S. Cleary, League organiser in Clare, was able at the beginning of May to contrast effectively the £1,351 given to Clare by the League with the £2 10s which constituted the total resources of the Clare Farmers' Club.[115] How much more, then, was this the case in areas which the League had specially favoured?

Neither the Duchess of Marlborough's relief committee nor the Mansion House Relief Committee was particularly efficient. It was a standing joke that farmers were feeding their pigs on the 'Duchess' —that is to say, on the grain provided by the Duchess of Marlborough's fund. James Hack Tuke had effectively pointed out that the Mansion House relief fund had a tendency to give assistance to wealthy unions.[116] This clearly left a gap which the Land League was quick to exploit. Davitt noted:

The distribution of seed and relief and/or seed potatoes amid the most distressed districts gave the organisation a growing prestige among the clergy. Most of the opposition from that quarter had died out in the face of the prompt and effective measures which were taken by the League Executive to cope with the partial famine. When no League organisation existed the parish priest or the curate was made the medium for the distribution of grants, the result being, in more instances of this kind, a formation of a branch of the movement, so that the work of combination kept pace with the relief operations among the people.[117]

It was true, of course, that conflict might still arise in connection with these funds. But the clergy were in a relatively weak position in this event. For example, Father Levingstone of Dunmore sent back the £50 he had received from the League for the defence of the Clondergan tenantry by Bodkin on account of a 'blasphemous' League placard advertising a meeting at Dunmore 'called without reference', as he put it, 'to any ecclesiastical authority or any responsible person'.[118] M. M. O'Sullivan, the League's assistant secretary, felt able to retaliate in Dunmore itself by pointing out that the money was given to Levingstone not for his own personal use but to help the tenantry, which he was, in effect, by his refusal of the money failing to do. At this meeting the possibility of cutting off clerical 'supplies' was raised.[119]

Levingstone hit back immediately by setting up his own private fund, to which Bishop John McEvilly and other sympathetic clerics subscribed. He alleged that the League had been known not to distribute relief to tenants unless they paid the League's membership fees.[120] He also called for a Land League statement on O'Sullivan's speech at Dunmore. O'Sullivan replied that he was not opposed to religion but that he had spoken of 'politics which had no more connection with religion than any other science'.[121] He added a few days later that while most of the priests believed that 'their priestly character . . . cannot be separated from any of their acts . . . I on the other hand believe that when a priest descends to engage in a political contest he becomes like every other man and that he does not possess any priestly prerogatives in that regard'.[122] The Irish Church would crumble if it supported Irish landlordism. Such a position was, of course, quite unacceptable to Father Levingstone, who did not regard the strength of the Church as being due to the effect of correct political choices.

The League executive was quick to close the embarrassing debate which O'Sullivan's forcefulness had brought about, and although

Davitt in particular was critical of Levingstone, Patrick Egan made it clear that O'Sullivan should not have given the impression that his personal views were also those of the League.[123] The most explicit and angry debate between the Catholic Church and 'Ribbon Fenianism' was thus brought to an end. The Levingstone dispute was atypical, however, and the pattern was one of increasing co-operation between the Land League and the priests.

This practical side to the Land League's activities was intensely important. It had, of course, a possible flaw. The League was now, through appeals to the judiciary, asking the dominant power to behave in a different way, or, more precisely, for 'British law' to intervene against the landlord class. This was very different from its initial emphasis upon self-help, that is, the immediate gains that could be won in the course of struggle. It was not simply that the legal structures appeared to receive a League sanction; it was also the case that within the new strategy there was a definite possibility of restricting the League's activities to legal disputes. The larger role of the Land League in creating a spirit of rural resistance was in danger of fading away. But the alternative was to see the forces of political and social radicalism in Connaught combined to produce an isolated and hopeless rebellion—for this is precisely what the moderate Home Rulers felt was likely to happen.

Moderate opinion, however, had been too impressed by the rhetoric and had missed the importance of much of what had been going on. James Louden later offered the *Freeman* an object lesson in translation of political rhetoric (in this case Dillon's) when he said:

> By a declaration of war Mr Dillon meant such a declaration as they made in the West of Ireland . . . against landlordism, which was successful, namely to use the Land Act—and all other legal forms, and every possible form of legitimate obstruction to prevent the landlords from exercising what they call their rights.[124]

But by 15 March 1880, in response to a massive demonstration in Phoenix Park which was expressly designed by Davitt to put pressure on the newspaper,[125] the *Freeman's Journal*, while regretting the 'socialist rhetoric' of certain Land Leaguers, admitted that the agitation was based on 'a substratum of solid fact'.[126] This admission made, the private hope of the *Freeman* was that the general election of April 1880 would produce a reforming Liberal ministry which would reopen the forum for discussion of a moderate solution.

5

The Land League Programme

I would empower the Sub Commission to give every
rack-renting landlord in Ireland, or the most rack-
renting among that number, twenty years' purchase of
the government valuation, and I believe that if such a
law were enacted and eight or ten million pounds given
to the Sub Commission, you would see rents in Ireland
coming down at such a rate as never entered the mind
of men at the present moment.

PARNELL, speech at Beaufort, Co. Kerry
(*Freeman's Journal*, 17 May, 1880)

1. *The General Election, 1880*

Parnell lost no time in committing himself to the electoral struggle.
In the first five days after his return from America he managed to
address five meetings—in Cork City, Kildare, Tipperary, Athlone
and Roscommon—called for the selection of candidates.[1] He
claimed, in fact, that he had been asked to intervene to help in the
selection process by over thirty constituencies, and despite clerical
cries of 'dictation', there is no reason to doubt him.[2] The degree of
Parnell's success is to be measured not so much in his personal
triumph in the constituencies as by his displacement of three Home
Rule candidates—Lord Browne in Mayo, The O'Conor Don in
Roscommon and the Chevalier O'Clery in Wexford—who were
perfectly acceptable to the *Freeman's Journal*. Nevertheless, al-
though Parnell had every reason to be pleased with the election, it
also revealed the somewhat narrow base of the Land League. In
Connaught notable victories had been won, particularly over The
O'Conor Don and in Sligo over King-Harman; and although
Leitrim had been unable to swallow the Parnellite Presbyterian, the
Rev. Isaac Nelson—the living link with the United Irishmen in his
own view, 'a clergyman of rather crazy political proclivities' in the
Freeman's[3]—he was soon accommodated with a seat vacated by
Parnell in Mayo. This was despite the opposition of the majority
of the Mayo clergy. But there is no evidence that the Land League
had any real effect on elections outside the province. Indeed, the
only Irish members elected at this time who had played any prominent part in the League were O'Connor Power, who was by no
means a Parnellite, Parnell himself, Biggar, Dillon, Sexton and J. L.
Finigan. Furthermore, three principal Parnellite candidates who

were also elected all subsequently admitted to a lack of substantial involvement in the land question in April 1880.[4]

The Waterford Farmers' Club had failed to back their champion, Joseph Fisher, newspaper editor and author, strongly enough to make it worth his while to stand against the Whiggish Villiers Stuart, whose major aim appeared to have been to win the renewal of his father's peerage from Gladstone.[5] (Villiers Stuart reneged on his Home Rule pledge given personally to Bishop Power of Waterford almost immediately after the election, much to the advantage of the Parnellites.)[6] In Co. Cork Andrew Kettle—admittedly rushed to the field at the last moment—provided an example of a prominent Land League figure defeated by clerical opposition. Recent research has indicated that Parnell had a greatly increased following after the election but no general mandate.[7] It was clear that there was a need to broaden the base of the agitation, but at the same time Parnell had to maintain his original support.

There is evidence that Parnell was almost overwhelmed by the problem of building an alliance of this sort. At an executive meeting of the Land League which he attended shortly after the general election Parnell spoke of the League committee drawing up a programme which would be acceptable not only to Ireland but 'by the sound portion, that is the majority, of the English Liberal Party'.[8] He concluded by saying that he hoped Shaw would not go through with his implied threat to split the Irish Party.

2. *The Land Conference, 1880: A Conflict of Interests and Perspectives*

The apparently conciliatory tone of this open appeal to the moderates was well received. However, matters were rather more complicated. Parnell was not a free agent: personally he did not hold a sufficiently strong position within the Land League to be able to push it in a less radical direction than that supported by the Land League executive. That body decided to call a national convention for the consideration and adoption of a plan of legislative land reform to be held at the Rotunda on 29 April 1880. On the night before this conference Parnell had the limitations on his ability to shape the agitation forcefully brought home to him.

At a meeting of a special Land League committee consisting of Parnell, Egan, Kettle, William Kelly, Louden, T. M. Healy (as Parnell's then secretary) and Michael Davitt, Parnell found his relatively cautious views brushed aside. This committee had met to prepare the Land League programme which was to be laid before the delegates at the conference. Michael Davitt's account of its deliberations is worth recalling:

We had an all-night sitting in Morrison's Hotel on the eve of the convention, and as a commentary upon Mr Parnell's then un-fixed ideas it may be mentioned that he had not a single sug-gestion to offer beyond the extraordinary proposal that we should recommend Mr Butt's land bill to the convention as the measure to be pressed for in the new parliament by the League party! He good-naturedly resigned himself to the utter rejection of this proposal, saying he would agree to anything upon which the majority would decide.[9]

This is a remarkable passage. According to Davitt, Parnell was recommending that Butt's proposals should be the target of the agitation. In 1876 Isaac Butt had framed and introduced a land bill on the lines of fixity of tenure and fair rents, with the Ulster custom of free sale for tenant right to be extended to all farmers. In November 1878 Parnell had advocated support for this admittedly unsatisfactory proposal, giving as his reason that 'he did not see how they were going to bring about a radical reform [i.e. the abolition of landlordism and the construction of a peasant pro-prietary] of the system of land tenure in this country'.[10] Apparently, even in the changed situation of April 1880, Parnell still thought this 'radical reform' was out of reach. This view was unacceptable to the majority of the Land League leadership, as Parnell must surely have expected; as a result the squire of Avondale felt it necessary to bury quietly his objections. Nevertheless, his abortive attempt to move the campaign on to a less militant basis should be noted.

However, it can hardly be a surprise to learn that the Land League's proposals, when they became known, shocked many of those previously linked with Butt's policy. The *Freeman's Journal* admitted that Butt's bill had been both complex and expensive. But the Land League's criticism applied not just to details but to the whole principle of the Buttite measure. The League had resolutely set its face against the concept of landlord–tenant partnership in the exploitation of the soil. Its uncompromising attitude was suc-cinctly expressed by Davitt:

The well-being of the state, the preservation of the people, the peace and prosperity of the country demand the dissolution of a partnership which has made financial ruin and social chaos the normal condition of Ireland; and the time has arrived when Parliament must decide whether a few non-working men or the great body of industrious and wealth-producing tillers of the soil are to own the land.[11]

One of the most important aspects of the League programme was a proposal that a state department be empowered to acquire the ownership of land at a price twenty times the Poor Law valuation and to let the land to tenants on generous terms (a rent equal to $3\frac{1}{2}$ per cent of the purchase money). To the Land League this was a reasonable and desirable proposal. To the *Freeman's Journal* it was 'confiscation pure and simple'.[12]

The Land League also proposed that a bill should be pushed forward with all speed suspending for two years ejectments for non-payment of rent in the case of all holdings valued at £10 a year and under, and also suspending for two years the right of recovering a higher rent than the Poor Law valuation in the case of any holding whatsoever. The *Freeman's Journal* 'translated' this proposal in the most critical way. The editorial commented: 'It was hardly necessary to comment on this proposal; if it were suggested as a remedy for a great commercial distress that there should be no recovery of any debt less than £10 and that, of larger debts, only 75% should be recoverable at law, such a suggestion should not have the slightest chance of being considered.'[13] Three days later it expanded the point: 'Such a general provision would protect many dishonest tenants able but unwilling to pay.'[14] In the context of these analyses in his own newspaper, it is hardly a surprise to find Edmund Dwyer Gray refusing to attend the land conference called by the Land League to discuss its programme.

However, the land conference did attract one particular group of tenants whose presence was to give it a rather unexpected shape and whose contribution to its proceedings was to provide vivid evidence of the contradictions inherent in Irish agrarian agitation in this period. In the late 1860s and 1870s several dozen farmers' clubs were set up in some southern and eastern counties. Their members were often tenants with large holdings of grazing land. One of the most active of these clubs was proud to admit that its members were 'big graziers'.[15] The conference at the end of April 1880 saw some of these men begin their intervention in Land League affairs.

It was an ambiguous intervention right from the start. The leaders of the Land League were by no means opposed in principle to some kind of participation by the more affluent farmers, and even the left-wingers within the organisation believed that the League should not be based simply on the smallholders of the West. As Michael O'Sullivan wrote to Matthew Harris as early as January 1880, continued failure to open a dialogue with the farmers of other regions, such as those taking part in the land conferences which were already being held in the North and the South, would effectively confine the League to a region of Connaught and would prove fatal to its aspirations to be a truly national body.[16] But these Mayo-based radicals resented the actual presence of the stronger farmers at the April conference. Far from listening with respect to their new 'friends', they poured scorn on their proposals. The Land Leaguers had demanded that the eviction of smallholders—from whatever cause—should be stopped. The larger farmers now argued that the League should demand that *all* evictions—including those affecting the wealthier farmers—should be stopped. The Mayo radicals reacted with exasperation.

The course of the debate was therefore a somewhat surprising one. Parnell had great difficulty in keeping the Land League within the confines of its original proposal of total protection for the smaller farmers only. He was harried by W. J. O'Doherty, the recent unsuccessful Home Rule candidate for Kilkenny City, whose views may be said to represent the Kilkenny Tenants' Defence Association, to provide protection for the interests of much larger farmers. The reason is not hard to find. As the *Kilkenny Journal* reported in the following month, 'Several good farms of Kilkenny that are normally let for grazing were this year let at one pound per acre less than usual, and other farms where grazing cattle used to be taken are in all directions waste.'[17] The conference clearly signalled the increasing frustration of the graziers with the deteriorating conditions brought about by the economic and social crisis.

Patrick Cahill of the Leinster Independent Club spoke in a similar vein in favour of the claims of the more comfortable farmers. Yet this man—who was now urging the League to make a more militant short-term demand for *total* security from eviction in the interests of the strong men—was a supporter of the 'three Fs'[18] and, according to his later admission, was even at this time at best a reluctant believer in the principle of a nation-wide Land League.[19] He was not apologetic about the group whose claims he advanced: 'He did not see why a tenant should not have the right to hold three or a dozen farms just as the landlord had the right to hold three or a dozen estates.'[20]

The Western militants were appalled. 'No! No!' they cried during Cahill's speech. Their vigorous refusal to do anything to help the larger farmers was the vital factor enabling Parnell to hold the conference to the line of complete protection for small farmers only. Joseph B. Walsh and Matthew Harris, in a major speech, were particularly vehement. The small farmers were as hostile to the graziers as to the landlords. The graziers had opposed the struggle for land reform. Harris told his audience that 'If they united with the grazier class . . . in endeavouring to get a land bill, it would be . . . the union of the shark and the prey.'[21] He produced statistics which showed the extent of the destruction of the small farmers by which the graziers had benefited enormously. It was questionable whether the interests of the public and the grazing system were identical. Anyway the political power of this class was 'nil'[22] in Ireland.

It was only the lack of time that prevented further conflict. William Kilroe later put forward a proposal (seconded by Harris) calling for a new valuation.[23] It was widely believed that this would favour the small tenants against the graziers, for it was felt that the existing valuation overvalued the tillage products of the small farmers and undervalued the meat products of the graziers.[24] Had such a proposal been raised at the land conference, it would have further divided the ranks of the tenantry.

The ambiguity of the situation is apparent. The representatives of the stronger farmers, who were quite explicitly sceptical of the Land League's ultimate objectives, were doing everything possible to force the League to adopt a more militant short-term programme. The balance of forces inside the League at this point was such that the Western radicals—those very 'Ribbon Fenians' who sought to extend the power of the League—rejected the idea and were unwilling to countenance demands which would attract the large and even the medium farmers who formed, proportionately, a much larger share of the population outside Connaught. The paradoxical outcome of all this was that, in a certain sense, Western suspicion of graziers was allowing Parnell to maintain the more 'moderate' stance of seeking to offer total defence against ejectment only to the small farmers. (Of course, the Western leaders would have said that their view was not a moderate one—merely a principled and consistent defence of those who were really suffering.)

But there was a more long-term significance. It revealed the absence of any strategy on the part of the League's neo-Fenian leadership for building *any* alliance with the stronger farmers. Harris had explicitly denied that he wanted any such alliance, as had Dillon in New York in January.[25] But what was the alternative alliance? Harris's reference to the fact that the large grazing system was not 'for the public good' implied the reintroduction of extensive tillage, the abolition of large grazing farms, and the employment of a larger agricultural labour force. He might perhaps have relied on the small farmers and sections of the agricultural proletariat[26] to support such a programme. But what of the middle range of the Irish tenantry who were numerically so significant outside Connaught?[27] Did Harris still hold that tenants valued at over £50 should be excluded from the benefit of land reform?

The failure to touch on these problems is noteworthy. In effect,

Harris merely expressed the resentments which were prevalent in the West. His comment that the political power of the grazing class was 'nil' had a certain shrewdness. In the sense that the graziers had traditionally identified with those forces on the right of the Irish political spectrum ('Whig' or 'nominal' Home Rulers, Liberals and even Irish Conservatives)[28] which were now coming under considerable popular attack, their 'political power' was decreasing but it was hardly nil. Considered as a whole, Harris's speech must be seen as the suppression of the admittedly difficult but nevertheless vital problem of the construction of a popular alliance.

Nevertheless, the conference was definitely a success in that it confirmed the Land League's steady progress towards national stature. Many important figures were won over, and a number of key provincial newspaper editors now identified with it in an unreserved fashion. These included men like Timothy Harrington of the *Kerry Sentinel*, who had not been committed to the League's policy up to this date,[29] Joseph Fisher of the *Munster Express*, who had been involved in the land conference of the South,[30] and T. S. Cleary of the *Clare Independent*.

Support for the 'three Fs' at the conference was surprisingly muted. It came in the main from The O'Donoghue, with some help from the Rev. J. Jordan. Davitt responded with vigorous attack on The O'Donoghue's record. Besides, he added, there was no evidence that the landlords would accept Isaac Butt's compromise. The O'Donoghue was further discomfited two weeks later by a meeting sponsored by Harrington in his political base at Beaufort, Co. Kerry, at which Parnell strongly opposed the 'three Fs'.[31]

3. *The Debate on the Programme, April–May 1880*

Parnell also supported Davitt's militant stance with his 'bread and lead' speech, delivered at a public meeting called on 29 April to ratify the line of the land conference. This speech contained a militant-sounding anecdote about an American who had offered Parnell twenty dollars for lead but only five for bread. The point was that the Irish tenants could expect more money from America only if they took up the land struggle in earnest. This did not, however, prevent Fenian disruption of the Rotunda meeting where the speech was made,[32] and John O'Leary commented on behalf of the traditionalist section of the IRB who were still opposed to Parnell : 'I think I may content myself with saying that there is at least one region where Parnell must suppose lead to exist in vast quantities and that is in the heads of his audience.'[33]

The *Freeman's Journal* editorial on the next day, by no means surprisingly, reiterated its opposition to the League proposal for peasant proprietorship. At the rate of compensation proposed by the Land League, the scheme, it was argued, would cost £224 million. Neither Ireland nor Britain could afford to pay such a price. It added explicitly: 'The details of this scheme could never be carried save by revolution, and the details in this case mean mainly everything.'[34]

The compulsory purchase scheme, it went on, was visionary, and Griffith's valuation was certainly not an adequate basis. The valuation on poor tillage lands was often a rack-rent, while on the good grazing land it was in some cases not even half the fair rent. A purchase scheme which had Griffith's valuation as its basis would have a severe bias in favour of the graziers and against the small farmers. But, at any rate, if the government did sanction any compulsory purchase scheme, it would certainly insist that the landlords should receive the full market value of their land. This would be a ruinous bargain for the tenantry, especially if the value of the land fell in the years to come, as many expected. The policy of peasant proprietorship was necessarily gradualist, and it was insisted that in the meantime the tenants required security of tenure.[35]

The next day the *Freeman's Journal* developed the theme. The Land League was giving an ideological weapon to British opponents of Home Rule, who could point to this wild scheme and declare it the type of legislation which a Home Rule parliament was likely to enact.[36]

Parnell and Davitt immediately attempted to reply from Mayo platforms. Davitt explained at Balla that he never expected that such a vast sum would be advanced, knowing as he did the 'prejudice' and 'bigotry' of the British parliament, but that he expected that £15 million or £20 million would be advanced in order that they might begin to buy out rack-renters, absentees and waste lands to create a peasant proprietary. But in the main this reply was hardly reassuring—in particular Davitt's reference to settling the land question once and for all in two or three years and his statement that he wanted to give the landlords only six years' compensation. This speech was very likely to create the impression that Davitt's main intention was to rule out any compromise with the British government.[37]

Parnell added his comment the next day at the meeting at Irishtown which was intended to celebrate the first anniversary of the Land League. He referred to the clause calling for the government to appoint a commission with the power to acquire the ownership of any estate upon tendering the owner a sum equal to twenty years of the Poor Law valuation, and to let this estate to the tenants at a rent equal to $3\frac{1}{2}$ per cent of the purchase money. 'This is the clause which has evidently misled the *Freeman's Journal,*' he said, 'but this clause does not contemplate a wholesale purchase of the land of Ireland by this department upon these terms. By no means.'[38] Rather the idea was that the possession of this potential power by a commission would put an end to the rack-renting landlord. The very existence of such a commission possessing such substantial powers would make any landlord think twice before acting in a repressive fashion. It would not actually be necessary for the commission to preside over a massive transfer of the land of Ireland. The threat alone would be sufficient to improve the peasant's lot. This 'power to pounce down upon any rack-renting or exterminating landlord'[39] was a far more workable method of protecting the tenant than the legal fiction of Butt's fixity of tenure bill.[40] The limitation of the operation of the commission's powers to rack-renters which Parnell now made (and to rack-renters, absentees and waste lands in the case of Davitt) was an innovation. It opened the way for an interpretation of the League's programme as decidedly reformist and non-revolutionary. The original account of the department of land administration in the Land League proposal had made no such limitation.[41]

The *Freeman's Journal*, which kept its attention on the actual programme, was in no way comforted by Parnell's profession of moderation. The Land League programme had, for example, proposed that any tenant should have the right to purchase upon tendering to the landlord twenty times the Poor Law valuation. In mid-1880 this was less than market value of the land, and many Irish tenants would surely try to use this golden opportunity to purchase the land. A total of £20 million or £30 million would be applied for within a week, and it was felt that nothing short of the capitalised value of the fee simple of the country would suffice for the operation. On the other hand, if the principle of peasant proprietorship was accepted and the compulsory sale was carried out at market value, what happened to the *ad interim* protection of the tenantry?[42]

In other words, the Land League was in danger of proposing a solution which was too radical and visionary. It was likely to be discounted by any British government. However, in the unlikely event of a British government conceding a peasant proprietorship scheme it would certainly not subsidise a transfer of land from the landlord to the peasant at less than the market value. It would insist that the peasant must pay for the full value of the land. Such a solution would effectively ignore the need of the bulk of the peasantry for a short-term remedy to the economic problems of 1880.

There was another side to the argument. There was, as the Land

Leaguers said, a definite antipathy among English land reformers to the principle of fixity of tenure. John Bright's major speech on the Irish land question at Birmingham in January was one indication of this. It was feared that they would seize upon the Land League's repudiation of it as an excuse to introduce a gradualist scheme for peasant proprietorship which would, in fact, overcompensate the landlords without giving the tenants the immediate help they needed. But the 'three Fs' could be won forthwith by a strong and united Irish Party.[43]

Parnell, speaking at Navan in May, felt compelled to make a second reply. He declared his agreement with Davitt's view that fixity of tenure meant fixity of landlordism. He claimed—to the *Irish World*'s delight—that the citizens of a nation had as much right to the land of a country as to the air thereof. He insisted that his proposal would not result in such a demand for land that £20 million or £30 million would be used in a week. On the other hand, fixity of tenure would lead to an overwhelming pressure on the courts. It would take, he predicted, thirty county court judges something like fifty years to deal with all the applications for rent reductions.[44] Commenting on the full implications of Parnell's proposal, a Parnellite supporter complained to the *Freeman's Journal*:

> The object of land reformers appears to be that a State department and not all tenants indiscriminately should be empowered to purchase compulsorily the estates of rack-renting landlords. This appears to be different matter to empowering tenants everywhere to buy under the market value whether they were rack-rented or not.[45]

On 16 May Parnell maintained his position at the meeting at Beaufort, Co. Kerry. His policy, he claimed, would ensure a speedy and large-scale rent reduction.[46] The capacity of the proposed commission to come down hard on the oppressive landlord would see to that. But on the same day the Limerick Farmers' Club held a meeting which, although obviously sympathetic to the long-term objectives of the League, clearly felt that in the short term no British government would grant them.[47]

4. *The Land League Programme and Parliamentary Politics*
In the context of this debate Parnell's election to the chairmanship of the Irish Parliamentary Party on 17 May by 23 votes to 18 added a complication for which he was almost certainly unprepared.[48] He had apparently hoped that Justin McCarthy, a compromise candidate, would be elected. It is clear that the extreme men would have preferred Shaw to continue as chairman while Parnell led the left.[49]

Was support for Parnell in the Irish Parliamentary Party the same thing as parliamentarian support for the Land League? The matter was soon put to the test as Parnell made a serious attempt to win the parliamentary party to a Land League position. Parnell's method was to attempt, first of all, to reduce the support for the land reform or 'three Fs' proposals associated with Isaac Butt, the erstwhile Home Rule leader.

For example, Butt's proposal had assumed that a jury of an equal number of landlords and peasants would agree on contentious cases. Parnell made it clear that he regarded any such unanimity as highly unlikely. Many people, Parnell acknowledged, felt that a peasant proprietorship scheme would take too long to carry out. However, Butt's reforms would also take considerable time, since they required a new valuation of Irish land.

Parnell then proposed the Land League solution. He adopted a firm tone: 'The Land League had been accused of making extreme demands but that League did not demand as much as he was now asking the . . . [party] to adopt.'[50] He made it clear that he thought that the level of rent ought to be fixed not just for two years but until the question was settled. He insisted that Griffith's valuation was all the tenants could afford to pay—though he would make exception for some of the graziers. He noted that only one English Liberal MP, Leonard Courtney, had supported the principle of Isaac Butt's proposal; John Bright, Shaw Lefevre and Gladstone had all been against. But the real living heart of Parnell's speech came in his conclusion. Up to this point he appeared to stick to a Land League-prepared brief. However, the voice that ended the speech was distinctively Parnell's own. It was a striking exposition of the essentials of his conservative nationalism:

Now there is another and greater reason why the reformers ought to strike at the root of the land evil and the system of landlordism. . . . The greatest reason why the upper and middle class—and he spoke more especially of the Protestants to which he himself belonged—had remained aloof from the national aspirations of Ireland and had refused to give them any assistance had been the institution of landlordism. They could not expect the landlords of Ireland to work for the good of Ireland as long as they supplied the landlords with every inducement for the maintenance of the English system of government (hear! hear!). Would they proceed to ask for a Bill which in order to give the tenant the first claim to this right makes it necessary for him to go against the landlord? The Land League had been charged with setting class against class. He took it as no surer way of perpetuating the system which England had introduced into this country, viz of setting class against class, could be desired than Mr Butt's proposal (hear! hear!). He for one believed that they would never obtain the national rights of the country until they united all classes in support of those rights.[51]

This speech illustrates, perhaps more clearly than any other, how Parnell was able to pose simultaneously as a conservative and a radical—to appeal to both Fenians and Home Rulers. The *Limerick Reporter* stated in an editorial that

> Mr Parnell explained his sensational views on the land question in a manner moderate and reasonable . . . that many of those who but lately appeared the most determined followers of Mr Shaw have hastened to accept the inevitable and in some cases to worship the rising sun in the most unmistakable manner.[52]

There is no doubt that in general terms the speech was a success and Parnell's personal standing certainly rose, but in the crucial area of Irish parliamentary policy very little changed. For while Parnell's peculiar Anglo-Irish ascendancy/radical creed might give him an ambiguous appeal to two very different sorts of constituencies, he was nevertheless going to have to back one or the other before very long, for his own ideology had no substantial force behind it. For the present it seemed as though Parnell had decided to rely on the Irish Parliamentary Party rather than the Land League.

His position was severely criticised by the party. Shaw said at the beginning of his speech that Butt's bill had been worked out in conference with the representatives of the tenant farmers throughout the country. He argued that in many estates peasant proprietorship was a sure recipe for peasant bankruptcy: it would create a gombeen man's paradise. Parnell's assessment of Griffith's valuation displayed a remarkable naïvety. Parts of Isaac Butt's bill were unworkable, but the basic principle was sound. Shaw also displayed the hollowness (or, from a different viewpoint, the danger) of the slogan 'The Land to the Tiller' when he claimed that if this was to be the case, then the land ought to go to the labourer not the farmer. D. H. Macfarlane, MP for Carlow, provided an 'example' of the 'three Fs' working in practice when he pointed out the case of Bengal.

The Land League report had implied opposition to the principle of fixity of tenure when it described it as having nothing to offer except the attractiveness of its name; but Parnell was compelled to declare that his opposition was to the details of the Butt plan before the party. Parnell seems to have won a paper commitment to the principle of peasant proprietorship, but such a commitment had already been given without his personal pressure at an Irish Parliamentary Party meeting on 20 January 1880.[53] In exchange, he was forced to abandon a significant part of his short-term recommendations for the alleviation of the peasantry. The conference agreed only to pass the first part of his resolution, suspending for two years ejectments on holdings valued at under £20—and even here some speakers made it clear that they voted only in a 'moral sense' and that they did not regard themselves as bound by the express terms of the resolution. The second part of the resolution, concerning the limiting of the power of recovering rent to the government valuation, was referred to a committee composed of Shaw, O'Shaughnessy, Marum, T. P. O'Connor, Lalor, Parnell, The O'Gorman Mahon and Biggar. The *Freeman's Journal* editorial happily concluded that if this spirit of compromise actuated the Irish members in future, there need be little fear of the result.[54]

The Suspension of Ejectments Bill was entrusted to the safe keeping of Dwyer Gray, who unsuccessfully balloted for a place for it. Gray then found that, owing to the weight of his official engagements, he was unable to take charge of a bill for which he had not been able to get a place. He communicated this to the meeting of the Irish Party on 1 June and requested that it should be entrusted to some other member.[55]

His suggestion was not taken up. Healy reported in Parnell's name[56] that the committee which had been appointed to discuss the question of *ad interim* protection had now decided to adopt the measure drafted by Dr Commins and introduced by O'Connor Power with the encouragement of Shaw Lefevre.[57] Power's measure was practically reduced to one clause: that the tenant should have the right of compensation where eviction took place for the non-payment of rent. But the bill did not suspend eviction for a single day, let alone the two years demanded by the land conference resolution. This was an attempt to work within the principle of the 1870 Land Act. It was a high price to pay for the unity of the Irish Parliamentary Party. Not only the League proposal but also Parnell's 'more radical' suggestions were abandoned. There was an immediate explosion of dissatisfaction.

5. *Strategies in Conflict: 'A Nation by the Roadside'*

At Irishtown, where the agitation had, of course, started, the Fenians held a well-attended meeting on 27 June to denounce the vain hope of parliamentary agitation. There had, in fact, been signs of discontent at the Irishtown anniversary meeting addressed by Parnell, and these now came into the open. The *Connaught Telegraph* remarked: 'It is scarcely necessary to point out that they [the organisers of the meeting—P. W. Nally, J. O'Keane and D. O'Connor] were from the beginning prominently connected with the agitation particularly in its early stages.'[58] In fact all these men figure in either Davitt's[59] or Daly's[60] list of the principal organisers of the first Land League meeting. O'Connor had addressed a League meeting at Ballyglass, Claremorris, only two weeks before.[61] This meeting cannot have surprised the leadership of the League— there was a worried correspondence between Dillon and Harris about the unruly mood of Mayo as early as 4 April 1880[62]—but neither can it have pleased them. Irishtown did not mark a definitive Fenian break with the League. But it was a sign of things to come if the League leadership failed to pursue a more militant line.

There was a predictable Land League executive revolt, recalled many years later by Healy:

> At the opening of the session the extremists of the Land League in Dublin yelped at Mr Parnell's heels. They demanded instant legislation to stop eviction. From their standpoint this was natural and they carried what amounted to a vote of no confidence in Mr Parnell's new party. [Healy was then asked by Parnell] to frame a letter to squelch the fault-finders. I dispatched in Parnell's name a lively rebuff.[63]

On this issue the 'fault-finders' felt it necessary to surrender gracefully, but the League executive continued to be unhappy about the general direction of the movement. There was increasing criticism of the policy of 'fighting points of law' in the Connaught land courts. Patrick Egan, the League treasurer, had in early May[64] thought that all attempts to utilise Section IX of the Land Act to win compensation for evicted tenants should be supported. By early June he was less sure.[65] He felt that, except in cases of special hardship or where victory was certain, it would only be putting money into the hands of the lawyers.[66] The background to his change of mind is clear.

On 25 May Thomas Brennan had noted that the League was flooded with requests to give assistance in resisting ejectments.[67] On 15 June he claimed that in the past week alone he had received a thousand letters making such requests. This was not a source of pleasure to the Land League. In the first place, the legal defence of ejectments was often an expensive business. The Westport Land League, for example, received a bill for £75 which covered the costs of legal defence on a mere six cases. How much more would a thousand cost? In the second place, it was now becoming clear that the desire to offer legal defences in cases of ejectment had reached the proportions of a mania in parts of the West of Ireland.

Many peasants were offering legal defences who had not the slightest chance of benefiting from any interpretation—no matter how liberal—of the 1870 Land Act.[68] On the following day T. Rice Henn, the judge at the Tuam land sessions, made precisely this point with some vigour: refusing to grant a stay of execution, he told the League-sponsored solicitor that the case of the thirty-two tenants he represented was different in every major respect from the case of the Clondergan tenantry.[69]

But there was a second factor involved in this dissatisfaction. A section of the Land League executive was hoping to move towards a more dramatic and intense form of struggle. The important thing to note about this new strategy is that it required a mass willingness among the peasantry to face eviction. It was fundamentally a politics of catastrophe. The idea was to mount a massive exposure of the crisis in Irish agrarian relations. The Irish were to become 'a nation by the roadside' while the outraged world looked on. Such a visible proof of the inherent rottenness of the Irish land system would be its kiss of death.

On the same day that Brennan first revealed that the League had been flooded with requests to assist in defending ejectments Andrew Kettle raised the possibility of restricting the application of relief funds so that they would be used only to help the evicted tenantry.[70] On 8 June Kettle moved a motion to the effect that no further relief ought to be given to the ordinary applicant and that the relief funds should be held over to assist evicted tenants only.[71] Kettle's comments on this point before the ordinary relief books were finally closed on 24 August are of some interest. On 10 August he added that there was a proviso attached to the allocation of a £10,000 sum for the relief of evicted families to the effect that the persons so relieved should place themselves in the hands of the Land League, and that the League should provide dwellings for them within sight of the expropriated land; this would enable them to see that if they did not get the crops, nobody else would.[72] On 24 August Kettle dramatically concluded that 'he wanted the people of Ireland to furnish evidence . . . 100,000 of them encamped like gypsies and the land lying idle'.[73]

The necessary context to these views is the argument about the unique nature of the harvest which had followed the economic crisis year of 1879. In early April 1880 Dillon in America had produced his 'Hold the Harvest' slogan. The people must have the food before any food was permitted to be sent out of the country to satisfy the greed of the landlord.[74] This new slogan appealed to what the Conservative press called the 'petty tenantry'. Dillon had insisted on his first arrival in New York that he did not want the larger farmers to join the Land League, as they were the enemies of the small men. He also appeared to think that larger farmers lacked the solidarity of the small men as demonstrated by the Balla affray.[75]

He spelled out the implications of the new line on his return from America in a speech at the Land League's central branch which the *Freeman's Journal* noted as having initiated an 'animated conversation'[76] and which repaid 'careful perusal'.[77] 'One of the policies of the Land League', Dillon argued, 'should be that any man who was supported by American charity during the last winter should not be called upon to pay rent during the time he was on the charity of foreign nations and that any attempt to levy rent for the year of the famine should be met with firm resistance.'[78] If, as a result of this move, Irish tenants who had been supported by American charity were evicted that winter, the League had a right to rely on a 'considerable organisation' in America that would supply them with a 'steady income'.[79] His conversations with Irish-Americans had convinced him of their intensity of feeling on this point.

It is possible to make two further points about the policy advocated by Kettle, Dillon and Egan. Parnell's American tour had collected £50,000 for relief purposes and £10,000 for the political purposes of the Land League. By holding over £10,000 out of the relief funds for the use of evicted tenants only, the League was able to give some, at least, of its relief funds a more direct use in the struggle against landlordism. This would at any rate appear to have been Kettle's idea. Secondly, as the leading detective Mallon explained to his superiors,[80] the decision to grant relief to evicted tenants only gave the League a basis for refusal of applications from those local leaders who had misused their money in selfish expenditure.

But were the tenantry ready to face the risk of eviction involved in the League's new policy? Were they prepared to allow the abandonment of legal intervention against ejectment processes? It may be significant that Michael Boyton, who was actually carrying out organising work in the country, was more sympathetic to the tactic of legal defence than either Egan or Kettle, whose activities were largely confined to Dublin.[81] Five days after Egan had declared that it would be a mistake to spend their money fighting legal quibbles, a meeting of priests and people was held in Claremorris which decided to offer legal defences in forty out of a total of a hundred recent cases of ejectment. The only reason why sixty were omitted was because there was no possible legal defence in their case. All the tenants at the meeting made it clear that they looked to the Land League as their 'only real hope and shield'.[82] It was surely a very difficult task for the League to refuse such requests and at the same time retain popularity in these areas.

James Daly in the *Connaught Telegraph* sharply reminded the Dublin leadership of Western feeling:

> Several struggling tenants have called on us during the week showing copies of their ejectments served upon them by their landlords invariably for two months' rent due May last. . . . We read of land meetings held after the process of eviction has taken place. Would it not be better to hold these meetings before the people are thrown adrift into the world? We hold that it would be the duty of the Dublin branch to defend legally more poor serfs on the grounds that . . . eviction on the part of the landlords is barbarous and cruel.[83]

The money expended on defending ejectments, he added, would be more judiciously and better spent than paying first-class railway fares and hotel expenses for attending meetings held at the ruins of devastated homesteads after their occupants had been driven homeless into the world. This sort of pressure was very hard to resist, implying as it did that selfishness alone prevented the League using its money to defend ejectments.

It is not surprising, therefore, that the money continued to be used for the purpose of exploiting loopholes in the Land Act. On 28 July Thomas Brennan, who was, in Davitt's absence in America, the new Dublin correspondent of the *Irish World*, cabled America to the effect that the Land League had defended many ejectment processes in the court in the past week and had succeeded in most of them. But he added—with obvious pessimism—that in his view the whole question would be disposed of fully by a higher court in the near future.[84] It is clear that Brennan regarded the policy as unsound and that it was persisted in only with the greatest reluctance. But the fact was that such 'legalistic' resistance had a great attraction for the peasantry. Carroll, the editor of the *Clare Advertiser*, agreed that Dillon's heady proposals to the League executive immediately upon his return from America sounded very fine. But Carroll spoke for many when he went on to ask:

> But were the people of this country in the same way of thinking as our Transatlantic friends? Four or five thousand pounds would be a small sum wherewithal to fight the battle of landlordism in the law courts. If not in the law courts, are the peasantry up to the fighting-point? That is the question.[85]

6

The Expansion of the Land League

It is pretty evident, I submit, that the leaders of the present . . . agitation have borrowed their tactics largely from the 'no tithe' agitation of 1831-2.

COUNTY INSPECTOR ALAN REED, in a memorandum of 4 March 1882, which was circulated in the cabinet, with Gladstone's strong commendation (BM, Gladstone Papers. Add. MS. 44160)

Though, for reasons sufficiently well-known, the Land League had not been introduced into the county for a considerable time after it had been founded, its main principles were identical with those of the Kilkenny Farmers' Tenants' Defence Association for years existing in Kilkenny. No sooner had some objectionable features of the movement disappeared—no sooner had its policy been known not to be in antagonism to what had been the policy of the former agitation, than the priests and people united to a man and formed in every branch in the parish of the diocese of Ossory parochial branches of the Land League which are at present in operation.

MAURICE HAYES, editorial in *Kilkenny Journal*, 26 Mar. 1881

1. *The Beginnings of Expansion*

At the end of May 1880 the Land League was still basically a Connaught phenomenon. At this moment Archbishop Croke of Cashel intervened decisively on the League's behalf. Croke took his opportunity at the ceremony of laying the cornerstone of Emly cathedral to give his large audience an exposition of his ardent Catholic nationalism—and here that term is used precisely. William O'Brien described it as the purpose of Croke's life to perfect that 'alliance of religious and national fervour—his enemies would suggest of the Altar and Revolution . . . of which he was himself the living embodiment'.[1] The Emly speech potently combined the themes of religious and national persecution endured by the Irish people in former times. Croke recalled the fate of a former Bishop of Emly, 'thoroughly loyal and devoted to his creed and country', whose head was cut off at Ireton's command and 'set up on St John's Gate where it remained as a symbol of British rule and Irish fidelity'.[2] Croke then moved with typical and significant ease from the sphere of history and politics to that of morality and argued that the bulk of the Irish people were incapable of contemplating any movement incompatible with morality. The Archbishop of Cashel's speech, although couched in the most general terms, had a significant ideological effect. The land agitation had been judged as an authentic expression of the Irish spirit—not a materialist Jacobin importation—by the most substantial authority on the subject.[3]

Croke's remarks certainly made it easier for the Land League to gain a foothold in his territory of Tipperary. The conflict between the locally distinguished Meagher family—'racy of the soil, as old as the hills in that quarter, and always acknowledged by every title of education, lineage and rank to associate among the gentry of their county and that of Kilkenny'[4]—and their landlord provided a more than suitable occasion. The Meaghers of Kilburry were certainly people of substance. Mrs Meagher, with the blood of the martyred Father Nicholas Sheehy in her veins, had brought her husband a dowry of £1,400,[5] which she had been furious to see swallowed up by their rent of £512 per annum. The *Freeman's Journal* editorial noted of this rent that it revealed that 'Even upon one of the largest farms and in one of the richest districts of the country the rack-rents . . . were piled up under cover of the bloated prices of ten years ago.'[6]

The judgment for ejectment in the Meagher case had, in fact, been obtained in January 1880, and Meagher had given up possession on 22 April. But on 25 April the bailiffs who were sent to resume possession found a number of persons in the house. A gun was pointed at them, a dog was set on them, and they were obliged to withdraw. On 20 May the sub-sheriff, who was accompanied by the RM and the sub-inspector, plus a large force of constabulary and several bailiffs, arrived at Kilburry. They found the avenue leading up to the house blocked up by large trees and the gate firmly clamped by an iron band. The house was strongly barricaded and occupied by a large number of men armed with various weapons, who refused to allow the sub-sheriff to enter and threatened to kill anyone who attempted to do so. After a period of violent resistance during which showers of missiles were thrown from the house, fourteen of the persons in the house, including the Meaghers, were arrested. After a magisterial investigation they were returned for trial at the Clonmel assizes but admitted to bail.[7]

The Meaghers easily became an object of popular sympathy, and the newly founded Slievenamon League called a meeting at Cloneen on 6 June.[8] Michael Boyton, the League organiser who was playing a major role in the Kilburry affair,[9] shared the platform with a representative selection of the local clergy including Archdeacon Kinane and also the local MP P. J. Smyth. The meeting was a considerable success and strengthened the local militants. On 13 July the League's central branch further supported them by agreeing to assist financially the defence at the Clonmel assizes.[10] The trial was postponed, a result which Boyton found 'very encouraging'; at the same time he was able to report to the central branch that 'the Land League was making rapid progress in Tipperary'.[11]

In such an atmosphere of self-confidence it was hardly surprising when, on the night of 28 July, a party of men with their faces blackened visited Kilburry House and, presenting a pistol at the bailiff's head, swore him to leave the place and have nothing more to do with it. The men then reinstated the evicted tenant, Henry Meagher, who, with several others, was arrested on the following morning by the police, brought before a magistrate, and held to bail to appear at the Mullinahone petty sessions. On the evening of 29 July, however, the police returned to Kilburry House to find Mrs Meagher in possession and refusing to admit them. The landlord's solicitor then requested the authorities to station police in Kilburry House or place an iron hut there for the protection of life and property. The Law Adviser, however, informed them that they would first have to get a renewal of the writ of *habere*, for as long as the Meaghers remained in possession it was illegal for the police to be involved in any retaking by force. On 17 August Justice Lawson granted the renewal,[12] but Meagher's allies retorted by swarming into the farm and cutting and carrying off the crops.[13] On 22 August there was a second large demonstration at Slievenamon.[14]

It was in the context of this dangerous state of affairs that the landlord and the tenant finally settled. The terms were very favourable to the tenant. The two years' arrears of rent were wiped out by a payment of £384. The yearly rent was reduced from £512 to £400. Finally, the landlord agreed to spend a sum of £300 in such a way as the tenant determined.[15] There was even a rumour that the final settlement was sealed by glasses of champagne. One journalist noted how 'tragedy passes into comedy all too easily in Ireland'.[16] But the Meaghers indignantly denied the story about the champagne.[17]

The Meagher affair was obviously a major success for the Land League. It combined all possible forms of resistance—illegal (resistance to bailiffs; forcible reinstatement; seizure of crops) and legal (League financial aid for defence at Clonmel; the forcing of the renewal of the writ of *habere*; two massive demonstrations at which 'the priests and the people were united . . . the indignation caused by the eviction was very temperately expressed and the farmers unequivocally pledged themselves that the farm should be allowed to

E

lie waste').[18] All this was marred only slightly by Meagher's £20 fine (with short prison sentences for three others) at the December assizes in Waterford.[19] In discussing the question of aid for these men, and with the benefit of hindsight, Joseph Fisher noted at the beginning of 1881: 'It has over and over been recognised that the Kilburry case has done more to establish the principles of the Land League in the South of Ireland than anything that had occurred.'[20]

But the Meagher case might have remained only a signal of the League's potential appeal to the more prosperous tenantry. It might have had only the status of a promising anticipation. After all, the government's decision at the beginning of June to set up a commission of inquiry into the Irish land question was a great encouragement for the more moderate tenantry. Thomas Robertson, a leading land reformer of the 1870s, demanded on 1 August that the Land League clarify its position by giving evidence before the Land Commission. It was whispered, he claimed, that the League planned to efface all tenants holding over a £30 valuation and redistribute the land among the poor people.[21] On the same day Matthew Harris, speaking in Frenchpark, Co. Roscommon, had with justification complained that Connaught's potential allies, Leinster and Munster, were not coming to the rescue. These farmers were 'our brothers' he claimed in the face of cries of 'Down with them!' but he wished they would take action instead of waiting for the priests.[22]

Apart from the Kilburry-inspired agitation in Tipperary, there was little to boast of. The Cork Land League had not yet penetrated rural Cork, while the Clare organiser, T. S. Cleary of Ennis, who had gone out into the field, had become disheartened by the time he reached Kilrush. The local Home Rule paper commented sympathetically: 'A Land League propagandist recently paid a visit to Kilrush and after interviewing some of the finest sons of the sod shook his head in a kind of mute despair. "I don't like the look of your finest peasantry," he said, "they're neither this nor that . . . cute to a degree but . . ." he ended this emphatic sentence with an emphatic shake of the head.'[23] On 31 July the same paper added:

> To be sure we have heard of information in Clare of the formation of League branches. But with all respect that is due to the organisers, and that is a great deal, we are still not very much impressed with the enthusiasm manifested up to the present. . . . Farms are said to be almost as rapaciously and voraciously snapped at now in parts of the country as in olden times.[24]

The League's effect in Munster, and still more in Leinster, was clearly a limited one so far. The expansion of the agitation was by no means certain. But the rejection of the Compensation for Disturbance Bill on 3 August by the majority of even the Liberal peers, combined with the earlier fact of the setting up of the Land Commission, gave real impetus to the League's struggle to expand outside Connaught.

2. The Effect of Political Developments

The Compensation for Disturbance Bill had been designed as a temporary measure to terminate at the end of 1881. A tenant evicted for non-payment of rent could claim compensation for disturbance if he could prove that he was unable to continue his tenancy because of the two last bad harvests and that the landlord had refused just terms. It applied only to a part of Ireland, and to tenancies at £30 a year or under. As the debates proceeded Forster tried to buy off opposition by amendments that would have weakened the bill in important ways: one limiting it to tenancies under £15, the other excluding cases where the landlord was willing to let the tenant sell his interest in the holding. The opposition of Parnell compelled the government to withdraw the first and to make the second much less controversial.

The conduct of the bill had placed the government under some strain. Some members of the cabinet (for example, Spencer, Hartington and Argyll) supported it with the greatest reluctance. The weakest point in the Compensation for Disturbance Bill, Spencer wrote to Cowper, the Lord Lieutenant, was the lack of evidence that numerous evictions of a really harsh kind were taking place.[25] Cowper replied that most of those evicted *did* owe some rent, but the problem was the *high* level of the rent. In his view a tenant who had made improvements surely ought not to lose his right to remain undisturbed because of a famine. If Gladstone's Land Act of 1870 had been just, then Forster's case for a compensation for disturbance reform was impregnable.[26]

In another letter Cowper added that there 'have been some [cases of hardship]; but what impresses me most is that they might be innumerable. Landlords might take the opportunity in all directions of clearing their estates and the temptation would be very strong; and we should have to assist by police and military throughout the winter.'[27] But the government had a difficult task in providing a factual basis for this fear. Gladstone in an early speech on the bill claimed that it was required to avert the eviction of 15,000 persons.[28] But after opposition criticism Lord Selborne, in the final government speech in the House of Lords, scaled the figure down to 3,500.[29] The bill's rejection by a majority of even the Liberal peers in these circumstances was hardly a surprise.

The House of Lords had been placed in a difficult position. 'If they pass this Bill,' noted the *Freeman's Journal,* 'they arm Liberal land reformers with all the powers implied in the consent that the present land laws are iniquitous, whereas if they reject the Bill they confess that they approve of oppression and they challenge the humane and popular force of the kingdom to put on its war paint.'[30] Barry O'Brien later elaborated the point: 'Timely concession from Ministers would have strengthened the hands of Shaw and the "moderates", and might have broke up the union between Fenians, farmers and priests. The refusal of concession in time consolidated this union, discredited the policy of the moderates and threw the game into Parnell's hands.'[31] The Compensation for Disturbance Bill was certainly a missed opportunity for conciliation.

There was no more successful, if unintentional, application of the much-sought-after carrot-and-stick principle in the history of Anglo-Irish relations. The decision to set up the commission in itself had acted as a calming force in Leinster and Munster. There were many local leaders of the Robertson type who were prepared at this stage for a strategy of graceful support and acceptance of Liberal proposals. But the rejection of the bill greatly strengthened those who argued that a nation-wide agitation was required to stiffen the cabinet's resolve and to unnerve the forces of the right in British politics. The moderates who now accepted this argument did so, however, with the knowledge that the government's decision to set up the commission had revealed the situation as a fluid one in which there was a definite possibility of victory.

Forster, the Chief Secretary, after all, had been totally committed to the Compensation for Disturbance Bill. Richard Hawkins has described Forster's stance in parliament: 'Forster was deliberately putting the situation in the harshest terms he could, trying to make the point he had told Burke he wished to make: that the law would be enforced but that it must be altered, or the house would face the responsibility for further collisions.'[32] Behind the scenes Forster had even gone so far as to consider the use of soldiers to support evictions in cases of particular tenant hardship such as Carraroe in order to provoke an 'outcry . . . to prove that the law need be altered'.[33] But he had failed to provide enough pressure to get the bill through the House of Lords. Only massive Irish pressure could achieve that aim.

The terms of the Compensation for Disturbance Bill began to receive an attention they would never have received if the bill had been passed. The very way the legislation had been framed became an argument for the stronger tenantry joining the Land League. The bill had been designed to benefit only tenants valued at £30 and under in the scheduled districts. By a skilful play on this fact, the League convinced many of the tenantry valued at over £30 in unscheduled districts that reform would only benefit them if they joined in the agitation. Parnell's speech at New Ross in September put the case explicitly:

> When the Compensation for Disturbance Bill was brought forward in the last session to the House of Commons, the counties and the people whom I am now addressing, namely the four counties of Waterford, Wexford, Kildare and Carlow were excluded with the exception of a small portion of Co. Waterford. . . . Now, why were you left out? It was because you had not organised yourselves and shown yourselves the determination and the power of the thousands of people who live in these counties (*cheers*). But I think that after today and after the practical work it will be our duty to see follows the proceedings of today, there will be no fear that the people of these counties will be left out of the coming Land Bill.[34]

3. *Leinster and Munster: 'Rent at the Point of the Bayonet'*

The Land League moved on to the offensive, but it was a particular kind of offensive which was determined very much by the nature of this newly formed rapprochement with the prosperous farmers of the East and South. On 10 August, a week after the rejection of the Compensation for Disturbance Bill, Michael Boyton reported that ten new branches of the Land League had been formed in Tipperary.[35] At the same meeting of the Central League Patrick Egan proposed a resolution which was passed unanimously calling for a refusal to pay 'unjust rent', an end to land-grabbing and the buying of property seized for rent, and the formation of an industrial union against landlord monopoly. Egan presented this resolution as a compromise in which he had deferred to the wishes of other members. He made it clear that he would have personally preferred a general strike against all rent pending the settlement of the land question. But while Egan's revolutionary credentials are not in doubt, it is significant that he had adopted this compromise, and also that in the course of his speech he argued for a policy based on an analogy with a previous struggle—the tithe war of the 1830s. He claimed that they 'should compel the landlord to collect rents at the point of the bayonet as the tithe rents were formerly collected'.[36]

The introduction of the old 'rent at the point of the bayonet' policy at this particular moment had crucial implications. In the first place, the analogy with the tithe war was misleading. The tithe war had been fought out against the isolated figure of the tithe-proctor with support from all rural classes.[37] But of far greater importance was the fact that Egan (for all his militancy) had implicitly adopted a policy which was to prove perfectly suited —with its low level of risk and easy martyrdoms—to the rural bourgeoisie of South Leinster who had taken the initiative during the tithe war. 'Even in the event of a seizure of goods', Gearóid Ó Tuathaigh has written of this conflict, 'a conspiracy to boycott or "fix" the ensuing auction could render it a Pyrrhic victory for the tithe owner.'[38]

'Rent at the point of the bayonet' involved the tenant in a decision to refuse an unjust rent until the landlords placed sufficient pressure on him (through sheriff's sale or some other method) to make it important for him—if he wanted to stay in the holding—to pay his rent and usually the hefty legal fees incurred by the process of delay. The case of the Pallas tenantry in Queen's County—the first major Land League exploit in Leinster—had made it clear that it was the League which was likely to pay these legal costs.[39] The policy had been the expression of the hegemony of the prosperous tenantry within the anti-tithe alliance which they had led from the first. After a somewhat slower start it was to be the means of re-establishing this hegemony in 1880.

The significance of all this is clear. *The Land League had failed to break with one of the classic organisational forms of struggle of the better-off Irish peasantry.* This is the key to the adoption of the 'rent at the point of the bayonet' strategy: the League was building, albeit very slightly, on the spontaneous local practice of the stronger peasantry. It was by no means obvious that there was any real alternative. The project envisaged by the most radical section of the League in July, and most precisely articulated by Andrew Kettle, required a mass willingness to face eviction for its success. In the first place, there is no evidence that any section of the Irish tenantry, either small or large, was prepared to face eviction if it could at all be avoided. In fact they regarded the Land League as a weapon for preventing ejectments. Parnell, speaking at Newcastle-upon-Tyne immediately after the rejection of the Compensation for Disturbance Bill, had claimed that the landlords would say: 'This is our last chance of clearing the land and getting it into our possession. They would say to themselves that though we have avoided legislation this year, we cannot hope to escape it next year, so let us make hay while the sun shines.'[40] But in reality the only way to ensure large-scale evictions was to attempt a total rent strike. The clergy would have been totally opposed to such a policy, and only the left of the Land League and the newly formed Ladies' Land League would have supported it. (The Ladies' Land

League had been called for in New York in August 1880 by
Fanny Parnell, but it was not until the end of the year that Fanny's
sister Anna began to build up its organisation in Ireland.) Anna
Parnell, who was often sharply critical of her brother's caution,
later claimed that there had been an outside chance of victory for
a rent strike:

> The most essential condition for success in a general resistance
> to rent was that the tenants themselves should wish to resist.
> If they did not wish it, they had powers of wasting money in a
> pretended resistance such as no other strikers have. That they
> did not wish it is certain. The only question is, might they have
> come to wish it, if they had been induced to begin it and per-
> ceived the possibility of success before them? . . . My own
> opinion is that about the early part of 1880 we were getting
> nearer to reality in our doings than at any time in the nineteenth
> or twentieth centuries.[41]

But when Michael M. O'Sullivan, the League's assistant secretary,
did, however, try to put forward a 'no rent' policy in August at
Sessiagh, Co. Monaghan, he found himself forced off the platform
by an outraged clergyman.[42] It is not difficult to see why the League
baulked the task and issued private instructions to all its branches
enjoining the payment of rent 'at the last'[43] and promising to
defray all the legal costs incurred by the delay, which tenants were
instructed to make as long as possible by interposing every obstruction they could to the collection of the money they owed to the
landlords. As well as legalistic forms of obstruction, the League
always attempted, in particular, to make seizure of cattle for rent
as difficult as possible. This had involved hiding cattle in the fields
of neighbours, blocking roads, complex early-warning systems and
other such devices. A typical exposition of the proposed general
strategy was that issued by the Westmeath Land League:

> In view of the law proceedings now threatened throughout this
> county for the recovery of rack-rents, we, the delegates of the
> Westmeath Land League convention assembled in Mullingar,
> exhort all those who will or may have received ejectment pro-
> cesses to hold out (where no legal defence can be offered) until
> the sheriff seizes, as in every case the League will render assis-
> tance, and indemnify for all pecuniary loss attending such
> resistance.[44]

Such a policy of obstruction, although it may not have been
realised at first, was fatal to the more confrontationist line advocated by Kettle.

'Rent at the point of the bayonet' was supplemented by another form of struggle which has traditionally received more attention. The Land League has been conceived as a combination whose immediate aim was to keep rents down by bringing back public opinion to bear on particularly hard cases of evictions for arrears of rent, and by making life difficult for the 'grabbers' who took on holdings of evicted tenants.[45] This points immediately to the famous 'boycott' system, first explicitly applied to an unpopular English land agent in Mayo, but more generally applied to the land-grabbing Irish tenant, as suggested by Parnell in his famous advocacy of the more Christian and charitable method of social ostracism at Ennis in September. There is no doubt that boycotting was a very valuable Land League weapon, but it should be noted that had it been the only one, the League would have been restricted to a largely defensive strategy. A campaign which had as its only object the aim of keeping down rents and drawing forceful attention to the particularly hard cases of eviction for arrears of rent would have been limited to a relatively small area of the country. In the period of six weeks in the autumn of 1880 when the League established its power in Munster there were, as Forster noted, only two evictions in the province.[46] The point is that the League's object was to bring down rents, not just to keep them down while large numbers of Irish tenants prosecuted the land war to this end without having to undergo evictions in their midst. 'Rent at the point of the bayonet' did, at least, offer some sort of offensive strategy, particularly in Munster and Leinster. The conception of the Land League as an essentially defensive organisation has led to a neglect of the importance of 'rent at the point of the bayonet' as against the renowned 'boycott' system. The role of 'Land League courts' has also been exaggerated. After the prosecution of Timothy Harrington for holding such a court in early 1881 the League itself tended to discourage them.

The predominantly legalistic methods of the early part of the year were also continued. The expense and political nature of these policies had brought them under critical review in May and June, when Egan and Brennan, in particular, had expressed their doubts. But now they were expanded, for not only were small tenants valued at £15 and under defended, but so also were the larger tenants. There was a gamut of complex 'legal' ways of making trouble for the landlords. With good reason Davitt spoke of the 'blessed elastic law' in this context,[47] and many of the legal actions undertaken by the League strained every loophole of the law.[48] One case, which the League organiser Michael Boyton described as of 'national importance' involved Lord Clarina and his tenant

George Smith; the case was undertaken in the first flush of Limerick's enthusiasm for the League. The project was to fight the landlord up to a certain point in the bankruptcy court and then by handing in the amount claimed to escape costs, thereby placing them on the landlord. Although Smith would not so far recognise his landlord's right—he had to be reimbursed by the Limerick League—Boyton recommended this policy for future use.[49]

The reports of the Central League meetings and the internal correspondence of the organisation reveal that these legal defences took up a considerable amount of time.[50] It is hardly surprising when one considers the promise made by Boyton at Waterford: 'They had £30,000 on hand and £50,000 to get for the asking . . . to fight their cause in English land courts.'[51] Even Brennan and Egan seemed to regard them as a necessary part of the League's work. What better way was there to assure strong farmers (particularly Protestant farmers) that the League was committed to their cause and could do something for them than by covering their legal costs? With Land League assistance one Protestant farmer in Co. Meath successfully claimed £1,654 10s 9d for improvements from his landlord, Major-General Guy Rotton, at the Trim land sessions. He also won an agreement out of court from the landlord to pay £200 instead of £600 total rent for the next three years, followed by a permanent reduction of rent to £135 per annum for the rest of a fifty-year lease.[52] In this context—at the very moment when the League was trying to get a foothold in Ulster— it is not surprising to find Brennan gleefully publicising the results of that very legalistic activity he had previously doubted.[53] Patrick Egan went so far as to describe the Meath case as 'one of the best fights that had been made since the League had commenced'.[54] But the price was high: the total legal costs ran to £92 7s 5d, of which the tenant was capable of paying only £20.[55]

But if 'rent at the point of the bayonet' was one of the decisive Land League slogans—a slogan whose meaning must be deciphered before the nature of the movement can be understood—the appeal to Griffith's valuation was another. By the end of the year 1880 the League was successful in that the demand for Griffith's valuation had been made by tenants in most of southern and western Ireland. The demand seems to have been put forward by the farmers themselves, particularly in the more prosperous areas. It was, in fact, opposed at first in Co. Clare by the League organiser, T. S. Cleary, who wanted to see a deeper commitment to the League before sanctioning such an objective.[56] Cleary was, however, soon overruled.[57]

The appeal to Griffith's valuation, with its implications of official legitimacy, was hardly one the League could afford to neglect (even though Parnell had acknowledged that the land held by graziers was often worth rather more). It set a target for rent reductions of 20 or 30 per cent which was in most cases potentially achievable. Nevertheless, this target of a percentage reduction was a controversial one. It revealed again the divisions with the Land League alliance. The *Roscommon Herald* wrote bitterly of the ranchers: 'In many places they have wormed themselves into the Land League; they have had poor men fighting for rent reductions which were practically worthless to the struggling tenants but great boons to the owners of the bullock-walks.'[58] The crisis of the small farmers was so great that they needed more than a percentage reduction in rent. Anyway, the rent reduction which was often, in absolute terms, a substantial sum for the strong farmer was usually a pittance for the small man. But a pittance was better than nothing, and there was always the hope of something more. By the end of 1880 it appeared that the majority of the Irish tenantry supported the Land League.

4. *Leinster and Munster: The League's Difficulties*

But behind this apparent success lay some major problems for the League leadership. Their actual control over their new recruits was remarkably loose, and there were considerable barriers which made it difficult for them to get their political line across effectively. The leadership in many of the recently recruited areas was drawn from previously existing Farmers' Clubs, Independent Clubs or Tenant Defence Associations. These local groupings accepted that the Land League had far greater financial resources than anything they might muster. The older Farmers' Clubs accepted the need not to organise on an exclusive basis. As John O'Connor explained at the meeting at which the Cork Farmers' Club transformed itself into the Cork Land League,

> The Farmers' Clubs were formed on the narrow principle that a man should be a farmer before he should be admitted. He believed that, the farmers being so far apart, there was an absence of that cohesion which was absolutely necessary to carry out the object they had in view. . . . They should make use of all the elements of power around them.[59]

In the end some 45·8 per cent of those interned under the Protection of Person and Property Act were not farmers or farmers' sons:[60] in fact 14·4 per cent of the total arrested were traders, business proprietors and shopworkers; 8·1 per cent were innkeepers and publicans; while 10·1 per cent were artisans and non-farm labourers.[61] Association with these elements involved the risk for many farmers of becoming more involved with Fenianism than they would have liked—but it was a risk they were prepared to take. However, the pre-existing rural leadership was not prepared to go beyond that point.

They regularly ignored League advice. On 17 August 1880, for example, the League leadership declared its opposition to the Land Commission and told its supporters not to give evidence to it.[62] This was partly because they disapproved of the allegedly pro-landlordist nature of its composition, and partly because they felt that the tenants who gave evidence to the commission would in some way be binding themselves to the conclusions of the commission. The Limerick Farmers' Club immediately resolved to send along representatives to the commission[63]—a decision which did not stop it deciding to join the League a few weeks later on 2 October.[64] Worse still, the Tipperary Independent Club decided to send representatives to the Land Commission at the very same meeting at which it decided to join the Land League.[65] The Kilkenny Tenants' Defence Association, later the nucleus of the Land League in that area, decided also to give evidence to the commission,[66] as did the Queen's County Independent Club.[67]

The Waterford Farmers' Club did not appear to be even aware of the League line when it asked Joseph Fisher, their chairman, to give evidence to the commission on their behalf. Fisher, although he had publicly supported such an idea—probably before he knew of the League's decision—was too closely identified with the Central League to take such a step, and he had to refuse in rather embarrassing circumstances.[68] On 19 March 1881 Fisher was to claim in his *Munster Express* that the Land League in other counties had been built up by the aid of paid organisers and pecuniary assistance. He contrasted this with the almost spontaneous nature of the movement in Waterford as revealed by another massive demonstration. But not surprisingly, a spontaneity based on the Waterford Farmers' Club did not particularly impress the Land League. It is significant that just before his arrest Dillon was hoping to begin an organising tour in Waterford.[69]

It was only after an angry debate that the League line was enforced at the Cork Land League. In condemning the Queenstown raid on the *Juno* for arms—the last gasp of Stephensite Fenianism —this particular branch had contradicted the spirit, at least, of the New Departure. It had been heavily censured by the Central League[70] and was, in fact, reconstituted in early October[71] around a rump of figures like Harrington, Heffernan, and P. P. O'Neill,[72] League employees whose loyalty to the Central League was undeniable, and moderate Fenians like John O'Connor and the more militant of the old Farmers' Club members. The branch was purged of extreme Fenians and ultra-moderates alike. But the League's control over the Cork branch had required exceptional effort—such as the importation of Harrington from Kerry—and did not translate itself into control of rural Cork. The Cork[73] and Cloyne[74] clergy had after all publicly committed themselves to the 'three Fs' solution to the land question, and they agitated on that basis with unusual explicitness. The Cork League considered asking them to change publicly their position, but they wisely backed down.[75] The matter was quietly buried by a resolution declaring that it had been learned from trustworthy sources that the majority of the clergy 'were not in favour of any legislation that would help to perpetuate landlordism in Ireland'.[76]

The activity of the clergy in Munster and Leinster must be seen as part of the resistance of the pre-existing rural leadership to the full claims of the new movement. In these areas the priests did not, as in Connaught, participate in the agitation as men whose local power had been shown to have limits; and as a result they tended to modify their traditional politics only slightly.

When the League first attempted to penetrate the Birr area of King's County, the local priest, Dr Bugler, refused to chair the meeting unless Matthew Harris left the platform. It was only on the previous day that Dr Bugler had so far sanctioned the proceedings as to promise his attendance at the demonstration itself. However, he intimated that his action was undertaken more for the purposes of securing peace and good order than for forwarding the avowed objects of the Land League. Bugler's attitude to popular agitation was clearly revealed in his speech: 'Let them bear in mind above all things, that they were not created solely for this world, that they should trust rather in the Providence of God than in violent exertions of their own.'[77] In these circumstances it is hardly a surprise that on the day of the first full-scale League demonstration in Birr in November the local band carried a banner bearing a handsome likeness of Parnell and, and on the reverse side, conspicuously figured, a 'three Fs' motto. ('A theory which, by the way,' the local Conservative press pointed out, 'Mr Parnell is credited with having utterly repudiated.')[78] It is hard to imagine a more appropriate symbol of the gap between the political objectives of the leadership and those of the farmers in this area—a gap which the Birr clergy had done everything in their power to accentuate. It is small wonder that Matthew Harris regretted that his involvement in a state trial prevented his intended organisational tour of the area at the beginning of 1881.[79]

These were not isolated cases of clerical opposition. It was felt, for example, that in both Meath and Westmeath clerical disapproval was responsible for low attendances at early League meetings.[80] This was despite the fact that the League tended to give prominence to its most ostentatiously Catholic leaders in this area. In other areas opposition, although less public, was real enough.

The resistance of the clergy was linked with the resistance of a certain section of the Home Rule MPs. In Carlow, for example, Dwyer Gray and Macfarlane were able to refuse to join the League while at the same time speaking at its meetings.[81] Land Leaguers naturally applied as much pressure as possible with such MPs, but only in the case of Bernard Molloy of King's County were they successful—and even in this case Molloy evaded too close an association with the League by joining its local but not its central branch.[82]

The limitations on the power of League organisers—in Leinster particularly—are made clear by the account of Michael Boyton's major efforts to intervene in Kildare. In a spell of hectic activity he burnt the infamously stringent Leinster lease[83] in the market place of Athy, and the Duke of Leinster's tenants were pledged to accept only Griffith's valuation.[84] Within a few weeks, however, at a meeting chaired by the Rev. Dr Kavanagh, the tenants agreed to accept the 20 per cent reduction which had been offered by the landlord, which in this case was less than the League's target.[85] The League was not even mentioned at this meeting, although another organiser, J. T. Heffernan, was present and was obviously unhappy about the clerically orchestrated compromise. The vice-president of the Athy Land League claimed in a resignation letter later that year that the acceptance of the Duke's offer had broken the backbone of the local Land League.[86]

5. *The Agitation in the Original Base*

Connaught, however, continued to develop its own distinct pattern. In the first half of 1880 the sharp nature of the economic crisis, the strength of neo-Fenian sentiment and the adoption of effective methods of struggle had all helped to give the Land League a strong position in many parts of the province. For many of the more articulate leaders the demand for peasant proprietorship was not a mere tactic—a necessary exaggeration in view of the British government's tendency to scale down Irish demands—but rather it was advocated because the 'three Fs' would fix the present distribution of the land.[87]

Roscommon and Sligo were effectively roused by Jasper Tully,

The Land War in Connaught: Incidents in the Agitation

P. J. Sheridan and Matthew Harris in the first months of 1880, as the dramatic election results in these areas proved. In August Sheridan claimed that there were eighteen League branches in Sligo alone.[88] It is no surprise to find the local Sligo police reporting that many persons belonging to secret societies made a 'cloak' of the land agitation to enable them to carry on their secret practices.[89] Davitt later admitted that where the clergy were unfriendly towards the agitation the open organisation of the League often fell under the control of the extremists, and while the general work of the League was carried on on its merits, the branch was used as a shield for the more ulterior ends of the advanced movement.[90] Many areas in Connaught appear to illustrate the truth of this remark.

The clergy of Mayo, Sligo and Roscommon had come to an accommodation with the Land League by early 1880. In Galway, despite the influence in the area of the pro-League bishop Dr Duggan, there was some delay. But after a meeting between the two parties on 11 October, it was agreed that the clergy should share the platform at Kilreecle on 31 October.[91] Only the Leitrim clergy seemed to have any chance of winning a struggle with the Land League. Dr Langan, the dominant priest in the Leitrim area, was powerful enough and confident enough in his opposition to the Presbyterian Parnellite parliamentary candidate, the Rev. Isaac Nelson (whose position on the Catholic university question was unsatisfactory), to threaten Parnell himself with a crowd of bludgeon boys.[92] Indeed, despite the efforts of an imported team of Mayo agitators, Nelson came behind the clergy's candidate in a poll where the split Home Rule vote gave victory to the Conservatives. By June the League had still made little headway, but an incident in which a young landlord, Acheson, shot dead one of his tenants during an affray over the fencing of land gave it a golden opportunity.[93] Sheridan claimed at the beginning of November that every parish in South Leitrim had a branch in good working order.[94] The clergy after some hesitation mounted the League platform at Cloonturk in that month.[95]

That the small farmers held the initiative in these campaigns is not in doubt. Even the relatively moderate James Kilmartin insisted that the South Galway League should exclude graziers from its ranks.[96] By June 1881 in Leitrim a quarter of the grazing lands of the neighbourhood were not stocked. This was superfluous meadowland which the Leitrim graziers had usually let at from £6 to £8 per acre; but with the League's boycott of the graziers in operation, this land lay vacant, while the small farmers could not be prevailed upon to send out young cattle at a moderate tariff.[97]

The *Times* correspondent, Finlay Dun, reported from Roscommon:

> Rents and prospects of grass farms are not what they have been; even substantial men have demurred to meet rents. Many who have rendered themselves obnoxious to the Land League have had their gates and fences broken down, their cattle of different sorts driven together, and sometimes sent in the night several miles along the roads while their herds are terrorised into resigning office. This programme is obviously designed to deter graziers taking more grass farms and thus to coerce landlords to divide them among smallholders.[98]

It was clear that the project was to take advantage of the graziers' predicament and turn the agricultural division of labour against them. The *Roscommon Herald* pointed out that the losses occasioned by foreign competition, by disease and sheep rot, the stoppage of credit by the banks, extravagance and other causes had driven the grass farmers into very sore straits. Where they had been excluded from the League they had collapsed under the strain; their farms were advertised to be let or laid down in meadow. It was quite evident that if the tenant farmers who could afford it refused to send beasts to the graziers on these farms and refused to take the meadow grown there and the hay sown there, then the tenure of many a grazier who eagerly supplanted the starving multitude in the famine years would come to an end.[99]

From the point of view of the radical section of the League executive, Connaught was a province where organisers had considerable political control, where the clergy were subdued and the militant small farmers and their Fenian allies were well to the front. This was partly because of special economic circumstances. The gravity of the crisis in 1879 was revealed by one simple fact—that pig numbers in 1880 were the lowest on record except in the years 1847 and 1849. (Pigs, traditionally vital to the 'poor man's economy', were fed largely on surplus potato.)[100] Only Mayo presented a major problem for the League organisers—and that was because in this county the forces of extremist activity had got out of control. As early as April 1880 this problem had been noted.[101] Among the Fenians the traditional militarist line began to regain ascendancy. The compromise which had led to the acceptance of O'Connor Power's bill (see p. 110) had been the context of the Irishtown meeting in July which had been a signal of potential Fenian dissatisfaction. In September and October there was some physical strife between the defenders of the League and its Fenian opponents in the Louisburgh area. On 11 October what was billed as a 'Nationalist' land meeting was held at Ballyhaunis, at which the Fenians heard criticisms of the League but nevertheless committed themselves to an agrarian agitation.[102]

The Boycott affair had an unfortunate effect on this compromise.[103] The organisation of large-scale passive resistance against the Orange labourers and their military guard brought in to harvest Captain Boycott's crops must be seen not only as a major propaganda coup—which it was—but as a pre-emptive intervention led by Father O'Malley (who was closely associated with O'Connor Power) and James Daly against a Fenian outbreak. Although in one sense the Boycott affair was an undeniable success for the Land League—£350 worth of potatoes and other crops had been harvested at an expense of £3,500 to the state and the supporters of the expedition—it was not surprising that it further alienated a section of the Mayo Fenians who were keen to attack the military. 'I have been down at the Lough Mask expedition and the young men were at that time talking in a terribly wild way,' William O'Brien later recalled. 'I do not believe the Land League had any power in Mayo after the Lough Mask expeditions.'[104]

In November, at the Manchester Martyrs' Day celebration, Thomas Hastings explained the position of an increasing number of Mayo Fenians. In the early days of the land movement they had given it the greater part of its enthusiasm. If of late they had shown an inclination to draw behind the line of demarcation, it was because they were disappointed in their fond hope that behind the land movement there was a strength and power such as compelled the British government to yield to the demands of the glorious Volunteers of '82.[105]

The political frustration of the Fenian activists combined with the growing social frustration of the small farmers. At a meeting at Leenane in August Joseph B. Walsh, a prominent League figure —he was to have the distinction of being the first Mayo man to be arrested under the coercion act—called for the breaking up of the consolidated farms.[106] James J. Louden made an obvious attempt to cool the ardour of Walsh and those who thought like him. The time was not yet ripe, he said, for a discussion of that subject. Possibly next year or the year after the League would take up the question of the area of the land occupied by the tenantry. Their present object, however, was to keep the people on the land they were now occupying.[107]

But the problem was not so easily suppressed. Walsh described a resolution at a meeting at Kilbree at the turn of the year which demanded that the landlords stripe their lands into fifteen-acre residential holdings as a 'new phase of the land agitation'.[108] A week later, however, he had retreated. The division of the grass farms, he claimed, was a 'secondary' consideration.[109] Nevertheless, on 10 January 1881 'Transatlantic' in one of his most notorious *Irish World* articles reported that 900 men at Milltown, on the border of Mayo and Galway, believing that the land belonged to them by some new law, had met to divide it among themselves. He enthusiastically proposed a ballot system to make for the most fair distribution.[110]

It was clear that there existed a degree of repressed social and political militancy in Mayo. The chaos thus produced was aggravated by internal squabblings of various kinds among the 'official' Land League leadership; these dissensions eventually led to the defection of the leading Land League newspaper. James Daly, believing that the Louden section of the League was guilty of misuse of funds and machinations to set up a rival Mayo League journal—not to mention atheism—regularly criticised the League in late 1880 and 1881. What was more, although Daly's own position was basically to the right of the League and close to that of O'Connor Power, his *Connaught Telegraph* gave increasing space to Fenian criticisms of the League in this period.[111]

This failure of leadership combined with the militancy to produce a critical situation. 'The branches of Mayo,' Parnell told the Special Commission, 'according to the information which I received at the time, ceased to exist during the year 1881. . . . In the beginning of that year, I always heard that the physical-force party had driven the Land League out of Mayo.'[112] Parnell was exaggerating the case in order to distance himself from Fenianism, but his remarks had some validity. This confusion in Mayo, the birthplace of the agitation, at a time when the Land League was being joined by the more prosperous farmers had the effect of weakening the forces in the struggle against compromise—a struggle which Michael Davitt saw as increasingly necessary.

6. *The Response of the Leadership: Harris, Davitt and Parnell*

The career of Matthew Harris, a prominent Land League organiser, may be taken as a perfect illustration of the tensions of the League alliance. Harris had spoken in April 1880 of an alliance of the grazier and the small farmer as an alliance of the shark with the prey. In August, just before the rejection of the Compensation for Disturbance Bill, he had expressed irritation that Connaught's potential allies, Munster and Leinster, had not come to the rescue. But he was clearly at this point prepared to envisage co-operation.

By November he was prepared to offer the graziers reluctant acceptance:

Whether it was through sincerity or through policy a great number of the grazing class—perhaps on account of the loss they had sustained through the depreciated value of stock—were quite willing to go with the people. If they advanced and worked honestly in their hearts and minds to identify themselves with the people, they might go a short distance in forgetting the past.[113]

A few weeks later he developed his position still further. While in Limerick on an organising tour he openly admitted that his role was minimal.[114] On his return to the West, he explained at Kilconnell:

> For this last month I was down in the South of Ireland organising, and early in this movement I regretted to say that the Southerners did not come to the front as we would expect them. But a most wonderful and extraordinary thing has come upon the people of the South, with regard to this great struggle for land reform in which we are engaged; and I have the honour to announce to you that if you do not exert yourselves, the people of the South will surpass the people of the West in this movement. Throughout Limerick I found the wealthy graziers joined in the cause. I found these men with heavy accounts in the bank and surrounded by everything that constitutes wealth and comfort quite as much in favour of this land movement as their humblest neighbours. They have all determined not to pay a halfpenny more than Griffith's valuation.[115]

But by 3 February Harris had completed a pamphlet[116] which, as he later went to great lengths to explain, represented his considered views on the land question. He gave it to Davitt to proof-read, and although the latter was arrested while half-way through his task,[117] the pamphlet appeared on 17 February 1881. The text, which was couched in the form of a letter to the council of the League, attracted some comment. Harris was like certain landlord spokesmen, the *Irish Times* editorial noted, in that he 'thinks or writes as if he thought that it is only the small farmers who stand in any violent need of legislative relief'.[118] The leading proposal in his plan was that farmers holding thirty acres and under should be enabled to purchase their holdings; sale was to be made compulsory on landlords, and repayment was to be extended over a period of twenty years. The purchase money was to be issued by the imperial exchequer without interest (Harris's estimate of the cost of the operation was described as 'absurdly low'.)

Harris had no such generous scheme in mind for the graziers. 'Those divisions', he argued, 'in poor law unions should be rated highest from which the least number of paupers would come, and those divisions lowest which contained, or from which came, the most paupers.'[119] By such a tax system Harris intended that the burden would fall on the grass farms and the 'worse than useless class which occupies them'.[120] Harris seemed to have gone a very short distance indeed in forgetting the past. It is no surprise that 'Transatlantic' found Harris his favourite land reformer.[121]

By April 1881 Harris was reported as having reverted totally to his traditional views. At a meeting of the Ballinasloe branch of the Land League he publicly lamented the loss of the League's original purity. The graziers who regarded themselves as a kind of second-ary gentry had tried to wipe the people out in certain localities. But it had been felt necessary as an act of policy to embrace all classes in the League movement. He concluded that however apparent for a time was the strength such men gave the movement, experience told the people that the graziers would do great harm in a crisis in which their own interests were involved.[122]

What is at stake here in this discussion of the evolution of Harris's views is not simply the disappointment of one man. Nor does the analysis reveal simply an uneasy coexistence of forces in the Land League alliance of strong farmers and small peasants who had hitherto been at one another's throats. The arrival of the substantial tenantry had definite implications. The ultimate effect of the evasion of the problem by the League leadership was that, the League having failed to impose its aims on the rural bourgeoisie, the rural bourgeoisie went a long way in imposing its aims upon the League. This process created a situation of crisis for the League leadership and, in particular, for Michael Davitt.

Davitt's own views on the ultimate solution of the land question were probably in a state of flux. He seems to have been moving in the autumn of 1880 towards the idea that land nationalisation and not peasant proprietorship was the final answer to the Irish social question. At a meeting held in New York, which Davitt attended just before he left America, resolutions in support of land national-isation were passed and Henry George himself, the famous apostle of this creed, was also present.[123] However, Davitt's movement in this direction was a confused and hesitant one. He had earnest discussions with Henry George, but he rejected George's arguments on one decisive point. In late 1880 land nationalisation was un-acceptable to Davitt if it was to be land nationalisation under a British government.[124]

However, Davitt—whether intentionally or not is unclear—did take one step at this time which increased the influence of land nationalisation supporters. He refused to allow any secretary to take his place in the American Land League.[125] In the absence of a proper working organisation in America, the role of the *Irish World*, which always promptly acknowledged funds sent to Ireland via its offices, was greatly expanded. The *Irish World*, of course, was the leading supporter of the land nationalisation solution. Irish-American moderates moved away in irritation, while John Devoy and others who had separatist priorities regarded this development as an unnecessary intrusion of social reforming faddism.[126]

Nevertheless, it is right to see Davitt and Devoy as allies who still shared basically the same perspective. Davitt's rejection of land nationalisation *within the Union* makes that clear enough. At most, at this stage it is correct to speak of Davitt having a sentimental preference for land nationalisation as an ultimate settlement. Both Devoy and Davitt still hoped that the land question could be made the material for nationalist victory, and Devoy was soon to be consulted by Davitt about the crisis in Land League affairs. Davitt in his last New York speech had urged the principle of 'no man to have more land than he can till', but on his arrival in Ireland he found men with very much more land than they could till beginning to dominate the Land League. On 14 December 1880 he issued a memorandum to the organisers and officers of the League which stated: 'Evidence is not wanting that numbers of men have formed and are joining the League who give but a half-hearted allegiance to the League programme . . . men who denounced the programme of the League but six months ago.'[127] On 16 December he wrote to Devoy:

> There is a danger, however, of this class and the priests coalescing and ousting the advanced men or gaining control of the whole thing and turning it against us. I am taking every precaution, however, against this Whig dodge. Already I have carried a neat constitution by a *coup de main* and on Tuesday next I intend to carry the election of an executive council of fifteen in whose hands the entire government will be placed. The Council will consist of six or seven MPs, and the remainder men like Brennan, Egan and myself.

But was such a manoeuvre adequate to deal with the serious problems faced by Davitt? These 'damned petty little outrages' gave the government grounds for coercion, while the offer of the 'three Fs' would, he believed, split the movement. Davitt outlined his solution to Devoy:

> I only see one way in which to combat it and neutralise the evil

it would work upon the country—that is, by calling a Convention.
The Delegates that would come from the country would be
certain to support the No Partnership platform of the League
against the compromise of the three Fs. If we could carry on this
Movement for another year without being interfered with we
could do almost anything we pleased in this country. The courage
of the people is magnificent. *All classes are purchasing Arms
openly.*[128]

This analysis of Davitt's is remarkable and requires some comment. It seems that Davitt saw the Land League's problem largely
as one of *leadership*. Hence it was enough to carry out a *'coup de
main'* against the 'Whig' intruders and place power in the hands of
more reliable men. He seems to have been sure that the broad
feeling in the countryside would have rejected any compromise.
There is a considerable element of over-simplification in Davitt's
views. A simple purge of the leadership was a very inadequate
reaction to the change in the social composition of the Land League
mass movement.

Davitt's position was very clear in his letter to Devoy. The 'three
Fs' must be avoided at all costs, or else the nationalist potential of
the movement would be lost.[129] He was perfectly prepared to
envisage a considerable delay of land reform if this was the price
of avoiding a middle-of-the-road solution. In late November he
claimed that he did not want a land reform until after there had
been an electoral reform which broke the Whig influence in British
politics.[130] But would he be able to avert the compromise? Outside
the West the pre-existing rural leadership was often able to curtail
the influence of the League's leadership, while even in the West
itself the Mayo League was divided.

Parnell, however, was content to reflect the nature of the movement he led. At Ennis on 19 September 1880 he had given his
exposition of the more Christian and charitable way of dealing with
land-grabbers: total social ostracism.[131] At New Ross a week later
he insisted that peasant proprietorship was the only possible solution
to the Irish land question.[132] But was this really all that Parnell had
to say on the land question? Would he settle for nothing less?

Parnell's position in all its ambiguity emerged in reply to an
application from Richard O'Shaughnessy, MP, to join the Land
League. Parnell had in the early days of the League project asked
O'Shaughnessy to join, but O'Shaughnessy had at that time declared
himself opposed to compulsory expropriation of all landlords, 'good,
bad or indifferent'. Parnell had replied that he did not think that
the programme of the League bound itself to favour the expro-

priation of the whole landlord class. By September 1880 both men were prepared to work together.

O'Shaughnessy's application of 28 September declared his principles: 'Peace and goodwill to the landlords who will give their tenants secure and inviolable tenure at fair rent; compulsory expropriation at a fair price of the landlords who refuse to give such tenure or insist on exorbitant rents.'[133] Parnell offered an interpretative response. He thought that O'Shaughnessy meant that landlords who were prepared to accept a low rent with eternal leases, even in the face of continued agricultural depression, should be exempted from the compulsory purchase scheme of the Land League. Parnell did not want to discuss these matters in too great a detail lest he lower his terms while the British government looked on, but he felt that O'Shaughnessy's proposal deserved attention. He declared that, 'without wishing to bind myself in any way', it would be 'practically an occupying proprietary'. The tenants would be in the position of occupying proprietors, except, of course, that their annual payments would go on for ever. The landlords would be converted into rent-chargers, and as rent-chargers they would be strongly inclined to sell voluntarily to their tenants. Meanwhile O'Shaughnessy still allowed for compulsory purchase for those landlords who refused to accept their new status. Parnell took the opportunity to reiterate his view that unless the government took the power of dealing compulsorily with a certain class of landlord, it would fail to solve the land question.[134]

This comment, for all its qualifications, was Parnell's most definite exposition of his views on a possible basis for a settlement of the land war in the second half of 1880. O'Shaughnessy had obviously made a move away from the Shaw section of the Home Rule Party by his decision to join the ranks of the League, but Parnell had moved away from his 'extreme men' in his response. He appeared once again to be returning to the programme which had lured the CTDA into the Land League ranks—certainly this is how the *Freeman's Journal* saw it[135]—and to be once again contemplating the 'three Fs' rather than peasant proprietorship as the solution for the majority of the Irish tenantry.

After this declaration Parnell refused to make any further clarification of his position. By implication, however, he adopted a steadily more extremist tone. In Kilkenny in October he refused to back a locally sponsored resolution with strong clerical support which demanded the 'three Fs'—an *ignis fatuus* in Parnell's vocabulary.[136] More reasonably he pointed out that Gladstone, Bright and Shaw Lefevre had repudiated the principle of government arbitration of rents and had said that land reform must be along the lines of the 1870 Land Act.[137] In other words, British statesmen were contemplating a compromise which would dissatisfy even the moderate 'three Fs' Irish supporters. The implication was that unless the tenantry kept up the pressure for peasant proprietorship, they would end up with less than the 'three Fs'.

Nevertheless, Parnell now began to face considerable criticism from a group of land reformers which included P. J. Smyth,[138] James Kilmartin[139] and A. M. Sullivan[140] for not displaying more interest in the practicalities of land reform.

> I observe that Mr Parnell never seems to have read the Port-carron lease or the Longfield lease [noted A. M. Sullivan]. I contend that in the face of these memorable charters of tenant right no one can say that a way has not been found to effect with perfect justice and satisfaction to the landlord, perpetuity of tenure at an equitable and self-adjusting rent with jury verdicts and valuators' decrees.[141]

Many people assumed that Sullivan was offering a detailed proposal for land reform, and his position was given great prominence on that basis. But Sullivan retreated abjectly as the land war grew more intense in the course of October. He admitted that he had associated himself with certain schemes, but he announced that he expressly disdained any idea of proposing them in the present circumstances as offers on the tenants' behalf. He believed in his soul that if Divine Inspiration suggested a plan divinely just and perfect, moderate and fair, the landlords would nevertheless vilify it as 'extreme' if it was put forward from the tenant camp. A people engaged in a great struggle with a class may sometimes be wise in accepting a compromise, but they were seldom wise in urging one.[142] Sullivan's discovery of the wisdom of Parnell's position was completed a few days later when he added that the landlords had refused to save themselves and, having been weighed fairly in the public balance, were found lamentably, irresistibly guilty.[143]

Sullivan's capitulation meant the end of effective opposition to Parnell on the nationalist side. Parnell was able to continue his style of agitation. At Cork in October he offered a vital footnote to his comments on compulsory expropriation in reply to O'Shaughnessy's letter. The unanswered question had been: how many landlords did Parnell want to see bought out? He spoke now of two-thirds of Irish land being transferred within a few months.[144]

At Longford later in October he appeared to go even further. He claimed that there was a line between the Bishop of Ossory, who had asked for restitution to the tenantry—a puckishly literal interpretation of that cautious bishop's ritualistic phrases about the hardships of the farmers—and those who felt that the tenants by paying rack-rents for many centuries had long since paid the fee simple of the land. He added that the Land League had not decided where along that line it would stop.[145] Having opened up this original perspective of compensation being paid *to* the tenantry, Parnell proceeded to Galway where he made a famous announcement that he would not have taken his coat off for the land question alone.

At a meeting at Limerick a few days later E. J. Synan, the local MP, attempted to force Parnell to define his position. Parnell was again very reluctant to do so, but he did remark with some effect that although the legislature might ratify rent reductions won in the course of struggle, it would never initiate them. He saw the state resuming the title to the land within three years.[146]

At this point Parnell's task was made much easier by the government's announcement of the decision to prosecute the Land League leaders. These included five MPs (Parnell, Biggar, Dillon, T. D. Sullivan and Sexton), along with Egan, Brennan and seven other prominent Leaguers. The charges against them dealt mainly with conspiracy to prevent payment of rent, to resist process of ejectment, to prevent 'land-grabbing' and to create ill-will against Her Majesty's Government. Already mere rumours of a prosecution had produced applications from Justin McCarthy, MP,[147] and F. H. O'Donnell, MP,[148] to join the Land League. On the day when the news of the prosecution broke, The O'Donoghue, MP, applied to join the organisation.[149] On 4 November the *Freeman's Journal* set up a defence fund. Three members of the Irish hierarchy on their *ad limina* visits in Rome sent in their contributions, and despite the disapproval of Archbishop McCabe of Dublin, the majority of the hierarchy followed suit.[150] By 16 November even J. C. McCoan, MP for Wicklow and a particularly noted trimmer, was ready to apply to join the League.[151]

Parnell was able to take a harder line. In December after an absence of three weeks with Mrs O'Shea, he culminated the year's agitation with a very strong speech at Waterford which in some ways marks the high point of his revolutionism. He claimed that the landlords of the Irish grazing counties were no longer to be allowed to let out their lands for the purpose of grazing, but must instead now let it out for agricultural purposes to the people now crowded together on the barren land of the West.[152]

Parnell's tactics were undeniably effective. There was on the Irish side virtually no discussion of the details of a possible land reform. The onus was placed firmly upon the government. This achievement was all the more remarkable because one of Parnell's main arguments—the absence of support for such a compromise among major British politicians[153]—had been removed in mid-November when Bright gave public notice of his support for fixity of tenure at fair rents.[154] But the reality remained that the discussion of details would, in fact, only have divided the Land League. As he himself insisted at Longford in October, the peasant proprietorship demand was a bare minimum if the labourers were to be won to the League.

Parnell's position on the question of the labourers, in fact, is a perfect illustration of the nature of his politics during this period. At the beginning of October 1880 there was considerable friction between the farmers and the labourers. After the first meeting of the League in Co. Wexford at Barntown the labourers issued a placard protesting that 'land sharks' dominated the local League leadership.[155] In Shanagarry, Co. Cork, a landlord, Mr Penn-Gaskell, divided up a farm for his labourers and thus created some friction between them and the farmers. Few landlords could afford to be so generous; but it was nevertheless a worrying incident.[156] The *Limerick Reporter* hoped, for example, that the Limerick labourers were not going to follow the example of the labourers of Carberries, Co. Cork, and oppose the League.[157]

Limerick was an area in which the labourers' question had particular prominence. In giving evidence before the Richmond Commission on 29 June, O'Flaherty, the president of the Limerick Farmers' Club, had declared himself as supporting in a vague way some scheme of internal migration. But when he was asked if he was willing to give up ten or twenty acres of his 180 acres to some cottier or labourer, he had nervously replied: 'No . . . I do not think it would be fair or just to deprive any man of his holding.'[158] It is not surprising in this context that the Limerick League's address of conciliation to the labourers—promising them out of Parnell's bill the blessings of a comfortable house, half an acre of ground and (thrown in at the last as 'a grand idea') the grass of a cow[159]—was widely regarded an unsatisfactory sop.

Parnell, sensitive to the need to win over the labourers, quickly intervened. He rejected the Limerick plan. He also rejected the ideas of settling the labourers on the waste lands. The task of the League was to undo the work of the famine. He spoke, he said, not so much of the really fattening lands, but rather of the lighter grazing lands which were cleared at the time of the famine and which were fast becoming unproductive owing to their having laid down too long in grass. The result had been, according to the *Gardener's Chronicle*, that they were becoming year after year more unproductive; the quality of the grass was becoming worse, and the yield of butter per acre and of fat cattle per acre was less and less. It was absolutely necessary that something should be done to these lands— perhaps four or five million acres in extent—in order to make them productive and a source of wealth to the nation at large. The League should discourage the seasonable letting of these grasslands next summer. In that way they would facilitate the action of the legislature in enabling the small farmers and the labourers to get back upon the less rich class of grazing lands.[160]

It is interesting, however, to note the way in which Parnell's remarks were interpreted in Limerick. The *Limerick Reporter* (which usually expressed the view of the local Farmers' Club) noted that to realise this provision for the labourers would take time— like some other parts of the programme—and that Parnell did not give a detailed statement of how the plan was to be carried out. But they felt that the statement was justified politically. By no other land scheme were the labourers' claims so liberally recognised, and by no other means could Parnell have extended his influence among this very numerous class more effectively—and this at the very time when it was proving especially necessary as an act of policy to make friends of this class upon whom the prosperity of the tenant so greatly depended.[161]

Parnell had spent much of his time in the latter half of 1880 persistently raising the stakes in the land war. He rarely made an accurate statement when there was a suitable exaggeration available. Parnell was exceptionally fortunate that the solution did not require an Irish leader with a detailed grasp of the technicalities of land reform. There is no sign that he possessed it. However, even if he had possessed it, he would have been wise in this period to repress it. If to know when to let an agitation have its head is the hallmark of a great leader, then Parnell was a great leader.

But there is something else to be noted about this period of Parnell's apparently unqualified militancy. Even at their most radical his ideas never appeared to be incompatible with the opportunism of the rural bourgeoisie. He certainly never intervened—as Davitt had attempted to—to strengthen decisively the hands of those who explicitly supported the small farmers and the labourers within the Land League organisation. He was in this fundamental respect capable of being all things to all men.

7. Conclusion

The basic form of class struggle employed by the Land League in the latter half of 1880 is clear. In the newly recruited counties the tenants refused to pay more than a 'fair rent', usually judged to be Griffith's valuation. Success was likely because of the breakdown of the landlord's means of retaliation. The numbers of those evicted fell from 3,447 in the third quarter of 1880 to only 954 during the last quarter of the year.[162] The landlord might distrain but he had apparently no chance of selling the crops and stock under seizure. He might perhaps obtain a judgment decree for his rent, but it was a difficult matter to enforce it. If he seized the crop or stock, he was in the same position as if he had distrained. If he put the tenant's interest* in the farm up for sale, he again had no buyer. If he registered his judgment as a mortgage against the holding, how was he to procure payment of either principal or interest? The policy was, within its limitations, very successful in late 1880. Why, it was asked in Dublin's Conservative press, should the tenants settle for the 'three Fs' when they had already won a stronger position in the course of the agitation?[163]

Why also should the 'three Fs' prevent the new movement from compelling the landlords to sell their pasture lands in smallholdings to tenants who were to break them up as Parnell boasted they would? In some places it had already almost assumed the form of a conspiracy to compel the tenants of the large grazing farms to surrender them for the same purpose.[164] The appearance of an editorial on these lines in the Dublin *Daily Express* marked the high point of Land League success.

* Mention of the tenant's interest in the land may require some clarification. However, as E. D. Steele has helpfully pointed out, tenant right was widespread outside Ulster. He quotes from a 1870 Poor Law inspector's report on a district that reached from King's County to Kerry and Limerick: 'There can be no doubt that, from a remote period, a certain limited right of property, and a distinct value has been attached by tenants . . . to the occupancy of a farm. . . . And it is this right which they are disposing of when selling the goodwill'. (Steele, *Irish Land and British Politics*, 20.) The 1870 Land Act legalised the 'Ulster custom' (which included the right of free sale of the tenant right of occupancy) wherever it existed, as well as any similar customs in the other parts of Ireland. In fact it appears that, despite the efforts of some landlords, this tenant right enjoyed wide recognition by the early 1880s. In W. E. Forster's words, 'It is an undoubted fact that, notwithstanding all the attempts that have been made in some parts of the South and West of Ireland to prevent it, tenant right has been sold . . . over and over again on estates where its sale has been forbidden. It has been done under the rose, but sometimes more or less with the acknowledgment and consent, of the landlord or agent, and sometimes against the nominal prohibition of the landlord, but in reality with his knowledge.' (Quoted in *ibid.*, 21–2.)

7

Coercion, Landlords and Gladstone's Land Bill, 1881

And is this 35% reduction, within landlordism as a firmly rooted institution, to be the outcome of the land agitation? Let not Mr Parnell deceive himself.

Irish World, 7 May 1881

Their great anxiety now is lest the Government may pass a Land Bill to satisfy the great majority of the Farmers and on the other if the Farmers are not satisfied with the Land Bill of the Government they may precipitate a rising about May next and the Council cannot restrain them. He heard repeatedly from Davitt, Brennan and O'Sullivan that no Land Bill would satisfy the Nationalists.

JOHN MALLON, report on information given by Bernard, a Fenian informer, 2 Dec. 1880 (SPO, INL Papers, Spec. Comm. docs, 1888, carton 9)

1. *The Coercion Act, 1881*

By early January 1881 it was clear that the Liberal government intended to respond to the land agitation with a coercion bill followed by a land bill. It was not until 25 January that the state trial finally ended with the expected acquittal of the Land League leaders owing to a jury disagreement. This outcome had been obvious by the end of December 1880; not only were eight of the twelve jurors Catholics, but two of the remaining four Protestants turned out to be pro-Land League. In Davitt's view this was the first jury in the history of Irish state trials which was not carefully packed, and the result was therefore beyond doubt. But the government had never set any great store by this enterprise: its real object had been to demonstrate the impotence of the ordinary law. The crucial decision on coercion had already been made following a revealing debate within the cabinet.

There had been considerable controversy in the cabinet over the decision to introduce coercion. By early November 1880 the Lord Lieutenant, Cowper, was at any rate declaring that there was a need for greater powers.[1] He was effectively a supporter of internment. He pointed out that the suspension of *habeas corpus* in the whole of Connaught except Sligo (where, according to Davitt, the head of police was secretly sympathetic to the Land League)[2] had been recommended by the police inspectors in their answer to a recent circular. On 13 November he reiterated this view in a private letter to Gladstone.[3]

Forster, the Chief Secretary, was, however, wavering. At a cabinet meeting on 10 November his uncertainty gave the impression that there was doubt in Dublin Castle as to the necessity for coercion.[4] He failed to put forward a note from Cowper recommending suspension of *habeas corpus*.[5] He leaned towards coercion, but he also recognised the parliamentary difficulties which proposals for such legislation would cause the government, and he constantly sought to throw some of the responsibility on the cabinet.[6] He made the error of saying that he believed that if the 'three Fs' were granted, the agitation would cease at once. This statement was a gift to the non-coercionists.[7]

Indecision was to be a characteristic feature of Forster's secretaryship. From November 1880, at least, he generally tended to favour strong repressive action. However, he was restrained by two factors. The first and most important was his fear of opposition from within his own party. This fear in 1880 was probably exaggerated. It is unlikely, for instance, that a Bright or a Chamberlain would have actually resigned over the issue of Irish coercion. Forster was also restrained by his sense of the justice of some of the tenantry's demands. The outcome of all these conflicting pressures on Forster produced his typical response—uncertainty.

The Chief Secretary comforted himself with the illusion that his strong military demonstration in support of the beleaguered Captain Boycott in Mayo would have a controlling effect on the agitation sufficient to enable the government to avoid taking stronger repressive measures.[8] By 15 November such hopes were clearly shattered. On that day Forster finally told Chamberlain of his intention to propose the suspension of *habeas corpus*.[9] On 16 November Gladstone wrote to Forster that such a suspension should be based on danger to life, which was not the defining characteristic of the present agitation.[10] 'Statistics' he had queried in pencil beside Forster's claim that the government was failing in its duty to protect the person.[11] Despite Forster's argument that the more criminal element was coming to the fore, Gladstone stood firm for his alternative plan at the cabinet meeting on 17 November. The premier explained later that he felt the agitation was too big, wide and strong for Forster's mode of coercion to be successful. The suspension of *habeas corpus* was effective against secret societies but not against open, organised, popular conspiracies like the Land League. Chamberlain felt that imprisonment without trial was comparable to 'firing with a rifle at a swarm of gnats'.[12] Gladstone wanted to alter the law in regard to incitement to break contracts and mischievous speeches and make these offences punishable by summary jurisdiction with severe sentences.[13] Forster referred the idea back to Dublin Castle, but both Cowper and T. H. Burke, the permanent Under-Secretary, were strongly opposed. Cowper replied on 18 November that the disturbed districts had got beyond the stage in which harm could be done by further meetings. He doubted whether many of the people for whom warrants had been issued by Resident Magistrates could be caught; and such men would anyway be let out at the next assizes. As to the peaceable counties, Gladstone's alternative plan would stop the mischief from spreading—but only if the miscreants did not elude the law by holding meetings under another name.[14]

On the same day Forster sent Burke's view, with his endorsement, on the Gladstone plan on to the premier.[15] But the letter did not have much effect, for Gladstone's view remained unchanged on 19 November.[16] Cowper on 23 November then increased the pressure by informing Gladstone that if the situation had not improved by January and if *habeas corpus* was not suspended, he would resign.[17] On 24 November Gladstone replied to Cowper that the cabinet's acquiescence in the situation was justified (unless there was an increase in outrage affecting actual life) while they endeavoured to provide a remedy applicable to the whole of the mischief. He was still doubtful about the value of the suspension of *habeas corpus*—in the face of opposition of two-thirds of the Irish representatives plus their British allies—in dealing with such a widespread conspiracy embracing in certain districts large fractions of the population and largely armed with means other than material. But he did offer to defend property rights without any mawkish susceptibilities in January if the situation had not improved by then.[18]

The Viceroy reluctantly accepted the delays on the grounds that a measure with Bright and Chamberlain against it and only reluctantly supported by Gladstone would take a long time to pass the House of Commons.[19] In the opinion of Cowper,[20] Spencer,[21] Hartington[22] and Chamberlain,[23] Forster's irresolution at the beginning of November had made the delay inevitable anyway. But the situation continued to deteriorate, and on 12 December Cowper reported to Gladstone: 'The state of the country becomes worse every day. Outrages have increased and the Land League has taken a much deeper root.'[24] The rate of increase of agrarian outrages was remarkable: of the 2,590 listed for 1880, nearly 1,700 were committed in the last three months of the year.[25] On 14 December Forster finally persuaded the cabinet to introduce a coercion bill which included the suspension of *habeas corpus*.

Forster's memorandum of 15 November had claimed to a

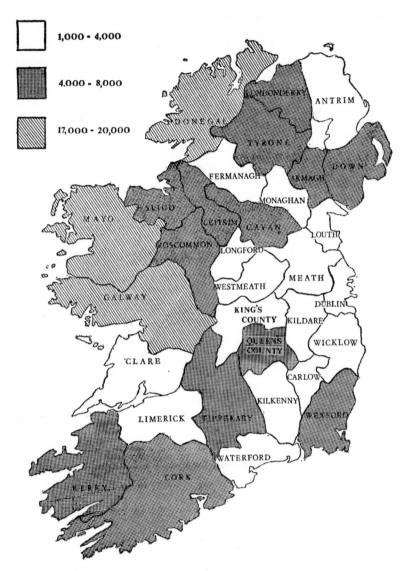

Distribution of Small Agricultural Holdings throughout Ireland,
1880

Holdings whose annual value was £4 and under (Griffith's valuation).

Source: R. Richardson, *The Irish Land Question* (1881)

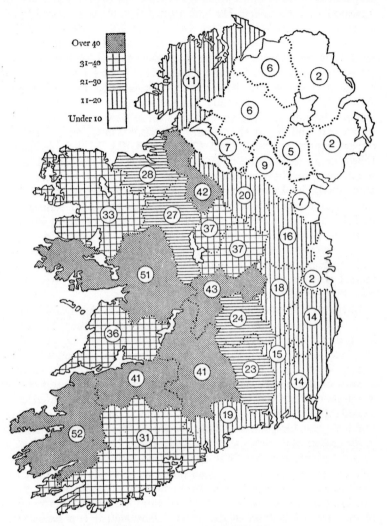

Agrarian Outrages, 1880–82

The number of reported outrages per 1,000 of the population. The city populations of Dublin, Cork, Limerick and Derry have been excluded from the calculations.

Source: E. Rumpf and A. C. Hepburn, *Nationalism and Socialism in Twentieth-Century Ireland* (1977)

Reproduced by kind permission of Liverpool University Press.

F

sceptical Gladstone that the purely criminal as opposed to anti-rent agitation was increasing. He had argued that those responsible for crime were known to the police. But he had also made a significant admission. It was true, he said, that the Land League had stimulated men to commit outrages, but its principal leaders had not planned or perpetrated crime themselves. It had been the result of the activity of old Ribbonmen, Fenians and *mauvais sujets.* Although they were generally League members and local League leaders, he did not believe that they were now under the control of Parnell and his parliamentary friends.[26] Many years later the official report of the Special Commission did, in fact, assume,[27] following an implication of Parnell himself,[28] that the Land League organisers may have organised crime. But although at least fourteen provincial Land League organisers (excluding MPs and full-time central officers who sometimes took on this role) were active in 1880-81, they were not suspected by the RIC of direct involvement in violence. They had, of course, been involved in strong advocacy of boycotting, interventions at sheriffs' sales, interference with graziers, etc., while Matthew Harris was believed to have incited persons to injure Pollock, the Galway landlord, but otherwise the record was surprisingly clean.[29]

In his public advocacy of coercion Gladstone clearly felt that it was necessary to imply a closer connection between the Land League as an organisation and the existence of crime. He attempted to place the responsibility for crime firmly at the door of the League by a heavy emphasis on the fact that primary distress had greatly diminished by mid-1880.[30] (He might also have added that a number of relatively isolated areas which had experience of considerable distress were without crime.)[31] But this attempt to implicate the League more directly was to be answered by Sexton in the course of a widely admired reply during the coercion debate.[32] Sexton pointed out that there were sixteen counties in which nearly half the total number of League meetings took place, and yet the average of crime was less in those than in counties where there had been no meetings. Two-thirds of the total agrarian crime was in the zone of distress in the West.[33] Although it is a naïve view which sees crime simply as the product of distress and does not take into account, for example, the pre-existing strength of Fenianism in an area, Sexton's reply did sharply reveal the inadequacies of Gladstone's attempt to link directly League meetings with crime.[34] The shaky nature of the public Gladstonian justification of coercion gave the Parnellites every incentive to fight against it.

On 24 January 1881 Forster brought in his coercion measure,

the Protection of Person and Property (Ireland) Bill, and obstruction increased in intensity. The terms of the bill were assessed by the constitutional lawyer A. V. Dicey as giving the Irish executive 'absolute power of arbitrary and preventive arrest'. John Morley summed it up by saying that the measure enabled the Viceroy to lock up anybody he pleased and to detain him as long as he pleased while the act was in force. The government could also in the case of certain crimes abolish the right to trial by jury, could arrest strangers found out of doors at night under suspicious circumstances, could seize any newspaper inciting to treason or violence, and could prohibit any public meeting which the Lord Lieutenant believed to be dangerous to the public peace or safety.[35]

The fact that there were about thirty members with the determination to 'obstruct' made the work of the House, under the existing circumstances, impossible. The sitting of 25 January took up twenty-two hours: and on 31 January a sitting began which lasted forty-one hours. On 2 February the speaker's intervention brought the forty-one-hour sitting to an end. By the application of the closure he ensured that the House divided, and the first reading of the bill was thus passed.

The opening of the session had already seen the revival of parliamentary obstruction. The debate on the address lasted eleven nights. Parnell took the opportunity to make a major effort to explain his own position and also to threaten the government with strong retaliation if it maintained its course of action. It was quite true, he admitted, that in his speeches in Ireland he had frequently said that the indirect consequence of the land movement would be to do away with British misrule and restore the Irish parliament. He could understand that such expressions of opinion, if not gone into very fully, may have given rise to the idea that prevailed in parliament, that he was seeking to use the land agitation for the purpose of violently destroying British power in Ireland. The Viceroy, at any rate, believed that this was so:

> When I was in Ireland [he recalled] we considered Mr Parnell the centre of the whole movement. We thought him the chief, if not the only, danger. . . . I certainly thought that his aim was separation. I thought that he used agrarian discontent for separatist purposes. There was very little said about Home Rule at that time. It was all agrarianism, with separation in the background, and Parnell was the centre of everything.[36]

However, Parnell insisted that he had not advocated the use of violence: he explained that in his speeches he had done no more than point out that if peasant proprietorship was achieved, Irish landlords would have no further incentive to look to England to help them enforce their unjust rights; and in such an eventuation

> There would then remain no class in Ireland interested in the maintenance of English supremacy there; and we should, in a rational and peaceable way, without any violent revolution, in my opinion, without jingle of arms, but by the union of all classes in Ireland obtain the restoration of our legislative independence.[37]

He wanted, he added, the right for the Irish to 'make our own laws under a system of constitutional government such as prevails in this country'.

Parnell's attempt to distance himself from the Fenian ideal of armed insurrection—which he praised while declaring it to be utterly impracticable—was a failure. He was over-optimistic in his belief that he had satisfied the House that, in speaking of the land movement as being designed to knock away one of the props of British misrule, he was merely indicating his desire for a friendly settlement of the differences between the two countries. H. O. Arnold-Forster commented, in a note on this speech: 'It may seem strange that after this explanation the misapprehension referred to should still exist. Yet, beyond all doubt it does exist in the minds of many.'[38] The pro-landlord Dublin *Daily Express* ironically felt that Parnell had at least reminded forgetful British Liberals of the vital role played by Irish landlordism in upholding British power in Ireland.[39]

But the important point is that it was Parnell's short-term tactics, not his professions of ultimate moderation, which interested British political leaders. Parnell claimed that he had done his best to resist the call for 'no rent', but in the event of coercion he would be powerless. Surely it was better that Irish landlords should be without their money for two or three months while the House discussed a land bill in an atmosphere of relative calm rather than one of mounting eviction and crime?[40] Sir Stafford Northcote's reply illustrated Tory feeling about the tone of such sentiments. Parnell had spoken as if he was supreme over the organisation which was now the virtual ruler of a portion at least of Ireland.[41] Northcote's overwhelming disquiet on this point was a sign that the confrontation between government and Land League was unavoidable.

While these parliamentary developments had been occurring Parnell was in close touch with the League executive. Discussion shortly after the collapse of the state trial upon the inevitable disagreement of the Irish jury on 25 January 1881 had revealed a sharp division on Parnell's left. Conor Cruise O'Brien has well illustrated the lesson of these 'demonstration trials': they 'had the usual effect of political prosecutions in Ireland. Enthusiasm for the "traverser's" case rose . . . a classic example of the self-defeating nature of the attempt to combine colonialism and demo-cracy.'[42] But how was the government's embarrassment to be capitalised upon by the Land League?

Davitt and Dillon (and probably, therefore, Egan, Brennan and Harris) wanted Parnell to go to America to collect funds. This was a radical project in certain ways. It would have removed Parnell's ability to restrain the dangerous developments at home, while at the same time increasing Irish-American donations. But it was certainly not a project of immediate revolution. The ideas of Kettle merit that description very much more accurately. Kettle opposed what he called the policy of 'dispersion' (that is, Parnell's removal to America) and called instead for the Irish Parliamentary Party to withdraw from parliament. Kettle later wrote: 'The trouble about the whole thing seemed to be that the revolutionary policy of the Land League Movement was being pushed by an outsider.'[43] What this comment catches is the way that Kettle's intervention had wrong-footed the neo-Fenian hardliners of the Land League alliance.

Kettle was outside the circle of neo-Fenianism which looked to an apotheosis of the New Departure—the winning of an inde-pendent Irish parliament—and had merely the objectives of agrarian radicalism. His policy (including the withdrawal of MPs) was designed to secure the settlement of the land question on the most radical basis and had no other political aim. With their larger political concerns, and perhaps also their healthy respect for govern-ment repression, the neo-Fenians were inclined to be more cautious and more long-term in their perspective. This tendency is revealed in Davitt's correspondence with Devoy in December 1880 and in Brennan's speech at the convention of April 1881.[44] Kettle's inter-vention came, as he himself put it, 'like a blizzard for which they were not prepared'.[45] Davitt was prepared to allow Kettle's motion to be discussed before his own, which he was prepared to drop if Kettle's was accepted.[46] He later claimed, in fact, to regard Kettle's plan as the right one in the circumstances.[47] Egan, Harris[48] and Dillon[49] were very much more reluctant. Harris perhaps experi-enced a revival of his earlier resistance to any agitation which placed parliamentarians in the leading role.

But Parnell rather surprisingly adopted a solution which was close to the Kettle scheme—perhaps simply to prevent a full dis-cussion of the policy of dispersion. The party would fight coercion in parliament as long as they could. They would then cross to

Ireland, where every member would go at once to take charge of his constituency and Parnell would announce that the first arrest under the coercion act would lead to a general strike against rent. This policy was unanimously supported, not simply by militants like Kettle and Davitt, but also, rather more surprisingly, by Dwyer Gray, who appeared to offer the support of the *Freeman's Journal*.[50]

On 3 February 1881 the real depth of this commitment was put to the test. Forster announced the arrest of Michael Davitt, and thirty-six members of the Irish Party were expelled in the ensuing uproar. Was the revolutionary promise to be kept? Irish indignation created by Davitt's arrest was considerable. It was certainly as favourable a moment as was likely to occur. Why wait for the coercion bill to be passed when coercion—as demonstrated by the arbitrary arrest of Michael Davitt—had already begun in practice? Davitt himself had no doubt that this presented the party with a golden opportunity to secede from parliament. 'Opportunity means almost everything in the fortunes of war,' he later wrote, 'and the one great chance of the present campaign arrived when Mr Parnell and his men were ignominiously ejected from the British Parliament and despotic law was about to be enforced in Ireland in defiance of all the boasted principle of British rule.'[51]

But there were major difficulties about such a course. Although thirty-six members had been expelled, probably only twenty would have obeyed a party decision to secede and certainly not more than five would have advocated such a policy.[52] The League leaders hurried off to Paris, where they awaited the arrival of Parnell. He, however, saw no need for haste and spent a week in the company of the conservatively inclined Katharine O'Shea before his arrival.

On 4 February Dillon revived again the notion which Kettle had described as the 'policy of dispersion.' On that day, according to the *Freeman's Journal*, Dillon 'conveyed to Mr Parnell the desire of the Land League executive that he should go to America'. Parnell refused this suggestion, reasserted the potential value of parliamentary work and offered the radicals the sop of widening the agitation to include the English masses. It was widely appreciated that in substance this meant very little except maintaining the traditional alliance with the small section of minor English left-wing political figures, for example, the Democratic Federation. In fact Harris, Kettle and Sexton—all of whom had been present in Paris—were publicly sceptical of this left-wing alliance when it was advocated in Ireland by John Ferguson and James Louden.[53]

Davitt did not blame Parnell for refusing the revolutionary step. He believed that Parnell could have commanded the support of only half his nominal following for such a policy.[54] Nevertheless, the retreat was obviously a serious blow for the militants.

The immediate result of Parnell's decision was to strengthen the position of the Irish Parliamentary Party in relation to the Land League. At the end of December 1880 Dillon had told the parliamentarians that

> They knew that the greatest power in the country was a power that told the people that Parliamentary representation was a sham. They all knew that if they wanted to decide on a Land Bill, they must go up to Sackville Street, and ask the Land League before they could decide upon a plan of action. That might not be a very acceptable truth, but it was the truth.[55]

This statement was an exaggeration; but the party was divided and unsure of its power as compared with the new force. However, as T. P. O'Connor put it, 'The nine weeks' struggle against coercion *made* the Irish party.'[56] The state trial had illustrated the fact that many Irish MPs who did not agree with Parnell on the agrarian question would support him when the issue appeared to be the constitutional liberty of Irishmen. The coercion debate proved the point all the more strongly. On the second reading of the Protection of Person and Property Bill the opponents numbered fifty-six, of whom seven were British Radicals; on the third reading the figure was forty-six, of whom five were British Radicals. It was clear that Parnell was working in co-operation with rather more than the twenty-three MPs who had voted for him as chairman of the Irish Parliamentary Party. Many of the parliamentarians made a considerable reputation for themselves in Ireland and were much less likely as a result to accept League 'dictation'.

2. *Landlord Reaction: The Property Defence Association*
The Land League now found itself in a difficult position, not simply because it had lost a possible chance to intensify the struggle, or because of the increased strength of the parliamentary party, or even because of impending coercion. All these problems might have been faced with much more confidence if it had not also become clear that the existing mode of struggle which had brought such success in late 1880 was becoming increasingly unsatisfactory. It had become obvious in the early months of 1881 that where the landlords were prepared to finance agents to bid for interests of farms or cattle and other goods sold at sheriff's sales, they had the power to unnerve the tenantry.

A landlord who desired to sue a tenant had the choice of two available processes. He could bring either an ejectment for non-payment of rent or an ordinary action for debt. If the landlord brought an ejectment, there was no sale of the farm after the judgment, but the sheriff, acting under writ of *habere,* took possession of the farm and evicted the tenant. Then what was known in law as the tenant's 'right to redeem' came into play. The meaning of this was that the tenant had a right at any time within six months from eviction, on payment of rent and costs to the landlord, to obtain a decree from the court restoring him to possession of the farm and compelling the landlord to account for the profit he had made of the farm during the period the tenant was out of it. If, on the other hand, the landlord brought an action for debt, the consequences were these: under a 'writ of *fi. fa.'* the sheriff seized the land and stock of the tenant and proceeded to sell them by auction. If the tenant did not 'buy in' at this point and pay his debt plus costs, he lost all right of redemption and, in fact, lost all claim to or interest in the farm. It was the adoption of this second course of action which seriously weakened the League.

The Property Defence Association (or 'Emergency Committee') had been set up in an atmosphere of landlord demoralisation on 11 January 1881. Its members had appointed one Norris Goddard as their chief officer in the field, and he was to be assisted in his activities in defence of the landlords' interest by a group of paid officers who came to be popularly known as 'emergency men'. At first their efforts came to little, but in early February, according to Lord Courtown, the PDA chairman, 'came the decisive action of the sheriff's sale at Dungarvan when Mr Goddard showed that energy, courage and judgment for which he has become so well known'.[57]

What was that decisive action? Norris Goddard, in fact, moved swiftly from sheriffs' sales in one part of the country to another in pursuit of his calling as the PDA's leading agent. He brought with him gangs of 'emergency men'. His main job was to engineer sales of stock and interest to these supporters of the landlord cause —while the local peasantry, who, of course, were under pressure not to bid, looked on and hooted with displeasure. The effect was dramatic. After the sale at Dungarvan the rents on the property at which the seizure was made and on an adjoining property were paid at once. The tenant involved in the case, Walsh, claimed to have lost £400 out of the affair, and when he received £150 from the Land League (personally handed over by Dillon) he immediately paid his full rent, thus provoking an outcry in the Waterford Land League.[58]

The PDA's increased intervention at sheriffs' sales had a further significance. It increased the importance of 'rent at the point of the bayonet' as against the boycott. The first reported example in Co. Cork after the initial Waterford incidents is of some interest. W. Baldwin Seely, a Kilbrittain landlord, had been boycotted after his refusal to accept Griffith's valuation in September 1880. This did not deter Seely, who took legal proceedings against Dineen, the most solvent of his tenants, for the recovery of the half year's rent due. On 28 February 1881 judgment was marked against the tenant in the superior courts and a writ obtained under which six cows were seized. On the occasion of the sheriff's sale the boycott came back into its own: cars were denied to policemen, sheriff, bailiff and parties from the PDA by Land League order. But despite all this, the sale went ahead. The cattle, though sold at half value, brought in about 15s in excess of the rent and costs when bought in on behalf of the League.[59] From this case it is obvious that we are dealing with a very novel interlacing of forms —both the boycott and 'rent at the point of the bayonet'—but it is equally obvious that 'rent at the point of the bayonet' was the more important of the two.

This pattern was determined by the form of defence which the landlords had resolved to adopt. There were at least ninety sales of stock or interests at sheriffs' sales reported in the area of Cork Land League operation from March to September 1881. From April the majority of these were sales of interest.[60] This figure for sales, large as it is, seriously underestimates the significance of the problem. As in the example given of Baldwin Seely, landlords usually took action against their most solvent tenant (or tenants) as the method of bringing the whole estate (almost forty tenants in Seely's case) to heel.

At the end of February Dillon felt it necessary to remind the Irish tenantry in the most explicit terms of the advantages which the Land League had won for them.[61] It had put something like £4 million into the tenants' pockets; it had saved thousands from the workhouse; and it had compelled the landlords to refrain from pressing their tenants for the last half-year's rent. Moreover, he asserted, these advantages had been won at small cost to the tenantry. A few men were sent to prison at Drumlish, some others were at present in Nenagh jail; these were the only persons, to Dillon's knowledge, who had suffered in the cause of the League. At Birr, in the moderate King's County, where Matthew Harris had been forced off the platform in October 1880,[62] the League, he said, had shown by hostile demonstration how to deal with the 'emergency men'.[63] On 3 March Dillon admitted, however, that the PDA was causing the League more trouble than the fear of coercion: the number of sheriffs' sales was immense.[64]

In March, at any rate, Dillon was still reasonably satisfied with 'rent at the point of the bayonet'. Morale was high: it was important, he said, that in hardly any district did the people show signs of giving way or being terrified by these operations. If the people stood together and compelled the landlords to levy unjust rents at the point of the bayonet, there could be no doubt in the world that such a stand would break down the system—not the slightest doubt.[65] He gambled that the expenses of the campaign would in the end prove too much for the landlords. At Thurles he explained: 'They must remember that each sale costs the landlords a lot of money, and the landlords had less money than the League had, and the people, if they kept up the fight, could wear out the Emergency Committee [i.e. the PDA] before they wore the League out.'[66]

This was inevitably—in the context of his recent rejection of 'no rent'—Parnell's line also. In an open letter to the Land League from Paris he had written:

> I am glad to find that our people persist not to offer for stock sold at such sales. . . . Our purpose is served whether it becomes necessary to buy in the stock or no, for it is evident that only in a very few instances can the landlord organisation and forces of the government be sufficient to enable a landlord to collect rent by these means.[67]

Dillon was captivated by the opportunities which the sheriffs' sales offered for militant display and was still at the end of the month referring wistfully to the 'bold front' and 'magnificent demonstration' at Birr.[68] He hoped that the high morale of the peasantry, combined with a landlord financial collapse, would make 'rent at the point of the bayonet' a success after all. The essence of the policy, he explained, was that all the tenants should stand together and do what was resolved in their own district.[69] At Fourmilewater in March he added:

> The policy of united action was . . . the chief plank of the Land League . . . the policy by which the tenant refuses to make terms for the landlord by himself, by which the tenantry on each estate decide that they should stand together or fall together. . . . That policy . . . has put four million pounds into the pockets of the Irish tenantry. . . . Wherever they got a favourable reduction they must be prepared to stand by their neighbours on other estates who have not been so fortunate.[70]

He hoped, in fact, as he said at Woodford later in March, that the tenantry who had got reductions of 25 to 20 per cent by the action of the Land League should give at least a quarter of that reduction to help their neighbours on other estates who were still struggling against their landlords.[71]

It was clear that sheriffs' sales of stock and (more importantly) sales of interest,[72] were having a significant effect. Now that the landlord had increased his chance of collecting his rent, 'rent at the point of the bayonet' stood revealed as a contradictory double-edged weapon. It is not surprising, therefore, that a section of the Land League radicals continued to feel that a 'no rent' call was by far the best policy. The direct point of application of the existing strategy was not the weakest part of the enemy's defences, his lack of financial resources. The chronic poverty of Irish landlordism was potentially its Achilles' heel. If only this could be exploited, it was felt, there was a chance of a total Land League triumph. In effect, however, the Land League was following a different line. It was pitting its purse against the British government. The existing mode of struggle adopted by the League posed one question only : had the state the capacity to enforce the law, particularly with regard to peasant efforts to evade attempts to enforce payment of rent, or had it not? There was little doubt that it had.

On the other hand, a 'no rent' strike, it was argued, would not only have exposed the poverty of the Irish landlord in a most dramatic way, but it would also have highlighted the limitations of British state power in Ireland. It was a simple fact that no British government could possibly provide enough troops to extract rent from every peasant who refused to pay it.[73]

There was very considerable doubt in radical Land League circles about the value of the resistance offered at sheriffs' sales. Father Norris of Buttevant summed it up all too aptly for League militants when he addressed the landlords: 'If you want your rack-rents we will not give them quietly but you may come and take them.'[74] He might have added 'plus the legal costs as well'. The behaviour of Walsh, the Dungarvan tenant who had been the first to suffer at Goddard's hands, was a bad omen. The case of Nugent, the second Dungarvan tenant to have his cattle seized by agents of his landlord, Count de la Poer, is of symbolic interest. The local pro-Land League journal analysed the situation thus :

> If the Irish farmers want a reduction of rents, they [i.e. the Land League] must face the cost of proceedings to recover the rents. . . . Mr Nugent has manfully fought for a principle and should not be allowed to suffer in consequence. . . . The mistake which was made in Mr Walsh's case was not repeated. . . . The landlords should not be allowed to obtain their cattle as a sacrifice.[75]

But the advocates of the existing policy had one major argument.

Dr Clarke, an English delegate of the Democratic Federation, at a joint conference of the Land League of Down and Armagh explained that the 'rent at the point of the bayonet' strategy was unpopular in radical circles in England as it appeared to be something of a sham fight. However, he continued, he himself now understood its *raison d'être*.[76] On the estates all the tenants, poor and rich alike, agreed upon what they would pay the landlords. If that offer was refused, they all refused to pay. The landlord, of course, knew which of them had money, and he then conspicuously sold the farms of those who had money and were prepared to pay. But if the League did not pay the 'rich' man his costs, what motive had he to stand besides his poorer brothers?

Even with 'rent at the point of the bayonet', it was still open to the landlords to operate 'divide and rule' strategy. For example, the Land League frequently encouraged tenants to refuse all reductions until those who could pay nothing were included in the settlement. But there was evidently no use in the tenant or any number of tenants rejecting arrangements satisfactory to themselves when it only meant that they would in the end have to pay the whole rent and the other tenants would be no better off for their self-denial. There was thus a constant tendency for the 'rich' man to settle for a percentage reduction which was satisfactory to him but which the small man found relatively useless. This was a sore point in the most radical pro-Land League provincial newspapers.[77] J. R. Heffernan, the Cork League organiser, concluded that 'the large tenant with the rent of £200 a year who gained most by the Land League' should maintain solidarity with his fellow-tenants.[78]

Linked with this problem was the rise in the number of evictions. In the last quarter of 1880 the number evicted had been 954, but in the first quarter of 1881 the figure rose to 1,732 before jumping to 5,262 for the second quarter and to 6,496 for the quarter ending 30 September.[79]

The abandonment of the catastrophist policy of Kettle in mid-1880, which had envisaged hundreds of thousands of evicted tenants, left the Land League with a difficult legacy. It was specifically for the relief of such evicted tenants that the League had asked for aid. Nevertheless, it was felt that the majority of them were evicted as a result of accumulated arrears and that they were making no particular stand for League principle in allowing themselves to be evicted. Once evicted, they tended to look to the League for support, and this was now given more and more reluctantly. On 16 March 1881 Thomas Brennan went so far as to cable the *Irish World* that there 'is a general feeling with regard to the ejectments throughout the Land League that the people should allow the evictions to take place and that the League should provide on the evicted farms'.[80]

But an incident at the end of March revealed the depth of the problem the League now faced. At a League executive meeting Tim Healy pointed out that the League could no longer afford to pay out cash to what were, in effect, charity cases. These cases should in future be dealt with through the Poor Law. It was in the power of the Poor Law Guardians to strike a special rate; the League should therefore now take advantage of its recent victories in the Poor Law Guardian elections. Outdoor relief should be applied, so that the landlords would be compelled to pay for the support and maintenance of the tenants they had evicted.[81] James Daly, editor of the *Connaught Telegraph*, who was also present at this meeting, was strongly opposed to Healy's position. The landlord would find a way of shifting the burden onto the Poor Law Guardians, he argued, and it would be a great mistake to let the people think that they could rely on outdoor relief.[82] Healy does not seem to have pushed his idea, but he had already given impetus to an existing feeling in Mayo that the League's use of its funds was open to severe criticism.

Anna Parnell went out of her way to reassure the tenants on the next day:

> I think that theory [Healy's] would only work where all the tenants are evicted; but I believe in any place all the tenants, or half the tenants won't be evicted. I must tell you if you hear talk of Mr Healy's theory don't be frightened. Half the money collected by the Land League will be to assist the tenants. So long as they act on the instructions of the League they will be assisted.[83]

Anna Parnell's remarks did not constitute a blanket reassurance for the evicted tenants—a fact which emerged very clearly a few weeks later. Writing in correction of a report from Drogheda, she claimed that she had explained that the Land League could not give large grants to tenants who had not furnished any proof of their determination to refuse a rack-rent when they had the power to pay it, as there would always be a danger that these persons might, if it was made possible for them to do so, misuse the money granted to them and pay their rent with it.[84]

3. *The Land Bill, 1881*
While these policy debates were going on within the League Gladstone introduced his new Land Bill. He claimed that its cardinal

principle was the institution of a land court which had the capacity
to acknowledge tenants' rights of tenure and assignment.[85] Although
Gladstone felt that he had stopped short of a full recognition of
the 'three Fs' claim,[86] he did satisfy the majority of 'three Fs'
supporters.

Parnell, who shortly before the bill's publication had talked of
accepting any measure which improved the lot of the Irish tenantry,
greeted the proposals aggressively.[87] He argued that although the
majority of the Irish tenants believed they were entering an
'Elysium', the composition of the land court which was to fix the
judicial rents was landlordist in sympathy. Solicitors' costs, he predicted, would be huge. But he did not simply object to the deficient
machinery. The exclusion of leaseholders and those in arrears was
disastrous. Furthermore, the land court was not allowed to take
into account the case of the tenant who had been paying a rack-
rent for twenty or thirty years. He proposed instead the Land
League policy of a compulsory expropriation of bad landlords and,
secondly, state advancement of money for the establishment of a
peasant proprietary. There would be some certainty about such a
scheme. There would be none as to the proceedings of the new
land court. He noted that the provisions of the second part of the
bill were taken almost line for line from the recommendation of
the committee of the Land League in April 1880, but there again
he had to object to the emigration clauses. Karl Marx regarded
Parnell's speech as the gist of what should be said about Gladstone's
new Land Bill.[88] The next day, at an ordinary League executive
meeting, Parnell asked the representatives of each of the four
provinces to give him opinions. They all poured scorn upon the
bill.

John O'Doherty of Ulster, Father Eugene Sheehy of Munster,
James Louden of Connaught, Richard Lalor of Leinster—all denounced the bill.[89] However, there was no evidence that they
reflected popular feeling. This was particularly so in the case of
the Ulster representative. William O'Brien commented on the
Northern attitude of a few months later to Gladstonian land
reform: 'That hardfisted body of men having done nothing themselves to win the Act, thought of nothing but turning it to their
immediate use and repudiating any solidarity with the Southern
and Western rebels to whom they really owed it.'[90] Even in April
1881 predominant opinion among the Ulster tenantry was friendly
towards the Land Act. As for the other provincial representatives,
Lalor, for example, claimed that the subdivision of the grasslands
from which the fathers of the smallholders had been evicted was
the only real solution of the problem.[91] But this was to criticise

Gladstone for not being in advance of the League's publicly stated policy. Louden's subsequent involvement in the moderate report of the League executive on the bill is a more accurate guide to popular attitudes. Some insight into the pragmatism that underlay the pugnacious rhetoric of that day is given by the fact that Parnell had already rejected Harold Rylett's militant resolutions on the Land Bill which had been drafted probably on 11 or 12 April, telling Rylett: 'We must have a back door.'[92]

There was therefore a certain air of unreality in this early militant reaction to Gladstone's proposals. There was, of course, no advantage to be gained by praising the premier's statesmanship. The only likely result of that would have been a reduction in the impetus for reform. Nevertheless, it is hard to escape the impression that men like O'Doherty, Lalor and Louden did not really mean all that they said.

But John Dillon, at least, was a genuine opponent of the bill. He saw it as a major ideological victory for the Irish landowners. He noted: 'The landlord was in the position of saying, "If you think your rent is unjust there is a court to give you a just rent." Consider the moral effect of that upon the tenantry.' Freedom of sale he saw as a direct incentive (amounting to £30 or £40) to every small farmer who was lying under a sentence of eviction to sell out and break away from the combination of the Land League. He felt that the bill had been prepared by a man who had been sent to study the whole history of the organisation and its working and had been instructed to draw up an act which would kill the Land League.[93]

Dillon's analysis was never seriously challenged, it was simply ignored. The executive of the Land League drew up a series of amendments to the Land Bill which were nothing more than echoes of objections already made by moderates such as Charles Russell and William Shaw. This response infuriated the more militant members of the League executive.

It was decided in April to call a national land convention (on a suffrage basis, it was claimed, of one representative for every 500 members) to consider the bill. Michael Davitt, in particular, had believed that such a convention would throw out any compromise based on the 'three Fs'. At first glance, Davitt's view of the likely result of such a convention appeared to be correct. Perhaps only one speaker, Canon Magee of Queen's County, really spoke in favour of the principle of the bill, and even he retracted within a few days.[94] The Ulster delegates spoke strongly against the bill, and there was also unqualified opposition from the South and the West. But all this should not be interpreted as evidence of a determination to accept peasant proprietorship or nothing. It was very simply the case that there was no point in being conciliatory towards the government as long as there was a hope of amending the bill still further in favour of the tenantry.

Responding to this mood, Parnell withdrew the resolution adopting the report of the executive and also the amendment to it and substituted a much larger and stronger pronouncement more in harmony with the tone of the assembly. The pronouncement stopped little short of denouncing the Land Bill, principle and details, root and branch; but it was so worded that it remained quite possible for the Irish Party, hearkening to the voice of the convention, to accept the measure if certain amendments to it, including those in the report of the executive, were adopted by parliament.[95] The convention was a major defeat for the radical section of the executive. Admittedly, the convention had not sanctioned the bill, but it was far more important at this stage that they had refused to condemn it outright. Significantly, the demand on behalf of the labourers was made in a completely general form without any real content whatsoever.

In frustration, Brennan may have been driven to make the more militant views of the Land League 'triumvirate' explicit. He feared that Irish-America would refuse its support when it realised that it had been appealed to under false pretences. The agitation had only just begun, he declared; let not Davitt's fear that a Whiggish compromise would kill the movement be fulfilled. He concluded:

The Land League should take care of the poor men. How were the poor men of Connemara who had bought their holdings over and over again by the payment of a rack-rent to go before a commission to have their rents revised? It appeared to him that lawyers alone would be able to get any benefit from the Act. . . . Something had been said with reference to leaseholders. Well, if these leaseholders were large owners, he did not mind their exclusion, for whatever the benefits the Act conferred . . . the graziers of Ireland had yet to show they were worthy of consideration. If this pilot balloon of a measure would not touch them, their only hope was to throw in their lot with the people and join with the democratic union. . . . The Bill which was wanted was such a measure as would benefit not only the people in the country but also the people in the cities and towns as well— a Bill that would replace poverty by plenty and secure to the many the fruits which were yielded by the earth. He believed that such a result could only be obtained by a National government and that the time was fast coming when they would be forced to step beyond the mere social question (*applause*). The country

was organised as it never had been before. They were approaching the centenary of a time memorable in the history of the
country, and if gentlemen from the North who spoke there that
day would remember Dungannon in connection with their demand
for free land, they might associate it with a demand for liberty
(*applause*).[96]

All the important elements of the 'triumvirate's' thinking were
present in this speech: the danger of a compromise around the
'three Fs'; the suspicion of the graziers; the strategy of putting
forward demands that could only be satisfied by a national parliament. The real choice before the convention was not simply whether
to accept or reject the bill but whether to accept or reject the
Brennan strategy.

The most articulate opposition to the Brennan strategy came
from the parliamentary section of the executive—Sexton, T. P.
O'Connor and J. J. O'Kelly—who were quite convinced by the
Paris débâcle that a moderate course was required. O'Kelly's comment was decisive. Brennan's position, he pointed out, inevitably
raised the question of force:

> If we take up that position that there is only one logical course
> for us—if we will accept no compromise with the government—
> if we will accept only certain things that we ourselves lay down—
> then we must be prepared to support our opinion outside parlia-
> ment. Well now, the question that suggests itself is are we pre-
> pared to do these things? Are we prepared to take the con-
> sequences of this act? (No.) Very well, if we are not, if we are
> not, there is only one thing to do and that is to fall back in the
> lines of legality.[97]

Shortly after the convention Brennan's attack on the large
farmers received a reply from one of their number, Thomas Robertson. In at least a fair proportion of instances, he pointed out, large
leaseholders had joined the Land League; in supporting the principles of the League they had had writs served on them and their
stock seized and auctioned. Not even the semblance of a line should
be drawn between one class of tenants and another at a crisis so
serious as the present one.[98] Brennan can only have contemplated
such a comment with extreme irritation.

8

'Let the Farms Go!'

> They, the tenants, were therefore making no sacrifice.
> The League was assisting the people, so that after all
> they had not much to boast of. In the matter of defend-
> ing legal proceedings the Land League was prepared to
> compete with the landlords of the country in the funds
> which they would provide for the purpose.
>
> TIMOTHY HARRINGTON, speech at Timoleague
> (*Cork Weekly Herald*, 22 May 1881)

> There is one thing I wish to impress on the minds of
> the Irish serfs. Let the Emergency Men buy the farms.
> The landlords are laughing up their sleeves at the great
> strain which is put upon the League funds through the
> heavy expenses which are incurred by sheriffs' sales.
> The Emergency Men have no money of their own—it
> is the landlords who are paying them and the landlord
> is not such a fool as to continue paying them to live on
> farms which would not yield a penny of rent. Besides
> no Emergency Man would venture to live on a farm
> without a regiment of peelers to guard him and the
> Government cannot answer every call.
>
> 'Letter from Westmeath', 1 Aug. 1881
> (*Irish World*, 21 Aug. 1881)

1. *A Setback for the Militants*

The convention of the Land League in April 1881 had resolved on
a policy of continuing the agitation and of rejecting the bill in
principle; but also, and most importantly, it had allowed the Irish
Parliamentary Party due discretion in its struggle to amend the bill.
This implied a fundamental change in the nature of the agitation.
Davitt had always insisted that the principle of the League was that
the Irish people should rely on themselves and not look to the Irish
Parliamentary Party. But had not the decision of the April convention created the possibility that this principle would become
more and more eroded? Brennan, sensing American fears on the
subject, in his capacity as secretary of the Land League claimed
in a cable sent to the *Irish World* on 19 May 1881 that the Irish
people took no interest in what was going on in parliament.[1] Patrick
Ford might be forgiven for his interpolation in the text of Brennan's
cablegram to the effect that if this was so, Parnell should follow up
his logic in refusing to vote for the sham bill and withdraw from

parliament.[2] But Parnell's mind was not working in this direction. In May he repeated his 'extremely anxious' opposition to a 'no rent' policy to Sexton, who had just taken over from Dillon as the director of the League's affairs in Ireland.[3]

It has been argued—on the basis of Parnell's alleged interview with the spy Le Caron—that in the situation of May 1881 Parnell may have considered the question of a possible insurrection, or at any rate a guerrilla phase of the struggle.[4] But the constitutional nature of Parnell's political practice in this period as opposed to his reported conversations does not bear out this interpretation.[5] Another interpretation of the Le Caron interview suggests that the Home Rule leader's object was to secure Clan na Gael intervention against the inconveniently ardent spirits of the home organisation of the IRB.[6] This theme may certainly be found in Le Caron's account,[7] and it is by no means unlikely that Parnell should wish to secure such an intervention.

For it appeared that events in Ireland supported Brennan's analysis in his *Irish World* cable. It really did seem that a section, at least, of the Irish people had no interest in what went on in parliament. The focus of the land war swung to the southern counties of Ireland, where the situation had suddenly become very hot. As a New York *Herald* reporter later put it, 'The mere reckless element of the League was showing itself.'[8] William O'Brien described the situation as one in which Fenians were beginning to return the hostility of the clergy with interest as the League fell increasingly under the control of secret societies.[9] At New Pallas, Co. Limerick, these forces achieved a major victory. Five hundred troops and one hundred police who had set out to serve notice of eviction on Colonel Hare's estate found the tenantry installed in the nearby castle of Castletown and armed with rifles. They opened fire, with the consequence that Majors Rolleston and Vandelim, the commanding officers of the troops, decided to go back for reinforcements and artillery to storm the castle. The next morning one of the five flying columns in Ireland organised for present emergencies was put in marching order from Limerick with two pieces of artillery to force the barricaded ruin. But they never reached it. To prevent the possibility of artillery being brought to bear on the fortified castle, three bridges on the three relevant roads had been cut through, leaving at each bridge a chasm twelve feet deep by nine wide. The flying column had to retreat to Limerick. The troops then attempted to starve out the defenders of the castle, but the besiegers found themselves boycotted by the suppliers of food in the neighbourhood and had to retreat yet again.[10] This minor outbreak of guerrilla warfare had led to a significant embarrassment of the military. It was also a problem for those on the Land League side who felt that an insurrection—or even merely the increased prestige of secret societies—would have been disastrous.

'The resistance to authority had gone one step too far,' noted the New York *Herald*. 'Archbishop Croke saw the position. It was a difficult one but his genius was equal to it.'[11] Croke, in fact, made use of the occasion of his biennial visitation to make his second decisive intervention in the land war. His first speeches had been full of bitter denunciations of the dominant class, but he gradually began to offer more and more moderate advice.[12] 'When he began the people were fully aroused; they had been overfed with strong words and national sentiments and would listen to nothing else. Dr Croke gave them what they wanted and having gained their attention, he proceeded to temper his words with reasonable advice. I have heard it said that had the Archbishop delivered his last speech first, he would have lost his case.'[13] William O'Brien certainly felt that Croke had succeeded in winning back the broad basis of the League, and also in winning back the clergy's privileged relationship to it.

Forster also felt that resistance to authority had gone one step too far and was determined to vindicate the forces of order in the South, which had now taken over from the West as the key trouble-spot. He took an initial step by allowing the arrest of Father Eugene Sheehy, an important figure in the Kilmallock area and the first priest to be interned. The arrest of Sheehy led to some of the most dramatic scenes of the land war. As Clifford Lloyd, the arresting officer, recalled,

> I shall never forget the scene as he proceeded up the street. The people fell upon their knees as he passed, seized his hands and the skirts of his clothes, while begging his blessing before he left them. Shouts of defiance and loud awful cries greeted my appearance.[14]

But the government's effrontery in interning a priest had some effect, at least, in quietening the area, and Forster's determination to combat local resistance was strengthened. On 29 May he wrote to Gladstone:

> It is clear that we cannot allow a repetition of what took place last Saturday week in Co. Limerick. Not merely must the sheriff and his officers be protected, but an obstructing, stone-throwing mob must be dispersed. Further legal processes must be carried out within a few days and, if let alone, the mob will be much larger and more dangerous than before. I am taking steps to send

an overpowering force of soldiers and police, and I intend at the same time to have a proclamation posted throughout the district, warning people that an assembly to obstruct the law is unlawful, will be dispersed, and they will attend it at their peril.[15]

The government issued a circular to the press expressing its determination to assist process-servers. In future the sheriff had to give information of his movements to the authorities so that the military would have ample time for preparation. The Land Leaguers argued that the system of procedure had been reversed. Formerly the sheriff had had to appeal to the government for armed assistance.[16] The armed forces of the crown were now apparently to be forced upon the sheriff.

The government's evidence of its determination had the desired effect. On 1 June a peasant lost his life shortly after 'a regular guerrilla engagement' at Tulla, Co. Clare, on the occasion of a writ-serving.[17] On 3 June Colonel Hare finally succeeded in carrying out evictions on his New Pallas estate.[18] This was a beginning, but Forster looked in particular to Clifford Lloyd, his new Resident Magistrate in the area, to bring peace to the South. Lloyd later described the area around Kilmallock, where he was stationed, as 'rich pasture land, the farms are large, and the people are generally very well-to-do'.[19] He set to work against the Land League forces in this area with considerable resolve and energy.

Lloyd had already attracted considerable hostile attention from the League in Co. Longford. His own account, *Ireland under the Land League*, suggests that he had a very different conception of his duties from that of the average RM. In Lloyd's view, the typical RM felt that he bore no 'responsibility for maintaining order',[20] which was felt to be the 'attribute of the Castle'[21] owing to the passivity created by an over-centralised executive. He concluded a critical account:

Beyond being supposed to attend large fairs or gatherings of the people, it cannot be said that in peaceable times, the Resident Magistrate was called upon to perform any executive duties. He had no general control over the police, which was ruled by the Inspector-General in Dublin, through the officers of the force in the counties. He was in no manner responsible for the maintenance of order within his petty sessions district, which often comprised portions of different counties. The fact that the Resident Magistrate's petty sessions district comprised two or three sub-inspectors' police districts, and of two or more counties, and that different portions of one police district were within the jurisdiction of more than one Resident Magistrate, will show how

extremely difficult, indeed impossible, it was to exercise authority
or to fix responsibility when the urgent need of doing both became evident.[22]

In June Lloyd, in the key area of Co. Cork and Co. Limerick
which included such trouble spots as Kilfinane, Kilmallock, Charle-
ville and Ballylanders, began a campaign to break the back of
resistance to the payment of rent. This was a task of some difficulty.
At Ballylanders, in Lloyd's opinion the worst district,[23] practically
the whole population turned out to resist the forces of order. This
was hardly surprising, as Ballylanders was virtually an independent
agrarian republic by mid-1881, with every farmer obliged to give
work to a labourer and rent him a rood of ground for a garden for
every twenty acres he farmed.[24] Nevertheless, the Chief Secretary
had high hopes that Lloyd had the capacity to defeat such agrarian
militancy.

Forster backed up his repressive actions with the arrests of
Andrew Kettle and Thomas Brennan. Kettle, casting around for a
way to deepen the struggle, had suggested to Parnell that he recommend the neighbours of an evicted tenant to plough up his land to
make it unsuitable for grazing. This was a mistake which might
have had serious consequences, for it placed the Home Rule leader
under the scope of the 'old Whiteboy act'.[25] Parnell had therefore
to withdraw quickly this advice.[26] Kettle had then launched his
personal 'no rent' call. In this step he was quickly followed by
Thomas Brennan. Kettle had acted merely on the assumption of
agrarian radicalism. Brennan, on the other hand, felt that the
struggle to smash landlordism inevitably raised the question of
self-determination. His last telegram to the *Irish World*, just before
his arrest, stated the position: 'Before this year has run to its full
course,' he wrote, 'some of us may be called to ascend the gallows.
And before another year shall have rolled away—who knows?
Ireland may be summoned to take her place among the nations.'[27]
The arrests of Brennan and Kettle in late May, combined with the
earlier arrests of Harris and Davitt, apparently smashed the militant
core of the League executive.

2. *A Radical Initiative: 'Letting the Farms Go'*

It might, therefore, have been expected that 'rent at the point of the
bayonet', for all that it was a compromise policy, would have been
continued. However, the policy was increasingly criticised by the
most notably pragmatic members of the League executive. At the
Central League meeting which followed immediately upon Brennan's
arrest Timothy Harrington suggested that the farmers might make

less use of 'rent at the point of the bayonet'. He had come to the conclusion, he said, that the tenants who had not made large-scale improvements should seriously make up their minds not to bid for farms in which they had little or no 'interest'. Instead they should simply leave them to the 'emergency men'. They would thus throw upon the landlords the costs of auction fees and the new conveyances, plus the onus of taking back the tenants after a short while when they could get nobody to touch the land.[28]

Throughout June 1881 support for this position mounted. Thomas Sexton was in obvious sympathy with Harrington. At the meeting of the Central League on 7 June he was quick to draw attention to the case of four farms in Co. Tipperary sold at the writ of the landlord for rent. Within three weeks the landlord had judiciously considered the state of public opinion in the country and had relieved the 'emergency men' of any further trouble or responsibility in connection with the farms. He had given back the farms at Griffith's valuation and had paid all the costs.[29] At the same meeting T. D. Sullivan, who was certainly on the right of the League executive, added that he thought that it would be desirable to let many of the farms for which the 'emergency men' were bidding go into their possession. He added the proviso that in some cases the interests of the tenant might be too valuable to risk.[30] Despite this qualification, however, it was clear that opinion was beginning to swing away from the old strategy.

But no decision of any sort was made for the time being. Later in the month, on 21 June, Sexton explained with some obvious discomfiture that since the beginning of June the executive, while vigilantly guarding the expenditure of every penny, had deemed it their duty to expend (under the heads of legal resistance, relief to evicted tenants, assistance of payment of costs at sheriffs' sales, maintenance of prisoners and their families, and generally keeping the League at a high pitch of efficiency throughout the country) no less than £2,700.[31] There was no sign of a cutback. It was felt that a large expenditure would be necessary for some time to come. This would certainly be the case if the League was to back to the hilt someone like J. T. Heffernan of Leinster, who at that very moment was wooing the prosperous farmers of Kilcullen (an area which Sexton regarded as quite hopeless)[32] with extravagant promises of financial support.[33]

On 28 June Sexton noted that the League had roughly £30,000 or £40,000 in reserve. This was a sufficient sum to deal with the landlords, of course, but he felt that, on the present scale of League expenditure, this amount would be quite soon drastically reduced unless the branches assisted the central body.[34] O'Neill Larkin, the

Irish World reporter, claimed that if the landlords doubled the present financial pressure on the League to £2,000 a week, it would be in severe danger.[35]

The crisis was clearly coming to a head. In fact on 2 July the secretary of the Limerick League explained that the Land League's central branch had resolved, except in peculiarly exceptional circumstances, to let Norris Goddard and his colleagues in the PDA purchase the interest of farms up for sale and thus put on those gentlemen the onus of getting tenants for them.[36] The policy had at last been changed.

The Land League's legal department took some care to explain the new policy in detail to the local branches. 'When the tenants hold out against rack-rents the League pays the expenses incurred by sheriff's sales of stock,' wrote William Dorris, the Land League solicitor to the Freemount/Charleville branch of the League, on 19 July, 'but in future, when the tenant's holding is set up for sale we cannot allow costs if he buys in.'[37] The point was further elaborated in a later letter of the League's legal department to another Cork branch. 'But with reference to sale of the tenants' interest in the holdings', it claimed, 'so long as landowners know they have only to put the sheriff in motion to get their costs, [they will do so,] while if the farmers let go to the Emergency Men, the landlords, finding that heavy expenses have to be borne, would very soon, we anticipate, have to abandon sales of interest.'[38] In other words, by discontinuing the practice of subsidising tenants who wanted to buy back their interests in their holdings, the League was forcing the PDA to bear the heavy responsibility of finding new tenants— considered to be an extremely difficult task in the circumstances of 1881.

The landlord's agent who purchased a cow or a horse at a sheriff's sale could be reasonably sure of obtaining a fair sum for it, but it was a very different matter in the case of a farm. The League thus felt it necessary to draw a crucial distinction between sales of interest and stock. Otherwise it would at the very least be implying a lack of confidence in its ability to block up the market for land.

The financial reasons for the change are clear. At the beginning of July Sexton toyed with the idea of getting more money from the provincial branches. He claimed that they wasted their money on frivolous festivities and actions at law undertaken without the full consent of the executive.[39] He again raised Dillon's hope of asking from the farmers a percentage of the rent abatement which they had won through the working of the Land League.[40] But although Sexton was prepared to speculate hopefully, he realised that no firm reliance could be placed on the Irish branches. This was only common sense, for, as it happened, in the whole month of July, as Forster pointed out, the Irish tenantry contributed only £163 to the Land League.[41] John Callanan commented sharply in the *Western News* on 6 August that out of £2,436 15s 9d subscribed to the League the previous week only £82 12s 7d had come from Ireland. He called for subscriptions to be raised to 2s 6d and 5s, except for the poorer farmers and labourers. Father Cantwell, Croke's Administrator at Thurles, had to admit failure in this respect at the Central League meeting on 9 August.[42]

Admitting the seriousness of the problem of local subscriptions, the nervousness of Sexton and the *Irish World* correspondent O'Neill Larkin may still appear to be without foundation. The reality of their fears, however, may be seen when it is noted that before the Chicago convention which opened on 30 November[43] the League's funds had fallen to £37,000.[44] At this moment it was facing a crisis which necessitated the Ladies' Land League paying out between October 1881 and the end of May 1882 sums of money estimated by Davitt to total £70,000.[45]

But if the financial argument was the most pressing reason for a modification of policy, there were certain other arguments of importance. It had become obvious that the sheriffs' sales were becoming more and more farcical. They had ceased to provide any real basis for mobilising the peasantry. The militancy of the Birr tenants—Dillon's prime example of staunch resistance to sheriffs' sales—collapsed, and Birr sales were more or less docile events by May. 'There were none of the lusty groans or hearty hoots of prior days, and if the "Emergency Men" did not exactly sigh for the days that were past, they must have been struck with the marked contrast,' noted the Conservative *King's County Chronicle* with some pleasure.[46]

The increasing apathy displayed towards these formal contestations was partly caused by the disenchantment of the smaller, more militant tenantry and the agricultural labourers. Sexton was conscious of the growing antipathy of these sectors towards 'rent at the point of the bayonet'.[47] There was a remarkable instance of this feeling in Midleton, Co. Cork, in March 1881, when the local League branch expelled their chairman, Denis McCarthy, 'a rich man', for having allowed his cattle to be sold without a sufficient fight. The Midleton League had successfully rescued McCarthy's cattle following a seizure, and they were—not surprisingly—infuriated when they found that McCarthy had already given in to the landlord. 'McCarthy had his rent in his hand for seven or eight days ready to pay it and, at the same time, he was preaching the opposite doctrine,'[48] noted J. Hyde, one of the Midleton militants. The lesson was clear:

> The poor man depended upon the rich man, and the rich man too depended upon the poor man, and that being so it was necessary for them to support one another. The poor man could not afford to have his cattle seized, while the other could easily support himself if such should happen to him, and he is doubly guilty of cowardice if he yields to force against him in such a way.[49]

If the 'rich' man took up a strong position and caused his landlord the maximum inconvenience, 'the example could not be practised upon the poor man'.[50]

But had not McCarthy caused his landlord a sufficient quantity of inconvenience by delaying the payment of his rent? The official Land League view was that he had. Both J. R. Heffernan and P. P. O'Neill, the Cork branch secretary, felt that McCarthy had put the landlord to enough trouble and that he was deserving of League financial support in the matter of costs. The rejection of this view by the Midleton militants was an indication of the crisis of the 'rent at the point of the bayonet' strategy.[51] In fact the Land League felt that however galling it might be to the smaller peasantry, there was no sense in changing the policy on sales of stock. The landlord, after all, could easily enough find buyers for stock thus sold. It was a different matter with the interest of a holding. If Land League boasts meant anything, it should have been possible to keep the land vacant and, therefore, to deprive the landlord of his income. The sale of interest should therefore have been a paper tiger. The reversal of policy on the sale of interests, therefore, was as far as the League could go in conciliating the smaller peasantry.

It also became particularly important that the Land League took steps to conciliate the labourers. Theodore Hoppen has recently argued that 'So long as labourers remained a significant element within the rural community and so long as the land agitation ignored their plight, no national movement could successfully mobilise the Irish countryside. What was significant about the land war of 1879–82 was that it reflected the "coincidence of unrest among smallholders and among the larger farmers" at the precise moment when labourers were beginning to constitute a rapidly declining proportion of the population.'[52] There is a substantial insight here. Nevertheless, it is clear that this comment underestimates the potential influence of the labourers in the period 1879–82.

The labourers had the capacity not only to split the alliance of the labourers and the farmers, but also to split the farmers themselves. For example, the demand of the labourers in Tipperary that every farmer should use only his own mowing machine would have hit most of those farmers who had to hire out their machines to pay off the cost.[53] The Tipperary League managed to avert the crisis by condemning all use of machines if mowers were to be had at reasonable wages.[54] But what were reasonable wages? The summer of 1881 in Co. Cork, in particular, was to see a number of strikes on this question.

As the harvest-time neared it became more and more common for meetings to pass resolutions of sympathy with the labourers' cause. In fact Land League meetings would have been sparsely attended but for the labourers' support. Yet the April land convention's protest on their behalf had been almost a pure matter of form. It had been not unusual, according to critics, for the *Freeman's Journal* to fail to report the speeches tagged on at the end of land meetings in support of labourers' demands.[55] The Munster labour convention of May had all the appearance of being a mere sop. Not a single speaker at this meeting, which was chaired by the Mayor of Limerick, was from the labouring class itself.[56]

By June it was clear that the League had to strengthen its line in order to maintain the existing level of commitment among the labourers. The labourers naturally supported the new policy on the question of the sales of the tenantry's interest. In this connection a Wexford labourer wrote:

Anyhow if there is to be a redistribution on equal terms, it will be all right if all present holdings were given up voluntarily. I believe that redistribution will come to pass and I will get my share, though just how it is going to be inaugurated I do not see clearly. However, I suppose we will see ahead as we go along and what seems almost impossible now will appear as clearly as the noonday sun after it is accomplished.[57]

The new policy got off to a good start. On 12 July Sexton reported that a return of the sale of farms attended by the agents of the League revealed that out of 120 farms put up for sale, two were withdrawn, eleven were bought in by the tenants, and 107 went to the 'emergency men'. He added the pledge that no settlement of the land question would be regarded as satisfactory which did not place such tenants—as well as the 3,000 who had suffered eviction—in as good a position as if they had never risked their private interest for the good of the public.[58] Those, however, who put their private interest before the public good were warned a week later that they could do as they pleased but they need not expect the League to pay their law costs.[59]

By 27 July it was clear from Sexton's figures that out of the ninety-three sheriffs' sales he had noted since 12 July, only twenty-five farms had not gone to the 'emergency men'.[60] This record was still fair and it was strongly supported by O'Neill Larkin. The new policy was on morally superior ground, while the reduction in eviction also illustrated the weakening of the landlords.[61] A week later Larkin noted:

> The land is utterly useless to the thieves themselves. I could give you the names of several of these big graziers and agriculturists, who thought not so long ago that they could clear the country-side . . . but who are now poorer than the unhappy men they drove out.[62]

The policy continued throughout the month of August. O'Neill Larkin cabled on 24 August that out of 143 farms sold the previous week, 116 had gone to the 'emergency men'.[63] But the editor of the *Irish World*, Patrick Ford, noted with unusual caution: 'We do not see how this thing is to wind up in the immediate future.'[64] There were signs that a significant number of the Irish tenantry agreed with him.

3. *The New Policy Under Attack: The Revolt of the Strong Farmers*

It appeared to many that the League was asking them to throw away the property about to be created for them by the Land Act. Joseph Fisher, the editor of the *Munster Express*, had written to Parnell on this subject; his letter had raised the spectre of the new policy depriving tenants of the fruits of the forthcoming Land Act. Parnell had replied that the advantages of the Land Act were so problematic that he doubted if the tenants who had permitted their farms to be sold would have any reason to regret their decision. It was necessary for Irish tenants to stand together and stick by the Land League: by these means they would win more favourable terms than those in the Land Bill. In the face of such a strongly expressed opinion, Fisher had little choice but to declare himself satisfied.[65]

But the fact remained that where a tenant permitted his interest to be sold under a writ he lost all his claim to compensation for improvements or disturbance from the landlord. If the sale did not realise the amount of the writ, the landlord was permitted to bide his time and seize, whenever it suited him, as much of the defendant's property as was necessary to realise the balance. Mean-while all the rights of the tenantry had definitely passed on to the new tenant, most probably an 'emergency man'.

Healy made every effort in parliament to reduce the possibility of a tenant meeting such a loss. The government accepted an amendment on 28 July stipulating that where there was a tenancy subsisting at the passing of the act, any new tenancy should be a 'present' tenancy, that is, the tenant should have the power of applying to the court for a declaration of fair rent. In other words, any peasant who enjoyed a tenancy on 22 August 1881, the day when the Gladstonian land reform became law, had the right to exploit the full benefits of the measure even if he was put out of his holding at a later date. But what was to happen to those tenants who were losing their holdings even while the Land Bill was being debated in late July? This was to prove a sore point for the agrarian leaders.

Healy sought to strengthen the amendment in order to make it applicable to the holdings which were at that moment being acquired by the landlord through the instrumentality of sheriffs' sales. The government, however, refused to agree to this proposed extension. Mitchell Henry was quick to point up the implication. In his view many of the farmers who had allowed their farms to be sold were in great difficulties.[66]

It is therefore not surprising that the criticism of the new policy grew more intense. On 1 August, only a few days after this debate in parliament, Patrick Cahill, editor of the newly founded Home Rule journal, the *Leinster Leader*, had declared his opposition at a Queen's County land convention to the policy of 'letting the farms go'.[67] On 9 August a meeting of the Central League was disrupted by an angry priest who claimed that a group of tenants at Free- mount, Co. Cork, who had 'let their farms go' had not received the promised compensation from the League. He received support from a Kildare priest who had attended the meeting in order to make the same point.[68]

It was no accident, however, that the most significant and explicit open revolt broke out at a Land League meeting in the area of Clifford Lloyd's magistracy. Despite strong opposition, Lloyd claimed that he and his police and soldiers[69] had collected many thousands of pounds of rent due, plus the costs (which averaged about 25 per cent of the debts).[70] He had failed, he said, only on one occasion. By sheer pressure he forced the League to break its promises with regard to the payment of the costs of those farmers who had had their cattle seized. 'Putting down the costs at an average of £15 in each case', he wrote to Cowper in August, '. . . would bring the costs in this district alone—not the country even—to about £10,000. Can the wildest Irishman believe for a moment that the League funds [could] stand this strain, even if there was an inclination on the part of the purseholders to apply it.'[71] The League's failure in this respect was obviously creating the conditions for defections.

At the Kilfinane League meeting on 23 August 1881 a group of graziers, furious at having been jeered at when they had recently bought in their farms, complained that 'If the Land League executive did not change their course, they [the farmers] would change theirs and they would not go behind doors to tell it either.'[72] A grazier named Thomas Power insisted that his farm would not be allowed to go to the 'emergency men' unless the League first gave him the sum of £200. The Kilfinane secretary nervously and baselessly told members that he had received special instructions from the executive stating that all costs would be paid. But at a meeting of the Cork League, which was reported in the *Cork Examiner* on 22 August, R. Walsh, the secretary, had stated:

> With regard to the future programme of the League, Mr Sexton, MP, had written to him to state for the information of tenants that out of every 10 or 12 farms put up for sale the League would purchase one or two, and that the tenants should plainly understand that these one or two farms were to shelter the other evicted tenants as well as themselves. The League would build houses on these farms for the other tenants. They would not ask the tenant of the farm to pay any rent, and they would be all supported during the entire time.[73]

Power, who had obviously read his *Cork Examiner* the day before, was not convinced. The Kilfinane fracas had an immediate effect. The central Limerick Land League weighed in to condemn criticisms of a policy which, they pointed out, had been in operation for some time, a fact which Kilfinane did not seem to have grasped. Limerick went on to condemn the local secretary Thomas Docherty's misrepresentation of Land League policy.[74] But opponents of the League's policy seized the chance to exploit the case. On 20 and 22 August the *Cork Examiner* had denounced the 'precarious character' of the terms of the living offered to the expelled tenant in Sexton's letter to the Cork Land League.

> Advice is offered to the tenants about to be sold up to let their farms go to the Emergency Men and, in the case of evictions, to submit to being put out of their holdings rather than pay what they consider an excessive rent. . . . Now in order that people should quite understand what this means we think it right to let them see what the consequences are likely to be. In the case of allowing an interest to be sold to the Emergency Men the tenant

absolutely parts with his tenant right; he forfeits all claim that he may have to compensation for improvements and, even if retained in the farm by his landlord, he ceases to be in the position of present tenant and occupies the less advantageous position of a future tenant. . . . Even if he be put back on redemption, what gain will it be to him to find his crops destroyed, his fields choked with weeds, his fences broken down by his neighbours' cattle and his dwelling injured by neglect? As a sacrifice for the cause, we must, even supposing it were necessary, confess it to be an extraordinarily hard one to extract from an individual.[75]

The *Cork Examiner* argued that in a matter of such importance a convention alone should have the power to decide. When the Kilfinane uproar occurred it commented: 'We have little doubt that when this question comes to be considered carefully throughout the country, the feeling expressed by that branch will be very widely spread.'[76]

The question was also raised in a critical spirit at the Cork Land League. James O'Connor, the usual chairman, objected strongly to the practice of the League in cases where farmers who had a large cash interest in their farms were obliged to let them go to the 'emergency men' for £5 or £10. The League gained nothing, while, on the other hand, O'Connor was personally acquainted with several cases in the midlands in which farmers had been ruined. Henry O'Shea of the Limerick Land League, who was chairman for the day in Cork, replied somewhat weakly that the 'League had not yet pronounced firmly upon that subject; but there was no question that they approved of farmers who allowed their farms to go to the landlords'.[77]

There was also protest about the Land League's use of its funds in the West. The League's increasing reluctance to assist the evicted small tenantry on the grounds that their eviction had nothing to do with the Land League meant that it had trouble with both extremes of its alliance. The graziers of Kilfinane and the smallholders of Westport were simultaneously dissatisfied. The League in Westport, James Daly claimed, was reduced to Louden and one ally who periodically sent farcical telegrams to the *Freeman's Journal* from the Westport Land League. 'Here we are,' complained Daly, 'not alone in Castlebar but in every town in the West of Ireland, surrounded by those who have been evicted calling assistance from the League without avail. The Castlebar branch of the Land League has made six ineffectual appeals to the central office for assistance.'[78]

A Conservative journal pointed out on 10 August that only 10 per cent on average of the League's weekly income went to the evicted tenantry.[79] Parnell, anxious to reassure Irish-America on this point, produced his own figures which put relief in the region of 35 per cent. 'The strain upon our present resources', he concluded, 'is at present very great.'[80]

It became increasingly common to find spokesmen who believed that the League was needlessly endangering the interests of the tenantry. This feeling increased after the passing of the Land Act. When Bishop Gillooly declared his strong opposition on 28 August to the policy of 'letting the farms go' he was not expressing an isolated opinion.[81] On 31 August Archbishop Croke, who had already clashed with Parnell over the latter's failure to give full support to the recently passed Gladstonian land reform, introduced to the public an anonymous journalist writing in the *Freeman's Journal* under the *nom de plume* of 'The Farmer's Friend'. This writer insisted that a tenant's interest in his holding was extinguished if he allowed it to go to the 'emergency men', and that, even if he got back his farm from the landlord, he would come in as a 'future' tenant, that is, he would not be entitled to get his rent fixed by the land court.[82] D. H. Macfarlane, MP for Carlow, claimed in support of the same issue that 'Several hundreds of tenants . . . permitted the sale under the impression that they could redeem within six months as in a case of eviction.'[83]

Sexton felt it necessary to reply at once. He claimed that the good condition of the League organisation ensured the safety of these tenants. For the *Cork Examiner* at least, this was 'rather an uncertain prospect on which a man is to run the risk of a shipwreck for himself and his family'.[84] Healy pointed out that a 'future' tenancy could not be created until 1 January 1883 on any farm when a 'present' tenancy subsisted at the date of the passing of the Land Act.[85] The implication is that the landlord had nothing to gain by putting out the tenant. But Healy's partially unsuccessful efforts in parliament on 28 July in this context had not gone unnoticed.

His weak point was all too apparent. 'The Farmer's Friend' hit back by emphasising the fact that Healy's letter had not covered the case of those tenants sold out before the act was passed.[86] Healy replied that this was

> partly true but not all the truth. I have already called attention to the fact that to produce the result not alone must the sale have taken place before the passing of the Act but the sheriff's conveyance must have been executed before that date. Now it is notorious that these emergency sales were instituted simply to

terrorise the tenants into submission and the bidders thereat
were never regarded as *bona fide* purchasers. In nine cases out
of ten when the sale was over the matter was, for the time being,
dropped by the landlords, and no sheriff's conveyance was
executed at all.[87]

He seemed to be admitting that in the rare cases where the 'emergency men' had purchased for themselves, the tenant had in fact
lost the holding. But for Healy the vital point for the future was
the fact that the landlord would gain nothing by any sales after
the passing of the act 'unless he was prepared to keep the holding
on his hands until 1883'.[88]

The Land League at any rate continued to resist the pressure.
Parnell explained on the day that the second 'Farmer's Friend' letter
appeared that a number of attempts had been made by 'more or
less learned men' to frighten the tenant farmers into the belief that
if they allowed their farms to be sold, they would lose everything.
He could not see that they would lose anything at all where it was
possible for the Land League to keep the farm vacant. If the League
had gone on encouraging the tenants to buy in their interests at vast
expense in the shape of legal costs, the League itself would have
failed: the fundamental principle that a tenant should not pay an
unjust rent would have been violated. He thought it extremely
doubtful that the sales that had taken place since the Land Act was
passed were legal. In fact he expected them to be set aside by the
new rules of the Land Commission.[89]

Parnell was here referring to a theme which had been developed
first by William J. Walsh of Maynooth[90] and then by Joseph Fisher
of Waterford. The point was this: in Section I of the 1881 Land
Act (which dealt with sale of tenancy) it was distinctly provided
in Subsection 14 that 'Where a sale of tenancy is made under a
judgement or other process of law against the tenant . . . the sale
should be made in the prescribed manner.' However, Section LVII
(which contained the definition of the terms contained in the act)
defined the word 'prescribed' to mean 'prescribed by rules in pur-
suance of this Act'. These rules had not yet appeared. They were
to be made by the Land Commissioners, who in September 1881
were still fully engaged in preparing them. But the act itself was
fully in force—which raised the question as to whether it could
be made 'suspensory', at least to the extent of checking the sales,
which, since they were not taking place in accordance with a set of
procedural rules, might be regarded as illegal. Fisher went so far as
to write directly to Gladstone asking him to stop the 'illegal' sales.[91]

Sexton also replied to his critics. His basic point was that the

G

strategy of the Land League depended not upon the rights granted
by English law but on the position which the League considered
justified by morality and public necessity.[92]

But the Land League's efforts to halt criticism were failing.
Healy's claims about sales made after the Land Act was passed
were challenged in the *Freeman's Journal* on 13 September. Healy
had claimed that the landlord would gain nothing by any such sales
unless he was prepared to keep the holding on his own hands until
1883. However an anonymous 'Barrister' declared:

> But I think it can be shown that even if they relet before that
> date, their gains will be very substantial. By the purchase from
> the sheriff the landlord becomes the absolute owner of all the
> improvements on the farm. . . . It must be borne in mind that
> the Emergency Men will buy for a merely nominal sum, but the
> landlord will, of course, be entitled to the full benefit of his
> bargain, and probably in fixing a rent on the incoming tenant
> will make him pay well for the improvements which the old
> tenant made, but has lost forever. If the new tenant wants to
> sell, what has he? A mere right of occupancy; and what
> be the true nature of this in the opinion of the court is hard to
> say. If he wishes to have the rent fixed he has the right to come
> to the Court, but he has no improvements—at least only such
> as may hereafter be made—and will come before the Court in
> a very different position from the old tenant.[93]

The resilience of the Land League critics was remarkable. It
may be fruitfully compared with the collapse of the efforts made
by moderate men to pin Parnell down on his precise land reform
proposals in the second half of 1880. Then they had tried to open
up a discussion on the technicalities of the land question in order
to expose the dangerous inexperience of the League leadership.
They had failed in this venture. However, in the late summer and
early autumn of 1881 they succeeded. This is the essence of the
complicated disputes over 'present' and 'future' tenants and other
such questions.

It was now clear that 'The Farmer's Friend' and his allies were
winning this particular struggle. They had succeeded in creating
a degree of panic. Joseph Fisher, who had earlier doubts which
Parnell had personally quelled, began to have doubts again about
the whole course of action. His editorial in the *Munster Express*[94]
expressed particular concern about the success of the proceedings
taken at Woodsgift, Co. Kilkenny, where the tenants had sold out
their interests to 'emergency men' and were in some considerable
state of demoralisation.[95] There were over 200 tenants in Tipperary

alone in this invidious position.[96] *The Nation* diplomatically summed up that while, of course, the Land League could not take the position of English law, special safeguards should be given to those who had a considerable interest in their farms.[97] The agitation was clearly losing its momentum.

4. *Political Developments*

At the same time as his debate with 'The Farmer's Friend' Healy had acted in such a way as to greatly increase the attractiveness of the Land Act. When the Land Commissioners issued their official summary of the act Healy attacked them for misrepresentation. The issue of contention was what became known as the 'Healy clause': 'No rent should be made payable . . . in respect of any improvements made by the tenant and by his predecessor in title.'[98] This clause had been passed in an atmosphere of confusion. 'Apparently nothing very particular had occurred, the whole business had passed off in unbroken tranquillity and overflowing amiability,' wrote T. P. O'Connor, 'but the prime mover knew what he had done. With a face of sphinx-like severity Mr Healy whispered to a friend at his side: these words will put millions in the pockets of the tenants.'[99] Healy himself admitted that if Edward Gibson, who was leading the Conservative opposition to the bill, had finished his dinner five minutes earlier, the Healy clause would never have been passed.[100] The *Freeman's Journal* recognised the event as a moderate victory. 'For the future,' it concluded, 'the improving tenant will work not for the landlord but for himself.'[101] But did such a comment recognise the full scope of the change?

In early September the interpretation of the Healy clause became a key issue of debate. Did the clause suggest that tenants should be protected from rent-raising on their improvements made in the future, or did it apply to improvements made before 1881 also? Healy's suggestion that it was retrospective conflicted with the official summary of the Land Commissioners, but it soon emerged that Healy had correctly construed the government's intention. Gladstone had expressed the point of principle on 10 August in a speech which was to be resurrected and frequently cited during the controversy.[102] The *Freeman's Journal* editorial claimed that Gladstone had decided that as he could not limit the right of the landlord to his improvements, no matter how far back in time they had been made, so he could not limit the right of the tenant to *his* improvements, no matter how far back they had been made.[103] In one sense this was a victory for the Land League, but in another sense it increased peasant desire to exploit Gladstone's reform.

There were other problems for the Land League leadership at this time. The heavy defeat of the Land League in the Tyrone by-election was also widely interpreted as a significant blow to the land movement. Parnell's decision to contest the Tyrone by-election was an early indication of his lack of grasp of Northern political realities. Andrew Kettle, in particular, felt strongly that to contest the seat was a mistake, although his message reached Parnell too late to affect the latter's decision.[104] Few people really expected the Land League to win many Orange votes in this area, but in the event it failed also to take many Catholic votes from the Liberal candidate, Dickson. Even the *Pall Mall Gazette,* as William O'Brien recalled, was delighted.[105] For Gladstone it was a decisively important event. He noted in a letter to Cowper on 9 September that Parnell was in a minority *among the Catholics themselves.*[106] In fact Catholic support for Dickson was hardly a surprise. In the first place, Dickson had a good reputation as a consistent land reformer, and the Tenant Right Associations were still the dominant agrarian radical force in Ulster. Secondly, there was the influence of the traditional pattern of politics in those parts of Ulster where the population was more or less evenly divided between Catholics and Protestants.

Although the Liberal Party had traditionally been able to rely on the Catholic clergy and population for support, they had usually needed a small percentage of Protestants to vote Liberal to give them victory. The remarkable fact here was the way in which this Protestant Liberal minority was able to impose terms for its support. As a rule they had refused to accept Catholic Liberal candidates, and also as a rule the Catholic clergy had accepted their wish as a price for defeating the Conservative. This system still operated in 1880, when Charles Russell was refused the Monaghan candidature on this basis, while the Catholic Liberal candidate who was accepted for Newry failed to secure the necessary handful of Protestant Liberal votes to win the seat—despite being the largest employer of labour in the town.[107] The effect of all this was to keep Catholic politics in this region a step behind that of the southern and western regions. It is little wonder that even after two years of land agitation the very limited, almost subservient, objectives of Catholic politics remained. But nevertheless, Parnell's defeat was important politically at the time, and he himself believed it determined his imprisonment; writing to Katharine O'Shea from Kilmainham, he declared: 'I am convinced that had it not been for the unfortunate result of Tyrone I should not be here.'[108]

5. *'Testing the Act'*

The loss of momentum signalled by these events made a compromise with the 1881 Land Act more or less inevitable. In the period before the massive land convention met in September 1881 to decide the Land League's attitude only the *Roscommon Herald*, of all the nationalist provincial press, offered any real opposition. The imprisoned editor, Jasper Tully, argued that the Land Act would split the tenantry, while free sale would again legitimatise land-grabbing.

> The Land Act might suit the big selfish farmers very well, but it benefits nothing to the starving peasants in the bogs and on the mountainsides and to the traders in the town, the sturdy artisans and the labourers—classes who had really suffered the most.[109]

But even Tully had to withdraw his attack on the Roscommon land convention (held just before the national convention) when he realised that it had the support of J. J. O'Kelly, MP, and a substantial element of Land League opinion in the area.[110]

Parnell assessed the situation in a comment recalled by William O'Brien:

> This Act won't settle the question. . . . But so far as it works it will only help the farmers. It will bankrupt one-third of the landlords which is more than any No Rent campaign of ours could do, and it will make the rest only too happy to be purchased out as an escape from the lawyers. . . . There is the Act and you either lay hold of it or others will and crush you. . . . If we had rejected this Bill, the farmers of Ireland would very properly have chased us out of the country. If we are not to make the best of it now, the only effect would be that it would be used in spite of us, but that the landlords would get off with half the reductions [which] we can, with judicious handling, knock out of these Land Commissioners.[111]

Parnell's speech at the land convention on 15 September was of some importance. Some of the League executive proposals for the labourers had appeared to be slightly less generous than the Land Act itself. Parnell took the opportunity to restate the view that there was no reason for any separate labourers' movement, but he managed at the same time to give the impression that he was particularly sympathetic to their cause. The vast tracts of semi-waste land of Leinster, Munster and Connaught which had been cleared in 1847–48 would, he suggested, be suitable for the labourers.

In the sense that he spoke of giving the labourers 'semi-waste' land as opposed to the 'lighter grazing lands',[112] he had apparently toned down his emphasis on the issue. He had already retreated from the revolutionary implications of his internal migration scheme in a speech on the second reading of the Land Bill: 'There is no practical necessity of bringing the people from Mayo to Meath. There is plenty of improvable land for everybody there.'[113] His new proposal, combined with the promise to lead personally a labourers' movement if the farmers did not give the labourers fair play, met the situation.[114] Although there were difficulties over the details of certain resolutions on this subject, the labourers' movement did become part of the Land League on fairly easy terms. The farmers were in future to pay a subscription in accordance with their valuation (in a typical case, that of the secretary of the Waterford Land League, this was an increase from 15s to £2 10s). The labourers were only to pay 1s per year.[115]

The bulk of Parnell's speech, however, developed a typical theme. He maintained that the disputes between landlord and tenant prevented the unity of classes in an Irish national movement. The British government, realising this, had deliberately produced a mechanism in the 1881 Land Act which would maintain the existence of these disputes. 'Parnell [at the convention] was at one and the same time', William O'Brien commented, 'as truly conservative as the most staid ecclesiastic in the assembly, and to any necessary extent more truly revolutionary than the most blatant of the young lions who roared at him for revolutionary measures.'[116] But he admitted that Parnell's analysis of the effects of the Land Act 'passed unnoticed at the time'.[117]

For the hard political core of Parnell's convention decision was his appeal to 'test the Land Act, not use it'. The League in each area was to hold back the tenants from a rush into the land court and submit only selected cases. Patrick Ford attempted to intervene by telegram. The view of the 'suspects' interned in Kilmainham that the Land Act should be rejected outright was widely known. There was also opposition from the North (where the League was not particularly strong); from J. M. Wall, the acting editor of the *Roscommon Herald,* and a small group of rural militants; from the *Irish World* reporter O'Neill Larkin and the Dublin City Commercial Branch; and there was a remarkable speech from Father O'Farrell of Kildare. The majority of the Land League strongholds were decisively opposed to an outright rejection of the act. On 16 September Parnell gave an effective concluding speech, but before he spoke all six immediately preceding speakers had declared their support for his policy.[118] In the end, when the matter was put to the vote, only five or six hands were raised in opposition.[119]

The convention also saw the League's final retreat from its policy of the months from July to September 1881. Parnell announced that every man who got notice of the approaching sale of his farm should forward such a notice and his particulars of the case to the Land League executive, who were to advise him on the course he should adopt 'so that he may incur no loss nor injury'.[120] The *Freeman's Journal* declared itself 'rejoiced that the Land League executive are taking steps to meet a danger which gravely imperilled not alone the property of many deserving farmers, but the very existence of an organisation which depends in the long run upon the substantial character of its deeds—the only solid basis of lasting prestige'.[121] A week later Parnell expressed his regret that since his speech at the convention sales had taken place which they had not been informed of. The League would have prevented these sales, he said, and the tenants would not have been obliged to pay the exorbitant rents which they had had to pay owing to the fact that the sheriff had put up the interest in their holdings.

The decision was greeted with relief in the country. Dr Kavanagh, a leading figure in the Kildare Land League, expressed a general feeling at Rathangan when he stated, 'No farms . . . to the Emergency Man. . . . It would be a crime to sacrifice the tenant farmers of Ireland, if we can attain the same end without the loss of a single homestead.'[122]

But what was the new policy? The following exchange between Parnell and Michael Terry of Carrick-on-Suir reveals the fact that Parnell did not want to see any falling back into the pre-July ways of paying the costs for those tenants who 'bought in'. It also reveals much else of the atmosphere of the time:

Mr Michael Terry of Carrick-on-Suir mentioned the case of the tenants of Lord Waterford who refused an offer of settlement of half a year's rent and no costs, and allowed their farms to go to sale for a year's rent and £17 costs. They bought in the farms and hoped the executive would take the matter of the costs into consideration.
Chairman [Parnell]: You said they did not give in.
Mr Terry: Not until they were sold.
Chairman: They might just as well have given in first as last. That is what we have been telling you all along. I would much rather these tenants had gone and taken the abatement offered than that they should have given a half fight and given in in the end (hear! hear!). You are asking the executive after Lord Waterford

had got his full rack-rent, a thing against all the principles of the League (*applause*), actually to pay a lot of costs out, money contributed by the hard-working Irish and American people, many of whom work ten times as hard as many Irish farmers. I have seen these people going to their work two hours before daybreak and working until after dark and then bringing perhaps a week's wage to the League to help you rich farmers make a sham fight (*applause*). The application is a perfectly disgraceful one, and one which I cannot sanction (*applause*). We have a good legal opinion that all the sales since the passing of the Land Act are illegal, and if the Marquis of Waterford's tenants had held out, the sales would have been perfectly invalid, and they would have had a good action against the sheriff for damages (hear! hear!).[123]

It was left to William Dorris, in a letter to League branches, to explain the meaning of Parnell's convention claim that tenants could prevent their farms being sold without paying 'impossible' rents. There were two possible methods. Firstly, the tenant could execute a deed of mortgage. Secondly, he could have a shopkeeper, or some other person to whom he owed money, proceed against him in court, and when judgment had been obtained it could be registered as a mortgage against the tenant's interest in the farm. Neither course would necessarily prevent the sheriff going through the form of the sale, but either would render the sale, if carried out, a nullity, provided the directions were properly carried out.[124]

What was the worth of the testing policy and of the new scheme to overcome the problem created by the sheriffs' sales of interests? It is necessary to stress that the value of the new lines of action was completely unknown. There were grave doubts as to the viability of these policies. Also it was felt that many tenants would not understand them. It was a time of major uncertainty for the League leadership, and much depended upon the response of the British government.

6. *Conclusion*

The main object of this chapter has been to demonstrate the crisis of 'rent at the point of the bayonet', which it has been argued was the dominant form of class struggle in this period of the Irish land war. This was part of a wider crisis for the Land League. This exposition has of necessity involved considerable rather complex detail. It may be helpful, therefore, to draw together some of the main points.

In the course of the year 1881 the differential class nature of the

Irish land war became increasingly clear. The number of evictions in Munster actually fell in that year, while those in Connaught doubled. The clue to understanding this fact is the increasing role played by 'rent at the point of the bayonet' outside Connaught. This should hardly be a surprise: it has been argued that it was fundamentally the weapon of the rural bourgeoisie. In Tipperary, for example, in August 1881 there were said to be over 200 tenants who had let their interests go to the landlords under this policy. Yet in that county during the whole year of 1881 there were only 37 evictions. Mayo, on the other hand, had 234 evictions in the same period of time.[125]

The Land League was therefore facing major problems with the extremes of the elements of the class alliance which composed it. The Land League was quite simply failing to protect the interests of its members. Since February 1881 it had been clear that a properly organised intervention by the Property Defence Association at a sheriff's sale of stock or interest could achieve decisive results for the landlord. If the PDA had the resources to buy in the stock or the interest of a farm, it was capable of demoralising sections of the tenantry. At first the Land League had fought this by purely financial means: it had paid the legal costs for the tenantry involved in such conflicts and thus enabled them to retain their holdings.

However, even following the arrest or flight of those militant sections of the Land League executive who hankered after a dramatic 'no rent' policy, this practice came under increasing criticism within the organisation. The sheer expense of the policy was one reason. Its political nature was another. The Land League appeared to be subsidising what could be represented as a purely formal conflict between substantial tenants and landlords. The substantial tenant delayed payment of his rent until the landlord pressurised him through the agency of the sheriff's sale; the tenant then paid up not only his rent but also, with Land League cash, the costs incurred by his delaying tactics. There is clear evidence that to maintain the existing level of commitment among small farmers and agricultural labourers the League had to ask for more sacrifices from the stronger farmers who, it was argued, were gaining most from the Land League.

In July the Land League changed its policy. It told the tenants that they ought to allow the landlords to buy in the interests of their farms. To some extent, illusions about the power of the boycott to keep such land vacant lay behind this decision. By August it was the turn of the more substantial tenantry to make clear their dissatisfaction with Land League policy.

At the same time in the West there was a strongly expressed fear that Connaught was becoming the forgotten region of the Irish land war. As evictions steadily mounted, so too did the political disunity of the Mayo Land League in particular, partly as cause, partly as effect. There was bitter resentment at the Land League's failure to devote more than a small fraction of its income to the cause of the evicted tenants—on whom so much emphasis had been laid in mid-1880 by Andrew Kettle and others. The Land League clearly felt that these tenants were not displaying any particular adherence to a cause in being evicted and that to answer every call for aid would have broken the organisation. Such developments undeniably sapped the organisation's popular appeal.

All this has considerable significance for the effects of the parliamentary debate upon and eventual passing of the 1881 Land Act. Despite the efforts of T. M. Healy both inside and outside parliament, it was not possible to prevent the idea growing up among tenants that the Land League's new policy of 'letting the farms go to the landlord' (which effectively abandoned 'rent at the point of the bayonet') involved the severe danger of a possible loss of the benefit for the farmer to be gained under the new Land Act. The situation was further complicated by the idea beginning to develop in certain local League branches in the West that as the Land League had failed the West, it was best to extract whatever benefit was possible from the new land law.

The implication of this is clear. It has been argued that one of the most significant factors in the explanation of the Land League is the increasing unity of the Irish peasantry.[126] In contrast, the interpretation in the present study has been concerned to stress that the Land League phenomenon is inexplicable without reference to internal class divisions within the peasantry. It would, of course, be absurd to deny the existence of an anti-landlord sentiment which provided the basic cement for the Land League alliance. Nevertheless, the whole pattern of events in 1881 cannot be understood simply as a conflict of Land League *versus* landlordism and the British state. Again and again the class divisions within the peasantry force themselves on the attention, and a close examination of them shows clearly how they helped to determine the shape of the wider conflict. For example, it may be seen how the class struggle within the Land League alliance forced the adoption of a particular form of strategy ('letting the farms go' as against 'rent at the point of the bayonet') and how this, in turn, deeply affected the Land League's reaction to the 1881 Land Act. And it was this act which now posed major problems for the Land League.

9

Land League *versus* Government, 1881–82

> When I was arrested, I did not think the movement
> would have lasted a month, but this wretched govern-
> ment have such a fashion of doing things by halves
> that it has managed to keep things going in several of
> the counties up to now.
>
> Parnell to Katharine O'Shea, 14 Feb. 1882, quoted in
> Katharine O'Shea, *Charles Stewart Parnell* (1914)

1. *The Testing Policy in Difficulties*

After the passage of the Land Act the crucial question became:
how did Forster perceive the drift of Parnell's politics? On 11
September 1881 he had written to Gladstone counselling against
over-optimism on account of the government's success in the Tyrone
by-election—'Ulster is not Connaught or Munster'—and reminding
him that Limerick, West Cork and the Loughrea district of Galway
showed no sign of improvement. Nevertheless, he was still prepared
to consider a general release of all 'suspects' in order to conciliate
Ireland. He finally proposed to study closely the development of
the League and, if it appeared to be losing power, to run the risk
of a general release of all suspects except suspected murderers.[1]

But the September convention of the Land League convinced
Forster that the risk could not be taken. The League was visibly
diminishing in support, while Parnell's leadership had taken a
dangerous turn to the left. Forster accepted at face value Parnell's
suggestion in his telegram to America that the testing policy was
designed simply to show the hollowness of the Land Act. On 20
September he wrote to Gladstone:

> I send Friday and Saturday's *Freeman*, as I think you ought to
> read Parnell's speech before you speak at Leeds. He means all the
> mischief possible; and the Land League under his advice will
> take what they call test cases into court; that is cases in which
> they know the Commissioners must decide against them and
> they will say to the farmers, 'Trust to us and outrages and pay
> no attention to the Land Act.'[2]

Forster was alive to the difficulties of Parnell's position. He
felt that he was 'moved by his tail',[3] but he felt also that the
League's intransigence made a general release of suspects imposs-

ible and the strengthening of coercion inevitable. The large Dublin demonstration in Parnell's favour on 25 September and Parnell's speech on that occasion finally resolved Forster to ask for his arrest.[4] He was determined to defeat boycotting. He felt that the leaders of the agitation would give up its advocacy if they saw that it meant imprisonment. In the last resort he saw no alternative 'unless we allow the Land League to govern Ireland: to determine what rent shall be paid; what decisions by the Commission shall be obeyed; what farms shall be taken; what grass-lands shall be allowed; what shops shall be kept open; what laws shall be obeyed, etc., etc., etc.'[5]

Accordingly on 26 September Forster wrote to Gladstone suggesting that Parnell himself should be arrested. On that very day the League had held a militant convention at Maryborough, Queen's County, where Parnell again declared his support for the system of boycotting, which was also advocated with particular rigour by a priest, who spoke of the 'all-powerful weapon . . . the power of boycotting, the power of crushing by social ban as by a Nasmyth steam hammer of a thousand tons every traitor to his country'.[6] Although Forster read a report of this speech to three Catholic bishops who called on him to discuss educational matters, he had no expectation that the Catholic hierarchy would take any action.[7] After all, in all five of the bishops' declarations issued during the Land League crisis there was no mention of boycotting.[8] At the same meeting Parnell also sanctioned a new threat to the Land Act in the Land League's 'assessors' idea. It was resolved that League assessors should estimate the value of every farmer's land and that no farmer should pay in excess of this valuation (regardless of any commission's decision) on pain of incurring the League's displeasure. The Queen's County initiative was accepted with obvious reluctance by the League conventions in Waterford[9] and Kilkenny[10] and also, in the immediate aftermath of Parnell's arrest, at Kildare.[11]

Nevertheless, although Forster was confirmed in his resolve by these events, he decided on 2 October to wait for a fortnight, by which time the land court would be at work, thus providing a distraction which would favour drastic action. However, he did not think it possible to wait longer than a fortnight, for the end of September and the beginning of October would see a desperate effort by the landlords to get in their rents, and if the League was to be paralysed at all, it had to be done by this date.[12] On 4 October Forster became even more determined to strike when he learned that the League had just received a large remittance from America and was in consequence increasing its activity.[13]

But in actual fact the League, far from strengthening its position, was at this moment facing a major crisis. The 'testing' policy, the manoeuvre which had saved the September land convention, was proving to be unworkable. The League had thought it best not to pursue test cases where the rent was 20 per cent over Griffith's valuation. It had no intention of allowing the land court to gain easy credit by substantial reductions of the most highly rented farms while the situation of the vast majority remained unchanged.[14] Instead the idea was to press the case of the 'average'-rented tenants, for they held at rents which the League considered to be still too high. In J. J. O'Kelly's words,

Instead of putting into court cases of men who were heavily rack-rented and thereby allowing the court to cut a very good figure without doing any possible benefit to the people . . . they intended to select cases where the rents were in a certain sense moderate, and yet where they were of such a character [that] the tenants were not able to pay them.[15]

But O'Kelly's further comment at the Galway land convention that many of the cases submitted by local League branches to the Central League as possible test cases were very badly selected is revealing.[16] At first sight such a policy was clearly in the interests of the vast majority of the tenantry and might have been expected to enjoy considerable popularity. In fact the situation was rather more complex.

The high-rented tenantry found it very hard to believe that any-one would benefit from their holding back from the land court. They wanted an immediate and official redress of grievance. Although the League did its best to explain that they at least were certain to benefit from the Land Act and would suffer in no way from the testing policy, this did not satisfy the tenantry. 'Such a man says in his heart,' reported Edward Cant-Wall, ' "How can it be better for any other tenant that I should go on paying a high rent when I need not do so?" '[17] Cant-Wall, who accompanied the League law adviser, Healy, on a Cork trip to find test cases, con-cluded:

After some further research it became clear that no cases of the desired description [i.e. in accordance with the testing policy] could be here obtained, it was finally decided by the emissary of the League to take two of alleged rack-renting, and prepare them for entry. I would call particular attention to this fact, because, in confirmation of what has been previously stated, it shows that the League cannot, even if they would, **prevent cases** of rack-renting from coming before the Commission, or hinder the administrators of the Act from establishing the remedial and beneficial character of the new legislation. Mr Healy might have been desirous to keep these two cases out of court, or not; but my point is that he could not help himself.[18]

The League's decision to pursue test cases on behalf of evicted tenants, although unavoidable, also played a part in weakening the overall objectives of the testing policy. Parnell explained on 7 October at the Central League that the League hoped in the next few days to file applications on behalf of 100 evicted tenants. But he warned against optimism about their prospects. The League found that 1,000 of the evicted tenantry had valuations below £8 or £9 a year, and unless they could reduce their rent by 700 or 800 per cent, it would be absolutely impossible for them to pay rent at all. He expected that the League would have to take very strong action hereafter in these cases 'when it was ascertained that the court had failed to give them the protection and justice to which they were entitled'.[19] The militant tone of this speech ought not to hide the fact that the League's policy of refusing to pursue the cases of the most obviously oppressed tenantry before the Land Commission was suffering a severe setback.

2. *The Arrest of Parnell*

Parnell, having made this speech on Friday evening, set off with J. J. O'Kelly for a week-end shooting party at Aughavanagh, Co. Wicklow. He did not hear until he met Healy on the way to a Wexford meeting on Sunday that Gladstone had denounced him in a speech at Leeds on Friday night.[20] Gladstone had picked up Parnell's statement to the effect that rental of Ireland should be reduced from £17 million to £2 or £3 million and linked it with the testing policy to produce a case that Parnell's basic aim was to sabotage the Land Act.[21] (Parnell had, in fact, made such sweeping statements during the controversy over the meaning of the Healy clause.)[22] His conduct was compared unfavourably with that of Dillon (to Dillon's considerable annoyance) and that of Gavan Duffy. Gladstone's decision to threaten Parnell with 'the resources of civilisation' obviously could not remain unanswered.

Parnell obviously had to reply. Even the Irish leader's friends acknowledged that 'the Chief's' remarks about rent levels had been 'unguarded' and 'obviously wide of the exact facts'.[23] It was, however, relatively easy for Parnell to change the terms of the debate. In his retaliatory speech at Wexford on 9 October he dismissed Gladstone's post-mortem tributes to the statesmanship of O'Connell and Butt, in contrast with their degenerate descendants, with the remark 'In the opinion of English statesmen no man is good in Ireland until he is dead and buried, and unable to strike a blow for Ireland.'[24] He demonstrated that on two separate occasions it was the vote of the Irish Party that had saved the bill they were now taunted with conspiring against. Perhaps most acutely of all, he quoted with great force Gladstone's confession that 'the Government had no moral force behind them in Ireland'.[25] Gladstone would be compelled to recognise, Parnell argued, 'that England's mission in Ireland has been a failure, and that Irishmen have established their right to govern Ireland by laws made by themselves, for themselves, upon Irish soil'.[26] The tone of these arguments, it was later recalled, 'had the touch of fire that thrilled the country, but were above all characterised by a provoking coolness, a merciless strength of argument, and a suspicion of contempt for the thunders of his angry antagonist that gave him most decidedly the best of the duel'.[27]

Parnell probably did not deliberately go out of his way to court arrest. He had only just been informed of Gladstone's denunciation when he delivered his speech at Wexford, and it is unlikely that he would have made up his mind on such an important topic so quickly. William O'Brien records his strong personal distaste for the prospect of arrest at this time. Parnell was also hoping to go on a continental holiday,[28] which he probably intended as a cover for a spell in the company of Mrs O'Shea.[29] Nor was the speech responsible for his arrest except in the sense that he failed to follow it up with an abject apology which would probably have averted it. F. H. O'Donnell described it as Parnell's most legal speech for over two years,[30] while Parnell himself pointed out that his warrant revealed that he had been arrested for an earlier speech in Dublin.[31] Nevertheless, the impression which Forster had hoped to prevent prevailed in Ireland—that Parnell had been arrested because of the manner of his reply to Gladstone.

The circumstances of Parnell's arrest allowed him the possibility of escape, and he seems to have briefly considered this option.[32] At 6 a.m. on 13 October 1881 the porter at Morrison's Hotel in Dublin, where Parnell was staying, was called up to receive a visit from John Mallon, the chief of the Dublin detective division, with a warrant for the arrest of Parnell as one 'reasonably suspected of treasonable practices'. The porter managed to keep the detectives in the hall while he communicated the ill news to Parnell in his bedroom. Parnell was told that every servant in the house would die for him, and he was also shown a passage along the chimney-pots over which he could easily reach the attic window of a neighbouring friendly house. Parnell considered this idea for a moment but finally replied: 'Thanks, no—I don't think so.' 'Kindly bid them wait below,' he added, issuing his order to the detectives, according to one account, 'with a hauteur of which his own servants never knew a trace'.

Parnell was certainly very angry. He succeeded in cowing those who had arrested him: Mallon 'veiled his eyes deferentially'; a red-bearded fellow-detective staggered and looked faint—so much so, in fact, that Parnell assumed at first he had been drinking but soon realised that it was 'emotion quite unmixed'. Parnell's dislike of arrest burst forth again when the prison warders tried to search him. 'How dare you!' he cried angrily. Wisely the warders did not persist in their task.

But although Parnell probably did not deliberately seek arrest, there is a sense in which it was certainly welcome to him when it came on 13 October. 'Politically it is a fortunate thing for me that I have been arrested,' he wrote to Mrs O'Shea on that day, 'as the movement is breaking fast and all will be quiet in a few months, when I shall be released.'[33] The crisis of his 'master stroke' of the testing policy was sufficient reason for Parnell's relief. His newly acquired aura of martyrdom would prevent criticism from his left, in particular from Irish-America.

3. *The 'No Rent' Manifesto*
Parnell reacted to his arrest by his decision to issue the long-awaited 'no rent' manifesto. William O'Brien, the draughtsman of the manifesto, insisted that Parnell was the most resolute in favour of 'extreme measures'.[34] There is a good reason to accept this account. The other League leaders in Kilmainham who signed the manifesto were Kettle, Brennan, Dillon and Sexton. Kettle[35] and Dillon[36] felt that the right opportunity had been missed and were at this time basically pessimistic about a 'no rent' policy. Brennan's and Sexton's views are not known, but it is likely that Brennan agreed with Kettle and Dillon with whom he had been so closely associated. It is impossible, anyway, that Parnell could have been coerced into signing anything he did not want to sign.

But what reason did Parnell have for this action? The official reason was that the arrest of many 'subordinate leaders' had made the complex task of testing the act impossible.[37] It was not possible to accept the act in these circumstances, and the League, it was argued, had no alternative but to strike a blow of retaliation. There is no reason to dismiss this account—although the testing policy was in a state of internal dissolution anyway—but neither is there any reason to dismiss F. H. O'Donnell's view that Parnell deliberately sought the suppression of the League[38] as 'hyper-machiavellian'.[39] As O'Donnell pointed out, J. J. O'Kelly, Parnell's closest lieutenant at this time, later told Davitt that the suppression of the League was a 'benedicted good job'.[40]

Parnell knew that the combined pressure of clergy, coercion and, most important, the Land Act gave the 'no rent' manifesto very little chance. Joseph B. Walsh, recently released from Kilmainham, wrote to his still incarcerated brother on 31 October: 'The people are coming in with a hiss. What you will read in the local newspapers on that subject is literally correct.'[41] He added that there was no reason for 'my dear martyrid [*sic*] brother' to remain in prison any longer, as the Westport people had quite forgotten that anyone was in jail. One thousand tenants, it was reported, had immediately flooded in to Castlebar for a ruling from the land court.[42] There is, therefore, good reason to suggest that Parnell sought a propaganda coup in Irish-America which would simultaneously give Forster the obvious opportunity to suppress the Land League.

It is a noteworthy fact that almost all the revolutionary faction were opposed to the decision to issue the 'no rent' manifesto. Davitt, Dillon and Kettle all felt that the moment of early 1881 had been missed and that the policy was bound to fail. Devoy felt that it was 'premature' at best, forced on the League by the 'ill-considered and reckless action' of the *Irish World* faction.[43] Father O'Farrell of Kildare, the priest who had eloquently called for the rejection of the Land Act at the September convention, regarded the manifesto as a tactical mistake which had turned the Land League branches of the country into debating clubs, with the likelihood of much present disagreement and the certainty of greater future coercion.[44]

Anna Parnell also insisted on placing the 'no rent' decision in the context of the League's financial affairs. She noted that 'The deluge of costs was rapidly rising and the impossibility of keeping their wholesale promises as to the payment thereof had become daily more obvious.'[45] The change of policy in July, when the League had resolved not to pay the costs in the case of those tenants whose 'interests' were sold out, had saved some money, but there were many other remaining liabilities—not to mention 'special cases'. Anna Parnell herself had been present at a clash between landlord and tenants at Mitchelstown in August, in which incident alone the League had 'impliedly' agreed to pay £2,000 in costs.[46] There were the costs of numerous sheriffs' sales of cattle over the country to be paid for. In addition, there were already many other drains on the League's resources. There were the evicted tenants for whose aid money had been explicitly sought in July 1880. The League had to spend some money on them, although many League leaders felt that the great majority of the evicted tenantry did not owe their condition to any support for the Land League struggle. They were simply tenants who were unable to pay their rent. There was also the cost of maintaining the suspects in jail (according to Parnell, this had reached £400 a week by early November)[47] and, over and above this, the costs of maintaining their families. Finally, the League was conducting legal defences in various criminal cases all over the country.

In the context of this outflow of money, the 'no rent' manifesto had the decided virtue for the League leadership that it was a definitive break with the previous expensive forms of resistance employed by the Land League. In Anna Parnell's view the 'no rent' manifesto was a cover which allowed the executive to escape from an impossible position while at the same time allowing it to keep up the semblance of a continuous policy.[48] A circular from Patrick Egan on 25 October directed local League branches to request payment for guaranteed law costs from the Land League solicitor,[49] but Anna Parnell claimed that this applied only to costs actually incurred and that all promises to pay other costs were deemed by the League executive to be cancelled.[50]

It is doubtful if even the precise terms of Egan's circular were carried out. In one particularly worthy case in Ballydehob, Co. Cork, where the tenants were Protestants who had acted in solidarity with their poorer neighbours and whose costs had been personally guaranteed by Parnell, there was considerable difficulty over payment.[51] The implication must be that there was in other less significant cases a complete failure to pay.

There was another incident which made the work of the Ladies' Land League more difficult. A letter, apparently from the Kilmainham leadership, was sent out to the effect that it had been decided that funds should be refused to assist tenants—no matter how deserving their cases—who were unsupported by the other tenants on the same estate. It is hard to imagine anything more likely to sink the 'no rent' manifesto, but in defence of the Kilmainham leadership it should be noted that there was a claim that the circular was bogus. Bogus or not, Anna Parnell and Clara Stritch of the Ladies' League had to take urgent steps to minimise the demoralisation. They insisted that any tenant who was genuinely holding out—as opposed, of course, to those who were simply unable to pay—even if one among hundreds of others, would be supported.[52]

The Ladies' Land League, whose responsibility it was to administer the policy, were placed in an almost intolerable position.

Its members were uncertain as to whether they were supposed to be carrying out in earnest a policy for which both the official 'no rent' manifesto and the unofficial one issued by Egan had promised large grants of money. (Such money would have been used only for supporting tenants who were genuinely committed to the 'no rent' policy.) Many of the tenantry did not realise that the agitation had entered a new phase—*that 'no rent' really did mean no rent*. Jennie Wyse Power explicitly declared her agreement with Anna Parnell that ' "Rent at the point of the bayonet" was only a farce as a fighting strategy, seeing that the enormous costs entailed by the procedure had to be paid out of the funds collected.' But she added: 'A more serious consequence was the demoralising influence the policy of make-believe had when the time came to proclaim "No Rent".'[53]

The case of Lord Cloncurry's Murroe tenantry summed up their difficulties. Some seventy families had allowed their interests to be sold in the county court after the League had announced its decision not to pay rent and costs for tenants buying in their own farms. The tenants then offered to pay their rents and costs, but they refused to accept the judicial lease offered by Cloncurry. It was certainly not League policy to enter into conflicts of this sort if the tenants had the ultimate intention of paying up. On the other hand, it was reasonable to suggest that the collapse of the Murroe tenantry may have been determined by the breakdown of resistance all around them. The Ladies' Land League decided to treat them as League cases as their struggle dragged on and decided to build huts. The Land League refused to sanction the building of huts, but also refused to take public responsibility for this refusal.[54]

The local clergy often behaved with a highly sectional concern for their particular localities rather than with regard for the general interest. This, at any rate, was Egan's opinion. 'One of the bishops a while ago stated that there was £300,000 in the fund,' he told Henry George, 'and the clergy seem to act as if these exaggerated statements were true.'[55]

In these circumstances it became very difficult for the Ladies to know when to pay out and when not to pay out. Their relationship with the Land League over financial questions became more and more strained. Anna Parnell refused to acknowledge the Land League's financial control and personally took over the funds collected through the *Freeman's Journal*'s Sustenation Fund.[56] At this point in December 1881, according to Henry George's account, P. J. Sheridan came over from Paris disguised as a priest to 'harmonise certain alleged difficulties in connection with the Ladies' League'.[57] Sheridan himself said that he had gone to 'inquire as to some alleged neglects and abuses in connection with the expenditure of the Land League funds, arising out of the fact that the Ladies' League in Dublin, as well as Mr Egan and myself in Paris, had been deprived of the assistance of our trained organisers who were locked up as suspects'.[58] By May 1882 Egan seems to have given up the attempt to regain control, for at that time he asked that all applications should be sent to the Ladies' League and not to Paris in order to avoid wasteful duplication.[59]

It became apparent that the 'no rent' call had very little popular support. But with the slackening in the level of economic class struggle the crime rate rose. In fact Anna Parnell even suggested that the few areas where 'no rent' was supported had very low crime rates compared with those areas which ignored the call.[60] This was a significant phenomenon. From 1879 to late 1881 crime, whatever its form, was usually linked closely with rent resistance. This was particularly clear, for example, in organised resistance to seizures, sheriffs' sales and evictions; but even the proportionately more rare cases of straightforward intimidation and shooting of landlords, their agents or anti-Land League tenants might have been said to have this ultimate rationale. Agrarian crime was largely instrumental not 'expressive': it was a means of strengthening the campaign to reduce rents and not primarily a means of alleviating accumulated resentment as, for example, the murder of Lord Leitrim in the immediate pre-Land League period had been.[61]

What did the new development imply? Was the post-October 1881 crime now purely 'expressive'?—or had a new form of instrumentality developed? Was it, as Parnell claimed, spontaneous?[62] Herbert Gladstone, who had gained a certain experience of the Irish government as an assistant to Forster in the period, offered an analysis which took account of both factors while also stressing the new dislocation between rent resistance and crime. In his diary entry for 29 March he noted of coercion:

> It has succeeded in the most important particulars, namely, the enforcement of rent payment and the re-establishment of the common law as the only recognised law. . . . That outrages continue and even increase is a fact but it is intelligible. In addition to the crime committed for agrarian purposes, outrages are committed (1) for purposes of revenge—you can't lock up hundreds of men without creating bad feeling (2) in order to show the government are wrong and that coercion is a failure. Egan probably knows something about this.[63]

The assumption that crime had, apart from this new revenge motive against the government and its agents and supporters, the object of discrediting the government's decision to suppress the Land League had been part of Dublin Castle thinking since at least November 1881. Mallon in a report of 26 November claimed to have found (on the evidence of an informer on the League's temporary executive) that 'Nothing would satisfy Egan but to keep up a regular guerrilla warfare to demonstrate that the Land League had a restraining power.'[64] Patrick Egan, the League treasurer, appeared to be the central figure in this conspiracy as he distributed money from his Paris base. Mallon claimed that a secret system of eight Land League organisers or 'inspectors' may have played a direct role in instigating outrage. The sum of £1,000, which Egan had laid aside as a sop to the Fenians at the time of the state trials, was distributed in this cause.[65]

It is very difficult to give a satisfactory account of Egan's activities at this time. On 10 December 1881, for example, an informer's report suggested that Egan had ordered that *all* the available money should go to the evicted tenants,[66] but a report of 17 December expressed scepticism about this claim.[67] But it seems certain that some Land League money found its way into the pockets of Fenian militants. This was apparently because in the circumstances of the time Egan felt morally obliged to pay some form of compensation to the Fenians, for since the Land League's activities had brought about coercion, the League could be held indirectly responsible for the arrest of a number of Fenians, some of whom had no connection at all with the League.[68]

4. *Government Reaction: Forster and Gladstone*
The Irish government—and, indeed, the cabinet as a whole—began to regard the struggle against crime as of unique importance. With the decline in effective resistance to rents, they seemed to feel that they had done everything possible for the landlords. The Irish landlords, on the other hand, felt themselves to be deserted. At the beginning of January 1882 the largest-ever meeting of Irish landowners, with 3,000 present, was held in Dublin. The Duke of Abercorn chaired the meeting, an act which signalled a belated determination on behalf of the leading lights of the Irish aristocracy to come to the aid of the smaller landlords. The major grievance was obvious. Rent reductions under the Land Act were running at an average of 23·7 per cent; in Connaught the figure was as high as 28·5 per cent.[69]

There was a further aggravating factor. To carry its provisions into effect the 1881 Land Act created a new tribunal, the Irish Land Commission, presided over by a judge of the High Court, with power to organise sub-commissions which would sit in all parts of the country to deal with applications for fair rents. It was the political complexion of the sub-commissioners which worried the landlords. The landlords regarded them as a band of pro-tenant liberals who persistently operated a bias. These fears were shared to some extent by Cowper[70] but not by Forster.[71] It was also claimed that the Solicitor-General, A. M. Porter, in his campaign for Derry in November had threatened the sub-commissioners with loss of appointment if they did not give sufficient attention to the tenantry's case. The landlords demanded that either the chief commissioners should be empowered to reverse the decisions of the sub-commissioners on appeal, or the government should face up to the question, as Gladstone had acknowledged on 22 June it would have to do, if 'ruin' or 'heavy loss' was brought about by the legislation.[72]

The majority of Liberals however, had little sympathy for this argument. Chamberlain, in a major speech on the same day as the landlords' conference, dismissed the cry for compensation by claiming that the evidence before the Land Commission was ample justification for the legislation that had been passed. Who was going to compensate all those tenants who had now been deemed to have been paying more than a fair rent? Forster also had written to Harcourt in the same spirit: 'The nominal rents, especially in the West and far South, have been pushed up to the point at which rents could only be paid in good years, even without agitation.'[73] He was sceptical of the damage involved in giving up a rent that could not be got.

But the most significant thing about Chamberlain's speech was his claim that government policy was succeeding in restoring order to Ireland. He noted that the number of agrarian crimes in December 1880 had been 384, but in December 1881 the number had fallen to 235. As compared with the figure for November 1881, the December 1881 figure marked a decrease of 13, which was more satisfactory than it appeared, for the winter months were the worst period for outrage.[74]

This optimism about crime was a remarkable feature of cabinet attitudes in the first two and a half months of 1882. The consensus seemed to be that the Chief Secretary was doing a difficult job well and gradually getting on top of the situation. When at the end of this period Forster appeared to claim that things in Ireland were as bad as they had ever been, it is perhaps not altogether surprising that he found he had lost the sympathy of colleagues who had publicly claimed otherwise.

But when parliament met on 7 February 1882 this optimism was still high. The number of outrages in January had shown a further reduction to 189, and it was suggested that Forster's new system of Special Resident Magistrates was beginning to have an effect.[75] The Chief Secretary had in late 1881 seen the danger of an over-centralised system where a young sub-inspector was the main figure of authority in a locality[76] and where the RM was often only slightly superior in prestige to the JP.[77] T. O. Plunkett, C. D. C. Lloyd, W. Forbes, O. R. Slacke, A. Butler and H. A. Blake were appointed as Special Resident Magistrates in various troubled regions and were made directly responsible to the executive for the administration of their areas. Whereas previously RMs had tended to content themselves with executing the government's orders, these new Special RMs took it on themselves to initiate action for the restoration of good order.[78] On 4 March Forster had a meeting with these Special RMs, all of whom brought him good reports. The next day Gladstone received a very hopeful note from Forster declaring that there was an undoubted break in lawless agitation, that rents were being paid in the worst districts, and that the very bad characters were 'bolting'.[79]

But despite this optimism (the problems of criminal conspiracy apart), it soon became clear that the basis for a return to normality in rural Ireland did not yet exist. Firstly, there was the blockage in the land court: by the beginning of January only 1 per cent of those who had applied to the court had had their cases heard.[80] Secondly, there was the fact that the tenants in arrears, who had most need of relief—one-third of tenants throughout the country, nearly two-thirds in Mayo—as well as leaseholders, were ineligible for reductions. As had been foreseen by Forster,[81] the landlords made a considerable effort to collect the arrears which they were undoubtedly owed—but at the very same time the land court was declaring these rents to be too high. Thirdly, the *Adams v. Dunseeth* case ruling by the Court of Appeal implied that the tenantry would not after all receive the full benefit of the Healy clause.[82]

On 19 March the depressing Irish outrage figures released raised further doubts about Forster's policy, *especially in the context of his optimism of early March.*[83] Gladstone argued (in a letter to Forster) that the majority of Liberals would not stand for the renewal of the existing coercion act, and he repeated his opposition to the suspension of *habeas corpus.*[84] The government also had a problem in the new parliamentary combination (a section of the Conservatives plus the Parnellites) against the use of the closure. Gladstone clearly felt that with the Land Act working, resistance to process on the wane, and rents generally being paid, there was no basis for a renewal of coercion.

On 25 March Forster declared himself sceptical about the release of suspects and less than sanguine about the general condition of the country. He wanted a bill to supplement the ordinary law, the renewal of the Protection of Person and Property Act, and the release of the suspects on the passing of such a bill. He was determined not to face the parliamentary recess without having allowed for the possibility of rearrest if necessary.[85]

Gladstone disagreed with Forster's view. On 26 March his secretary, Edward Hamilton, noted in his diary that Gladstone believed that whatever the situation required must be met solely by supplementing the ordinary law with other forms. Hamilton added his own comment:

> My own belief is that the present means of coercion have wholly failed as regards shutting up prominent political agitators. For these the Act was not really intended; while for those committed to outrages such kid-glove confinement is a pleasant change. In spite of the difficulty of getting evidence which might even be enhanced when there was less likelihood of acquittal, I should be inclined to try the effect of substituting a Judicial Commission for trial by jury in agrarian cases.[86]

Two days later however, Forster told the Commons that the government had in mind further coercive measures.[87] This caused considerable irritation to Gladstone, for the cabinet had not yet considered the matter.[88] He told Hamilton that it could only be a premature conclusion and in all probability an erroneous one,[89] and he sent Forster a sharp note.[90] Herbert Gladstone also recorded the premier's irritation:

> W. E. G. much alarmed at Mr Forster's speech yesterday afternoon—not as positively wrong, but as so far wanting in balance as to give possible erroneous impression in the wrong direction. I thought him indiscreet and to some extent inaccurate in saying that the Coercion Act had failed.[91]

On 4 April Forster reacted to an article in the *Pall Mall Gazette* demanding his dismissal, telling Gladstone:

> If now, or at any future time, you think that *from any cause* it would be to the advantage of the public service or for the good of Ireland that I should resign, I most unreservedly place my resignation in your hands. You might come to this opinion, and come to it on good grounds, without any disapproval of, or indeed disagreement with, my official action; and I earnestly beg of you not to allow yourself to be influenced, for a moment, by personal consideration for me of any kind whatever.[92]

Gladstone replied:

> I do not admit your failure, and I think you have admitted it
> rather too much—at any rate, by omission; by not putting forward
> the fact that in the main point, namely, the deadly fight with
> social revolution, you have not failed, but are succeeding. Your
> failure, were it true, is our failure; and outrage, though a grave
> fact, is not the main one.[93]

Gladstone's letter should not be construed as indicating fundamental agreement with Forster;[94] rather it is a sign of fundamental
disagreement about the nature of the Irish situation. The prime
factor for Gladstone was the severing of the connection between
crime and rent resistance—the 'social revolution'. Herbert Gladstone
recorded on 6 April: 'Father . . . is accepting my view of the Irish
situation, i.e. that the no rent manifesto has failed and that crime
is more revolutionary in its character; and outrages committed
to prove the government wrong in coercing.'[95] For the government's
area of success—the Land Act and the defeat of the 'no rent'
manifesto—to be fully capitalised upon it was necessary to abandon
a coercion act which was, to use Herbert Gladstone's word, 'in-
operative'[96] for the suppression of crime and, in fact, very often the
cause of it.

Marxist and conservative historians alike have revelled in
exposing Gladstone's responsibility for the institution of internment
without trial in Ireland. The evidence produced by Gladstone's
sympathisers as to his qualms about this course of action has been
dismissed as mere liberal hypocrisy. This is perfectly reasonable
as far as it goes. It was hardly of any comfort to an Irish 'suspect'
to know that the British premier had reservations about internment.
But there is a great danger that the currently fashionable tough-
minded attitude towards Gladstonian cant may be misleading in
an important respect. It may impose an erroneous conception of
the monolithic unity of British policy in this period. It may make
it impossible to understand differing nuances of opinion and strategic
assumptions—for they certainly existed between Downing Street
and Dublin Castle.

In this exchange of views Gladstone was telling Forster that the
Chief Secretary had won the main struggle against social revolution
or rent resistance *if he would but see it.* As Gladstone helpfully
explained, 'Outrage, though a grave fact, is not the main one.' The
main fact was the slackening in the pace of the specifically economic
level of agrarian class conflict—that directed against payment of
rent. The purpose of Irish outrage was now simply to embarrass

the government and to demonstrate that Ireland could not be coerced.

There is undoubtedly an element of war-weariness in this argument. Everybody in the Liberal cabinet had been keen enough to claim a decrease in violence when it had seemed to be on the cards. Now that the optimism inspired by Forster on this point had evaporated, it was very tempting to contemplate areas in which British policy had been successful and to speculate on new initiatives that might extract the government from its unattractive impasse in Ireland.

By 5 April the gap between Gladstone and Forster was already wide. Although they agreed about the need to strengthen the Irish government, even this area of agreement could not hide the fact that Forster's position was weakening. Forster suggested that he be made Lord Deputy with a seat in the cabinet while the vice-royalty was placed in commission. Gladstone was quick to refuse this suggestion.[97] Edward Hamilton, who was unsympathetic to Forster, was already writing in his diary: 'However disagreeable and distressing it may be, they ought to sacrifice the poor old man for the good of the country.'[98]

On 7 April Forster sent a full analysis of the situation to Gladstone.[99] The Land League had been defeated in its attempts: firstly, to dictate what rents should be paid; secondly, to prevent any rents being paid. Nevertheless agrarian outrages continued. Exclusive of threatening letters, the quarterly totals were:

Oct.–Dec. 1880	717
Jan.–Mar. 1881	369
Apr.–Jun. 1881	622
Jul.–Sep. 1881	525
Oct.–Dec. 1881	732
Jan.–Mar. 1882	555

But these figures tended to conceal the deterioration in the situation in late 1881 and early 1882. For the three worst agrarian offences (murder, manslaughter, and firing at the person) the statistics were:

	Murder	Man-slaughter	Firing at the person	Total
Oct.–Dec. 1880	2	0	13	15
Jan.–Mar. 1881	1	2	4	7
Apr.–Jun. 1881	7	2	16	25
Jul.–Sep. 1881	1	1	12	14
Oct.–Dec. 1881	8	0	34	42
Jan.–Mar. 1882	6	0	27	33

And this was despite the fact that the government had in early 1882 established as many as 235 personal protection posts in Ireland.[100]

Forster asked for the renewal of the coercion act and also for a number of new powers, the most important of which was the suspension of trial by jury.[101] (Irish juries throughout the course of the agitation had shown a marked tendency to favour Land League suspects. Once the power of internment had been granted it is hardly surprising to find the police using it as an easy way out.) On 12 April Forster wrote further to Gladstone:

> My six special magistrates all bring me bad reports. These are confirmed by constabulary reports. The immunity from punishment is spreading like a plague. I fear it will be impossible to prevent very strong and immediate legislation.[102]

5. Coercion or Rapprochement?: Forster and Gladstone

On 10 April 1882 Parnell took advantage of his release on parole, in connection with the death of his nephew, to begin the negotiations leading to the so-called 'Kilmainham Treaty'.[103] At first Parnell communicated through Captain O'Shea with Gladstone and Chamberlain, and later through Justin McCarthy with Chamberlain. Forster did not react with any great enthusiasm. 'I return O'Shea's letter . . . ' he wrote to Gladstone. 'I do not believe he has the influence either with Parnell or the priests which he claims.'[104] He was sceptical about the possibility of release:

> We will release them as soon as we think it safe to do so. There are three events which in my opinion would imply safety: (1) the country so quiet that Parnell and Co. can do little harm; (2) the acquisition of fresh powers by a fresh Act which might warrant the attempt to govern Ireland with the suspects released; (3) an assurance upon which we could depend that Parnell and his friends, if released, would not attempt in any manner to intimidate men into obedience to their unwritten law.[105]

In a memorandum prepared for the cabinet on 17 April Forster reiterated his view that, in the public interest, the government's new method for dealing with crime should be prepared. It was later suggested by Gladstone that Forster's keen interest in the replacement of the 1881 coercion act, which was not due to lapse until September 1882, was misplaced. But Forster's view was that it was necessary to produce a counterbalance to concessions to the tenantry in the way of amendments to the Land Act. Motions on the Land Act and the Protection of Person and Property Act were expected in the near future, and Forster felt that it would be difficult to keep silent about the government's Irish intentions:

> I do not think it will be easy or safe to make any proposal with regard to further arrears or further facilities for purchase and at the same time to leave it doubtful what we intend to do with the Protection Act or whether we shall bring any measure to replace or accompany it. Further concessions to the tenantry unaccompanied by strong assertion of the law will make government almost impossible. . . . Let us try to govern Ireland without suspension of the *habeas corpus* but let us keep the power in reserve.[106]

But despite the expression of these strong views, there suddenly seemed to be a very real possibility that Forster would *not* after all insist on the maintenance of the 1881 Protection of Person and Property Act. Despite the stereotype of the Chief Secretary as the firm upholder—as against Gladstonian vacillations—of law and order in Ireland, Forster was, in fact, notoriously weak in the view of many of his cabinet colleagues. It was this weakness that had betrayed him in the discussions on coercion in the autumn of 1880, and it was to play a major role in isolating him in the spring of 1882. For his cabinet document was typical of the man: full of strong words about impending dangers and the need for decisive action, it capitulated at the last to his critics. He retreated on his view of a fortnight earlier that internment without trial was a *sine qua non* for the Irish executive.

Forster's memorandum proposed the re-enactment of the clauses of the Peace Preservation Act, 1870, which had made districts pay for their special police and compensation to injured persons and, further, gave power to arrest suspicious strangers and men out at night. The recent Arms Act, he added, required sharpening with regard to search rights. But the real root of the evil was immunity from punishment. To meet this, in part at least, summary jurisdiction should be extended so as to replace the uncertain prospect of a severe sentence from a jury by a more certain, less severe sentence from a magistrate. To deal with murder cases he suggested a strong legal commission. But although Forster made clear his preference for a renewal of the coercion act of 1881—with a promise to release all suspects on its becoming law—he admitted the strong parliamentary objections to this course and was prepared to make do with increased powers of police surveillance and repressive initiative from the magistrates. He seemed to be prepared to work with only the threat of a speedy renewal of the act in the event of an increased necessity to arrest on suspicion.[107]

He is still not sure that these additional powers will suffice without a renewal of the Coercion Act [noted Hamilton], but he seems to be willing to allow the question of its renewal to depend upon the state of the country. Meanwhile he is prepared to let out suspects by degrees.[108]

Chamberlain, for his part, noted the party-political implications of Forster's proposals:

I do not suppose it would be impossible to renew the Bill with the help of the Tory party, but I am certain it would hopelessly divide the Liberals both in the House and in the country.[109]

On 22 April the cabinet met to discuss the Irish situation. They had to deal with Cowper's resignation, which had been brought about by his uneasy relationship with Forster; a new Redmond–Healy Land Bill, which significantly indicated Parnellite willingness to work within the Land Act framework; Forster's memorandum; and 'approaches' from O'Shea and, less important, from F. H. O'Donnell. Despite Forster's obvious uncertainty, the cabinet was keen to see a solution of a crisis which had been dragging on, and Chamberlain was instructed to continue informal negotiations at his own discretion with O'Shea.

Forster was increasingly uncomfortable. The next day he had luncheon with Herbert Gladstone, whose contacts with F. H. O'Donnell were discussed:

He [Forster] thought that there was the greatest possible danger in this kind of negotiation, and not much chance of anything coming out of it. On what pretext, assurance or pledge could Parnell be let out? If crime stopped, if the state of the country allowed it, or if he would give any definite assurance of good conduct, he could be released. But how could this be done?[110]

On 29 April Forster insisted that unless he received from Parnell a public declaration against intimidation so expressed as to include boycotting, he would resign.[111] On 30 April O'Shea returned to London with a letter which he had extracted from a reluctant Parnell who would have preferred at this point to use Justin McCarthy as his agent. Parnell's letter repeated the need for an arrears settlement and his confidence that he and his colleagues could effectively stop intimidation and outrage, while it also noted in a general way his hope that some amendment of the Land Act which would favour leaseholders was imminent. It did not offer any public declaration. It did offer, however, probably under O'Shea's prompting, a perspective—felt likely to appeal to Chamberlain—of offering 'to co-operate cordially for the future with the Liberal Party in forwarding Liberal principles and measures of general reform'.[112]

Forster was not impressed with Parnell's letter. His response was distinctly cool. Forster felt that a promise to exert influence against outrages if the arrears question was settled allowed Parnell too much room for manoeuvre. O'Shea was forced to embroider on his achievement and told Forster (as the Chief Secretary quickly dictated to his wife) that 'The conspiracy which has been used to get up boycotting and outrages will now be used to put them down.'[113] O'Shea claimed that Parnell hoped to make use of P. J. Sheridan to help him put down the 'conspiracy (or agitation, I am not sure which word was used) as he knew all its details in the West'. No suggestion could possibly have angered Forster more. Sheridan's trips from Paris as Egan's emissary disguised as a priest had made him the *bête noir* of Dublin Castle. Forster wrote to Gladstone saying that Parnell had given less than even he had expected.

Gladstone took a different view. He was delighted that Parnell had expressed his belief that if the arrears question were settled, then he and his friends would be able to stop outrages and intimidation. Although Parnell had stated other aims under the amendment of the Land Act, he had carefully abstained from importing any of them as conditions of the basic statement:

> He then proceeds to throw in his indication or promise of future co-operation with the Liberal Party. This is a *hors d'oeuvre* which we had no right to expect. . . . Upon the whole Parnell's letter is, I think, the most extraordinary I have ever read. I cannot help feeling indebted to O'Shea.[114]

Gladstone's satisfaction virtually settled both the release of the suspects and the problem of Forster's continuance in office. On 1 May the cabinet met, and it was found that the difference between Forster and certain of his colleagues was irreconcilable.

It is rather difficult to reconstruct Forster's precise state of mind at this time. According to his biographer, Sir T. Wemyss Reid, he was still willing to allow the release of Parnell on condition that the new crimes bill, which had already been drafted in Dublin, should be introduced at once.[115] However, it is difficult to see why the Chief Secretary could not have been satisfied if this was the core of the matter. There seems to have been a majority consensus in the cabinet that this new crimes bill—presumably prepared along the lines of Forster's memorandum of 17 April—should be introduced. Indeed, as Lady Frederick Cavendish later noted in her diary, her husband's first task at Dublin Castle as Forster's successor was to put some finishing touches to this new proposed legislation:

> At one time Bobby Spencer came to see me, I think it was in 1882. He told me that Lord Spencer and Freddy had set to work at the Castle as soon as ever they were sworn in . . . going carefully through the different provisions of the crimes bill—putting in a plea for moderating it where he could.[116]

Furthermore, writing to John Morley in 1902 in connection with his biography of Gladstone, Lady Frederick was keen to deny that the

> coercion act 1882 was brought in in consequence of the murders in Phoenix Park. Nothing could have been more painful to me than this untruth, knowing as I did how abhorrent it would have been to Lord Frederick to have coercion introduced, when not contemplated on public grounds. . . . I remember asking Lord Selborne some time in the summer of '82 if it was not true that coercion had been decided upon before May. He replied 'Certainly' and added emphatically 'there were members of the cabinet who would have resigned otherwise'.[117]

The cabinet consensus on 1 May seems to have been to oppose the suspension of *habeas corpus* and to support a release of the suspects and the non-renewal of the 1881 coercion act; but at the same time they were anxious to adopt a strengthened form of the ordinary law, the main element of which was to be an increase in magistrates' powers of summary jurisdiction. They were unwilling to face the rigours of the Irish agrarian climate without at least some extra protection. Why, then, did Forster resign?

Suspicion of the premier was a large part of the reason. Gladstone, of course, might well have persisted in his opposition to coercion. In his *Nineteenth Century* article in 1888 he recalled that at that particular time in 1882 'the subject of coercion was viewed with very great jealousies'.[118] He also noted that, whatever the state of preparation of the bill in Ireland, it had not been seen by any other member of the cabinet on 2 May.[119] Although Gladstone's public pronouncements on 2 May acknowledged that a bill was agreed upon at least in principle, it is clear, as Lady Frederick Cavendish later admitted in her letter to Morley, that the premier (though not the cabinet) hoped that it would not be necessary to enforce it.[120]

It was therefore reasonable of Forster to suggest that Gladstone was likely to delay the introduction of a new crimes bill for as long as possible. There was now no possibility of bridging the gulf between the two men. On the evening of his resignation the former Chief Secretary also made the fair point that there was little to be gained—from Gladstone's point of view—in declaring a new faith in Parnell and simultaneously attacking his followers.[121] (Forster was on less firm ground when he appeared to condemn any 'disgraceful compromise'[122] with Parnell predicated upon a nationalist change of heart; after all, he had himself repeatedly raised this prospect.)[123] In general, then, Forster's defence of his decision to resign seems to be a reasonably sound one.

However, there is a further factor which Forster did not mention but which was surely a major influence in his decision to resign. For had he not resigned, he would have placed himself in an intolerable position—created by the weakness he had revealed in his confidential cabinet memorandum of 17 April when he had apparently retracted his former demand for the power to intern. Both in this memorandum and in his letters to Gladstone he had conceded a decisive point by declaring his willingness (however reluctantly) to do without the suspension of *habeas corpus*. In the circumstances of May 1882 the only form of coercion acceptable to the cabinet was the strengthening of the ordinary law. The suspension of *habeas corpus* had become increasingly unacceptable. Forster would have had to accept this with good grace in the light of his concession of 17 April.

The consequences, however, would have been a deterioration in the relationship between Forster, as Chief Secretary, and the leading figures in the Dublin Castle machine. It would appear that there was a majority among the relevant officials of the Irish government in favour of the renewal of the 1881 act combined with other supplementary forms of a strengthened ordinary law. In short, they still wanted the power of internment, together with other forms of repressive legislation. Cowper, in virtually his last act in office, had made it clear that this was his view in a cabinet memorandum of 19 April.[124]

The six Special RMs, in a report of 12 April, were divided equally on the question. Plunkett, Blake and Lloyd (who between them spoke for West Cork, Kerry, Limerick, Clare, Galway and King's and Queen's Counties) wanted an extension of summary jurisdiction combined with the suspension of trial by jury in certain proclaimed areas. They were prepared to do without the coercion act if given additional powers, although they were not prepared to say that its renewal might not be necessary.[125] Lloyd later presented a critique from a Special RM's point of view of the effect of the coercion act on police methods:

The police were harassed to the last degree. They procured little or no information, and murders were of frequent occurrence, while it can hardly be said that any serious effort was being made in detecting criminals. This was one of the most marked evil results of the suspension of the Habeas Corpus Act. The police considered their duty done when on a crime being committed, a person was reported as being 'reasonably suspected' of the offence.[126]

Porter, the Solicitor-General, was also in favour of allowing the coercion act to lapse, though he was strongly opposed to replacing it with any form of law involving the suspension of trial by jury.[127]

The other three Special RMs, Slacke (North and South Ridings of Tipperary), Forbes (Roscommon, Mayo and Sligo) and Butler (Westmeath, Longford and Leitrim), sought the continuance of the act.[128] Naish, the Law Adviser, agreed.[129] But most important of all, T. H. Burke, the permanent Under-Secretary and the Chief-Secretary's closest confidant and aide, wrote to Forster on 30 April telling him that he was opposed to the dropping of coercion in its 1881 form.[130] Burke's letter was circulated as a cabinet memorandum on 1 May.

If Forster had continued in office, he would have had to reconcile his closest colleague[131] in the Irish executive not only to the releases but also to the effect of his own reluctant surrender on the renewal of the 1881 act. Perhaps more important, he could hardly have cut a very impressive public figure. It is not surprising that he decided not to take the chance, choosing instead the role of standard-bearer for authoritarian liberalism. On 2 May 1882 the Chief Secretary resigned.

6. *The 'Kilmainham Treaty'*
In the aftermath of these events Gladstone strongly denied that there had been any arrangement between the government and Parnell. As early as 2 May, as part of this argument, he claimed that the 1881 act demanded 'the release of men no longer believed to be associated with the commission of crime'.[132] But in fact such a statutory obligation binding the government to release the suspects once suspicion had passed was non-existent.[133] But, making full allowance for Gladstone's error in this respect, it is still possible to argue that his attitude to coercion in Ireland differed markedly from that of Forster. It appears that Gladstone had consistently different criteria for judging the situation. This view has, however, recently been subject to criticism. A. B. Cooke and J. R. Vincent have written: 'What has tended to escape notice about Gladstone

H

because he was the obvious charismatic figure is how similar his views were to other people's.'[134] They also assert: 'In 1881–82 the cabinet contained no stronger supporter of coercion than Gladstone.' It is difficult, however, to accept the implication of the revisionist analysis on this point. Gladstone had originally opposed the suspension of *habeas corpus* and declared his scepticism concerning Forster's hopes. The resistance, he had felt, was too widespread for the arrest of 'village ruffians' to be of any avail. In September and October 1881, when Gladstone consented to the arrest of Parnell, he was clearly under the impression that the government had already made major progress in winning over the middle ground in Irish politics. (It has been noted above (p. 184) that Gladstone felt that the Tyrone election result indicated that the majority of Catholics now opposed Parnell.) On 31 October he had written to Forster:

> If Ireland is still divided between Orangemen and law-haters, then our task is hopeless, but our belief and contention always is that a more intelligent and less impassioned body had gradually come to exist in Ireland. It is on that body and its precepts and examples that our hopes depend, for if we are at war with a nation we cannot win.[135]

Gladstone's apparently absurdly unrealistic obsession with the hope of recruiting a non-sectarian body of special constables in Ireland to assist the forces of law and order must be seen in this light. Spencer, having passed Gladstone's theories on this subject on to Cowper on 19 October, added on the following day:

> The serious objections which I feel are that if you begin this, you might move the Orange feeling, and would either bring on a religious war or would confront the Orangemen if you refused their help which would probably be promptly given. The active support of Orangemen and Protestants is the ultimate resource of English rule in Ireland, but ought to be kept until every other card has been played.[136]

Forster's policy, likewise, was predicated upon no fond Gladstonian illusions of a non-sectarian special constabulary. In his reply to an earlier letter from Gladstone[137] he had already made clear to the premier his views on the matter:

> In the South and West we cannot get them and in the North, Orangemen would offer themselves, and we should probably have to put a policeman on the side of every S[pecial] C[onstable] to keep them in order.

Although Forster obviously sought to win the middle ground away from Parnell, he had a grasp of the full extent of the government's unpopularity and cautioned Gladstone against exaggerated hopes.[138]

Gladstone, for his part, felt that Forster was less than scrupulous in his operation of the coercion policy. The case of Dr Kenny, who was dismissed from his post as a medical officer with a Poor Law union as well as being interned, was rectified by the premier himself. He later claimed—however unjustly—that Forster felt he was 'entitled to use the powers given by the Act as *a point of departure* from which to set out in the exercise of arbitrary powers [my italics]'.[139] Naturally Gladstone's distaste for the illiberal policy of repression increased throughout 1882 as the full extent of Irish opposition became clear and as this policy, which appeared to be leading nowhere, became more and more politically unpopular. Resistance to rent payment had been defeated, and therefore the government had done its duty to preserve the social order. When Parnell made known his changed views and the Irish Party in parliament obviously accepted the Land Act, it would have been impossible to keep him in jail any longer.

On this basis the so-called 'Kilmainham Treaty' was arrived at. The understanding was that the government would release the prisoners, would deal with the question of arrears of rent in a manner satisfactory to the tenants, and would amend the Land Act of 1881 in certain ways, in particular by extending the benefit of its fair-rent clauses to leaseholders. In return, Parnell undertook to use his influence against intimidation and outrage in Ireland. If the Land Act was suitably altered, this would, he claimed, be perceived by the country as a practical settlement of the land question and would enable the Irish Party (in a phrase that was to cause trouble) 'to co-operate cordially for the future with the Liberal Party in forwarding Liberal principles and measures of general reform'.[140]

Formally this was a Parnellite surrender rather than a bargain. But in the changed circumstances of May 1882 Parnell lost nothing by it, for 'no rent' was a proven failure. Jennie Wyse Power claimed that the Ladies' Land League received definite official instructions from the demoralised leadership in Kilmainham to drop the 'no rent' call some time before the negotiations began. Parnell's letters to Katharine O'Shea (always an influence for moderation) reveal his determination to gain his release. The Ladies ignored the instructions, which at least left Parnell with a bargaining counter—although it was no more than that, for everyone in the League leadership knew by early 1882 that 'no rent' had failed to win mass support.[141]

For the agrarian radicals the 'Kilmainham Treaty' was a com-

promise of a basic principle.[142] For Davitt the Arrears Act which
followed was a 'curse',[143] despite the fact that the state paid
£800,000 rent for 130,000 tenants. In his view the spirit and meaning
of the Land Act condemned as legal robbery the extraction of rents
from land reclaimed entirely by the occupants' labour, and a recognition of arrears thus contracted was a surrender of the principle
fought for in the Healy clause.[144] If the League had maintained its
strength and resolution, such unfortunate people would never have
been evicted wholesale. But, although Davitt did not admit it, there
were few who believed that the Land League was capable in May
1882 of any such effort. In his view the murder of Cavendish and
Burke by the Invincibles on 6 May 1882 came as a 'cyclonic
sensation' which saved 'Mr Parnell from the perils which lurked
in the terms of the compact'.[145]

The political rationale for the 'Kilmainham Treaty' was obvious,
and it was supported by even such a militant as John Devoy. 'The
second of May 1882 will rank henceforth among the most memorable dates in Irish history,' he wrote in the *Irish Nation*. 'To future
generations it will mark the turning-point in the tide of adversity
against which Irish courage and constancy have been so long . . .
struggling.'[146] The resignation of Forster, more than any other single
factor, gave the 'treaty' credibility among nationalists.

While the 'Kilmainham Treaty' was regarded as being politically
justifiable, Parnell's offer of co-operation with the Liberals—the
admission of which was wrung out of him by Forster in a famous
House of Commons scene on 15 May 1882—radically affected its
ideological justification. The essence of Parnellism was the militant
assertion of nationalist principle (for example, support for the
morality of armed insurrection) combined with numerous tactical
compromises due to the unfavourable balance of forces. While it
was possible to get across the idea that such compromises were
unavoidable, and even desirable, in the long-term interests of the
nationalist movement, the offer of co-operation with the Liberals
appeared as a gratuitous compromise of the very basis of that
movement. Parnell made this error under considerable pressure
from Captain O'Shea. As far as Parnell's general conduct of the
nationalist movement was concerned, the error was the exception
that proved the rule.[147]

10

Conclusion:
People's War[1] or Historical Regression?

> Departure it was, but for where? It went back deep into the primitivism of peasant Ireland. . . . The Land League was not a movement for land reform, it was a wholesale crusade for the establishment of a peasant Ireland. As such it was not—despite Davitt's personal advocacy of land nationalisation—a forward-looking socialist solution to the problem of Irish freedom and identity, it was a backward-looking peasant solution. The Land League marked the popular beginnings of that massive fit of historical introspection which achieved cultural respectability in the Gaelic revival.
>
> PATRICK O'FARRELL, *Ireland's English Question* (1971)

> The absence of a strong populist or peasantist streak distinguishes Land League ideology from that of most other European rural movements. The League . . . rarely indulged in glorification of arcadian virtues. . . . [It] fostered few fond *narodnik* illusions about the intrinsic virtues of rural life. . . . It was not Land League but landlord spokesmen who romanticised pre-industrial society.
>
> JOSEPH LEE, *The Modernisation of Irish Society, 1848–1918* (1973)

In a three-year period the mass of the Irish tenantry had engaged in a struggle culminating in a measure of land reform which drastically reduced the power of the Irish landlord class. The political, ideological and economic effects of this process were of some complexity, and it is not possible to summarise them under a single rubric, whether it sees the movement in terms of a strengthening of an anti-urban,[2] specifically Catholic, backward-looking peasantism[3] or as part of the process of 'modernisation'.[4]

It is a mistake to inflate the purely Catholic determination of the land war.[5] The struggle of Catholic peasants against a largely Protestant landlord class and a Protestant British government must have a certain sectarian colouring. It is as easy to see this as it was for a Mayo peasant to jokingly mispronounce the name of the unpopular Chief Secretary Lowther as 'Luther'. The view of eviction as part of a Protestant plot to depopulate Catholic Ireland certainly existed, but it did not play a very significant role. It was subordinate to the secular/social analysis of the crisis of the

Irish tenantry,[6] and it was given no encouragement by a Land League leadership which had other priorities—as was made clear, for example, in the attempt in the summer of 1881 to reduce sectarian tension in Ulster.[7]

The critique of the transition to pasture and of its linked effects of consolidation and emigration may have been exaggerated. The fact that anti-nationalists also held it means that it cannot be dismissed as yet another nationalist myth. Nevertheless, the consensus of commentators both inside and outside the nationalist camp that—even in terms of the increase of livestock numbers— the transition had failed may have been too harsh. Perhaps even the Irish agricultural technocrats had a utopian notion of what could be achieved by a 'good mixed system' in Ireland. Certainly one of the commentators in this tradition, Karl Marx, implied that the mixed system on its own would not be an answer to the Irish social question. National independence and protective tariffs against England were also parts of the remedy. However, although this critique has also a certain 'social/national' component to it (a particular sympathy for the 'reclamation' tenantry, bitter resentments against absenteeism, and the historical experience of confiscation), it certainly cannot be described as a religious/sectarian world-view.

This fact reveals the dangers of projecting the sectarianism of the 1970s back into the 1870s. In general what is significant about the Irish land war as compared with other Catholic peasant nationalist movements in Europe is the relative insignificance of conflict over religious and cultural factors. This can be seen most clearly when the attitude of the Protestant Ulster tenantry to the land war is examined.

Beyond any doubt the Protestant Ulster tenantry were not terrified by the Land League as some rather far-fetched accounts have it. It is no surprise to find that 'local resistance' to Land League incursions required to be supplemented by trainloads of imported Orangemen.[8] Indeed, far from being terrified by the Land League, Ulster tenants exploited it. As their political representatives told Gladstone in December 1880, 'Any hesitation to deal with the question in a broad and liberal spirit would cause the present constitutional agitation in Ulster to assume a very serious aspect.'[9] In other words, they made their loyalty conditional on a good measure of land reform.

On the other hand, it is also difficult to portray the conflict as one essentially between a landlord class wrapped in rural obscurantism and a modernising peasant class.[10] The position of both sides contains much that—from the point of view of capitalist agriculture

—may be said to be obscurantist. The landlords exaggerated both the dangers of peasant proprietorship[11] and their own contribution to the efficiency of Irish agriculture.[12] The tenants opposed even the most necessary consolidation; but so, in the West of Ireland, did some of the landlords.

But this very obscurantism was simply part of the rhetoric of the clash between two social systems (and implicitly two political systems). It is very clear that both systems, an Ireland with or without landlords, with or without the British link, were variants of capitalist agriculture. However, the 'modernisation' thesis has the merit of emphasising the Land League's role in destroying some of the characteristic inequalities and relationships of deference in Irish rural society.[13]

Even so, it should be added that the Land League's radical scheme for a major transformation of social relationships in Irish agriculture was disappointed. The critique of consolidation and transition to pasture which had informed so many in the movement did not lead to any major reorganisation of Irish agriculture. Gladstone, although sympathetic to opposition to consolidation, explicitly declared his Land Act to be neutral on this point, concluding: 'It is a question, undoubtedly, of public policy; but it is one we cannot see our way to taking out of the hands of those entitled by law to adopt the measures they think requisite for the management of their own property.'[14] The radicals felt they had lost because the correct form of class struggle—a genuine 'no rent' call—had not been adopted at the right moment. Instead the disastrous 'rent at the point of the bayonet' policy had held sway. This is not a problem which can simply be analysed in terms of a betrayal by a 'middle-class leadership'.[15] The leadership of Parnell and others undoubtedly played a certain role in damping down militancy. Arguably such an activity served to protract a mutually unsatisfactory relationship between England and Ireland.[16] But the policies of the leadership can only be understood by reference to the nature of the Land League as a mass movement and, therefore, to the forms of struggle which it produced.

It has been a major object of this work to analyse these forms of struggle. In the analysis of rural class conflict many urban observers have been led astray by the seductive appeal of vivid and dramatic images. They appear to gesture towards an all too easily accessible 'concrete reality' of agrarian class struggle. However, the mechanisms of such a struggle can, in fact, only be constructed by means of a more circumspect and elaborate analysis. In other words, the straightforward description of that which is apparently most striking and visible often produces an extremely misleading account.[17] The powerful images of the Land League conflict are well known. One school stresses the role of rural terrorism, the opposing school the militant consensus of a 'risen people'. Most writers offer a more or less judicious mixture of what are fundamentally two competing interpretations. A typical example is to be found in Máire and Conor Cruise O'Brien's *A Concise History of Ireland:*

> There can be little doubt that intimidation—whether deplored or ordered by the leadership—was a significant element in the social reality of the Land League movement. . . . But what those who emphasised intimidation overlooked, or ignored, was that the Land League would have had no power to intimidate dissidents had it not possessed overwhelming rural support.[18]

Although both interpretations are basically opposed, they share the characteristic of being in thrall to superficially revealing, highly charged notions.

On the one hand are those accounts (often generally unsympathetic to the agitation) which emphasise the role of violent intimidation of landlords, landlords' agents and peasants who opposed the Land League's will. We are presented with a catalogue of shootings, mutilations and burnings. The role of agrarian violence (and its relationship to the progress of parliamentary nationalism) has been seen by one recent writer in this camp as one of the key suppressed problems in nationalist historiography.[19] All that may be said here on this topic is that violent intimidation was, of course, a significant component of the peasant struggle. However, on its own in the pre-Land League period it had never achieved more than a relatively limited success, and in the 1879–82 period itself murderous violence greatly increased in significance *after* the suppression of the League—in other words, in the absence of the characteristic Land League forms of struggle.

On the other hand are the accounts (often sympathetic to the agitation) which emphasise the supposed unity of the popular movement. One such account deserves quotation because it expresses this view in its essentials :

> An elaborate system of moral-force warfare was developed : process-serving and evictions were made the occasion of great popular demonstrations; families evicted for non-payment of rent were sheltered and supported; and an embargo was placed on evicted farms; persons involved in prosecutions because of their League activities were defended, and families of those sent

to prison were cared for; and the terrible weapon of social ostracism, the boycott, was perfected as the ultimate sanction of the League against those who violated its code.[20]

This account is perfectly true in the sense that all these developments actually happened. Nevertheless, it does not give an accurate description of how the struggle for the land operated. It falls victim to certain basic misconceptions which may be stated briefly. It overstates the capacity of the spontaneous solidarity of the peasantry to sweep all before them. It fails to ask the necessary questions about the effectiveness of different modes of struggle; it does not even properly identify all these modes.

It has been argued in the present work that the most important forms of struggle were different varieties of highly legalistic strategies. To take the themes of mass resistance to process-servers and succour for the evicted: Balla, Co. Mayo, in November 1879 saw one of the most tense cases of crowd opposition to eviction, followed a month later, it should be noted, by a successful eviction, after which the tenant immediately received financial aid from the Land League. Far from being seen as an example of the successful working of the League, the case provoked an acute crisis. The League had failed to be effective and merely lost money. The crisis was only resolved by new forms of struggle which involved large-scale intervention in the Connaught law courts in defence of the interests of the smallholders.

But what of the 'ultimate sanction'—the boycott? N. D. Palmer had claimed it as 'the most powerful weapon'[21] of the League, and this contention is repeatedly to be found in other writings on the Land League, even in works which imply a certain limitation to the power of the boycott.[22] 'The League's . . . chief weapon was the boycotting of rack-renters and land-grabbers,' wrote T. N. Brown in a typical phrase.[23] There is no doubt that the boycott did play a significant role, particularly as one of the methods of isolating backsliding tenants. In a more general sense the refusal to provide police with cars and other such actions are obviously part of the boycott tactic. But the 'boycott system', in so far as it operated in the main sense used by historians, appears to presuppose a landlord attack of some sort to which it was a response. To this extent it has fitted neatly with the traditional conception of the Land League as a *defensive* movement. This view is exemplified by Máire and Conor Cruise O'Brien:

> Its policy was to select estates especially notorious for rack-renting and eviction, concentrate public attention on those estates by means of mass meetings; and then by pressure of social

ostracism and refusal of services render life as difficult as possible for the landlord (if resident), and especially for grabbers—those who rented land from which the tenant had been evicted and which the League had placed under a ban.[24]

In fact, as my argument has attempted to show, the Land League was something very different: an *offensive* movement. During the crucial period of the Land League's offensive advance in 1880 the boycott played a minimal role in large areas of the country. It could only have played a larger role if there had been more eviction than the peasantry in many key areas were prepared to tolerate. It is impossible to estimate with total accuracy the role of the boycott, as we cannot know how many landlords were deterred from eviction or sale of an interest by its existence. Nevertheless, there is one significant fact to be noted. Despite its prominence in the rhetoric of this period—W. E. Forster was mesmerised by it—Bernard Becker, the journalist who had done most to bring the boycott to popular attention, was at the end of 1880 regarding it merely as a novelty whose full limitations were just beginning to appear.[25]

In reality, the *dominant* strategy was one which the textbook accounts have almost entirely omitted. It is now long overdue that its importance should be stressed. This strategy was denoted by the slogan 'rent at the point of the bayonet'. What this meant was that the peasantry delayed the payment of rent until the last possible moment, then paid the rent while the Land League defrayed the often hefty legal costs incurred by the delay. It is an incidental but important fact that it was here, rather than in financing outrage, where the Land League's Irish-American dollars found their most significant use. (The theory of massive League sponsorship of outrage first received widespread currency as a result of the obsessions of the Special Commission in 1888.) The low-risk nature of the strategy was, of course, objectively in the interests of the more substantial tenantry. But this very fact, plus also the high financial cost for the organisation, made it unpopular with sections of the poorer tenantry and the agricultural proletariat. It is the conflict around the validity and political nature of this policy which, in conjunction with the better-known coercion–concession dialectic, punctuated the rhythm of the land war in the crucial period from February to October 1881.

The boycott conception tells us only of the unity of the peasantry. In other words, the boycott image is perhaps even more misleading than that of mass resistance to process-servers. It presents us with a vision of the 'alien' landlord *excluded* by the intense unity of the

homogeneous peasantry, whose principal tactic might therefore be
seen as a precursor of the exclusive practices of the Gaelic Athletic
Association; this view is concisely expressed by Conor Cruise
O'Brien:

> I do not know that it has been remarked that the GAA, in effect,
> carried into what might very broadly be called the cultural field
> the great principle which had brought the Land League victory
> in the agrarian struggle: the principle of the boycott.[26]

The power of this image misled even James Connolly, who had
produced an unusually sharp appreciation of the Land League's
place in Irish history.[27]

The history of 'rent at the point of the bayonet', on the other
hand, points to the class struggle within the peasantry that was such
an important part of the League experience. 'Rent at the point of
the bayonet' was the critical price the League leadership had to pay
to win the allegiance of the rural bourgeoisie in the crucial phase of
the League's expansion in the late summer and autumn of 1880.
The problems of this period are suppressed by N. D. Palmer's
exaggeration of the role of the boycott and his economic catastroph-
ism; he even went so far as to claim that at the beginning of June
1880 'thousands of the Irish people were threatened with actual
starvation and the agitation was increasing daily in violence and
strength'.[28] This assumes a much too simple relation between the
progress of the agitation and the role of distress. The Land League
was above all a class alliance of the rural bourgeoisie, the middle
and poor peasantry, and the agricultural proletariat: one of the
most remarkable things about the League is the way in which its
different sections pushed in different directions. The large and
middle farmers were looking for rent reductions, the smallholders
of the West were looking for a land redistribution,* while the
labourers of the South were contemplating at least a general strike
for better wages. Nevertheless, it would be foolish to deny that
despite these differences there was an overall anti-landlord unity.
While accepting this, I do not accept Sam Clark's view that 'there
were no serious class divisions within the movement'.[29] The history
of the Land League is to a very large extent the history of the
relationship of these forces in their contradictory unity during a
vital phase of the Irish nationalist struggle against landlords and

---

* It is clear that it is justified to insist on the greater militancy of
aspiration of the smaller farmers. However, it should perhaps also be
stressed that they too were often reluctant to take the risks which the
League militants suggested were necessary in pursuit of these aspirations.

British government. This analysis helps to explain why the Land League should eventually have culminated in a compromise with the British government, despite the fact that (in Connolly's later words) it brought 'a political revolution within the grasp of the agitators'.[30]

It would be wrong to ignore the Land League's positive achievement. The 'three Fs' granted by the 1881 Land Act were a decided benefit. L. P. Curtis has noted: 'Although the act did not safeguard the tenants against eviction and rack-rents in any final sense, the land and county courts together fixed over 150,000 "fair rents" in the first three years of operation, with reductions averaging twenty per cent.' Perhaps more important, after some years' trial it became clear that reform of the landlord system along the lines of dual ownership was far from being radical enough to meet the problem. Conservatives as well as Liberals and Nationalists moved over to the peasant proprietorship solution.[31]

But it would be equally wrong to ignore the League's area of failure. This was most evident in the West of Ireland, where many of the most pressing social problems remained. As the agitation faded Forster noted: 'The poor cottier tenants are beginning to see that their only hope is emigration.'[32] In an attempt to draw attention to this fact, James Daly tried to revive a campaign for the breaking up of the grasslands in 1883. The *Connaught* newspaper editor insisted that this was the real answer to the problem of emigration. He criticised the Baldwin scheme for the reclamation of waste lands as a diversion.[33] Parnell had, of course, effectively associated himself with Baldwin in the claim that 100,000 families could be migrated onto improved lands.[34] A year after his comments on the Baldwin scheme Daly noted:

> Mr Parnell and his so-called party of action promised to see that a migration scheme would be adopted. How have they carried out their theory? They have done it faithfully and well to suit their own ends. They have started out companies in order to swell their private exchequers.[35]

William O'Brien, however, was one Parnellite lieutenant who did take some note of this sentiment in the West. In 1884 O'Brien attempted to inaugurate the National League in Mayo. Daly predictably described the meeting as 'abortive', and the *Irish Times* estimated the attendance at a paltry 300, while the sympathetic *Ballina Herald* commented: 'The enthusiasm of the Land League meetings are nowhere to be noted.'[36] O'Brien later admitted to the Special Commission that the meeting had indeed been a failure.[37] Nevertheless, O'Brien's visit to Mayo does seem to have reaffirmed his interest in the peculiar problems of Western smallholders which was to play such an important part in the later United Irish League.[38] But, as Daly bitterly noted, the small tenants of the West had already begun to 'solve' their social problem by the high rate of emigration in the area which dates from this period.[39]

It was not only in a social sense that the Land League was a disappointment to some of its founders and followers. There was also a major blow for political aspirations. It has not been an easy task for historians to reconstruct the precise nature of the objectives of those involved.

There are two main trends of thought on the relationship between the land and national questions. The first stresses the virtual identity of the national and social question, at least up to the Land Acts of the 1880s. 'Les deux adversaires coincident: le landlord et l'anglais,' as the French scholar François Bedarida has noted.[40] In this view the content of the national question in Ireland was the land question. Any mass agitation against the landlords is, therefore, in effect, a mass agitation against the British link. The clear kernel of truth in this argument should not, however, be allowed to obscure the fact that the priorities of the movement for national independence (at least in the view of some of its leaders) were not always identical to those of the movement for agrarian reform. It should also be stressed that the way that the republican elites saw the tie-up of the land and national questions did change over time. In the period of classic Fenianism between 1858 and 1867 it was insisted that a radical solution of the land question must await the achievement of national independence. By the late 1870s what had been the *end* of the movement for national independence had become its *means*. The radical nature of this change should be underlined. It was the *sine qua non* of the Irish Land League.

The second main trend in interpretation sees Fenian involvement in the land struggle as growing more or less spontaneously out of an already established association with rural class conflict. Here the neo-Fenian involvement becomes a confused attempt to exacerbate existing sources of discontent. This view has been expressed by Robert Kee:

> In this traditional agrarian activism many rank-and-file Fenians of the New Departure school [took] part in the *rather blurred* conviction that they were in some way promoting the national uprising to which their original creed had been dedicated [my italics].[41]

In fact, as I have argued, far from having a blurred conviction, this group had a clearly defined political objective which informed their practice even after the agrarian distress of 1879 had modified their original plans. Those in the Fenian orbit felt strongly that as the British government would never grant the full demand of the land agitation—the abolition of landlordism—the land struggle would inevitably become at some stage a struggle for nationalist revolution with mass peasant backing. Parnell, it has been stressed, did not share this view. In fact, in a sense, his position was the polar opposite. A good measure of land reform (which he clearly believed it possible to extract from parliament) would end the agrarian social conflict and thereby bring the landlords into the nationalist ranks and thus greatly strengthen the demand for Home Rule.

Parnell's attitude therefore places him within the Buttite tradition in a very important sense. He wanted a unity of all the classes of Irish society, and this meant involving landlords in the Home Rule movement. He had, however, a fundamentally different premise from that of Butt. He accepted that, given the existence of a land struggle in Ireland, it would have to be settled—preferably at the British government's expense[42]—before an all-class nationalist alliance could be achieved. His sister Anna, writing of the landlords, noted scornfully: 'Unable by reason of their very small intelligence to comprehend the simple laws which regulate their own and the rest of the country's relationship with the British Empire, it was a rude awakening for them to find that all the power of the machine could not, or would not, any longer help them to raise their rents.'[43] But she added:

> It will be seen that the design of the Land League was not as it has generally been taken to be . . . hostile to the interests of the landlords as a class, in spite of the excited rhetoric used by Land League speakers. And if the programme I have described had been carried out successfully, an enormous number of this class, including the holders of mortgages . . . would have been saved who have now been ruined. It is a matter of fact the Land League did point [this] out to them.[44]

Parnell's hopes in this respect suffered a setback with the increase in outrage of which Davitt informed him at the turn of 1880–81[45] and which did so much to alienate the landlords. In this context—and also, of course, in the context of a substantial although theoretically unsatisfactory land reform—he was ready to compromise. After 1882 and the 'Kilmainham Treaty' Parnell's new movement had the clergy and the 'right centre' ensconced in a particularly strong position. It is even quite possible that his alliance with the Conservatives in 1885 has to be seen at least partly in the light of his stated views and, therefore, as a 'package' making it easier for the landlords to accept a Home Rule Ireland.[46]

It is most likely that Parnell's position represented a double rationalisation. Firstly, it was the rationalisation of the nationalist but still conservative product of the Protestant squirearchy. It posited a day of reconciliation with his class. (A recent study of his personal background has noted that 'Even with regard to Parnell himself, a certain class solidarity [with the landlords] remained.')[47] With the benefit of hindsight such a view may appear naïve and sentimental: the Irish leader apparently thought that omelettes *could* be made without breaking eggs. Nevertheless, he stated it in so many private and public places that it is impossible to regard it as, say, a ploy to convince the Liberal cabinet of his essential moderation. The cabinet remained unconvinced until the spring of 1882, and the change of heart then was due to other factors. Secondly, and very much more importantly, it represented the rationalisation of Parnell's political will to lead the land agitation— an agitation which its other potential leaders (in 1879 they were F. H. O'Donnell and P. J. Smyth) had dismissed as a blind alley from the nationalist point of view. For Parnell, at least, the land question played a vital role in the strategy of nationalism. By taking up such a position he was able to seize the leadership at the vital moment. He did at least agree with the neo-Fenians that the land question was the key to the national question, but at the same time he remained, as he wanted, firmly within the sphere of constitution-alism. He retained a fundamental freedom of manoeuvre without becoming a mundane parliamentary land reformer. At one point he insisted that parliament could potentially grant such a major measure of land reform as to end Irish agrarian social conflict. At another point he claimed that such a result would increase class unity and make Irish nationalism irresistible. It was a unique com-bination: Parnell's ability to lead both nationalist revolutionary and constitutionalist was not based (so far as his political practice played a role) simply on demagoguery or even adeptness at revolutionary 'cape-work'. It was based on the fact that he combined both elements in his political personality. This positive (if incoherent) assessment of the relationship between land and nationality on the part of a major constitutional leader was also a *sine qua non* of the Land League.

Even in retreat, as William O'Brien has pointed out, he was thus able to pose simultaneously as a conservative and a revolutionary.[48] Of course, it is true that the importance of this personal ideology of Parnell's is strictly limited, that in day-to-day politics he responded to the balance of forces at any given moment. But this very responsiveness had to be taken in conjunction with his ideological concessions to neo-Fenianism, including not only his apparently revolutionary demands for land reform but also a certain militant nationalistic tone. It was thus possible for contemporaries—and this includes the important moderate nationalist *Freeman's Journal* as well as embittered landlord partisans—to see him as much more entangled in Fenian projects than, in fact, he was. Recent scholarship has indeed done well to stress the ultimate difference of position of Parnell and that of his neo-Fenian allies;[49] where it has been less successful is in demonstrating how the illusion that Parnell was basically a Fenian protégé developed to the extent that it was held by relatively sober observers, Home Rulers as well as Conservatives and Liberals.

There were, of course, many activists in the land agitation who did not hold either the Parnellite view or the neo-Fenian view of the relationship between the land and the national questions. There were some whose objectives were purely to improve the economic position of the Irish peasantry. There were others—J. J. O'Kelly is a prime example—who began with Fenian objectives and who moved towards this later more timid position. There were some who oscillated back and forth. But this much is certain: the history of the Land League, the Parnell–neo-Fenian alliance and the reaction to it cannot be written without placing substantial emphasis on the existence of a relatively elaborate and definite neo-Fenian strategy. It is only then that certain events, for example the controversy over the Land League's apparently revolutionary programme in April and May 1880, emerge with their full meaning clarified.

The picture of Parnell that is advanced in the present study is not the usual one. He does not appear as a major political strategist. He was wrong about the most important strategic problem in Irish politics—the land question and national question nexus. In fact the much-vaunted enigma of Parnell lies in the fact that it was possible for him to be so wrong about such a major question and for it not to matter greatly.

The true significance of Parnell lies in his role as a catalyst in the movement which he led. He held neo-Fenians and moderate Home Rulers together for long enough in the period 1879–82 to have reduced their mutual antagonisms. Both sides had suffered a specific defeat. The moderates had had to sanction a platform of peasant proprietorship, with national independence in the background. On the other hand, the militants had never been able to achieve a level of struggle of the necessary intensity and had had to accept, despite the adoption of a formal programme of peasant proprietorship, a compromise settlement. By 1882 such questions had a historical interest, but they were no longer matters of political contention. The inevitable result was the integration of these ex-Fenians (for example, James O'Kelly, who was 'tired, weary to death of playing roles,' as he wrote to John Devoy, 'of rolling impossible balls up impossible hills')[50] within conventional Parnellism.

O'Kelly was an early example of a trend the significance of which has rarely been fully grasped. It is a remarkable fact that, according to one RIC report marked 'very secret' of 1887, 21 out of 83 listed Parnellite MPs were believed to be probably Fenians, 4 were believed to be likely to support Fenian designs, while 2 were regarded as ex-Fenians.[51] This was bound to affect the ideological tone. Parnellism tended to insist (in a way that Buttism had not) that the Fenian ideal of armed insurrection was admirable, although, of course, utterly utopian. The insistence on the moral correctness of an obviously hopeless military struggle, combined with the experience of the practical worth of the agrarian class struggle, made Parnellism a qualitatively different political phenomenon.

This new tone in Irish politics was part of the reason why John Devoy regarded the Land League as a major step forward. The struggle for him had been a nationalist one because the landlords were a source of anti-national influence supported in the last instance by British bayonets. Perhaps also Devoy saw that with the decisive step taken in 1881 to abandon the landlord class Britain had greatly weakened its moral hold on Ireland. Patrick O'Farrell has well expressed this point: 'The eventual repudiation by Britain of support for the reactionary landed elite placed Britain in the position of having both tolerated and continued unsettlement of the Irish peasantry and then having refused to maintain the structure which both provoked and contained that unsettlement.'[52]

There was also the 'microcosm of independence' theory, which enjoyed a certain popularity at the time. It was expected that the Irish tenant, freed from his relationship with his repressive landlord, would show the sturdy characteristics of the independent man, including, naturally, a more ardent commitment to the cause of Ireland. Matthew Harris was rather sceptical on this point.

> I took the chance of the movement [Harris explained before the Special Commission], but I was rather inclined to think that so far from assisting in bringing about the independence of Ireland, that it would have the opposite effect; that when the farmers would be emancipated and get their lands, such men would look on the boundary of their farms as the boundary of their country, because farmers as a rule are very selfish men.[53]

This was the assumption, of course, which lay behind much of later Conservative policy in Ireland. F. H. O'Donnell in his *History of the Irish Parliamentary Party* (1910) devoted considerable space to demonstrating the disappointment of the specifically nationalist hopes of the Land League leaders.[54] Admittedly it was perfectly true that the 'solution' of the land question did not prevent the eventual victory of the forces of political nationalism.[55] But O'Donnell's comment does hit—however blindly—on a decisive point. One particular possible connection between the land question and the national question had been destroyed.

Devoy had hoped that the struggle for a peasant proprietary would inevitably lead to independence for Ireland, for only an independent Irish parliament would take the step of smashing landlordism. The movement had, however, been defused by Gladstone's Land Act. The conditions for a withdrawal from Westminster of Irish MPs to set up an Irish parliament with massive peasant support no longer existed. The Land Act had detached a sufficient number of Leaguers to make the project impossible. Davitt quickly accepted the implications of this fact and decided that, as there was nothing politically at stake, measures of land reform should be argued solely on their economic and social merits. As he said in his subsequent advocacy of land nationalisation, to allow the British government to become owner or steward of Irish land was no more anti-national than paying its taxes or calling upon it to advance the necessary funds for carrying out a scheme of peasant proprietorship.

In his first response to Davitt, John Devoy declared that although there was a great deal in the abstract to be said for such a scheme, he suspected that in practice it might prove as great a failure as Owenism. The slogan of 'a peasant proprietary' had emerged in triumph from the struggle.[56] He soon deepened his opposition to land nationalisation *per se,* claiming that the details of the scheme would not bear 'even cursory examination'.[57] But there is no doubt that his basic objection had its root in nationalist politics. He would not have the Irish farmers transformed into tenants in perpetuity to a foreign and hostile nation.[58] As Devoy noted, 'He [Davitt] said he preferred to have this done through an Irish parliament but even under the existing government he would prefer it to all other settlements of the land question.'[59] Davitt completed the breach by refusing to make his American tour of 1882 'under the guidance of the Nationalists'.[60] Even the *Roscommon Herald,* the most radical Irish provincial journal, although initially sympathetic to Davitt, dropped him angrily when it perceived the anti-national implications. This newspaper's censure, which appeared only two weeks after it had praised a pro-nationalisation address by Davitt as 'brilliant', is worth quoting in full:

> The pith of the nationalisation scheme is to make the English government the landlord of the Irish soil, and to transfer all taxes from the shoulders of the professional and other classes to the heavily weighted backs of the tenant farmers. It is rather inconsistent that the men who coolly propose that all rent for land should be paid to the British Exchequer are the very persons who have been preaching that rent was a blasphemy. Since according to their plans it is the government alone should levy rent, it follows that we must have Government agents to collect it and Government bailiffs to warn for it. And in plain language what they mean by the 'total abolition of landlordism' is the substitution of a hoard of English officials for the present race of landlords and their chieftains. Instead of the nationalisation of Ireland it would be the denationalisation of Ireland, and instead of rooting the Irish people in the soil, they would be consolidating and strengthening British rule in this country. One of the chief merits of peasant proprietary is that it effectively staunches the gaping wound created by absenteeism, and ensures that the money raised in the country will be spent in the country. . . . If we nationalise the land as proposed by Davitt and the *Irish World* . . . we will merely substitute a State rent for a landlord rent.[61]

As an epilogue, it may be noted that from this moment onwards creative reflection on the relationship between the Irish land and national questions became very much the concern of British politicians. Much has been written about the crude economic determinism of Conservative government ministers in Ireland. But the Liberals also had their ideas. Earl Spencer argued in an important contribution to the Home Rule debate that a large scheme of land reform could only be safely carried by establishing simultaneously an Irish government in Dublin to act between the imperial government and the tenants.[62] Lord Thring's essay in the same volume gave a fuller exposition.[63] The Irish tenant was in the toils of an irrational attitude towards the land. There was very little that could be done about this save to sell him the land. But given such an action, the only way to ensure that the tenant did not default on his payment was to set up a parliament in Dublin to which he would pay his debt rather than to an alien British government at Westminster.[64]

Such a concept had its origins in Gladstone's response to the Cavendish–Welby memoranda of 1882 when the premier had suggested that any land purchase scheme should be tied to a strengthening of the institutions of Irish local government lest it lead to even greater social demoralisation in Ireland.[65] This project had the advantage not only of giving the British government an apparent guarantee but also—as Charles Russell pointed out in a letter to Gladstone—of giving Ulster Protestant tenants an inducement to support Home Rule. No Home Rule, no generous land purchase scheme—so the argument ran.[66] In defeat, Gladstone explained to his colleagues that it was necessary to reconsider the proposed relationship between the land and Home Rule bills which was over-generous to Irish conservatism.[67] But the sophistication of the project ought to be noted.

To counter it Chamberlain produced a plan to achieve peasant proprietorship 'through Irish resources', with the transfer being carried out by the local authorities. This major effort to maintain Ulster Protestant unity by convincing the Protestant tenantry that agrarian radicalism was by no means incompatible with Unionism was gratefully welcomed by the spokesmen of Ulster Liberal Unionism.[68] It is significant that Chamberlain claimed that it was the anti-Unionist forces who were cynically blocking his proposal. Speculation about the connection between the land and national questions was now carried on in circles very different from those of the Irish revolutionary groups who had first brought the matter onto the political stage in the 1860s.

Appendices

1. TECHNICAL TERMS

Conacre

This term applied to a form of holding, varying from half a rood (a quarter of an acre) to two acres in size, rented from the farmer or landlord to grow potatoes (or less commonly oats) for one season. Conacre land was usually taken by those of labourer or near-labourer status, although it was sometimes taken by tradesmen and small farmers. Its main importance is in the social history of pre-famine Ireland, but it is still to be found in certain areas in the 1880s.

Cottier

Michael Beames has pointed out that this term has, in fact, three quite distinct usages in pre-famine Ireland.[1] In the counties of Clare, Limerick, Kerry, Tipperary, Waterford and parts of King's County it meant an occupier of a smallholding of up to about ten acres of land. In these areas the term has no connotations with labourer status; the cottier held land enough, or almost enough, to employ his own labour, and he paid his rent in cash. Secondly, in parts of Ulster and Leinster and in most of Connaught the term 'cottier' did apply primarily to one who paid all or part of his rent by labour services. In its third usage the term denoted simply the occupier of a cabin, without any reference to the size of the attached land. This usage was to be found in the counties of Dublin, Louth, Meath, Armagh, Down and Cavan. In post-famine Ireland, however, the term seems to have been used simply as a synonym for 'small-holder'.

2. LAND LEGISLATION, 1860–85

Landlord and Tenant Law Amendment (Ireland) Act, 1860

Deasy's Act (as it was generally known) was passed 'at a time when Irish parliamentary representation stood indeed at a very low and discreditable ebb'. It was based on the view that land is the exclusive property of the landlord, and that the tenant's interest is simply that of an individual who has agreed to pay a certain remuneration for the use of the land for a limited period. The act also increased facilities in the matter of proceedings in ejectment and made more stringent the law of ejectment for non-payment of rent and on notice to quit.

Landlord and Tenant (Ireland) Act, 1870

In 1869 Gladstone perceived the demand of Irish land reformers to be for fixity of tenure. He was largely sympathetic with what he took to be the Irish view. As E. D. Steele has put it, 'Celtic society could not be restored but the morality of its conquest was a live issue.'[2] In Gladstone's own words, 'What the Irishman may think with great semblance and perhaps with the full reality of historic truth is this: that, without at all questioning the landlord's title, he too had by the old customs of the country his share in a tribal property which, however rude in adjustment, gave a right to him and his race to remain upon the soil.'[3]

In the political circumstances of the day a land reform embodying the principle of fixity of tenure implied by such a statement was impossible. However, in the autumn of 1869 Gladstone took up the position that the legalisation of the Ulster custom in the North and its simulation in the South were the best available means to this end. (The Ulster custom is usually defined as giving fixity of tenure at fair rents and allowing the outgoing tenant free sale—in other words, the 'three Fs'.)

Eversley's *Agrarian Tenures* gives what has been regarded as a good short description of the act:

> This Act legalised the Customs of Ulster and any like custom in other parts of Ireland, and gave to tenants who held under them, the protection of the law. It then proceeded to enact for the rest of Ireland a somewhat analogous system. It reversed the presumption of law that improvements belong to the owner of the land and secured both past and present improvements to the tenants, and enabled them to claim compensation for them on the determination of their tenancies. It laid down a further scale of compensation in respect of holdings valued at less than £10 a year to less amounts for larger holdings, payable beyond the value of improvements on eviction for any other cause than non-payment of rent.[4]

To this account J. L. Hammond made two additions. In certain cases (for holdings valued at £15 or less)[5] ejection for non-payment might be characterised as disturbance and compensation might therefore be claimed. It has been shown in the present study that this provision played an important part in the land war, especially in Connaught in the early part of 1880. Moreover, the act contained what were commonly known as the Bright clauses, whose purpose was to aid and encourage the conversion of tenants into owners. These allowed the Treasury to advance two-thirds of the purchase money on the sale of any holding to its tenant, repayable by equal annual instalments, and interest spread over twenty-five years at the rate of £5 for every £100 advanced. On these terms the advance of peasant proprietorship made very little headway indeed in the Ireland of the 1870s.[6]

As Kolbert and O'Brien conclude, 'Although the 1870 Land Act failed, it was an important enactment inasmuch as it was the precursor of the great remedial measures on behalf of the tenants which were to follow. By making the landlord pay some compensation, at any rate, to the tenant for improvements and disturbance, it prepared the way for the system of dual ownership that the second Gladstone Act was to establish.'[7] It is, however, widely agreed that the 1870 Land Act was irrelevant to economic and social conditions in Ireland at the time. This is accepted by historians who appear to be largely sympathetic[8] to Gladstone's measure of reform as well as by those who are largely unsympathetic.[9]

Land Law (Ireland) Act, 1881

Gladstone's second Land Act was a far more substantial reform than that of 1870. This, of course, reflected the militancy of the mass agitation organised by the Land League. The act of 1881 legalised the 'three Fs'. This meant that the tenant was guaranteed by law

(1) a *fair rent* on his holding fixed by an independent tribunal;

(2) *fixity of tenure* in his holding so long as he paid his rent and observed his covenants;

(3) the *free sale* of his interest in his holding.

Clearly the granting of the 'three Fs' amounted to the recognition of the principle of dual ownership of land. The act, however, went even further. It forced the landlord to compensate the tenant fully for disturbance in the occupancy and for any improvements he may have effected on his holding.

One of the most important provisions of the act was the creation of an Irish Land Commission to deal with applications for fair rents.

The practical benefits resulting from the act were considerable. During the period of over four decades in which its fair-rent provisions were in force they greatly improved the lot of the Irish tenant. In the twenty-six counties which constitute the modern Republic some 275,000 original rents were reduced by about 21 per cent. Some 93,000 rents which had already been fixed for a first fifteen-year term were further reduced for a second fifteen-year term by about 18 per cent, and 3,000 second-term rents were reduced for a third term by 9 per cent. The act also played an important role in providing the impetus for further reforms in the direction of a peasant proprietorship solution.[10] The act's major shortcomings were the omission of leaseholders, meaning (in one estimate) that one-sixth of the Irish tenantry were outside the benefit of the act,[11] absence of any special provision for smallholders,[12] and the unattractive purchase clauses.

The act gave the newly created Land Commission the power to make advances to tenants for the purchase of their holdings and enabled it to purchase land for resale to the tenants. The limit of advance was increased from two-thirds of the purchase money (as allowed by the act of 1870) to three-quarters. The terms of repayment were the same: an annuity of 5 per cent for thirty-five years, subsequently reduced by the Land Act of 1885 to 4 per cent for a forty-nine-year period. As in the case of the 1870 act, these purchase provisions remained almost unused.

Purchase of Land (Ireland) Act, 1885

After some years' trial it became clear that dual ownership as embodied in the 1881 act was not the basis for a settlement of the Irish land question. It came to be accepted by British Conservatives as well as by Liberals that the only answer was a peasant proprietary.

The terms of purchase under both the 1870 and 1881 acts required the tenant to produce a portion of his purchase money as a guarantee of his solvency. Furthermore, it was pointed out by many commentators that the short term of repayment involved a high rate of annuity. Gradually British parliamentary opinion began to see the need for a more ambitious policy. In 1882 a select committee of inquiry into the working of the Land Act of 1881 recommended a wider extension of voluntary land purchase and the lowering of annuities over a longer period of repayment.

The Ashbourne Land Act (as it was generally known) of 1885 embodied such views. In a period of twenty-five years since Deasy's Act the whole basis of Irish agrarian legislation had been overturned. After a period of flirtation with dual ownership, the Ashbourne Act marked a return to the principle of single ownership of land. This was the principle of Deasy's Act, but now there was a very important difference, for *the tenant, not the landlord, was now to be the sole owner.* Later Land Acts, including Balfour's Act of 1891 and Wyndham's Act of 1903, built upon this principle, allowing ever more generous terms to the tenantry.

*   *   *

The results of the Land Acts under the Union were remarkable. Over 316,000 holdings, comprising an area of over 11,000,000 acres, were purchased for some £100,000,000. Even so, the system remained in principle voluntary, and in some areas (for example, Co. Clare) the changeover was rather slower than in others, a fact which had definite implications for Irish politics. Thus, with the failure of the voluntary system to conclude the purchase of the land, a compulsory system began to receive considerable support. Following the setting up of an autonomous Irish government in Dublin, such a system came into effect in 1923.

3. BIOGRAPHICAL NOTES

The Land League gave certain men a brief but very real significance in Irish history. For other men it destroyed promising careers. The men who fall into either of these categories are not so well known as men like Parnell and Gladstone who played a significant role in Anglo-Irish relations both before and after the land war. Short biographical notes on some of these lesser-known figures are given below. Numerals in parentheses indicate ages in 1879.

Michael Boyton (32 or 33)
Boyton's Irish parents became naturalised Americans in 1860. He was educated by the Christian Brothers at Pittsburgh, Pennsylvania, and at St Francis's College, Loretto, Pennsylvania. The brother of Captain Paul Boyton, the well-known swimmer, Michael Boyton himself returned to Ireland in the fateful year of 1867.[13] He was an ardent nationalist and, not surprisingly, became one of the Land League's first organisers, playing a key role in Co. Tipperary. He shared with Joseph B. Walsh the distinction of being placed first in Forster's list of suspects and was swiftly interned.

At this point the significance of Boyton's American citizenship came into play. A strong campaign developed in America demanding that Boyton be rapidly released or charged. The Franciscans took 'great pleasure' in publicising their opinion that 'Michael Boyton was a very exemplary youth, gave evidence of a high standard of virtue and moral conduct; he was, indeed, a model student, and from his ennobling qualities of head and heart endeared himself to all who knew him.'[14] Perhaps surprisingly (in view of the fact that Boyton's family was one of noted athletic prowess), his health seems to have been poor in Kilmainham. Despite the hulla-balloo that all this aroused—the *Philadelphia Sunday Herald* demanded that England 'must be brought to her senses . . . [and] respect the dignity of American citizenship in the person of Boyton'[15]—and the embarrassment generated for Forster, it must be insisted that Boyton's historical significance lies in the role he played in giving the League a firm foothold in the more prosperous regions outside Connaught.

Thomas Brennan (about 27)

Thomas Brennan was probably the most socially radical of the ex-Fenian leaders who joined the Land League. In his mid-twenties when the agitation started, he quickly gave up his job in Dublin to become full-time secretary of the Land League. Despite his considerable personal popularity in Ireland, he refused, as did Patrick Egan, to stand for election to the imperial parliament. (Brennan was linked personally to Egan through his uncle, James Rourke, who was one of Egan's business partners.) He was bitterly detested by the RIC, who suspected him of involvement in many nefarious designs. He was arrested in May 1881, but, as this had long been anticipated, the removal of the League secretary was not a heavy blow to the organisation's efficiency.

Following the 'Kilmainham Treaty' Brennan left for America, where he continued to adopt a militant stance in Irish-American politics. Davitt concluded: 'Mr Brennan has been, to those who knew him best, a high type of disinterested patriot—young, ardent and gifted with many qualities that would find in a self-governed Ireland the recognition which they have already won for him in the prosperous city of Omaha in Nebraska.'[16]

James Daly (about 43)

James Daly of Castlebar, Co. Mayo, the editor of the *Connaught Telegraph*, has been described as 'the most undeservedly forgotten man in Irish history'.[17] There is some truth in this. In the first phase of the land war (1879 and the early months of 1880) Daly put his considerable skills as an organiser and propagandist at the service of the Land League. When the break came it seems to have been over the use of funds. Perhaps Daly also felt that his early role was insufficiently recognised by the Land League's collective leadership in Dublin.

However, Daly's obscurity is not solely the fault of others. His later opposition to the Land League was highly personalistic and inconsistent. He would concentrate on the alleged infidelities of local leaders and then, perhaps in the same issue of his newspaper, print ultra-Fenian attacks on the organisation. Undoubtedly he remained a consistent and realistic land reformer, but there is no doubt that politically he lost his way.

This is hardly surprising. The currents in Mayo politics in 1879–82 were of quite remarkable complexity. The result was Daly's isolation from a national leadership which gave him scant notice in their memoirs. This is why one of the putative 'fathers of the Land League' has had so little recognition of his paternity.

Patrick Egan (38)

Born at Ballymahon, Co. Longford, where his father, Francis Egan, and all his relatives were farmers. At an early age he entered the office of an established firm of corn merchants in Dublin and after a short time became their chief accountant. From 1868 he was engaged in the flour and baking trade as a member of the firm of Egan & Rourke, one of the largest businesses of this kind in Ireland. He was also a Director of the Dublin North City Milling Company, the most extensive milling concern in the country.

His acumen in both business and politics was considerable. He was also a 'hard man' and was regarded as a fanatic by other nationalists. The *Irish World* claimed: 'While Mr Egan has taken an active part in all the agitations for years, it has ever been understood that he was something more than a mere Home Ruler.'[18] He had a large family of nine children and was believed to have made considerable personal sacrifice in the cause of Irish nationalism.

Egan was a founder and active member of the Amnesty Association, a Fenian organisation, in 1868. He played an important part in the eventful Longford election of December 1869, supporting the nationalist John Martin against Earl Grenville, the clerical candidate. He also supported Martin in his attempt to become MP for Meath, and it was he who introduced Parnell to the Meath selection committee which agreed on Parnell's candidature in place of Martin.

Egan first attracted police attention in 1870, when he was known to use his job in North City Mills to cover his work as a Fenian agent in the West and midlands. He rose within the Fenian organisation to become a member of the IRB Supreme Council, and for the next twenty-two years he was to figure prominently in police reports.[19] By 1879 he was established as a substantial businessman —by the Dublin standards of the 1870s—and as a committed if not doctrinaire nationalist. As early as 1870 in Longford he was interested in the possibilities of exploiting parliamentary elections for the nationalist cause.[20] He was the obvious choice to be treasurer of the Land League and in collusion with Thomas Brennan and Michael Davitt formed that 'triumvirate' which played such a significant role in the League's affairs. In February 1881, with the onset of coercion, he left for Paris and controlled the organisation's purse-strings as best he could from that base until December 1882. In this role he began to be seen by the authorities as the paymaster of outrage. A few days after the Phoenix Park murders he was linked with the crime in a report by Superintendent John Mallon: 'The Fenian suspects in Dublin are not capable to organise and carry out a desperate business like the Phoenix Park Outrages. They are sufficiently wicked but they have not sufficient brains or money. They would assist in the carrying out of such a thing and would I think keep the secret as well as any other people on earth.'[21] Egan was known to have approved of other outrages, for example the Manchester rescue of 1867 and the attempt to blow up the Albert Memorial. Mallon concluded: 'All this makes us incline to the belief that Egan supplied the sinews of war for the late outrage.'[22]

In fact Mallon's relationship with Egan was considerably more ambiguous. They were on first-name terms, and, as Leon Ó Broin has shown in a remarkable book, there were those who felt that Mallon might have closed the net more quickly on Egan.[23] Whatever the truth of the charge against Egan, it was a significant undercurrent at the time of the Special Commission. Charles Russell in his speech for the defence, however, insisted that no true bill had ever been found against Egan.[24]

Egan nevertheless decided to emigrate to America, where he continued his business activities and became a prominent figure in Irish-American politics. He concluded his varied career by becoming the American ambassador to Chile, where at the time of the military *coup d'état* against the progressive Balmacada government he apparently distinguished himself.[25]

Patrick Ford (45)

A native of Galway, Ford edited the *Irish World*, the extremist nationalist journal, in New York. Its readers and friends sent more financial help to the Land League than 'has probably ever been contributed by the efforts of a single weekly paper to any political movement'.[26] Ford's support for the League was unstinting, although he personally remained in favour of a programme of land nationalisation rather than peasant proprietorship. Later, for a time, he became an advocate of violent methods for breaking the British link. For this reason he became notorious in British government circles. In personal life he had, however, the reputation of being 'a kind-hearted man, a good citizen, a practical Christian and a philanthropist'.[27]

Matthew Harris (54)

Matthew Harris's life was devoted to the cause of Irish nationalism: he was in turn a supporter of Repeal, a Young Irelander, a leading Fenian organiser, and MP for South Galway. His grandfather, Peter Harris, had been a United Irishman and was hanged for his part in the 1798 rebellion. By occupation Harris was a small building contractor at the time of the Land League crisis, but he threw himself wholeheartedly into the agitation.[28] Although he never lost sight of his nationalist objectives, he was resolutely opposed to that sterile nationalism which neglected the social condition of Ireland. Much of his significance lies in his attempt to make Fenians see the folly of neglecting the Land League. The documents seized at his house at the time of his arrest in 1881 played a role in the Special Commission in 1888. Charles Russell in his opening speech for the defence acknowledged: 'These documents . . . showed that Mr Matthew Harris was revolving apparently at one time in his mind some very comprehensive schemes for national as well as for land reform.'[29]

Frank Hugh O'Donnell (31)

F. H. O'Donnell, the son of a ranker who had held a commission, was educated at University College, Galway, and was a Home Rule leader in the 1870s. He constantly nurtured illusions of possible O'Donnell aristocratic connections and had considerable arrogance of appearance and manner. T. P. O'Connor has left an interesting portrait of the man: 'Here . . . was a figure from Balzac: one of the self-confident adventurers like Lucien de Rubempré, who regarded life as a struggle between the world and his will to succeed.'[30]

O'Donnell undoubtedly supplied Parnell with much of his material during the obstruction campaign of 1877, but this (in T. P.'s view) was the clue to his downfall: 'He never could get rid of the idea that it was he who created Parnell, and in this way he became in secret the vindictive and jealous enemy of his chief.'[31] He was to learn in time that conflict with Parnell was a losing and fatal struggle. Indeed, unlike so many of the other Irish Catholic petit-bourgeois intelligentsia who were pursuing a political career at this time, O'Donnell did not believe in or profess to believe in Parnell's greatness. But his greatest mistake was his failure to perceive the importance of the agrarian mass movement of 1879–82. O'Donnell failed to throw himself actively into the land agitation, and this inaction ensured for him a marginal place in Irish politics in the 1880s. Nevertheless, his *History of the Irish Parliamentary Party,* although it has to be used with caution, is a valuable study.

James J. O'Kelly (34)

A Dublin-born Fenian who later became a leading member of the Irish Parliamentary Party, O'Kelly was to prove one of Parnell's most loyal followers. He was at different times an energetic soldier and journalist and also an active republican.

He had joined the Fenian organisation in 1860 and became a member of the Supreme Council towards the end of 1867. His defection to Parnell was always on the cards, however, after an interview with the squire of Avondale in 1877. 'I had a long chat with Parnell . . . a man of promise. I think he ought to be sup-ported,' he wrote to Devoy in August 1877. 'He has the idea I held at the start of the Home Rule organisation—that is, the creation of a political link between the conservative and radical nationalists.'[32]

O'Kelly was certainly a remarkable man. He could move easily from scooping other journalists to dreaming up bold stratagems of war. His absorption into Parnellism had perhaps distracted attention from the fact that many other Fenians in this period were also absorbed as a result of the Land League movement.

John O'Connor Power (33)

O'Connor Power had the three most likely attributes of a Parnellite lieutenant: he was intellectually able, an excellent public speaker and of poor background. T. P. O'Connor entitled his brief biogra-phical note on Power 'Workhouse Boy's Rise and Fall' and wrote: 'Smallpox was in those days a mark or form of class inferiority; only the children of the very poor ever bore its traces. When O'Connor Power was in one of his fits of rage, these little marks of smallpox would become white, and his face looked ugly and ferocious.'[33]

In his early days Power was an active Fenian. In disappointment he eventually turned to constitutional politics, although he never forgot to press the case of the imprisoned Fenian of the 1870s, Michael Davitt. Like F. H. O'Donnell, his knowledge of Parnell in the late 1870s did not dispose him to accept the squire of Avon-dale's leadership of the nationalist cause. In fact, also like O'Donnell, he found Parnell's leadership unbearable. His political career did not survive his open expression of opposition to 'the Chief'.

He had one piece of luck: he married the widow of a wealthy instrument-maker. But he failed both to get elected to parliament as a Liberal or to return to the Home Rule ranks. His later involvement in London high society disgusted many of his former friends. One judge, however, believed that O'Connor Power retained some of the instincts of Irish jacobinism. When Davitt was rearrested at the beginning of 1881 O'Connor Power had declared: 'If I were in control of things, three of these [Liberal] Ministers would be dead tomorrow.' T. P. commented: 'This was the old ferocity that lay behind the smooth-tongued guest of the fashionable ladies of London.'[34]

Thomas Sexton (31)

Later described by T. P. O'Connor as 'one of the most tragic figures of all the tragic figures in the Irish movement',[35] Sexton achieved a rapid rise to national prominence in 1880 and 1881. His reputation as a parliamentary orator is a high one. He had, said T. P., 'the southern sensitiveness, the southern versatility, the southern eloquence'. The same writer regarded Sexton as second only to Gladstone as a public speaker. F. H. O'Donnell, typically, was less impressed: 'His main faults were repetition and commonplace. All the venerable citations of Dublin patriotism were poured in a gentle stream.'[36] Sexton's later reputation as a parliamentarian has distracted attention from his role as a Land Leaguer in 1880 and 1881.

What did he give the Land League? Certainly an ability to make the sort of speech which earned him a place as a 'traverser' at the state trials and later a spell in Kilmainham as a 'suspect'. More important was his legendary—for an Irish agitator—financial and mathematical acumen. T. P. recalled: 'He had an extraordinary mastery of figures, and in mental arithmetic he was far beyond any man in the House. . . . His schoolfellows afterwards used to tell how they or the masters would pitch at him a great bundle of figures, and how, quick as lightning, he would give the proper answers.' He was the obvious candidate to examine the League's financial affairs in the summer of 1881.

This highly sensitive ascetic was driven out of politics by Tim Healy in later years. He lived in isolated retirement but not in penury. T. P. concluded: 'He has an income, I am glad to say, from some of the commercial companies over which he presides.'[37]

Patrick J. Sheridan (34)

Born in Co. Mayo, Sheridan lived in Tubbercurry, Co. Sligo, where he was 'unemployed' according to the police[38] but a hotel keeper and merchant grocer according to the *Irish World*. 'In independent circumstances and above want himself,' continued the *Irish World*,[39] his feelings revolted against landlordism, and 'since early manhood he had been active in every movement looking to the betterment of Ireland'. He quickly involved himself in Land League activities as an organiser and was one of the 'traversers' in the failed state trials that marked the commencement of the land agitation. He was arrested under the coercion act and spent from mid-March to mid-September 1881 in Kilmainham. Shortly after his release the Land League was suppressed. Sheridan then withdrew to Paris, where the Land League treasurer, Patrick Egan, had already taken up residence.

It was at this point that Sheridan's career became the centre of enormous controversy. His secret trip to Ireland as Egan's emissary when, disguised as a priest, he toured the country, aroused profound suspicions in Dublin Castle. Both Sheridan and Egan claimed that Sheridan's task had been to sort out the League's financial affairs and distribute some money to the evicted tenantry. Certainly the Chief Secretary, Forster, did not accept this innocent account. He was therefore alarmed rather than comforted by Parnell's claim in the 'Kilmainham Treaty' negotiations that Sheridan might be the sort of man to have a restraining influence on crime in the West of Ireland. Sheridan later claimed that Parnell had been right: 'I have no doubt but if myself and other active men then either in prison or exile were allowed to move about as usual amongst the people, society would be spared the horrible exhibitions, or most of them, that followed.'[40] He also claimed that Parnell had been motivated by a 'kindly consideration towards myself . . . knowing, as he did, the great financial loss and injury I had sustained by my imprisonment and enforced absence from Ireland'.[41]

However, Sheridan obviously felt that it was unwise to return to Ireland. He left for America and obtained a job working for Patrick Ford's *Irish World* in New York. He was in this employment when the news reached America in February 1883 that he had been named by the informer Carey as being implicated in plots of assassination and outrage. Sheridan stoutly denied Carey's allegations. However, he later made somewhat garrulous claims about his earlier activities in order to impress militant Irish-Americans.

By June 1884 Sheridan had fallen out with Patrick Ford over money (as he had done earlier with James Daly), and Ford quickly took the opportunity to expose his former friend. Sheridan was accused of play-acting in Paris: 'He procured a bandit's hat and a sword-umbrella, and with these, and assuming a tragic air, he posed as some terrible unknown in the most open places.'[42] Sheridan in America, it was alleged, launched a lecture tour in which he pretended to be 'Number One', the leader of the terrorist Invincibles. ('Number One is coming,' ran the advance publicity.) In fact Sheridan privately admitted that he was not 'Number One', and, indeed, Ford alleged that he had been expelled from the Invincibles eight months before the Phoenix Park murders occurred.[43] Davitt later summarised Sheridan's activities as 'bunkum speeches in New York about his reputed connection with the Invincibles—speeches which had much more of Byronic bravado than of actual criminality'.[44] Sheridan later regained some credibility as a nationalist by his refusal to co-operate with the *Times* investigation into 'Parnellism and crime' in 1889.[45]

P. J. Smyth (about 55)

P. J. Smyth's career is one of a spectacular decline from the nationalist grace of his early days in politics. In 1853 he was commissioned by his Irish-American compatriots to liberate the Irish leader John Mitchel from penal exile, and in the autumn of that year he successfully accomplished that task. In 1873 he gave his adhesion to Butt's Home Rule programme and a federal solution, but he was always unhappy with this position. He soon changed his mind and declared that he would favour nothing but 'simple repeal' and a return to 'the constitution of 1782'.

He held a Westmeath seat until 1880, but in that year moved to Tipperary and managed to get himself elected on Repeal principles. But although his nationalist record recommended him to the Land League leadership, he turned bitterly against this body, denouncing it as the 'League of Hell'. This act basically cut him off from the popular forces in Irish politics. In 1884 he accepted a small government post in Ireland: in 1885, three weeks after his appointment, he died. Only six years previously he had been seriously considered as a possible 'New Departure' leader.[46]

Abbreviations

The following abbreviations are used in the notes.

BM	British Museum (British Library)
CSO, RP	Chief Secretary's Office, Registered Papers (Dublin Castle)
CT	*Connaught Telegraph*
FJ	*Freeman's Journal*
IN	*Irish Nation*
INL	Irish National League
IT	*Irish Times*
IW	*Irish World*
NLI	National Library of Ireland
PRO	Public Record Office (London)
SPO	State Paper Office (Dublin Castle)

Notes

PREFACE
(pp. 1–5)
1. J. Connolly, *Selected Political Writings,* ed. O. D. Edwards and B. Ransom, London 1973, 211–12.

Chapter 1
FROM THE FAMINE TO THE LAND WAR
(pp. 7–33)
1. W. O'C. Morris, 'The Land System of Ireland' in *Oxford Essays, 1856,* Oxford 1856, 193–217.
2. For a recent discussion see P. J. Gibbon, 'Colonisation and the Great Irish Famine of 1845–49', *Race and Class* XVII, No. 2 (1975), 131–9.
3. L. M. Cullen, *An Economic History of Ireland since 1660,* London 1972, 137.
4. J. J. Lee, 'Irish Agriculture', *Agricultural History Review* XVII, Pt 1 (1969), 70–1.
5. W. O'C. Morris, *Letters on the Land Question of Ireland,* London 1870, ix.
6. W. N. Hancock, *Report on the Supposed Progressive Decline in Irish Prosperity,* Dublin 1863, 83.
7. *Ibid.,* 82–4.
8. *Irish People,* 28 May 1864.
9. But see P. M. A. Bourke, 'The Average Yield of Food Crops in Ireland on the Eve of the Great Famine', *Journal of the Department of Agriculture* LXVI (1969), 27–31, for criticism of Hancock by a modern authority. The major essay on the depression is J. S. Donnelly, 'The Irish Agricultural Depression of 1859–64', *Irish Economic and Social History* III (1976).
10. See *Irish People,* especially 28 May and 8 Oct. 1864.
11. T. W. Grimshaw, *Facts and Figures about Ireland,* Dublin 1893, Table XI, p. 25. The area under cereal crops fell from 3,213,000 acres (1847–50) to 1,814,000 acres by 1876–80.
12. *Agricultural Statistics of Ireland for the year 1876,* 8, H. C. 1877 [C.1749] LXXXV, 536. In the period 1841–76 the decrease of farms in the 5–15 acre category was 34·8 per cent, while those in the 15–30 acre category increased by 72·8 per cent and those above 30 acres increased by 228·8 per cent. Even in the period 1851–79, Gladstone noted, the number of farms under 15 acres fell from 280,000 to 227,000 (*Hansard,* cclx, 294 (7 Apr. 1881).)
13. B. M. Walsh, 'Marriage Rates and Population Pressure: Ireland, 1871 and 1911', *Economic History Review* XXIII (Apr. 1970), 157–8.

14. E. Larkin, 'The Devotional Revolution in Ireland, 1850–75', *American Historical Review* LXXVII (1972), 636.
15. K. H. Connell, 'Catholicism and Marriage in the Century after the Famine' in *Irish Peasant Society*, Oxford 1968, 113–61.
16. *FJ*, 24 Apr. 1880.
17. *Irish Farmer's Gazette*, 13 Aug. 1870.
18. R. O. Pringle, 'A Review of Irish Agriculture, Chiefly with Reference to the Production of Livestock', *Journal of the Royal Agricultural Society of England*, 2nd ser., VIII (1872), 53.
19. S. H. Cousens, 'The Regional Variations in Population Changes in Ireland, 1861–1881', *Economic History Review* XVII (Dec. 1964).
20. *Agricultural Statistics . . . 1876*, 8, H.C. 1877 [C. 1749] LXXXV, 536.
21. B. L. Solow, *The Land Question and the Irish Economy, 1870–1903*, Cambridge, Mass. 1971, 89–91, takes Pollock's estate as an image for Irish agriculture generally.
22. Sir G. Campbell, *The Irish Land*, Dublin 1869, 135.
23. P. G. Lane, 'An Attempt at Commercial Farming in Ireland after the Famine', *Studies* LXI (spring 1972), 54–66.
24. New York *Herald*, 3 Jan. 1880.
25. Cousens in *Economic History Review* XVII (Dec. 1964), 311.
26. S. Clark, 'The Political Mobilisation of Irish Farmers', *Canadian Review of Sociology and Anthropology* XII (1975), 494.
27. Solow, *op. cit.*, 105.
28. On this subject see C. Ó Gráda, 'Seasonal Migration and Post-Famine Adjustment in the West of Ireland', *Studia Hibernica* XIII (1973), 60.
29. F. Dun, *Landlords and Tenants in Ireland*, London 1881, 227.
30. *Royal Commission on the Depressed Condition of the Agricultural Interest* [Richmond Commission], *Assistant Commissioners' Report: Ireland, by Messrs Baldwin and Robertson*, 1, H.C. 1881 [C. 2951] XVI, 841 (hereafter cited as *Richmond Comm., Report by Baldwin and Robertson*). See also FJ, 19 Jul. 1881.
31. *Royal Commission on the Depressed Condition of the Agricultural Interest, Minutes of Evidence, Pt I*, 550, H.C. 1881 [C. 2778–I] XV, 578 (Qs 15722–3) (hereafter cited as *Richmond Comm.*)
32. *Ibid.*, 1000 (Q. 27424). See J. S. Donnelly, 'Cork Market: Its Role in the Nineteenth-Century Irish Butter Trade', *Studia Hibernica* XI (1971), 130–63, for a full discussion of the market itself. On this problem see pp. 141–3 in particular.
33. *Richmond Comm.*, 1000 (Q. 27424).
34. Despite the prominence of 'gombeen man' as a term of abuse in Irish political vocabulary, there is no extensive historical study. But see the review of the discussion, within Irish social anthropology, in P. J. Gibbon, 'Arensberg and Kimball Revisited', *Economy and Society* II, No. 4 (Nov. 1973), 479–98. The subsequent work of P. J. Gibbon and M. D. Higgins has provoked a substantial debate between them and L. Ken-

nedy which is at last expanding our knowledge of this area.
35. *Richmond Comm.*, 1025 (Q. 27989).
36. Ó Gráda in *Studia Hibernica* XIII (1973), 73.
37. *CT*, 25 Jun., 1881; *FJ*, 21 Jul. and 3 Aug. 1881.
38. *Richmond Comm.*, 400 (Qs 11151 and 11242).
39. *CT*, 25 Jun. 1881; *FJ*, 21 Jul. and 3 Aug. 1881.
40. *CT*, 25 Jun. 1881.
41. New York *Herald*, 19 Jan. 1880.
42. M. Davitt, *The Fall of Feudalism in Ireland*, London and New York 1904, 145.
43. N. Senior, *Journals, Conversations and Essays Relating to Ireland*, London 1868, II, 282.
44. *FJ*, 25 Sep. 1880.
45. *Ibid.*, 24 Sep. 1880.
46. The average number of cattle in all Ireland, yearly throughout the period 1851–60, was 3,480,623; in 1881 it was 3,954,479 (an increase of 473,856). Sheep: 3,297,971–3,258,583 (a decrease of 39,388). Pigs: 1,194,303–1,088,041 (a decrease of 106,262). Horses: 572,219–547,662 (a decrease of 24,577). These figures are taken from Appendix C, by A. M. Sullivan, in M. Davitt, *The Times–Parnell Commission: Speech Delivered in Defence of the Land League*, London 1890, 393.
47. K. Marx, *Capital*, Moscow 1961, I, 703. For Marx's statistics see pp. 698–701. These figures mainly cover the 1860–65 period. For some comments on Marx's views on Ireland see P. Bew, 'The Problem of Irish Unionism', *Economy and Society* VI, No. 1 (1977), 90–110.
48. C. S. Parnell, 'The Irish Land Question', *North American Review* CXXX, No. 1 (Apr. 1880). T. M. Healy, *Letters and Leaders of My Day*, London [1928], I, 87, suggests that this article was written by Parnell's sister Fanny. But it certainly reflected Parnell's views as expressed in his speeches in America, his speech of 19 October at a Land League meeting, his Waterford speech in early December and his speech of 18 April 1881 at Glasgow in reception of Gladstone's Land Bill.
49. *Hansard*, cclxi, 893 (19 May 1881).
50. *Western News*, 16 Jul, 1881.
51. J. N. Murphy, *Ireland, Industrial, Political, and Social*, London 1870, 203.
52. *Richmond Comm.*, 436 (Q. 12253).
53. Murphy, *op. cit.*, 125.
54. *FJ*, 24 Apr. 1880. See also *ibid.*, 19 Aug. and 2 Sep. 1880. Balfe's pamphlet, *One Cause of Ireland's Poverty*, is summarised in the *Clare Advertiser*, 26 Mar. 1881.
55. The letter of James Kilmartin, president of the Ballinasloe Tenants' Defence Association, to the *Irish Farmer's Gazette*, 21 Feb. 1880, revealed clearly the assumption that the technical journals of farming supported the Cloncurry approach.
56. Cited in *Irish Farmer's Gazette*, 18 Aug. 1870.

57. Morris, *Letters on the Land Question*, x.
58. L. Playfair, 'On the Declining Production of Human Food in Ireland' in Sir A. Grant, ed., *Recess Studies*, Edinburgh 1870, 241–60. Even foreign analysts, while critical of Gladstone's remedies, placed a large measure of blame on the grazing system; see interview with M. de Molinari, *Flag of Ireland*, 16 Apr. 1881.
59. *Richmond Comm., Report by Baldwin and Robertson*, 4. See also *Western News*, 9 Jul. 1881.
60. *Richmond Comm.*, 1063–98 (Qs 28968–29690) *passim*.
61. Pringle in *Journal of the Royal Agricultural Society of England*, 2nd ser., VIII (1872), 1–76.
62. *Ibid.*, 19–20.
63. *Ibid.*, 45.
64. R. O. Pringle, 'Illustrations of Irish Farming', *Journal of the Royal Agricultural Society of England*, 2nd ser., IX (1873), 401–12.
65. *Irish Farmer's Gazette*, 4 Sep. 1880.
66. *CT*, 25 Jun. 1881.
67. *Report from the Select Committee appointed to inquire into the Workings . . . of the Irish Land Act, 1870 . . .* [Shaw Lefevre Committee], 271, H.C. 1878 (249) XV, 313 (Q. 5005).
68. See, for example, their derisive critique (*Irish Farmer's Gazette*, 24 Apr. 1880) of Parnell's article in the *North American Review*.
69. *Kilkenny Moderator*, editorial, 20 Apr. 1881.
70. Marx, *op. cit.*, I, 704. Marx never completed a systematic study of Ireland. The political texts have traditionally received most comment, but, in fact, the passages in *Capital* mark his most serious contribution. Even here Marx failed in Vol. III to keep his promise (Vol. I, 711) to show how 'the famine and its consequences have been deliberately made the most of, both by the individual landlords and by the English legislature, to carry out the agricultural revolution'.
71. *Ibid.*, I, 711.
72. *Richmond Comm.*, 436 (Q. 12253).
73. *Report from the Poor Law Inspectors in Ireland as to the Existing Arrangements between Landlord and Tenant in respect of Improvements to Farms*, 43, H.C. 1870 [C. 31] XIV, 79 (hereafter cited as *Report from the Poor Law Inspectors* [1870]).
74. Morris, *Letters on the Land Question*, 231. Dr W. E. Vaughan in a recent review has said: 'In fact, as a destroyer of human life, disputes between landlords and tenants were only slightly more significant than deaths caused by lightning.' *(Irish Economic and Social History* III (1976), 93.)
75. It was, as *The Nation* saw it, an opposition to the 'extremes of legal tyranny'; the fact that few landlords attempted to apply such extremes was irrelevant. *(Nation, 4 Jun. 1870.)*
76. *FJ*, 9 Apr. 1881.
77. *Ibid.*, 30 Aug. 1880.
78. J. S. Mill, *England and Ireland*, London 1868, 12.

79. *FJ,* 9 Apr. 1881.
80. *Ibid.* As C. B. MacPherson has recently observed, it is a critical part of Mill's defence of capitalist property rights to point out that the capitalist had not obtained it by wrongful dispossession of those who had created it by their past labour. *(The Life and Times of Liberal Democracy,* Oxford 1977, 54.) In this respect Mill's liberal democratic theory was the English capitalist's meat but the Irish landlord's poison.
81. Argyll to Gladstone, 26 Dec. 1880 (BM, Gladstone Papers, Add. MS. 56446). These papers are in the new deposit MSS 56444–53, the history and contents of which are described briefly by M. R. D. Foot, 'A Revealing New Light on Gladstone', *Times,* 6 Nov. 1970.
82. E. D. Steele, 'Gladstone and Ireland', *Irish Historical Studies* XVII, No. 65 (Mar. 1970), 83. For the background in intellectual history see C. J. Dewey, 'Celtic Agrarian Legislation and the Celtic Revival: Historicist Implications of Gladstone's Irish and Scottish Land Acts, 1870–1886', *Past and Present* LXVI (1974).
83. *CT,* 23 Aug 1879.
84. Nationalist purists felt, however, that Healy lacked a grasp of the finer points. 'As a subject of legal argument,' noted Joseph Fisher in his review, 'it does not sufficiently dwell upon the change from the Irish to the English system in the reign of James I; it is disfigured by the suggestion that the first Earl of Cork was a horsestealer and forger.' (*Munster Express,* 15 Jan. 1881.) For a full exposition of Fisher's views see his 'History of Land-Holding in Ireland', *Transactions of the Royal Historical Society* V (1877).
85. T. N. Brown, *Irish-American Nationalism, 1870–1890,* Philadelphia 1966, 107.
86. J. J. Lee, *The Modernisation of Irish Society, 1848–1918,* Dublin 1973, 96 and 94.
87. E. D. Steele, 'Ireland for the Irish', *History* LIV (1972), 242; see also his *Irish Land and British Politics: Tenant Right and Nationality, 1865–1870,* Cambridge 1974, 28.
88. J. J. Lee, 'Gladstone and the Landlords', *Times Literary Supplement,* 9 May 1975.
89. *Report from the Poor Law Inspectors* [1870], 43.
90. *FJ,* 13 Apr. 1881.
91. C. Ó Gráda, 'Agricultural Head Rents, Pre-Famine and Post-Famine', *Economic and Social Review* V, No. 3 (Apr. 1974), 390.
92. *Ibid.,* 4 Jan. 1881.
93. C. Ó Gráda, 'The Investment Behaviour of Irish Landlords, 1850–75: Some Preliminary Findings', *Agricultural History Review* XXIII, Pt 2 (1975), 151.
94. M. Davitt, 'The Irish Social Problem', *Today: A Journal of Scientific Socialism* I (Jun. 1884), 249. Ó Gráda's comment helps to explain why the issue was so emotional: 'We would still argue that most of the improvement that went on in the pre-famine period was the tenant's own work; this consisted largely of reclamation of previously extra-marginal land during the post-Waterloo

decades. Perhaps over a million acres were put into use in this way.' Ó Gráda admits that much of this improvement was not permanent: most of the land fell back into its uncultivated state after the famine and was used afterwards for grazing purposes only or not at all. But he adds: 'In terms of subsistence for several hundred thousand people for twenty or thirty years, the value of such improvement, no matter how temporary, was enormous nevertheless.' (Ó Gráda in *Agricultural History Review* XXIII, Pt 2 (1975), 141.)

95. Davitt, *Fall of Feudalism*, 141–2.
96. J. H. Tuke, *Irish Distress and its Remedies: A Visit to Donegal and Connaught in the Spring of 1880*, 3rd ed., London 1880, 114. See *Spectator*, 11 Sep. 1880 (pp. 1154–5), for a lengthier exposition of Stickney's views. Tuke's pamphlet was of considerable importance. 'Of all the writings and speeches which the Irish land question has produced,' wrote Lord Sherbrooke in the *Nineteenth Century* of November 1880, 'there is none which has made so deep an impression on the English mind as the pamphlet of Mr Tuke.' (Quoted in N. D. Palmer, *The Irish Land League Crisis*, New Haven and London 1940, 271.)
97. Marx, *op. cit.*, III, 611.
98. *Richmond Comm.*, 724 (Q. 20900).
99. N. D. Palmer, 'Irish Absenteeism in the 1870s', *Journal of Modern History* XII (1940), presents a full study of the problem.
100. Quoted in C. F. Kolbert and T. O'Brien, *Land Reform in Ireland*, Cambridge 1975, 28.
101. *FJ*, 17 May 1880.
102. A. Parnell, 'Tale of the Land League: A Great Sham' (NLI MS. 12144).
103. Gladstone, cabinet memo, 9 Dec. 1880 (BM, Gladstone Papers, Add. MS. 44625).
104. Forster, cabinet memo, 27 Dec. 1880 (*ibid.*).
105. Irish Land Committee, *The Land Question*, No. 1: *Notes upon the Government Valuation of Land in Ireland*, Dublin 1880. For critical reviews see *FJ*, 15 Jul. 1880, and *Munster Express*, 31 Jul. 1880 and 15 Jan., 5 Mar., 30 Apr. and 21 May 1881.
106. Irish Land Committee, *op. cit.*, 20.
107. Cited in *FJ*, 19 Nov. 1880.
108. J. Ball Greene (Commissioner for Valuation), cabinet memo, Nov. 1880 (BM, Gladstone Papers, Add. MS. 44625).
109. *Nation*, quoted in *Limerick Reporter*, 30 Nov. 1880.
110. *Ibid.* See R. B. O'Brien, *The Irish Land Question and English Public Opinion*, London 1880, 90–118, for the same argument.
111. *FJ*, 26 Nov. 1880.
112. Solow, *op. cit.*, 67.
113. *Ibid.*, 70. But see *IT*, 4 Jan. 1881, for critical comment.
114. Marx, *op. cit.*, I, 703.
115. Ó Gráda in *Economic and Social Review* V, No. 3 (Apr. 1974), 390.

116. For the optimistic case see, in particular, Solow, *op. cit.*, Chapter 4.

117. *Ibid.*, 57–77.

118. Ó Gráda in *Economic and Social Review* V, No. 3 (Apr. 1974), 390.

119. *Ibid.*, 391.

120. Solow, *op. cit.*, 120.

121. *Richmond Comm.*, 102 (Q. 3169).

122. J. Ball Greene, cabinet memo, Nov. 1880 (BM, Gladstone Papers, Add. MS. 44625).

123. *FJ*, 10 Dec. 1880.

124. *Richmond Comm.*, 1012 (Qs 27693–7).

125. *Preliminary Report on the Returns of Agricultural Produce in Ireland in 1879*, Table V, 7, H.C. 1880 [C. 2495] LXXVI, 899; Palmer, *Irish Land League Crisis*, 64.

126. The statistics were: 1850 5·0; 1851 5·9; 1852 5·7; 1853 6·6; 1854 5·3; 1855 7·2; 1856 3·9; 1857 2·54; 1859 3·1; 1860 3·1; 1861 1·4; 1862 1·8; 1863 3·0; 1864 3·6; 1865 3·6; 1866 2·4; 1867 3·1; 1868 3·3; 1869 3·3; 1870 3·7; 1871 2·7; 1872 2·0; 1873 2·4; 1874 4·0; 1875 3·4; 1876 5·1; 1877 1·8; 1878 3·0; 1879 1·4. The sources are *Agricultural Statistics of Ireland for the year 1857*, Table VII, xi, H.C. 1859 [2461, Sess. 2] XXIX, 11; *Agricultural Statistics of Ireland for the year 1869*, Table VII, li–lxii, H.C. 1871 [C. 239] LXIX, 397–409; *Preliminary Report on the Returns of Agricultural Produce in Ireland in 1879*, Table VI, 9, H.C. 1880 [C. 2495] LXXVI, 901.

127. *FJ*, 17 Nov. and 21 Dec. 1880.

128. William O'Brien, cited in *CT*, 18 Oct. 1879.

129. *FJ*, 19 May 1880.

130. See, for example, J. S. Donnelly, *The Land and the People of Nineteenth-Century Cork*, London and Boston 1975, 6.

131. See J. B. O'Brien, 'The Land and the People of Nineteenth-Century Cork' [review of Donnelly, *op. cit.*], *Journal of the Cork Historical and Archaeological Society* LXXX, No. 232 (1975), 96.

132. Earl Spencer, Introduction to J. Bryce, ed., *Handbook of Home Rule. Being Articles on the Irish Question*, 2nd ed., London 1887, xi.

133. Davitt, *Fall of Feudalism*, 116.

134. *Richmond Comm.*, 501–2 (Q. 14224).

135. Cousens in *Economic History Review* XVII (Dec. 1964), 320: 'Far fewer women were married in the age-group 20–24 in 1881 than had been the case ten years earlier, and the decline was most emphatic in the West. In Leinster the proportion fell by 1 or 2 per cent, for example, in Louth from 18·9 per cent to 17·6 per cent, in Wexford from 14·8 per cent to 12·5 per cent, and in Wicklow from 13·4 per cent to 12·9 per cent. In Ulster changes were on much the same scale. In Connaught, however, the smallest loss, from 29·0 per cent to 23·2 per cent, was in Galway, and the largest, from 29·5 per cent to 20·9 per cent, in

Mayo. Losses in Munster were more variable, as low as from 20·4 per cent to 16·5 per cent in Waterford, and as high as from 34·4 per cent to 19·9 per cent in Kerry, a drop of 14·5 per cent. This meant that whereas in 1871 34·4 per cent of the 20–24 age-group were married in Kerry and 14·8 per cent in Wexford, the gap between them had very much narrowed by 1881, when the proportions were 19·9 per cent and 12·5 per cent respectively.'

136. See also J. J. Lee, 'The Estates of Cork', *Times Literary Supplement*, 17 Oct. 1975.

137. P. J. Gibbon, *The Origins of Ulster Unionism*, Manchester 1975, 117.

Chapter 2
AGRARIAN MOVEMENTS BEFORE
THE LAND LEAGUE
(pp. 34–45)

1. Lee, *Modernisation of Irish Society*, 39–41.

2. Morris in *Oxford Essays, 1856*, 201.

3. On this point see Steele, *Irish Land and British Politics*, 17. See also Table 2 (p. 36 below). While it is undoubtedly true that even compared with the years 1853–54 there was a far higher ratio of outrage to eviction in 1860, it should be noted that the significant increase in evictions in 1861, 1862 and 1863 does not appear to see a continuation of the trend of the period 1850–60.

4. J. J. Lee, 'The Ribbonmen' in T. D. Williams, ed., *Secret Societies in Ireland*, Dublin and New York 1973, 28–30. See also J. S. Donnelly, *Landlord and Tenant in Nineteenth-century Ireland*, Dublin 1973, 32–3.

5. *Report from the Select Committee on Outrages (Ireland)*, 137, H.C. 1852 (438) XIV, 155 (Q. 1386) (hereafter cited as *Report Sel. Committee on Outrages*).

6. *Dundalk Democrat*, 4 Mar. 1852.

7. Donnelly, *op. cit.*, 29.

8. *Report Sel. Committee on Outrages*, 195 (Q. 2012).

9. *Ibid.*, 118–21 (Q. 1258).

10. Davitt, *Fall of Feudalism*, 42.

11. E. Strauss, *Irish Nationalism and British Democracy*, London 1951, 147.

12. K. Marx and F. Engels, *Ireland and the Irish Question*, Moscow 1971, 90. (Published in the New York *Daily Tribune*, 11 Jan. 1859.)

13. *Ibid.*, 212. (From the preparatory material for the *History of Ireland*.)

14. See, for example, the evidence of Capt. B. Warburton and H. J. Brownrigg, Inspector-General, Irish Constabulary, *Report Sel. Committee on Outrages*, 11, 13 and 193–4 (Qs 90, 104 and 1991–6).

15. *Report from the Select Committee appointed to inquire into the State of Westmeath, &c., and the Nature of a Certain Unlawful*

Combination existing therein, Appendix 5, 164–74, H.C. 1871 (147) XIII, 720–30 (hereafter cited as *Report Sel. Committee on Westmeath*).

16. CSO, RP, 6424/1871.
17. *Hansard*, ccvi, 10 (2 May 1871).
18. *Westmeath Guardian*, 20 Jul. 1871.
19. *Ibid.*, 21 Dec. 1871.
20. Marx and Engels, *op. cit.*, 334, Engels to Eduard Bernstein, 26 Jun. 1882.
21. *Ibid.*, 124.
22. *Ibid.*, 147.
23. L. Ó Broin, *Revolutionary Underground: The Story of the Irish Republican Brotherhood, 1858–1924*, Dublin 1976, 21–2. This is a most valuable study.
24. Strauss, *op. cit.*, 147.
25. *Ibid.*, 145.
26. *Irish People*, 26 Dec. 1863 (p. 73).
27. Quoted in D. Ryan, *The Fenian Chief*, Dublin 1967, 65.
28. L. Ó Broin, *Fenian Fever*, London 1971, 76 and 112.
29. Ryan, *op. cit.*, 328. See Davitt, *op. cit.*, 42.
30. Quoted in S. Ó Lúing, 'A Contribution to the Study of Fenianism in Breifne', *Breifne* III, No. 10 (1967), 157.
31. *Ibid.*, 155.
32. 'State of the Country as to Fenianism', conclusion, 1 Dec. 1869 (SPO, Fenian Papers).
33. *Ibid.*
34. T. W. Moody and L. Ó Broin, ed., 'The I.R.B. Supreme Council, 1868–78', *Irish Historical Studies* XIX, No. 75 (Mar. 1975), 298.
35. *Report Sel. Committee on Westmeath*, 44 (Qs 1147 and 1149).
36. 'State of the Country as to Fenianism', Meath County Inspector's report, 30 Nov. 1869 (SPO, Fenian Papers).
37. Westmeath County Inspector's report, 30 Nov. 1869 (*ibid.*). It notes cautiously: 'These reports are not grounded on any information received, for that is impossible to be had, but merely on opinion from general observation of the people.'
38. *Ibid.*
39. Meath and Westmeath County Inspectors' reports, 1 Mar. and 20 Sep. 1870 (*ibid.*).
40. Informer's report, 20 Dec. 1871 (*ibid.*).
41. Steele, *op. cit.*, 30.
42. *Westmeath Guardian*, 7 Apr. 1870.
43. Morris, *Letters on the Land Question*, 128.
44. For considerable detail on this point see *ibid.*, 112–13 and 124–5.
45. *Westmeath Guardian*, 8 Apr. 1869 and 24 Mar. 1870.
46. Lee, *Modernisation of Irish Society*, 58.
47. Dublin Castle report, 24 Sep. 1871 (SPO, Fenian Papers). These comments appear in a report on the activities of Patrick Egan, an audit clerk with North City Mills, who used his job for good cover for travel as a Fenian agent in the West and midlands. It is

the first of many such reports on the activities of Egan, later the treasurer of the Land League and alleged paymaster of the Invincibles; for a résumé see the report in SPO, Crime Branch Special, 1892.
48. Informer's report, 20 Dec. 1871 (SPO, Fenian Papers).
49. Informer's report, 20 Feb. 1870 (*ibid.*).
50. Longford County Inspector's report, 30 Mar. 1871 (*ibid.*).
51. Cavan County Inspector's report, 30 Nov. 1869 (*ibid.*). See also Ó Lúing in *Bréifne* III, No. 10 (1967), 173–4.

Chapter 3
LAND AND THE 'NEW DEPARTURE', 1879
(pp. 46–73)
1. *Devoy's Post-Bag*, ed. W. O'Brien and D. Ryan, Dublin 1948–53, I, 151, Carroll to Devoy, 29 Mar. 1876.
2. According to Superintendent Mallon of the Dublin Metropolitan Police, Stephens held that where a man succeeded in bringing a certain number of recruits into the organisation he became an officer whether 'he was intelligent or not'. (Mallon, report, 2 Dec. 1880 (SPO, INL Papers, Spec. Comm. docs, 1888, carton 9).)
3. See Ó Broin, *Fenian Fever*, 47–51, for Millen's betrayal.
4. *Devoy's Post-Bag*, I, 288, Millen to Supreme Council, IRB, 23 Dec. 1877.
5. *Ibid.*, I, 296, Carroll to Devoy, 19 Jan. 1878.
6. T. W. Moody and L. Ó Broin, ed., 'The I.R.B. Supreme Council, 1868–78', *Irish Historical Studies* XIX, No. 75 (Mar. 1975), 298.
7. *Devoy's Post-Bag*, I, 312–13.
8. Ó Broin, *Revolutionary Underground*, 23.
9. For an analysis of the social composition of the Fenians see Ó Broin, *op. cit.* (This work is discussed by its author in 'Creative History', *This Week*, 31 Aug. 1972.) But see also E. Larkin, 'Church, State and Nation in Modern Ireland', *American Historical Review* LXXX (1975), 1261.
10. Ryan, *Fenian Chief*, 65.
11. Davitt, *Fall of Feudalism*, 117.
12. *Ibid.*
13. *Ibid.*
14. For a full discussion see Brown, *Irish-American Nationalism*, Chapter 3.
15. J. F. Lalor, *James Fintan Lalor: Patriot and Political Essayist* [collected writings, ed. L. Fogarty], Dublin 1918, 57.
16. Their grasp of the realities of Irish life, however, should not on this account be exaggerated. Even John Devoy was unable to tell Parnell, in reply to his question of June 1879, how many of the farmers were Fenians. He later learned that although the Fenians had strong rural support in Connaught, they had less in Munster and virtually none at all in Leinster. On this point see J. Devoy, 'Michael Davitt's Career', Pt xiv, *Gaelic American*, 22 Sep. 1906. Patrick Ford, more spectacularly, refused to believe that the right

of free election to city councils existed in Ireland. (*Ibid.*, Pt iii, 23 Jun. 1906.)

17. *Devoy's Post-Bag*, I, 272, Carroll to Devoy, 27 Sep. 1877.
18. T. W. Moody, 'Irish-American Nationalism' [review of Brown, *op. cit.*], *Irish Historical Studies* XV, No. 60 (Sep. 1967), 444.
19. *Devoy's Post-Bag*, I, 372. For Dillon's attitude as revealed in his diary between late 1877 and early 1878 see F. S. L. Lyons, *John Dillon*, London 1968, 23.
20. Devoy (Pt iv) in *Gaelic American*, 30 Jun. 1906.
21. *Ibid.*, Pt ii, 16 Jun. 1906. A resolution to this effect was passed at Davitt's Cooper Institute meeting of 23 September 1878. (*IW*, 5 Oct. 1878; see also *Devoy's Post-Bag*, I, 346.)
22. J. Devoy, *The Land of Eire*, New York 1882, 42.
23. *FJ*, 27 Dec. 1878 (letter dated 11 Dec.).
24. Devoy (Pt xiv) in *Gaelic American*, 22 Sep. 1906.
25. *Ibid.*, Pt xv, 29 Sep. 1906.
26. *Ibid.*
27. Mill, *England and Ireland*, 22.
28. *FJ*, 2 Jul. 1880.
29. *IN*, 11 Feb. 1882. This admission appears in the course of a largely critical review of an article by John Boyle O'Reilly in the *Catholic Quarterly Review*.
30. *FJ*, 2 Jul. 1880.
31. *Ibid.*
32. *IN*, 11 Mar. 1882.
33. *Ibid.*, 4 Mar. 1882.
34. *FJ*, 2 Jul. 1880.
35. This evidence is assessed in Brown, *op. cit.*, Chapter 6.
36. For Davitt's personal contribution to the New Departure see T. W. Moody, 'The New Departure in Irish Politics, 1878–9' in H. A. Cronne, T. W. Moody and D. B. Quinn, ed., *Essays in British and Irish History in Honour of James Eadie Todd*, London 1949; Brown, *op. cit.*, Chapter 5; T. W. Moody in *Irish Historical Studies* XV, No. 60 (Sep. 1967), 438–45.
37. *Devoy's Post-Bag*, I, 482–4, Davitt to Devoy, 6 Feb. 1880; *ibid.*, II, 21–5, Davitt to Devoy, 16 Dec. 1880.
38. New York *Herald*, 12 Mar. 1881, quoted in *Cork Weekly Herald*, 19 Mar. 1881.
39. Davitt, *op. cit.*, 151.
40. B. O'Reilly, *John MacHale, Archbishop of Tuam*, New York 1890, II, 669–70.
41. *FJ*, 2 Jun. 1881.
42. A. J. Kettle, *The Material for Victory*, ed. L. J. Kettle, Dublin 1958, 21.
43. *The Irish Crisis of 1879–80: Proceedings of the Dublin Mansion House Relief Committee, 1880*, Dublin 1881, 2.
44. See *Western News*, 22 Feb. 1879, for a clear exposition from William Kilroe.
45. Dublin *Daily Express*, 3 May 1881.

46. *FJ*, 23 Jan. 1879.
47. *Western News*, 25 Jan. 1879.
48. P. H. Bagenal, *The Irish Agitator in Parliament and on the Platform*, Dublin 1880, 21.
49. *Richmond Comm.*, 389 (Q. 10793).
50. *FJ*, 4 Feb. 1879.
51. *Ibid.*, 6 Feb. 1879.
52. *Ibid.*, 14 Aug. 1880.
53. *Ibid.*, 23 Aug. 1880.
54. *Western News*, 15 Feb. 1879.
55. Kettle, *op. cit.*, 21.
56. M. Sullivan, *No Man's Land*, Dublin 1943, 13.
57. Kettle, *op. cit.*, 22.
58. *Ibid.*
59. *CT*, 23 Aug. 1879.
60. D. B. Cashman, *The Life of Michael Davitt*, Glasgow [1882?], 213.
61. *Western News*, 17 May 1880.
62. *FJ*, 25 Aug. 1879.
63. *Western News*, 4 Oct. 1879. Not surprisingly, Irish conservative comment on this relationship tended to echo Balzac, who claimed that the peasant, 'that indefatigable sapper, that rodent who sub-divides and parcels out land and cuts an acre into a hundred bits' was 'always invited to the banquet by the petty bourgeoisie which makes of him its auxiliary and its prey at once'. (Introduction to *The Peasants* (1911), 4.)
64. William O'Brien, reprinted in *Western News*, 6 Sep. 1879.
65. *Ibid.*
66. W. N. Hancock, statement at meeting of the Statistical Society, 27 Jan. 1880, reported in Dublin *Evening Mail*, 28 Jan. 1880; see also Palmer, *Irish Land League Crisis*, 66.
67. *FJ*, 25 Aug. 1879.
68. *Western News*, 6 Sep. 1879.
69. *FJ*, 25 Aug. 1879.
70. *Ibid.*
71. Sir H. James, *The Work of the Irish Leagues*, London 1890, 135.
72. For Davitt's fears on this subject see *Devoy's Post-Bag*, I, 483, Davitt to Devoy, 6 Feb. 1880.
73. *CT*, 14 Jun. 1879.
74. *Ibid.*, 21 Jun. 1879.
75. Harris, with the benefit of hindsight, later claimed that he was not so optimistic but 'took the chance'. (*The Special Commission Act, 1888. Reprint of the Shorthand Notes of the Speeches, Proceedings and Evidence taken before the Commissioners appointed under the above-named Act*, London 1890, X, 179 (hereafter cited as *Spec. Comm. Proc.*).)
76. Devoy (Pt viii) in *Gaelic American*, 28 Jul. 1906. For Harris, A. B. Finegan, 'The Land War in South-East Galway, 1879–90' (unpublished M.A. thesis, University College, Galway, 1974),

20–5, should be consulted. For his great-grandson's view see U. O'Connor, *A Terrible Beauty is Born*, London 1975, 1–5.
77. *Spec. Comm. Proc.*, X, 188.
78. *Galway Vindicator*, 20 Apr. 1881.
79. *Ibid.*
80. *Western News*, 7 Dec. 1878.
81. *IW*, 7 May 1881.
82. *Spec. Comm. Proc.*, III, 601–2.
83. *Devoy's Post-Bag*, II, 108, Egan to Devoy, 17 Feb. 1882.
84. Devoy, *Land of Eire*, 50.
85. Davitt, *op. cit.*, 112.
86. Devoy, *op. cit.*, 46–7. Parnell later claimed that the action of the Fenians in joining the 'constitutional' movement was 'quite honest . . . and they had no *arrière pensée* of any sort'. (*Spec. Comm. Proc.*, VII, 88.)
87. F. H. O'Donnell, *A History of the Irish Parliamentary Party*, London 1910, 381.
88. *FJ*, 4 Feb. 1879.
89. *CT*, 14 Jun. 1879.
90. Kettle, *op. cit.*, 34. Kettle also recorded Parnell's attempt to win over Toomey, the Conservative election agent for Wicklow. He had never heard, he later claimed, a more interesting conversation between two men—Toomey bantering Parnell for leaving the landlord lines, Parnell defending and striking back all round. Parnell later asked Kettle to tell him seriously who had had the best of the bout. (*Ibid.*, 27.)
91. *Boston Pilot*, 11 Dec. 1880, quoted in *FJ*, 23 Dec. 1880.
92. W. O'Brien, *Recollections*, London 1905, 202.
93. *FJ*, 14 Oct. 1881. For particularly clear expositions of this theme see Parnell's speeches at Liverpool (*ibid.*, 1 Dec. 1879), New Ross (*ibid.*, 27 Sep. 1880) and in parliament (*Hansard*, cclv, 2017–18 (24 Aug. 1880)). Two other major examples are discussed on pp. 152 and 186 below.
94. *IW*, 1 Jun. 1881 (cabled 23 May).
95. *FJ*, 24 Aug. 1880. See also especially Smyth's Clonmel speech (*Munster Express*, 14 Aug. 1880).
96. *Tipperary People*, 11 Jun. 1880.
97. *FJ*, 1 Nov. 1880.
98. Davitt, *op. cit.*, 174.
99. O'Donnell, *op. cit.*, I, 377.
100. *Ibid.*, I, 373.
101. *FJ*, 27 Oct, and 3 and 10 Nov. 1880.
102. *Devoy's Post-Bag*, I, 453, Davitt to Devoy, 23 Aug. 1879.
103. *Ibid.*
104. *Ibid.*
105. This statement is worth noting, as the bulk of P. J. P. Tynan's charge against the constitutionalists in *The Irish National Invincibles and their Times*, London 1894, is the claim that the Parnellites had committed themselves to the opposite position.

106. *CT*, 23 Aug. 1879.
107. *Ibid.*, 30 Aug. 1879.
108. *FJ*, 15 Nov. 1879 (Kavanagh's speech).
109. *Devoy's Post-Bag*, I, 453, Davitt to Devoy, 23 Aug. 1879.
110. *FJ*, 12 Sep. 1879.
111. Henry to Daunt, 11 Jan. 1880 (NLI, Daunt Papers, MS. 11446).
112. *Report of the Special Commission, 1888*, 21, H. C. 1890 [C. 5891] XXVII, 501.
113. *FJ*, 16 Oct. 1879 (Belfast speech).
114. Davitt, *op. cit.*, 160.
115. *Ibid.*
116. *CT*, 19 Jul. 1879.
117. Devoy (Pt xvii) in *Gaelic American*, 3 Nov. 1906.
118. Quoted in C. J. Woods, 'The Catholic Church and Irish Politics, 1879–92' (unpublished Ph.D. thesis, University of Nottingham, 1968), 47.
119. *Spec. Comm. Proc.*, III, 355–6.
120. *CT*, 23 Aug. 1879.
121. *Ibid.*, 27 Sep. 1879; Davitt, *op. cit.*, 159.
122. *CT*, 8 Nov. 1879.
123. *Clare Independent*, 10 Apr. 1880.
124. R. B. O'Brien, *The Life of Charles Stewart Parnell*, London 1899, I, 191–2.
125. Sir C. Russell, *The Parnell Commission: The Opening Speech for the Defence*, London 1899, 189.
126. Devoy, *Land of Eire*, 57.
127. The average number of peasant proprietors created through these means in any one year in the 1870s was 80. (Dublin *Daily Express*, 27 Jul. 1881.)
128. *Spec. Comm. Proc.*, IX, 28–9.
129. *FJ*, 27 Oct. 1879.
130. *Ibid.*, 6 Nov. 1879.
131. *Ibid.*, 1 Nov. 1879. See also *Devoy's Post-Bag*, I, 459–60.
132. *FJ*, 6 Nov. 1879.
133. *Nation*, 22 Nov. 1879.
134. *FJ*, 17 Dec. 1879.
135. *Ibid.*, 18 Dec. 1879.
136. Henry to Daunt, 11 Jan. 1880 (NLI, Daunt Papers, MS. 11446).
137. *Ibid.*
138. *Ibid.*
139. Moody in *Irish Historical Studies* XV, No. 60 (Sep. 1967), 444–5.

Chapter 4
LAND LEAGUERS *VERSUS* MODERATE HOME
RULERS
(pp. 74–97)

1. *Devoy's Post-Bag*, I, 454, Davitt to Devoy, 23 Aug. 1879.
2. R. B. O'Brien, *Parnell*, I, 198.

3. New York *Herald*, 2 Jan. 1880.
4. *FJ*, 22 Dec. 1879.
5. New York *Herald*, 2 Jan. 1880.
6. *Ibid.*
7. James, *Work of the Irish Leagues*, 172.
8. New York *Herald*, 3 Jan. 1880.
9. *IW*, 17 Jan. 1880.
10. *IT*, 18 Jan. 1880. This report from its special reporter on the Parnell tour is dated 5 Jan. It was a significant political fact in itself, which Land Leaguers publicly noted, that the *Freeman's Journal* did not send a reporter to cover the tour.
11. *Ibid.*, 7 Jan. 1880.
12. *IW*, 17 Jan. 1880.
13. *Devoy's Post-Bag*, I, 457, Davitt to J. J. O'Kelly, 22 Oct. 1879.
14. *IT*, 20 Jan. 1880 (report dated 6 Jan.).
15. *Ibid.*, 22 Jan. 1880 (report dated 9 Jan.).
16. F. S. L. Lyons, *Charles Stewart Parnell*, London 1977, 108–9, writes: 'There is reason to believe that the effect of . . . tragic stories from home was to give the relief of famine the dominant place in his thoughts and in his speeches at the expense of his other objective, the winning of financial support for the League.' It seems more likely that New York politics rather than stories from home lay behind this new development. For a wider discussion of this fine biography see P. Bew, 'The Hollow Man', *Books Ireland*, No. 17 (Oct. 1977), 198–9.
17. *IT*, 22 Jan. 1880 (report dated 9 Jan.).
18. *Ibid.*, 30 Jan. 1880 (report dated 15 Jan.).
19. *FJ*, 21 Jan. 1880.
20. *Ibid.*, 27 Jan. 1880.
21. *Spec. Comm. Proc.*, III, 603; see also *Western News*, editorial, 20 Dec. 1879.
22. *Western News*, 31 Jan. 1880.
23. *FJ*, 13 Feb. 1880.
24. *Ibid.*, 8 Feb. 1880 (speech of 30 Jan. 1880).
25. *Devoy's Post-Bag*, I, 486, Carroll to Devoy, 8 Feb, 1880.
26. R. B. O'Brien, *op. cit.*, I, 203.
27. F. S. L. Lyons, 'The Political Ideas of Parnell', *Historical Journal* XVI (Dec. 1973), 761.
28. *Spec. Comm. Proc.*, VII, 22.
29. R. B. O'Brien, *op. cit.*, I, 203.
30. James, *op. cit.*, 175–6.
31. *Devoy's Post-Bag*, I, 499–501, Carroll to Devoy, 11 Mar. 1880; *ibid.*, I, 504–8, Carroll to Devoy, 23 Mar. 1880.
32. *Ibid.*, I, 467–8, Carroll to Devoy, 7 Dec. 1879.
33. *Ibid.*, I, 332–3; see also *ibid.*, I, 534, Devoy to Reynolds, 21 Jun. 1880.
34. Devoy, *Land of Eire*, 67.
35. Davitt, *Fall of Feudalism*, 210.
36. *IW*, 17 Jan. 1880.

37. F. S. L. Lyons, 'The Economic Ideas of Parnell' in M. Roberts, ed., *Historical Studies* II, London 1959, 64.
38. *IW*, 7 Feb. 1880.
39. C. S. Parnell, 'The Irish Land Question', *North American Review* CXXX, No. 1 (Apr. 1880).
40. This phrase is taken from Parnell's speech of 19 Oct. 1880 at the Land League headquarters in Dublin. (*FJ*, 20 Oct. 1880.)
41. Claims about the increase in waste land have to be treated with care. T. W. Grimshaw claimed that this increase was a statistical illusion created by the increasing accuracy of the enumerators in carrying out their classifications, which had grown more rigorous. (*Facts and Figures about Ireland*, 20.) For an argument which lays stress on the increase in waste see A. M. Sullivan's paper, reprinted as Appendix C in Davitt, *The* Times–*Parnell Commission: Speech Delivered in Defence of the Land League.*
42. *FJ*, 22 Apr. 1880.
43. *Weekly Freeman*, 13 Sep. 1879.
44. *Ibid.*
45. *Richmond Comm.*, 122 (Q. 3728).
46. *Ibid.*, 1086 (Qs 29402–9).
47. *FJ*, 22 Apr. 1880.
48. *Western News*, 27 Aug. 1881 (interview dated 28 Jul.).
49. For a full report of this speech see *CT*, 5 Jun. 1880.
50. G. F. Trench, *The Land Question. Are the Landlords Worth Preserving?*, Dublin 1881, 42.
51. Dublin *Evening Mail*, cited in *Leitrim Advertiser*, 13 May 1880.
52. Quoted in Trench, *op. cit.*, 56.
53. *Ibid.*, 58.
54. *Census for Ireland, 1881*, Table 62, p. 214.
55. *Ibid.*, Table 48, pp. 165–6.
56. W. O'Brien, *Recollections*, 205. See also his report in *FJ*, 28 Aug. 1879, on this point.
57. *Roscommon Herald*, 13 Dec. 1879.
58. *Leitrim Advertiser*, 4 Jan. 1880.
59. *FJ*, 4 Jan. 1880.
60. *Ibid.*, 6 Jan. 1880; see also 'Transatlantic' in *IW*, 7 Feb. 1880.
61. *FJ*, 6 Jan. 1880.
62. *Ibid.*, 7 Jan. 1880.
63. *CT*, 31 Jan. 1880.
64. *Ibid.*, 23 Aug. 1879.
65. *Ibid.*, 13 Mar. 1880.
66. *Ibid.*, 29 May 1880.
67. *Western News*, 20 Sep. 1879.
68. *Ibid.*, 11 Oct. 1879.
69. *FJ*, 9 Oct. 1880.
70. *Western News*, 11 Oct. 1879.
71. *Ibid.*, 19 Jun. 1880.
72. *Weekly Freeman*, 19 Mar. 1881; *FJ*, 9 May 1881.
73. *Ibid.*

74. *Royal Commission on Labour: Assistant Commissioners' Reports on the Agricultural Labourer: Vol. IV (Ireland), Pt IV, by Mr Wilson-Fox*, 11, H. C. 1893/4 [C. 6894–XXI] XXXVII, Pt I, 352.
75. J. E. Handley, *The Irish in Modern Scotland*, Cork 1947, 170–1.
76. Dun, *Landlords and Tenants in Ireland*, 254.
77. J. A. Fox in 'Report to the Mansion House Relief Committee, 5 July 1880' in *The Irish Crisis of 1879–80: Proceedings of the Dublin Mansion House Relief Committee, 1880*, 110.
78. Dun, *op. cit.*, 255.
79. *Devoy's Post-Bag*, I, 483, Davitt to Devoy, 6 Feb. 1880.
80. *IW*, 24 Apr. 1880 (cable of 14 Apr.).
81. Dillon to Parnell, 20 Apr. 1880 (NLI, Land League MSS, 8291).
82. *IW*, 29 May 1880.
83. *Times*, 23 Apr. 1880.
84. See Chapter 1 above on this point.
85. *Devoy's Post-Bag*, I, 453, Davitt to Devoy, 23 Aug. 1879.
86. A. B. Finegan, 'The Land War in South-East Galway, 1879–90' (unpublished M.A. thesis, University College, Galway, 1974), 8–9.
87. For the Balla meeting see *Report of the Special Commission, 1888*, Appendix IV, 127–31, H. C. 1890 [C. 5891] XXVII, 607–11.
88. CSO, RP, 264/1880.
89. Davitt, *op. cit.*, 213.
90. *Ibid.*, 213–14.
91. *FJ*, 10 Jan. 1880.
92. *Ibid.*
93. *Devoy's Post-Bag*, I, 483, Davitt to Devoy, 6 Feb. 1880.
94. *Ibid.*, I, 490, O'Kelly to Devoy, 11 Feb. 1880.
95. Davitt, *op. cit.*, 264.
96. *Ibid.*, 219.
97. New York *Herald*, 2 Jan. 1880.
98. *Ibid.*
99. Louden's efforts are recorded at Westport (*CT*, 10 Jan. 1880) and at Swinford (*ibid.*, 24 Jan. and 10 Apr. 1880). For Bodkin see *Galway Vindicator*, 28 Jan. 1880.
100. *Ibid.*, 24 Jul. 1880.
101. *Hansard*, ccliv, 1376 (29 Jul. 1880).
102. Davitt, *op. cit.*, 219.
103. *IT*, 28 Jan. 1880.
104. *Western News*, 20 Dec. 1879.
105. *Ibid.*, 7 Feb. 1880.
106. *CT*, 10 Apr. 1880.
107. *FJ*, 21 Apr. 1880.
108. *Weekly Freeman*, 5 Mar. 1881; see also *ibid.*, 13 Jul. 1881.
109. Davitt, *op. cit.*, 219–20.
110. *IW*, 29 May 1880.
111. *Ibid.*, 24 Jul. 1880.
112. *CT*, 8 May 1880.
113. *FJ*, 2 Apr. 1880.
114. *Ibid.*, 19 Mar. 1880.

115. *Clare Independent*, 7 May 1880.
116. *FJ*, 19 Apr. 1880.
117. Davitt, *op. cit.*, 211.
118. *FJ*, 2 Apr. 1880.
119. *Ibid.*, 3 Apr. 1880. The area already had a reputation for extremist activity. As early as 21 June 1879 Dunmore had been singled out in a special report prepared for the Conservative Chief Secretary Lowther as a Fenian area of 'unenviable notoriety'. (CSO, RP, 10269/1879.)
120. *FJ*, 9 Apr. 1880.
121. *Ibid.*, 6 Apr. 1880.
122. *Ibid.*, 15 Apr. 1880.
123. *Ibid.*, 17 Apr. 1880.
124. *Ibid.*, 9 Feb. 1881.
125. Davitt, *op. cit.*, 227.
126. *FJ*, 15 Mar. 1880.

Chapter 5
THE LAND LEAGUE PROGRAMME
(pp. 98–114)
1. *FJ*, 27 Mar. 1880.
2. *Ibid.*
3. *Ibid.*, 30 Mar. 1880.
4. J. J. O'Kelly in his evidence before the Special Commission (*Spec. Comm. Proc.*, X, 169); T. P. O'Connor, *Memoirs of an Old Parliamentarian*, London 1929, I, 122; J. McCarthy, *The Story of an Irishman*, London 1904, 217. It should be added that William O'Brien argued that T. P. O'Connor was elected because he was thought to be an English radical. (*Recollections*, 244–5.)
5. Villiers Stuart to Gladstone, 23 Jul. 1881 (BM, Gladstone Papers, Add. MS. 44469).
6. *FJ*, 10 May 1880.
7. A. O'Day, *The English Face of Irish Nationalism*, Dublin 1977, 12.
8. *FJ*, 21 Apr. 1880.
9. Davitt, *Fall of Feudalism*, 241.
10. *Ibid.*, 141.
11. *Ibid.*, 242.
12. *FJ*, 27 Apr. 1880.
13. *Ibid.*
14. *Ibid.*, 30 Apr. 1880.
15. S. Clark, 'The Political Mobilisation of Irish Farmers', *Canadian Review of Sociology and Anthropology* XII (1975), 493.
16. *Spec. Comm. Proc.*, III, 602.
17. *Kilkenny Journal*, 22 May 1880.
18. *FJ*, 7 Jan. 1880.
19. *Leinster Leader*, 6 Aug. 1881.
20. *FJ*, 30 Apr. 1880.
21. *Ibid.*; see also *CT*, 8 May 1880.

22. *FJ*, 30 Apr. 1880.
23. *Ibid.*, 15 May 1880 (letter by Harris).
24. See p. 30 above.
25. New York *Herald*, 3 Jan. 1880.
26. For the recent struggles of the agricultural labourers to improve their conditions see P. L. R. Horn, 'The National Agricultural Union in Ireland, 1873–9', *Irish Historical Studies* XVII, No. 67 (Mar. 1971), 340–52.
27. See p. 87 above. Harris's position was based at least to a certain extent on statistical reality. The rate of decline of tillage had been considerably greater on large as against small holdings in the period 1854–74. (See J. Hooper, introductory essay in Department of Industry and Commerce, *Saorstát Éireann, Agricultural Statistics, 1847–1926*, Dublin 1928, xlv.) In fact, as Hooper pointed out, the situation changed in the period 1874–1912, when tillage decreased very much more rapidly on small as against large farms. But when Harris spoke in 1879 it was still possible to believe that the small farm was unequivocally the 'friend' of tillage production and the large farm unequivocally its 'enemy'.
28. See *FJ*, editorial, 8 Apr. 1880, on this point.
29. *Spec. Comm. Proc.*, IX, 229. Harrington's recollection may not, of course, have been entirely accurate. However, as late as 23 April 1880 his paper reprinted a typical moderate *Freeman's Journal* article on fixity of tenure.
30. *Munster Express*, 4 Jan. 1880.
31. *FJ*, 17 May 1880.
32. *Ibid.*, 30 Apr. 1880.
33. *Irishman*, 15 May 1880 (letter dated 4 May).
34. *FJ*, 30 Apr. 1880.
35. *Ibid.*
36. *Ibid.*, 1 May 1880.
37. *Ibid.*, 3 May 1880.
38. *Ibid.* See also the letter by J. A. Bermingham on this point in *ibid.*, 8 May 1880.
39. *Ibid.*, 3 May 1880.
40. *Ibid.*
41. Davitt, *op. cit.*, 242–3.
42. *FJ*, 3 May 1880.
43. *Ibid.*, 4 May 1880.
44. *Ibid.*, 5 May 1880.
45. *Ibid.*, 8 May 1880 (letter by J. A. Bermingham).
46. *Ibid.*, 17 May 1880.
47. *Ibid.*
48. O'Connor, *op. cit.*, I, 45.
49. R. B. O'Brien, *Parnell*, I, 223.
50. *FJ*, 19 May 1880.
51. *Ibid.*
52. *Limerick Reporter*, 21 May 1880.
53. *FJ*, 21 Jan. 1880.

54. *Ibid.*, 19 May 1880.
55. *Ibid.*, 17 Jun. 1880 (Gray's letter of explanation).
56. *Ibid.*, 23 Jun. 1880.
57. Lord Eversley [G. J. Shaw Lefevre], *Gladstone and Ireland*, London 1912, 115.
58. *CT*, 3 Jul. 1880.
59. Davitt, *op. cit.*, 147.
60. *CT*, 15 Jan. 1881.
61. *FJ*, 14 Jun. 1880.
62. *Spec. Comm. Proc.*, III, 603–4.
63. T. M. Healy, *Letters and Leaders of My Day*, London [1928], I, 94.
64. *FJ*, 12 May 1880.
65. *Ibid.*, 2 Jun. 1880.
66. *Ibid.*, 9 Jun. 1880.
67. *Ibid.*, 26 May 1880.
68. *Ibid.*, 16 Jun. 1880.
69. *Ibid.*, 18 Jun. 1880.
70. *Ibid.*, 26 May 1880.
71. *Ibid.*, 9 Jun. 1880.
72. *Ibid.*, 11 Aug. 1880.
73. *Ibid.*, 25 Aug. 1880.
74. *IW*, 10 Apr. 1880.
75. New York *Herald*, 3 Jan. 1880. (For the Balla affair see pp. 91–2 above.)
76. *FJ*, 21 Jul. 1880.
77. *Ibid.*
78. *Ibid.*
79. *Ibid.*
80. Mallon, report, 10 Aug. 1880 (SPO, INL Papers, Spec. Comm. docs, 1888, carton 9).
81. *FJ*, 9 Jun. 1880.
82. *Ibid.*, 14 Jun. 1880.
83. *CT*, 24 Jul. 1880.
84. *IW*, 7 Aug. 1880.
85. *Clare Advertiser*, 24 Jul. 1880.

Chapter 6
THE EXPANSION OF THE LAND LEAGUE
(pp. 115–144)
1. W. O'Brien, *Recollections*, 276.
2. *FJ*, 31 May 1880.
3. For a similar assessment see E. Larkin, *The Roman Catholic Church and the Creation of the Modern Irish State, 1878–1886*, Philadelphia and Dublin 1975, 41 and 52–3.
4. *Limerick Reporter*, 8 Jun. 1880.
5. *Tipperary People*, 28 Jan. 1881.
6. *FJ*, 27 Aug. 1880.
7. *Ibid.*, 17 Aug. 1880.

8. *Tipperary People*, 11 and 18 Jun. 1880.
9. *Ibid.*, 28 Jan. 1881: 'During the fray Mr Boyton was on the scene at all critical times, counselling and aiding the Slievenamon Land League and cheering on the determination of the people. He planted the flag at Kilburry and did not remove it till it bore fruit [*sic*].'
10. *FJ*, 14 Jul. 1880.
11. *Ibid.*, 21 Jul. 1880.
12. *Ibid.*, 18 Aug. 1880.
13. *Ibid.*, 28 Aug. 1880.
14. *Ibid.*, 23 Aug. 1880.
15. *Ibid.*, 27 Aug. 1880.
16. *Leitrim Advertiser*, 21 Sep. 1880.
17. *FJ*, 1 and 15 Sep. 1880.
18. *Ibid.*, 27 Aug. 1880.
19. Despite Justice Barry's claim that the evidence against the accused was of an overwhelming nature, several of the jurors held out for a considerable time for an acquittal but eventually agreed to a verdict of guilty on the terms of the entire jury joining in a strong recommendation for mercy. (Correspondence and statistics regarding cases of agrarian crime in the winter assizes of 1880 (PRO, Colonial Office, 904/182).)
20. *Munster Express*, 22 Jan. 1881.
21. *FJ*, 2 Aug. 1880.
22. *Ibid.*
23. *Clare Advertiser*, 6 Jul. 1880.
24. *Ibid.*, 31 Jul. 1880.
25. K. C. Cowper, *Earl Cowper, K.G. A Memoir by his Wife*, (privately printed) [London?] 1913, 375, Spencer to Cowper, 6 Jul. 1880.
26. *Ibid.*, 377, Cowper to Spencer, 12 Jul. 1880.
27. *Ibid.*, 330, Cowper to Hon. H. Cowper, 18 Jul. 1880.
28. *Hansard*, ccliv, 355–7 (13 Jul. 1880).
29. *Ibid.*, cclv, 49 (3 Aug. 1880). J. L. Hammond, *Gladstone and the Irish Nation*, London 1938, 176–81, gives the Gladstonian view of the debate. For Forster's view see R. Hawkins, 'Liberals, Land and Coercion in the Summer of 1880: The Influence of the Carraroe Ejectments', *Journal of the Galway Archaeological and Historical Society* XXXIV (1974–75), 54–7. For Selborne's misgivings see R. Palmer, Earl of Selborne, *Memorials*, Pt. 2: *Personal and Political, 1865–95*, London 1898, I, 490.
30. *FJ*, 2 Aug. 1880.
31. R. B. O'Brien, *Parnell*, I, 230.
32. Hawkins in *Journal of the Galway Archaeological and Historical Society* XXXIV (1974–75), 56.
33. CSO, RP, 15839/1880 (the 'Carraroe File').
34. *FJ*, 27 Sep. 1880.
35. *Ibid.*, 11 Aug. 1880.
36. *Ibid.* For my earlier discussion of 'rent at the point of the bayonet'

see P. Bew, 'Irish Histories', *Cambridge Review* XCIV (1973), 152–3.

37. G. Ó Tuathaigh, *Ireland before the Famine, 1798–1848*, Dublin 1972, 177. Anna Parnell argued also that 'Tithe and rent stood on different leases. Distraint was the only means by which the payment of tithes could be effected and distraint [was] . . . necessarily troublesome, expensive and ineffective. The government of that day was unable to employ further means because the landlords were behind the parsons and were by far the most important body of the two. Extremities to enforce payment of the latter's claims would have jeopardised the interests of the landlords and so the hands of the government were in a sense tied. The penalty of eviction had to be kept sacred for the landlord's use.' (A. Parnell, 'Tale of the Land League: A Great Sham' (NLI MS. 12144).)

38. Ó Tuathaigh, *op. cit.*, 176.

39. *Leinster Express*, 17 Jul. 1880.

40. *FJ*, 10 Aug. 1880.

41. A. Parnell, 'Tale of the Land League: A Great Sham' (NLI MS. 12144).

42. *People's Advocate*, 28 Aug. 1880.

43. A. Parnell, 'Tale of the Land League: A Great Sham' (NLI MS. 12144).

44. *Westmeath Guardian*, 8 Apr. 1881.

45. C. C. O'Brien, *Parnell and his Party*, Oxford 1957, 3.

46. Sir T. W. Reid, *Life of the Rt Hon. W. E. Forster*, 2nd ed., London 1888, II, 269, Forster to Gladstone, 18 Nov. 1880.

47. *IW*, 23 Oct. 1880.

48. See, for example, the League organiser J. R. Heffernan's account of his own case (*Cork Weekly Herald*, 5 Mar. 1881).

49. *FJ*, 6 Dec. 1880 and 9 and 14 Feb. 1881.

50. NLI, Land League MSS, 8291, PC 658–60.

51. *Waterford News*, 29 Oct. 1880.

52. *FJ*, 18 and 19 Nov. 1880.

53. *Ibid.*, 24 Nov. 1880.

54. *Ibid.*, 1 Dec. 1880.

55. NLI, Land League MSS, 8291.

56. *Clare Freeman*, 6 Oct. 1880.

57. *FJ*, 23 Nov. 1880.

58. *Roscommon Herald*, 16 Apr. 1881.

59. *IW*, 22 May 1880. John O'Connor was allegedly, according to a police report (SPO, B47), the main link between the Munster IRB and the Land League at this time. For O'Connor's own account of his evolution towards Parnellism see his evidence before the Special Commission (*Spec. Comm. Proc.*, IX, 628).

60. S. Clark, 'The Social Composition of the Land League', *Irish Historical Studies* XVII, No. 68 (Sep. 1971), 458. But see also, on the problem of 'town and country' during the land war, Lee, *Modernisation of Irish Society*, 97–9.

61. Clark in *Irish Historical Studies* XVII, No. 68 (Sep. 1971), 455.
62. *FJ*, 18 Aug. 1880.
63. *Ibid.*, 23 Aug. 1880.
64. *Limerick Reporter*, 5 Oct. 1880.
65. *FJ*, 8 Sep. 1880.
66. *Ibid.*, 10 Sep. 1880.
67. *Ibid.*, 30 Sep. 1880.
68. *Ibid.*, 18 Sep. 1880.
69. *Munster Express*, 28 May 1881 (evidence of Fisher in his Bally-jamesduff speech).
70. *FJ*, 18 Aug. 1880.
71. *Ibid.*, 11 Oct. 1880.
72. However, O'Neill refused to join the IRB after coercion, even on pain of losing his salary. (SPO, B47.)
73. *FJ*, 22 Oct. 1880.
74. *Ibid.*, 1 Oct. 1880.
75. *Ibid.*, 29 Dec. 1880.
76. *Ibid.*, 3 Jan. 1881.
77. *Ibid.*, 5 Oct. 1880; see also *King's County Chronicle*, 9 Oct. 1880.
78. *King's County Chronicle*, 25 Nov. 1880.
79. *Ibid.*, 17 Feb. 1881.
80. *FJ*, 11 Oct. 1880; *Irish Farmer's Gazette,* 16 Oct. 1880; see also *Westmeath Guardian*, 6 Nov. 1880.
81. *Carlow Sentinel*, 23 Oct. 1880.
82. *FJ*, 19 Oct. and 19 Nov. 1880.
83. The allegedly stringent terms of the Leinster lease, which were said to deprive tenants of some of the benefit of the 1870 Land Act, brought the Duke into severe conflict with Maynooth College and the Athy Board of Guardians—for both bodies refused to accept it. (*Leinster Express*, 23 Apr. 1881.)
84. *Kildare Observer*, 8 Jan. 1881.
85. *Ibid.*, 19 Feb. 1881.
86. *Ibid.*, 9 Jul. 1881.
87. *Roscommon Herald*, 23 Oct. 1880.
88. *FJ*, 4 Aug. 1880.
89. Sub-Inspector Hindley, report, 22 Jan. 1881 (SPO, Protection of Person and Property Act, No. 1).
90. Davitt, *Fall of Feudalism*, 311.
91. *FJ*, 11 Oct. 1880; see also *ibid.*, 1 Nov. 1880.
92. *Leitrim Advertiser*, 8 Apr. 1880.
93. *FJ*, 16 Jun. 1880.
94. *Leitrim Advertiser*, 6 Nov. 1880.
95. *Ibid.*, 11 Nov. 1880.
96. *Western News*, 27 Nov. 1880.
97. *Leitrim Advertiser*, 16 Jun. and 11 Aug. 1881.
98. Dun, *Landlords and Tenants in Ireland*, 211–12. One writer, Warburton, replied to Dun's cool account of the local League activity in the Roscommon press. He claimed that the poor Irish tenantry had been driven on to the bog and forced to reclaim it

by their labour. There were spots where twenty years previously it had been dangerous to shoot wild fowl which were now rented at 15s or 20s per acre. It was this history of oppression which, above all, justified the tenantry's demands. The writer added that he knew a farm of 150 acres which a grazier had been forced to give up and which the landlord intended to subdivide into four or five farms. He was expected to receive a rent equal to that which the outgoing tenant was unable to pay—and also the approbation of the tenantry. (*Roscommon Messenger*, 16 Apr. 1881.)

99. *Roscommon Herald*, 16 Apr. 1881.
100. Grimshaw, *Facts and Figures about Ireland*, 11. On this point see also Lee, *op. cit.*, 79–80.
101. *Spec. Comm. Proc.*, III, 603–4, Dillon to Harris, 4 Apr. 1880.
102. *FJ*, 12 Oct. 1880.
103. For a recent narrative see J. Marlow, *Captain Boycott and the Irish*, London 1973.
104. *Spec. Comm. Proc.*, VIII, 86–7.
105. *CT*, 20 Nov. 1880.
106. *FJ*, 18 Aug. 1880.
107. *Ibid.*
108. *CT*, 1 Jan. 1881.
109. *Ibid.*, 8 Jan. 1881.
110. *IW*, 5 Feb. 1881. See Dublin *Daily Express*, 15 Feb. 1881, for hostile editorial comment.
111. *CT*, 29 May 1880, marks the beginning of this split.
112. *Spec. Comm. Proc.*, VII, 56.
113. *Western News*, 6 Nov. 1880.
114. *Limerick Reporter*, 8 Nov. 1880.
115. *Western News*, 11 Dec. 1880.
116. *Spec. Comm. Proc.*, III, 610–16, Harris's diary. (The diary was confiscated by the RIC, and the portion relating to the period between November 1880 and 15 July 1882 was reproduced in *Spec. Comm. Proc.*)
117. *Ibid.*, III, 611.
118. *IT*, 18 Feb. 1881.
119. *Ibid.*
120. *Ibid.*
121. *Spec. Comm. Proc.*, III, 615–16.
122. *Western News*, 2 Apr. 1881.
123. *IW*, 20 Nov. 1880.
124. *Ibid.*, 19 Feb. 1881.
125. Devoy, *Land of Eire*, 83.
126. *Ibid.*
127. *Weekly Freeman*, 18 Dec. 1880.
128. *Devoy's Post-Bag*, II, 20–5, Davitt to Devoy, 16 Dec. 1880.
129. Davitt refused on 14 December 1880 to accept Sexton's argument that the League was purely a 'social movement' and that therefore green flags should no longer be carried at demonstrations in the North. Davitt was desperately keen to win support in the

North for the League, and his decision to place nationalist principle before this objective was significant. (*Weekly Freeman,* 18 Dec. 1880.)

130. *FJ,* 22 Nov. 1880.
131. *Ibid.,* 20 Sep. 1880. It is interesting to note that on 13 September Captain O'Shea had written to Gladstone informing him that he was, with the help of the priests, successfully opposing the League in Clare. (BM, Gladstone Papers, Add. MS. 56646.) By the time he received Gladstone's reply of 21 September congratulating him on the union of the people and the pastors against extremists (K. O'Shea, *Charles Stewart Parnell,* London 1914, I, 146) eight priests had joined Parnell on the Ennis platform.
132. *FJ,* 27 Sep. 1880.
133. *Ibid.,* 29 Sep. 1880.
134. *Ibid.*
135. *Ibid.,* 23 Dec. 1880.
136. *Ibid.,* 4 Oct. 1880.
137. *Ibid.*
138. *Ibid.,* 18 Oct. 1880.
139. *Ibid.,* 16 Oct. 1880.
140. *Ibid.,* 5 and 13 Oct. 1880.
141. *Ibid.,* 5 Oct. 1880.
142. *Ibid.,* 20 Oct. 1880.
143. *Ibid.,* 23 Oct. 1880.
144. *Weekly Freeman,* 16 Oct. 1880.
145. *FJ,* 18 Oct. 1880.
146. *Ibid.,* 2 Nov. 1880.
147. *Ibid.,* 27 Oct. 1880.
148. *Ibid.*
149. *Ibid.,* 3 Nov. 1880.
150. *Ibid.,* 13 Nov. 1880.
151. *Ibid.,* 17 Nov. 1880.
152. *Ibid.,* 6 Dec. 1880. See also the significant *Spectator* editorial of 11 Dec. 1880. Although Parnell utilised these themes in his critique of the Land Bill at Glasgow in April 1881, it was in a relatively restrained tone. In any case, his speech was criticised in the *Kilkenny Moderator,* 20 Apr. 1881.
153. Parnell may have been helped—though there is little hard evidence on this subject—by *The Times,* which flirted with the concept of peasant proprietorship. (*Times,* 13 Nov. 1880.)
154. *FJ,* 18 Nov. 1880.
155. *Wexford Independent,* 17 Oct. 1880.
156. *FJ,* 14 Oct. 1880.
157. *Limerick Reporter,* 17 Oct. 1880.
158. *Richmond Comm.,* 552 (Qs 15797–8).
159. *Limerick Reporter,* 19 Oct. 1880; see also *Irish Farmer's Gazette,* 23 Oct. 1880.
160. *FJ,* 20 Oct. 1880.
161. *Limerick Reporter,* 22 Oct. 1880.

162. Palmer, *Irish Land League Crisis*, 271.
163. Dublin *Daily Express*, 14 Jan. 1881.
164. *Ibid*. See also B. H. Becker, *Disturbed Ireland*, London 1881, 78–9, for further evidence.

Chapter 7
COERCION, LANDLORDS AND GLADSTONE'S
LAND BILL, 1881
(pp. 145–165)

1. Cowper, *Cowper*, 422–4, Cowper, cabinet memo, 8 Nov. 1880.
2. Davitt, *Fall of Feudalism*, 185.
3. Cowper, *op. cit.*, 427–8, Cowper to Gladstone, 13 Nov. 1880.
4. *Ibid.*, 438–9, Spencer to Cowper, 28 Nov. 1880.
5. *Ibid.*, 441.
6. C. H. D. Howard, ed., *Joseph Chamberlain: A Political Memoir, 1880–92*, London 1953, 6.
7. Cowper, *op. cit.*, 444, Hartington to Cowper, 8 Dec. 1880.
8. *Ibid.*, 428; see also Forster, cabinet memo, 15 Nov. 1880 (BM, Gladstone Papers, Add. MS. 44625).
9. Howard, *op. cit.*, 10.
10. Gladstone to Forster, 16 Nov. 1880 (BM, Gladstone Papers, Add. MS. 44157).
11. Comment by Gladstone on Forster, cabinet memo, 15 Nov. 1880 (BM, Gladstone Papers, Add. MS. 44625).
12. On this point see Hammond, *Gladstone and the Irish Nation*, 196.
13. A. B. Cooke and J. R. Vincent, ed., 'Herbert Gladstone, Forster, and Ireland, 1881–2', Pt 2, *Irish Historical Studies* XVIII, No. 69 (Mar. 1972), 75, H. Gladstone's journal, 23 Apr. 1882.
14. Cowper, *op. cit.*, 429, Cowper to Forster, 18 Nov. 1880.
15. Forster to Gladstone, 18 Nov. 1880 (BM, Gladstone Papers, Add. MS. 44157).
16. Cowper, *op. cit.*, 430. Indeed, Gladstone's reply of 18 Nov. 1880 (BM, Gladstone Papers, Add. MS. 44157) suggests that he felt that Burke had been shown his plan prematurely by Forster.
17. Cowper, *op. cit.*, 435, Cowper to Gladstone, 23 Nov. 1880.
18. *Ibid.*, 435, Gladstone to Cowper, 24 Nov. 1880.
19. *Ibid.*, 437, Cowper to Argyll, 28 Nov. 1880.
20. *Ibid.*, 443, Cowper to Hartington, 4 Dec. 1880.
21. *Ibid.*, 438–9, Spencer to Cowper, 28 Nov. 1880.
22. *Ibid.*, 444, Hartington to Cowper, 8 Dec. 1880.
23. Howard, *op. cit.*, 6.
24. R. B. O'Brien, *Parnell*, I, 262, Cowper to Gladstone, 12 Dec. 1880.
25. Hammond, *op. cit.*, 192. However, there was some dispute about these figures. Forster in his cabinet memo of 15 November cited a figure of 1,372 outrages since the beginning of 1880 (BM, Gladstone Papers, Add. MS. 44625), but a nationalist analysis which discounted threatening letters, duplications and non-agrarian offences in the RIC figures arrived at a total of 332 serious crimes for the first ten months of the year. See the series of articles

entitled 'Mr Forster's Fallacious Figures', *Weekly Freeman*, 12 Feb. 1881 (Munster and Ulster), 19 Feb. 1881 (Connaught), and *FJ*, 5 Feb. 1881 (Leinster). For a comment on the November and December figures see *ibid.*, 8 Jan. 1881.

26. Forster, cabinet memo, 15 Nov. 1880 (BM, Gladstone Papers, Add. MS. 44625).
27. *Report of the Special Commission, 1888*, 24, H.C. 1890 [C. 5891] XXVII, 504.
28. *Spec. Comm. Proc.*, VII, 37.
29. The organisers were Michael Boyton, T. S. Cleary, Joseph Cox, Patrick Fulham, Timothy Harrington, Matthew Harris, J. R. Heffernan (Cork), J. T. Heffernan (Kildare), James Lynam, Martin Mulleague, P. P. O'Neill, P. J. Sheridan, Jasper Tully and W. M. Veale. (SPO, Irish Crimes Records, 1881, Vols I–V.) In the case of T. S. Cleary of Ennis, for example, the local sub-inspector went out of his way to resist successfully the demand of the RM for his arrest. (Report, 27 Feb. 1881 (SPO, Protection of Person and Property Act, No. 1).) After the suppression of the Land League in October 1881 the RIC view of the role of the League organisers and their relationship altered considerably.
30. *Hansard*, cclvii, 1690–1 (28 Jan. 1881).
31. James, *Work of the Irish Leagues*, 215–39. S. Clark, 'The Land War in Ireland' (abstract of unpublished Ph.D. thesis, Harvard University, 1974), 7, has emphasised 'the presence of communication facilities (newspapers and railways)' as a factor in making for the strength of the agitation.
32. Davitt, *op. cit.*, 310: 'Mr Sexton's speech in defence of the Land League on the second reading of the Forster coercion Bill was his first great parliamentary achievement. I have heard it discussed by competent judges who were present as the finest piece of debating eloquence that had been heard in the House of Commons for many years.'
33. For Sexton's major speeches see *Hansard*, cclviii, 2008–27 (31 Jan. 1881) and 438–55 (9 Feb. 1881), particularly 452.
34. For a recent critique by a historian of the conspiracy thesis see Lee, *Modernisation of Irish Society*, 79–85.
35. Hammond, *op. cit.*, 211.
36. R. B. O'Brien, *op. cit.*, I, 248.
37. *Hansard*, cclvii, 905–7 (17 Jan. 1881).
38. H. O. Arnold-Forster, *The Truth about the Land League*, 3rd ed., London 1883, 25.
39. Dublin *Daily Express*, 19 Jan. 1881.
40. *Hansard*, cclvii, 913 (17 Jan. 1881).
41. *Ibid.*, cclvii, 914–16 (17 Jan. 1881).
42. C. C. O'Brien, *Parnell and his Party*, 55.
43. Kettle, *Material for Victory*, 39.
44. See also *Devoy's Post-Bag*, II, 12, 30, 57 and 93, for evidence of Clan na Gael caution.
45. Kettle, *op. cit.*, 45.

46. *Ibid.*, 40.
47. Davitt, *op. cit.*, 309–10.
48. Kettle, *op. cit.*, 45.
49. Dillon raised the 'dispersion' idea in Paris a few days later. (*FJ*, 15 Feb. 1881.)
50. Kettle, *op. cit.*, 38–42.
51. Davitt, *op. cit.*, 309.
52. C. C. O'Brien, *op. cit.*, 61.
53. *FJ*, 23 Mar. 1881.
54. Davitt, *op. cit.*, 310.
55. *FJ*, 28 Dec. 1880.
56. T. P. O'Connor, *The Parnell Movement*, London 1886, 228.
57. Dublin *Daily Express*, 28 Apr. 1881. For an account of the Dungarvan case see *Munster Express*, 12 Feb. 1881.
58. *Munster Express*, 16 Apr. 1881.
59. *Cork Weekly Herald*, 12 Mar. 1881.
60. See *Cork Weekly Herald* in this period.
61. *FJ*, 28 Feb. 1881 (speech at Borrisokane).
62. *Weekly Freeman*, 9 Oct. 1880.
63. See *King's County Chronicle*, 3 Mar. 1881, for a full report. See also RM's report (CSO, RP, 10030/1881).
64. Dublin *Daily Express*, 28 Apr. 1881, quoted by Lord Courtown, the PDA chairman.
65. *FJ*, 9 Mar. 1881.
66. *IT*, 29 Mar. 1881.
67. *FJ*, 1 Mar. 1881 (letter dated Paris, 24 Feb.).
68. *Ibid.*, 29 Mar. 1881.
69. *Ibid.*, 9 Mar. 1881.
70. *Ibid.*, 19 Mar. 1881.
71. *Ibid.*, 21 Mar. 1881.
72. *Kildare Observer*, 9 Apr. 1881 (report of speech made by Dillon on 2 Apr.).
73. The *Spectator* editorial of 25 Sep. 1880 is very clear on this point.
74. *Cork Weekly Herald*, 28 May 1881.
75. *Munster Express*, 19 Feb. 1881.
76. *IW*, 13 Aug. 1881 (speech delivered on 11 Jul.).
77. See in particular *Roscommon Herald*, 26 Apr. 1881.
78. *Cork Weekly Herald*, 2 Apr. 1881.
79. O'Connor, *op. cit.*, 231 and 244.
80. *IW*, 26 Mar. 1881.
81. *FJ*, 30 Mar. 1881.
82. *Ibid.*
83. *Spec. Comm. Proc.*, III, 109.
84. *Dundalk Democrat*, 21 May 1881 (letter dated 19 May).
85. *Hansard*, cclx, 905 (7 Apr. 1881).
86. Edward Hamilton, Gladstone's secretary, argued that the concluding paragraph of the more conservative Richmond Commission's report was the premier's guideline concerning the 'three

Fs'. (Sir E. W. Hamilton, *Diary, 1880–1885*, ed. D. W. R. Bahlman, Oxford 1972, I, 193.) This paragraph supported the demand for protection for tenants who faced the possibility of rent being raised on their improvements, but added that the 'three Fs' would involve injustice to the landlord. On 6 March 1881 Forster wrote to Harcourt that he was 'very melancholy about the Land Bill'. (Bodl., Harcourt MSS, deposit 81.) On 9 March Spencer explained to Cowper that he and Gladstone had agreed—as against Forster—on the impossibility of granting fixity of tenure. Gladstone had put his foot down and refused to introduce the bill if fixity of tenure was adopted. On 3 April Spencer added that although the bill approached the 'three Fs', there was 'enough difference to make an argument tell'. (Cowper, *op. cit.*, 481 and 493.) In his speech Gladstone opposed the system of fixed tenancy, where, in his view, the holding continued subject either to a perpetual fee-farm rent with revaluation by the court at fixed periods, and where all power of redemption by the landlord from any cause, however great and under whatever authority, was taken away. (*Hansard*, cclx, 915 (7 Apr. 1881).) Effectively by defining fixity of tenure as permanent tenure Gladstone convinced himself that he had stopped short of the full measure of fixity of tenure.

87. *FJ*, 28 Mar. 1881.
88. *Marx and Engels on Ireland*, introd. D. Greaves, London and Moscow, 1971, 330, Marx to Jenny Longuet, 11 Apr. 1881.
89. *FJ*, 13 April 1881.
90. W. O'Brien, *Recollections*, 322.
91. *FJ*, 13 Apr. 1881.
92. H. Rylett, 'Parnell', *Contemporary Review* CXXIX (1926), 477.
93. *FJ*, 13 Apr. 1881.
94. *Ibid.*, 27 Oct. 1881.
95. *Ibid.*, 23 Apr. 1881.
96. *IT*, 22 Apr. 1881 (full report of convention).
97. *Ibid.*
98. *FJ*, 30 Apr. 1881.

Chapter 8
'LET THE FARMS GO!'
(pp. 166–190)

1. *IW*, 28 May 1881.
2. *Ibid.*
3. *Spec. Comm. Proc.*, IX, 183.
4. Desmond Ryan's suggestion is to be found in *Devoy's Post-Bag*, II, 86–7.
5. C. C. O'Brien, *Parnell and his Party*, 31.
6. Desmond Ryan allows this as a possible reading. (*Devoy's Post-Bag*, II, 80.)
7. *Ibid.*, II, 84.
8. New York *Herald*, 1 Aug. 1881.

9. See W. O'Brien, *Recollections*, 276–9, for his discussion of this problem.
10. *IW*, 30 Jul. 1881, gives the most complete account of these events; but see also *Nation*, 28 May 1881, and *FJ*, 12 May 1881.
11. Preamble to a New York *Herald* interview with Croke which took place on 16 Jul. 1881 and was printed on 1 Aug. 1881.
12. W. O'Brien, *op. cit.*, 276–9.
13. New York *Herald*, 1 Aug. 1881. See also M. Tierney, *Croke of Cashel: The Life of Archbishop Thomas William Croke, 1823–1902*, Dublin 1976, 124–32.
14. C. D. C. Lloyd, *Ireland under the Land League*, Edinburgh 1892, 89.
15. Reid, *Forster*, II, 321–2, Forster to Gladstone, 29 May 1881.
16. *Nation*, 11 Jun. 1881.
17. *Ibid.*
18. *IW*, 18 Jun. 1881.
19. Lloyd, *op. cit.*, 77.
20. *Ibid.*, 58.
21. *Ibid.*, 48.
22. *Ibid.*, 47–8.
23. *Ibid.*, 157–8.
24. *Cork Weekly Herald*, 12 Feb. 1881.
25. Kettle, *Material for Victory*, 46–7.
26. *Ibid.*
27. *IW*, 4 Jun. 1881 (cable dated 23 May).
28. *FJ*, 25 May 1881.
29. *Ibid.*, 8 Jun. 1881.
30. *Ibid.*
31. *Ibid.*, 22 Jun. 1881.
32. *Kildare Observer*, 30 Jul. 1881.
33. *Ibid.*, 25 Jun. 1881.
34. *FJ*, 29 Jun. 1881.
35. *IW*, 16 Jul. 1881 (report dated 1 Jul.).
36. *Limerick Reporter*, 5 Jul. 1881.
37. *Cork Weekly Herald*, 20 Aug. 1881.
38. *Ibid.*, 17 Sep. 1881.
39. *FJ*, 6 Jul. 1881.
40. *Cork Weekly Herald*, 9 Jul. 1881.
41. O'Neill Larkin picked up this point in his speech at the land convention on 15 September 1881. (*FJ*, 16 Sep. 1881.)
42. *Ibid.*, 10 Aug. 1881.
43. *IN*, 10 Dec. 1881.
44. *IW*, 13 May 1882.
45. Davitt, *Fall of Feudalism*, 344–5. Davitt's claim is for the period from October 1881 to the end of May 1882. This money was spent at the rate of £10,000 a month, according to Henry George (*IW*, 13 May 1882), and this was a rate well above that allowed by Sexton in July. In fact the League was able to do this and still have £10,400 more on 6 April 1882 than on 1 October 1881

(*ibid.*), but this was an effect of the hard-won unity of the persistently warring factions of Irish-America at the Chicago convention—which nobody could have been sure of in July.

46. *King's County Chronicle*, 9 Jun. 1881.
47. *FJ*, 10 Sep. 1881.
48. *Cork Weekly Herald*, 2 Apr. 1881.
49. *Ibid.*
50. *Ibid.*
51. For the whole affair see *ibid.* and also *FJ*, 24 Mar. 1881.
52. K. T. Hoppen, 'Landlords, Society and Electoral Politics in Mid-Nineteenth-Century Ireland', *Past and Present* LXXV (1977), 64.
53. *Tipperary People*, 1 Jul. 1881.
54. *Ibid.*, 8 Jul. 1881.
55. Dublin *Evening Mail*, 25 Apr. 1881.
56. *IW*, 18 Jun. 1881 (report dated 23 May); see also *Limerick Reporter*, 20 May 1881.
57. *IW*, 10 Sep. 1881 (letter dated 3 Aug.).
58. *FJ*, 13 Jul. 1881.
59. *Ibid.*, 20 Jul. 1881.
60. *Ibid.*, 28 Jul. 1881.
61. *IW*, 30 Jul. 1881 (cable dated 20 Jul.).
62. *Ibid.*, 20 Aug. 1881 (letter dated 25 Jul.).
63. *Ibid.*, 3 Sep. 1881.
64. *Ibid.*
65. *Munster Express*, 30 Jul. 1881.
66. For this debate see *Hansard*, cclxiv, 50–5 (28 Jul. 1881).
67. *Leinster Express*, 6 Aug. 1881.
68. *FJ*, 10 Aug. 1881.
69. Lloyd, *op. cit.*, 157–8.
70. *Ibid.*, 156.
71. Cowper, *Cowper*, 511, Lloyd to Cowper, 4 Aug. 1881.
72. *Limerick Reporter*, 26 Aug. 1881.
73. *Cork Examiner*, 22 Aug. 1881.
74. *Limerick Reporter*, 30 Aug. 1881 (report dated 27 Aug.).
75. *Cork Examiner*, 20 Aug. 1881.
76. *Ibid.*, 25 Aug. 1881.
77. *Cork Weekly Herald*, 3 Sep. 1881.
78. *CT*, 20 Aug. 1881.
79. Dublin *Daily Express*, 10 Aug. 1881.
80. *Lowell Weekly Sun*, 2 Jul. 1881, reprinted in *Tipperary Free Press*, 19 Jul. 1881.
81. *Roscommon Messenger*, 3 Sep. 1881.
82. *FJ*, 31 Aug. 1881.
83. *Ibid.*
84. *Cork Examiner*, 2 Sep. 1881.
85. *Ibid.*
86. *FJ*, 9 Sep. 1881 (letter dated 7 Sep.).
87. *Ibid.*, 10 Sep. 1881 (letter dated 9 Sep.).
88. *Ibid.*

K

89. *Ibid.*
90. *Ibid.*, 6 Sep. 1881.
91. *Munster Express*, 1 Oct. 1881. This issue reprints the relevant correspondence with Hamilton's reply of 23 September that Gladstone did not find Fisher's 'exposition of illegality in this case a very clear one'.
92. *FJ*, 10 Sep. 1881.
93. *Nation*, 17 Sep. 1881, reprints this and all the other major contributions to the debate.
94. *Munster Express*, 10 Sep. 1881.
95. *Kilkenny Moderator*, 3 and 7 Sep. 1881; see also *FJ*, editorial, 6 Sep. 1881.
96. The Clonmel sheriff, cited in *Munster Express*, 27 Aug. 1881. Yet during the whole of 1881 there had been only 37 evictions in Tipperary, 12 of which were returned as caretakers and 2 returned as tenants. (*Returns of Cases of Evictions in Ireland . . . for 1881*, 4, H.C. 1882 (9) LV, 232.) These figures illustrate beyond doubt that eviction had faded into the background and that conflicts linked with 'rent at the point of the bayonet' and its successor policies were dominant in the region. It is the role of this policy which explains why the number of evictions in Munster actually fell in 1881 from 742 to 720. In Connaught, where the agitation had a very different character—'rent at the point of the bayonet' was after all the weapon of the rural bourgeoisie—the number of evictions rose from 387 to 784. Mayo alone had 234 evictions in 1881 as against Waterford's 46. (*Ibid.*, 4–6.)
97. *Nation*, 17 Sep. 1881.
98. *Hansard*, cclxiii, 1978–82 (27 Jul. 1881), especially 1980; see also Charles Russell's account (*FJ*, 21 Jan. 1882).
99. O'Connor, *Memoirs of an Old Parliamentarian*, I, 179.
100. Healy, *Letters and Leaders of My Day*, I, 125.
101. *FJ*, 28 Jul. 1881.
102. E.g. *ibid.*, 11 and 23 Jan. 1882.
103. *Ibid.* See also Hammond, *Gladstone and the Irish Nation*, 225n., which confirms the fact that the Healy clause was in accordance with Gladstone's ideas.
104. Kettle, *op. cit.*, 51–2. E. McCann, *War and an Irish Town*, Harmondsworth 1974, 128–31, tries to analyse why the League failed to change the terms of the Ulster problem. But see also P. Bew, 'The Problem of Irish Unionism', *Economy and Society* VI, No. 1 (Feb. 1977), 98–100.
105. W. O'Brien, *op. cit.*, 324. 'The *Freeman's Journal*', he added, 'cautiously rejoiced.'
106. Gladstone to Cowper, 9 Sep. 1881 (BM, Gladstone Papers, Add. MS. 56453).
107. Russell, memorandum to Gladstone on this subject, 17 Mar. 1886 (*ibid.*, 56447). The context is, of course, the Home Rule debate. Russell's object is to refute a characteristic claim of Ulster Liberalism to the effect that before Gladstone accentuated

extremism on both sides by accepting the Home Rule demand they were successfully proceeding on a principled non-sectarian basis with the task of defeating bigotry in Ulster politics. Russell's views clash directly with the views of Ulster Liberalism gathered by Bryce and noted in his earlier memorandum of 12 March, as it does with the implication of such classic statements as T. McKnight, *Ulster As It Is*, 2 vols, London 1896. For a valuable analysis of Ulster Liberalism see Gibbon, *Origins of Ulster Unionism*, Chapter 5.

108. O'Shea, *Parnell*, I, 221, Parnell to K. O'Shea, 21 Nov. 1881.
109. *Roscommon Messenger*, 15 Oct. 1881.
110. *Ibid.*
111. W. O'Brien, *op. cit.*, 328–9.
112. This was the phrase used by Parnell on 19 October when he had explicitly opposed the project of giving the waste land to the labourers. (*FJ*, 20 Oct. 1880.)
113. *Hansard*, cclxii, 893 (19 May 1881). For Parnell's later activities in this area see F. S. L. Lyons, 'The Economic Ideas of Parnell' in M. Roberts, ed., *Historical Studies* II, London 1959, 68.
114. *FJ*, 16 Sep. 1881.
115. *Munster Express*, 24 Sep. 1881.
116. W. O'Brien, *op. cit.*, 335–6.
117. *Ibid.*, 330.
118. William O'Brien in a widely accepted account claimed that Parnell 'bore the battle on his single shield'. (*Op. cit.*, 334.) He did, however, take a certain poetic licence. Parnell was not unassisted by his parliamentary lieutenants: J. J. O'Kelly, for example, spoke in support of the testing policy. The 'greatest oratorical success of the convention', the extremist speech of Father Rowan, CC, was delivered *after* the crucial vote had been cast.
119. See *FJ*, 16 and 17 Sep. 1881, for reports of the convention.
120. *Ibid.*, 17 Sep. 1881.
121. *Ibid.*
122. *Kildare Observer*, 24 Sep. 1881.
123. *Munster Express*, 8 Oct. 1881.
124. This letter is quoted in a comment in *ibid.*, 29 Oct. 1881, following Dorris's arrest.
125. *Returns of Cases of Evictions in Ireland . . . for 1881*, 4–6.
126. See in particular S. Clark, 'The Political Mobilisation of Irish Farmers', *Canadian Review of Sociology and Anthropology* XII (1975), 494. Undoubtedly certain changes in the class structure, in particular the diminution of the number of agricultural labourers in the post-famine period, reduced some of the sources of disunity in the Irish peasantry. Nevertheless, disunity within the tenantry itself remained a prominent factor. We do, however, need to know more about pre-famine class conflict; the work at present being undertaken by Michael Beames and Sam Clark will certainly be of help here.

Chapter 9
LAND LEAGUE *VERSUS* GOVERNMENT, 1881–82
(pp. 191–216)

1. Reid, *Forster*, II, 335–7, Forster to Gladstone, 11 Sep. 1881.
2. Hammond, *Gladstone and the Irish Nation*, 247, Forster to Gladstone, 20 Sep. 1881.
3. Reid, *op. cit.*, II, 340, Forster to Gladstone, 26 Sep. 1881.
4. *Ibid.*, II, 339, Forster to Gladstone, 26 Sep. 1881.
5. *Ibid.*, II, 343, Forster to Gladstone, 2 Oct. 1881.
6. *FJ*, 27 Sep. 1881.
7. Reid, *op. cit.*, II, 242, Forster to Gladstone, 2 Oct. 1881.
8. C. J. Woods, 'The Catholic Church and Irish Politics, 1879–92' (unpublished Ph.D. thesis, University of Nottingham, 1968), 77–8.
9. *FJ*, 9 Sep. 1881.
10. *Ibid.*, 13 Oct. 1881.
11. *Ibid.*, 14 Oct. 1881.
12. Reid, *op. cit.*, II, 344, Forster to Gladstone, 2 Oct. 1881.
13. *Ibid.*, II, 347, Forster to Gladstone, 4 Oct. 1881.
14. E. Cant-Wall, *Ireland under the Land Act*, London 1882, 33.
15. *FJ*, 13 Oct. 1881.
16. *Ibid.*
17. Cant-Wall, *op. cit.*, 36.
18. *Ibid.*, 35.
19. *FJ*, 8 Oct. 1881.
20. Healy, *Letters and Leaders of My Day*, I, 136.
21. *FJ*, 8 Oct. 1881.
22. *Ibid.*, 7 Sep. 1881.
23. W. O'Brien, *Recollections*, 338.
24. *Ibid.*, 343.
25. *Ibid.*, 344.
26. *Ibid.*
27. *Ibid.*, 343.
28. *Ibid.*, 345–8.
29. O'Shea, *Parnell*, I, 202, Parnell to K. O'Shea, 8 and 11 Oct. 1881.
30. O'Donnell, *History of the Irish Parliamentary Party*, II, 34.
31. *FJ*, 24 Oct. 1881.
32. The account that follows is based on W. O'Brien, *op. cit.*, 348–9.
33. O'Shea, *op. cit.*, I, 207.
34. W. O'Brien, *op. cit.*, 365.
35. Kettle, *Material for Victory*, 56.
36. Lyons, *Dillon*, 60.
37. *FJ*, 24 Oct. 1881.
38. O'Donnell, *op. cit.*, II, 25–6.
39. See C. C. O'Brien, *Parnell and his Party*, 73.
40. O'Donnell, *op. cit.*, II, 26.
41. J. B. Walsh to M. Walsh, 31 Oct. 1881 (NLI, Kilmainham MSS, 10700).
42. *FJ*, 28 Oct. 1881.
43. *IN*, 17 Dec. 1881.

44. *FJ*, 21 Oct. 1881.
45. A. Parnell, 'Tale of the Land League: A Great Sham' (NLI MS. 12144).
46. *Cork Weekly Herald*, 13 Aug. 1881. For further details see R. F. Foster, *Charles Stewart Parnell: The Man and his Family*, Hassocks 1976, 272.
47. *FJ*, 12 Nov. 1881.
48. A. Parnell, 'Tale of the Land League: A Great Sham' (NLI MS. 12144).
49. *Spec. Comm. Proc.*, III, 121.
50. A. Parnell, 'Tale of the Land League: A Great Sham' (NLI MS. 12144).
51. Ballydehob Land League correspondence for this period is reprinted in *Spec. Comm. Proc.*, III, 121–5.
52. For this incident see Anna Parnell's letter quoted in *FJ*, 19 Nov. 1881. Clara Stritch's letter to Edward Mahony, secretary of the Ballydehob Land League, 19 Nov. 1881, is also relevant (*Spec. Comm. Proc.*, III, 122).
53. *Sinn Féin*, 16 Oct. 1909.
54. A. Parnell, 'Tale of the Land League: A Great Sham' (NLI MS. 12144); see also *FJ*, 21 Feb. and 6 Mar. 1882.
55. *IW*, 13 May 1882.
56. Police report, 30 Dec. 1881 (SPO, INL Papers, Spec. Comm. docs, 1888, carton 9).
57. *IW*, 24 Mar. 1883.
58. *Ibid.*, 3 Mar. 1883.
59. *Ibid.*, 13 May 1882.
60. A. Parnell, 'Tale of the Land League: A Great Sham' (NLI MS. 12144). See also reports on Wexford, especially RM's report, 25 May 1882 (CSO, RP, 25092/1882), which bear out this view.
61. For this case see S. Brady, 'The Diaries of Lord Leitrim', *Irish Independent*, 2–7 Oct. 1967. See O'Connor, *The Parnell Movement*, 116–17, for the popular explanation of the murder. This should not be taken to mean that the murder of Lord Leitrim was typical of pre-Land League crime. It has been argued in Chapter 2 above that even in this period the basis of agrarian crime was not a simple revenge motive.
62. O'Shea, *op. cit.*, I, 241, Parnell to K. O'Shea, 29 Mar. 1882.
63. A. B. Cooke and J. R. Vincent, ed., 'Herbert Gladstone, Forster, and Ireland, 1881–2', Pt 2, *Irish Historical Studies* XVIII, No. 69 (Mar. 1972), 79, H. Gladstone's journal, 29 Mar. 1882.
64. Mallon, report, 26 Nov. 1881 (SPO, INL Papers, Spec. Comm. docs, 1888, carton 9).
65. Mallon, report, 24 Nov. 1881 (*ibid.*).
66. Informer's report, 10 Dec. 1881 (*ibid.*, carton 10).
67. Informer's report, 17 Dec. 1881 (*ibid.*).
68. Police report, 30 Dec. 1881 (*ibid.*, carton 9); 11 May 1882 (SPO, B14); see also Harrington to Miss Lynch, 28 Oct. 1881 (NLI, Kilmainham MSS, 10700). For Egan's relationship with violent

conspiracy see also T. Corfe, *The Phoenix Park Murders*, London 1968, 137–40, and L. Ó Broin, 'The Invincibles' in T. D. Williams, ed. *Secret Societies in Ireland*. These police reports give one side of Mallon's attitude to Egan, but for another detective's view of another side of this complex relationship see L. Ó Broin, *The Prime Informer*, London 1971, 31–4.

69. 'Effect of the Land Act in Ireland up to 28 Jan. 1882' (BM, Gladstone Papers, Add. MS. 56446).
70. Cowper, *Cowper*, 543, Cowper to Hon. H. Cowper, 13 Dec. 1881: 'I am afraid that these Ass. Commissioners, as they rightly write themselves, have gone in too much for the tenants. One feels now that it must have been a bad selection. It certainly was very wrong to put no Tories on the list.'
71. Forster to Harcourt, 24 Nov. 1881 (Bodl., Harcourt MSS, deposit 81) defends the record of the sub-commissioners.
72. *FJ*, 4 Jan. 1882.
73. Forster to Harcourt, 24 Nov. 1881 (Bodl., Harcourt MSS, deposit 81).
74. *FJ*, 4 Jan. 1882.
75. Reid, *op. cit.*, II, 385.
76. Lloyd, *Ireland under the Land League*, 56–8.
77. *Ibid.*, 46.
78. *Ibid.*, 227–30.
79. Reid, *op. cit.*, II, 395, Forster to wife, 4 Mar. 1882.
80. *FJ*, 5 Jan. 1882.
81. Forster to Gladstone, 29 Mar. 1881 (BM, Gladstone Papers, Add. MS. 44158). Forster noted that the forthcoming Land Act might tempt rack-renting landlords to evict.
82. *FJ*, 1 Mar. 1882. For the Healy clause see also p. 183 above.
83. Hamilton, *Diary*, I, 239, entry for 19 Mar. 1882. For an overall analysis of the crime figures see Forster's statistics on p. 206 below.
84. Reid, *op. cit.*, II, 406, Gladstone to Forster, 24 Mar. 1882.
85. *Ibid.*, II, 408.
86. Hamilton, *op. cit.*, I, 242.
87. *Hansard*, cclxviii, 199–203 (28 Mar. 1882).
88. Hamilton, *op. cit.*, I, 242.
89. *Ibid.*
90. Gladstone to Forster, 29 Mar. 1882 (BM, Gladstone Papers, Add. MS. 44158).
91. Cooke and Vincent (Pt 2) in *Irish Historical Studies* XVIII, No. 69 (Mar. 1972), 75–6, H. Gladstone's journal, 29 Mar. 1882.
92. Reid, *op cit.*, II, 412, Forster to Gladstone, 4 Apr. 1882.
93. *Ibid.*, II, 413, Gladstone to Forster, 5 Apr. 1882.
94. Such a reading is implied in Strauss, *Irish Nationalism and British Democracy*, 166, and also in A. B. Cooke and J. R. Vincent, ed., 'Herbert Gladstone, Forster, and Ireland, 1881–2', Pt 1, *Irish Historical Studies* XVII, No. 68 (Sep. 1971), 527.
95. Cooke and Vincent (Pt 2) in *Irish Historical Studies* XVIII, No. 69 (Mar. 1972), 77, H. Gladstone's journal, 6 Apr. 1882.

96. *Ibid.*, 79, H. Gladstone's journal, 22 Apr. 1882.
97. Hamilton, *op. cit.*, I, 247, entry for 5 Apr. 1882.
98. *Ibid.*
99. Reid, *op. cit.*, II, 416, Forster to Gladstone, 7 Apr. 1882.
100. Ross of Bladensburg, memorandum entitled 'Military on Protection Duty' (CSO, RP, 2214/1882), 11.
101. Reid, *op. cit.*, II, 417–19, Forster to Gladstone, 7 Apr. 1882.
102. *Ibid.*, II, 423, Forster to Gladstone, 12 Apr. 1882.
103. For the detailed course of negotiations see R. B. O'Brien, *Parnell*, I, 336–50; Howard, ed., *Joseph Chamberlain: A Political Memoir*, Chapter 2; H. Harrison, *Parnell Vindicated*, London 1931, Appendix C.
104. Reid, *op. cit.*, II, 425, Forster to Gladstone, 18 Apr. 1882.
105. *Ibid.*
106. Forster, cabinet memo, 17 Apr. 1882 (BM, Gladstone Papers, Add. MS. 44160).
107. *Ibid.*
108. Hamilton, *op. cit.*, I, 256, entry for 20 Apr. 1882.
109. Howard, *op. cit.*, 51–5, Chamberlain, memorandum, 21 Apr. 1882 (reproduced in full).
110. Cooke and Vincent (Pt 2) in *Irish Historical Studies* XVIII, No. 69 (Mar. 1972), 79, H. Gladstone's journal, 23 Apr. 1882.
111. Reid, *op. cit.*, II, 434, Forster to Gladstone, 29 Apr. 1882.
112. *Ibid.*, II, 438, Parnell to O'Shea, dated 28 Apr. 1882 (written 29 Apr.).
113. *Ibid.*, II, 437, Forster, memorandum, 30 Apr. 1882.
114. Hammond, *op. cit.*, 279, Gladstone to Forster, 30 Apr. 1882.
115. Reid, *op. cit.*, II, 440.
116. Cooke and Vincent (Pt 2) in *Irish Historical Studies* XVIII, No. 69 (Mar. 1972), 82, Lady F. Cavendish's diary, 23 Oct. 1884.
117. Lady F. Cavendish to Morley, 31 Jan. 1902 (BM, Gladstone Papers, Add. MS. 56453).
118. W. E. Gladstone, 'Mr Forster and Ireland', *Nineteenth Century* XXIV (1888), 461.
119. *Ibid.*
120. Lady F. Cavendish to Morley, 31 Jan. 1902 (BM, Gladstone Papers, Add. MS. 56453).
121. Reid, *op. cit.*, II, 441–2, Forster to Kimberley, 2 May 1882.
122. *Ibid.*
123. Gladstone in *Nineteenth Century* XXIV (1888), 461.
124. R. B. O'Brien, *op. cit.*, I, 326–9.
125. Forster, cabinet memo, 17 Apr. 1882, Annex (a): 'Reports made by the Special Resident Magistrates relative to the State of their Districts' (BM, Gladstone Papers, Add. MS. 44160).
126. Lloyd, *op. cit.*, 226.
127. A. M. Porter, 'Notes on Mr Forster's Memorandum of 17 April 1882', No. 3, 22 Apr. 1882 (BM, Gladstone Papers, Add. MS. 44628).
128. Forster, cabinet memo, 17 Apr. 1882, Annex (a): 'Reports made

by the Special Resident Magistrates relative to the State of their Districts' (*ibid.*, 44160).

129. J. Naish, 'Notes on Mr Forster's Memorandum of 17 April 1882', No. 4, 26 Apr. 1882 (*ibid.*, 44628).

130. Burke to Forster, 30 Apr. 1882 (*ibid.*).

131. It may be expected that Burke's status will emerge in *The Irish Journal of Florence Arnold-Forster, 1880–82*, ed. T. W. Moody and R. Hawkins, which is to be published by the Clarendon Press.

132. *Hansard*, cclxviii, 1967–8 (2 May 1882).

133. R. Hawkins, 'Gladstone, Forster, and the Release of Parnell, 1882–8', *Irish Historical Studies* XVI, No. 64 (Sep. 1969), 417–45, argues this point in detail. See also A. B. Cooke and J. R. Vincent, ed., 'Lord Spencer on the Phoenix Park Murders', *ibid.* XVIII, No. 72 (Sep. 1973), 589.

134. A. B. Cooke and J. R. Vincent, *The Governing Passion: Cabinet Government and Party Politics in Britain, 1885–86*, Brighton 1974, 51. This interpretation appears in the context of a broader critique of 'a sincere liberal tradition', linked particularly with the name of J. L. Hammond, that Gladstone's Irish reforms formed a single coherent programme. It is outside the scope of the present work to discuss this and the other arguments in *The Governing Passion*: Cooke and Vincent's work is, of course, part of a broader trend. In a valuable critical review article Derek Beales has noted: 'Conservative historiography of nineteenth-century British politics is now dominant, at least among students of what went on at the centre, in parliament and the administration.' He has suggested the existence of certain limitations to this approach. (D. E. D. Beales, 'Peel, Russell and Reform', *Historical Journal* XVII, No. 4 (Dec. 1974), 874.)

135. Hammond, *op. cit.*, 246, Gladstone to Forster, 31 Oct. 1881.

136. Cowper, *op. cit.*, 533–5, Spencer to Cowper, 20 Oct. 1881.

137. Reid, *op. cit.*, II, 348–50, Gladstone to Forster, 5 Oct. 1881.

138. *Ibid.*, II, 335–7, Forster to Gladstone, 11 Sep. 1881.

139. This comment appears in Gladstone's notes on his second cabinet (BM, Gladstone Papers, Add. MS. 56445).

140. Hammond, *op. cit.*, 277, Parnell to O'Shea, dated 28 Apr. 1882 (written 29 Apr.).

141. Jennie Wyse Power in *Sinn Féin*, 16 Oct. 1909.

142. For a different view see M. Hurst, *Parnell and Irish Nationalism*, London, 1968, 76, which sees the 'treaty' as involving only a tactical surrender on the part of Parnell.

143. Davitt, *Fall of Feudalism*, 264.

144. *Ibid.* Although the left of the Land League tended not to emphasise their case, 100,000 leaseholders could also point out that until 1887 they were excluded from the Land Act.

145. *Ibid.*, 362.

146. *IN*, 6 May 1882.

147. But cf. O'Day, *The English Face of Irish Nationalism*.

Chapter 10
CONCLUSION: PEOPLE'S WAR OR HISTORICAL
REGRESSION?
(pp. 217–232)

1. The term 'people's war' is used to describe the Land League agitation in P. Berresford Ellis, *A History of the Irish Working Class*, London 1972.
2. P. O'Farrell, *Ireland's English Question*, London [1971], 171.
3. *Ibid.*, 172.
4. Lee, *Modernisation of Irish Society*, 89.
5. O'Farrell, *op. cit.*, 177, for example, describes the Land League as a 'religious crusade . . . another variation on the Irish theme of holy war'.
6. See the preface to the present work.
7. As Sexton pointed out. (*Hansard*, cclxvi, 659–60 (14 Feb. 1882).)
8. Lloyd, *Ireland under the Land League*, 8.
9. T. McClure and all the Ulster Liberal MPs to Gladstone, 1 Dec. 1880 (BM, Gladstone Papers, Add. MS. 44158).
10. Lee, *op. cit.*, 97. It should be noted that there is enough evidence for Solow, *The Land Question and the Irish Economy*, to argue the opposite case.
11. Lee, *op. cit.*, 105.
12. It is on this point of the landlord contribution that much of Mrs Solow's argument flounders. See the review by J. S. Donnelly in *Studia Hibernica* XIII (1973), 185–90. See also the comments in the preface to the present work.
13. Lee, *op. cit.*, 89.
14. *Hansard*, cclxii, 42–3 (3 Jun. 1881).
15. As in D. R. O'C. Lysaght, *The Republic of Ireland*, Cork 1971, 26.
16. For this point see P. O'Farrell, *England and Ireland since 1800*, Oxford 1975, 169. This is in sharp disagreement with Conor Cruise O'Brien's interpretation in *Parnell and his Party*.
17. E. J. Hobsbawm and G. Rudé, *Captain Swing*, 2nd ed., Harmondsworth 1973, 166, 171, 244, etc.
18. M. and C. C. O'Brien, *A Concise History of Ireland*, London 1972, 110.
19. E. D. Steele, 'Ireland for the Irish', *History* LIV (1972), 246–7.
20. T. W. Moody, 'Fenianism, Home Rule and the Land War, 1850–91', in T. W. Moody and F. X. Martin, ed., *The Course of Irish History*, Cork 1967, 286.
21. Palmer, *Irish Land League Crisis*, 195.
22. Peter Alter in his study of the National League, *Die Irische Nationalbewegung Zwichen Parlament und Revolution*, Munich 1971, 110–14, notes that the boycott was often ineffective against the larger landlords, yet even so he takes as a key source Parnell's Ennis speech and writes that the boycott was the 'kernel of the agrarian agitation'. Nevertheless, the analysis of the stages of the development of the boycott on p. 112 is worth noting.

23. Brown, *Irish-American Nationalism*, 102.
24. M. and C. C. O'Brien, *op. cit.*, 109–10.
25. Becker, *Disturbed Ireland*, 326.
26. C. C. O'Brien, '1891–1916' in C. C. O'Brien, ed., *The Shaping of Modern Ireland*, London 1960, 16.
27. See his analysis of Land League methods in 'Michael Davitt—A Text for a Revolutionary Lecture' (1908), reprinted in J. Connolly, *Selected Political Writings*, ed. O. D. Edwards and B. Ransom, 211–12.
28. Palmer, *op. cit.*, 195.
29. S. Clark, 'The Land War in Ireland' (abstract of unpublished Ph. D. thesis, Harvard University, 1974), 7.
30. Connolly, *op. cit.*, 212.
31. L. P. Curtis, *Coercion and Conciliation in Ireland, 1880–1892*, Oxford 1963, 10; Kolbert and O'Brien, *Land Reform in Ireland*, 34–7.
32. Forster, cabinet memo, 17 Apr. 1882 (BM, Gladstone Papers, Add. MS. 44160).
33. *CT*, 13 Jan. 1882.
34. *Times*, 19 Apr. 1881.
35. *CT*, 9 Feb. 1884.
36. See *ibid.*, 4 Oct. 1884.
37. *Spec. Comm. Proc.*, VIII, 86–7.
38. J. V. O'Brien, *William O'Brien and the Course of Irish Politics, 1881–1918*, California 1976, Chapter 5.
39. B. M. Walsh, 'Marriage Rates and Population Pressure: Ireland, 1871 and 1911', *Economic History Review* XXIII (Apr. 1970), 161–2.
40. F. Bedarida, 'Irlande: La Participation des Classes Populaires au Mouvement National (1800–1921)' in *Mouvements Nationaux d'Independance et Classes Populaires aux XIXᵉ et XXᵉ Siècles en Occident et en Orient*, Paris 1971, 19.
41. R. Kee, *The Green Flag: A History of Irish Nationalism*, London 1972, 375.
42. Parnell was never averse to throwing burdens on the British tax-payer. See, for example, his remarkable secret proposal through O'Shea to Gladstone in June 1881 that the government should back a rent reduction to Griffith's valuation and compensate the landlords accordingly. (Hammond, *Gladstone and the Irish Nation*, 222.)
43. A. Parnell, 'Tale of the Land League: A Great Sham' (NLI MS. 12144).
44. *Ibid.*
45. *Spec. Comm. Proc.*, IX, 393.
46. Kettle, *Material for Victory*, 63–4.
47. Foster, *Parnell*, 207. In this section of his book Foster offers proofs that Parnell did not return landlord enmity. See also his conclusion.
48. W. O'Brien, *Recollections*, 335–6.

49. For a forceful defence of his work on this subject see C. C. O'Brien's review of Hurst, *Parnell and Irish Nationalism,* in *Irish Historical Studies* XVI, No. 62 (Sep. 1968), 230–6.
50. *Devoy's Post-Bag,* I, 538, O'Kelly to Devoy, 14 Jul. 1880.
51. List of Nationalist MPs, giving brief particulars about the political views of each, Feb. 1887 (SPO, Crime Branch Special, Police Reports, 1886–1915, No. 4).
52. O'Farrell, *England and Ireland since 1800,* 117.
53. *Spec. Comm. Proc.,* X, 179.
54. O'Donnell, *History of the Irish Parliamentary Party,* I, 371–2.
55. N. S. Mansergh, *The Irish Question, 1840–1921,* 3rd ed., London 1975, 314. In Chapter 3 of this recently further revised work Mansergh has made this point the basis of his attack on Marx's view that the Irish land question was 'inseparable' from the national question. For Mansergh this notion reveals an economic determinism which makes Marxism a useless tool for the analysis of Irish society. However, this is a remarkably harsh reading of a statement in a letter which was certainly true for the date (1870) at which it was written. It would have been remarkably speculative for Marx to have considered other possible relationships at this juncture.
56. *IN,* 3 Jun. 1882.
57. *Ibid.,* 22 Jul. 1882.
58. *Ibid.,* 3 Jun. 1882.
59. Devoy, *Land of Eire,* 90.
60. SPO, B36.
61. *Roscommon Herald,* 24 Jun. 1882.
62. Spencer, Introduction to Bryce, ed., *Handbook of Home Rule,* x.
63. *Ibid.,* 96–105.
64. *Ibid.*
65. Hammond, *op. cit.,* 258, quotes Gladstone to Granville, 13 Apr. 1883, on this subject.
66. Russell to Gladstone, 17 Mar. 1886 (BM, Gladstone Papers, Add. MS. 56447).
67. Gladstone, cabinet memo, 12 Jul. 1886 (*ibid.,* 56445).
68. McKnight, *Ulster As It Is,* II, 206–7.

APPENDICES
(pp. 233–245)

1. M. Beames, 'Cottiers and Conacre in Pre-Famine Ireland', *Journal of Peasant Studies* II (1975).
2. Steele, *Irish Land and British Politics,* 253.
3. *Ibid.*
4. Quoted in Hammond, *Gladstone and the Irish Nation,* 105.
5. Solow, *The Land Question and the Irish Economy,* 46.
6. Hammond, *op. cit.,* 105.
7. Kolbert and O'Brien, *Land Reform in Ireland,* 34–5.
8. E.g. E. D. Steele and J. J. Lee; see the latter's 'Gladstone and the Landlords', *Times Literary Supplement,* 9 May 1975.

9. E.g. Solow, *op. cit.*, Chapter 2, and W. E. Vaughan's review of Steele, *op. cit.*, in *Irish Economic and Social History* III (1976), 92–4.
10. Kolbert and O'Brien, *op. cit.*, 34–7.
11. Donnelly, *The Land and the People of Nineteenth-century Cork,* 378.
12. *Ibid.*, 314.
13. SPO, Irish Crimes Records, Vol. I. Boyton's name is top of this list that stretches through the pages of five volumes.
14. Quoted in *IW*, 7 May 1881.
15. *Ibid.*
16. Davitt, *The* Times–*Parnell Commission: Speech Delivered in Defence of the Land League*, 120.
17. Lee, *Modernisation of Irish Society*, 69.
18. *IW*, 24 Mar. 1883.
19. Police report, 24 Sep. 1871 (SPO, Fenian Papers).
20. T. D. Sullivan, *Recollections of Troubled Times in Irish Politics,* Dublin 1905, 161.
21. DMP report, 18 May 1882 (SPO, B9).
22. *Ibid.*
23. Ó Broin, *The Prime Informer*, 31-4.
24. Russell, *The Parnell Commission: The Opening Speech for the Defence*, 523.
25. Davitt, *Fall of Feudalism*, 227.
26. *Ibid.*, 169.
27. Davitt, *The* Times–*Parnell Commission: Speech Delivered in Defence of the Land League*, 61.
28. A. B. Finegan, 'The Land War in South-East Galway, 1879–90' (unpublished M.A. thesis, University College, Galway, 1974), 20–5, gives a very valuable account of Harris.
29. Russell, *op. cit.*, 252.
30. O'Connor, *Memoirs of an Old Parliamentarian*, I, 68.
31. *Ibid.*, I, 70.
32. *Devoy's Post-Bag*, I, 59, O'Kelly to Devoy, 5 Aug. 1877.
33. O'Connor, *op. cit.*, I, 84.
34. *Ibid.*, I, 86.
35. *Ibid.*, I, 137.
36. O'Donnell, *History of the Irish Parliamentary Party*, II, 458.
37. O'Connor, *op. cit.*, I, 139.
38. SPO, Irish Crimes Records, Vol. I.
39. *IW*, 3 Mar. 1883.
40. *Ibid.*
41. *Ibid.*
42. *Ibid.*, 7 Jun. 1884.
43. *Ibid.*
44. Davitt, *Fall of Feudalism*, 552.
45. *Ibid.*, 552–60.
46. For more details of Smyth's career see Sullivan, *op. cit.*

Bibliography

PARLIAMENTARY PAPERS AND OFFICIAL PUBLICATIONS

Hansard's Parliamentary Debates, 3rd series

Report from the Select Committee on Outrages (Ireland). H.C. 1852 (438) XIV, 1

Agricultural Statistics of Ireland
  for 1857. H.C. 1859 [2461, Sess. 2] XXIX, 1
  for 1869. H.C. 1871 [C. 239] LXIX, 347
  for 1876. H.C. 1877 [C. 1749] LXXXV, 549
  for 1877. H.C. 1878 [C. 1938] LXXVII, 511
  for 1878. H.C. 1878/9 [C. 2347] LXXV, 587
  for 1879. H.C. 1880 [C. 2534] LXXVI, 815
  for 1880. H.C. 1881 [C. 2932] XCIII, 685
  for 1881. H.C. 1883 [C. 3332] LXXIV, 93
  for 1882. H.C. 1883 [C. 3677] LXXVI, 825

General Abstract, showing the Acreage under Crops; also the Number and Description of Live Stock in Each County and Province
  for 1876. H.C. 1876 [C. 1567] LXXVIII, 469
  for 1876–77. H.C. 1877 [C. 1841] LXXXV, 601
  for 1877–78. H.C. 1878 [C. 2146] LXXVII, 587
  for 1878–79. H.C. 1878/9 [C. 2404] LXXV, 661
  for 1879–80. H.C. 1880 [C. 2652] LXXVI, 941
  for 1880–81. H.C. 1881 [C. 3071] XCIII, 773
  for 1881–82. H.C. 1882 [C. 3366] LXXIV, 169

Report from the Select Committee appointed to inquire into the State of Westmeath, &c., and the Nature of a Certain Unlawful Combination existing therein; with the Proceedings, Minutes of Evidence, Appendix, and Index. H.C. 1871 (147) XIII, 547.

[Shaw Lefevre Committee] Report from the Select Committee appointed to inquire into the Workings and Results of the 44th, 45th and 47th Clauses of the Irish Land Act, 1870, and to report whether any Facilities should be given for Promoting the Purchase of Land by Occupying Tenants; together with the Proceedings, Minutes of Evidence, Appendix, and Index. H.C. 1877 (328) XII, 1; 1878 (249) XV, 1

Preliminary Report on the Returns of Agricultural Produce in Ireland in 1879; with Tables. H.C. 1880 [C. 2495] LXXVI, 893

[*Bessborough Commission*] *Report of the Commission of Inquiry into the Working of the Landlord and Tenant (Ireland) Act, 1870, and the Amending Acts; with the Evidence, Appendices, and Index.* H.C. 1881 [C. 2779] XVIII–XIX

Reports and Tables Relating to Migratory Agricultural Irish Labourers for 1880. H.C. 1881 [C. 2809] XCIII, 807

[*Richmond Commission*] *Royal Commission on the Depressed Condition of the Agricultural Interest.*
   Preliminary Report. H.C. 1881 [C. 2778] XV, 1
   Final Report. H.C. 1882 [C. 3309] XIV, 1
   Assistant Commissioners' Report: Ireland, by Messrs Baldwin and Robertson. H.C. 1881 [C. 2951] XVI, 841
   Minutes of Evidence.
      Pt I. H.C. 1881 [C. 2778–I] XV, 25
      Pt II. H.C. 1881 [C. 3096] XVII, 1
      Pt III. H.C. 1882 [C. 3309–I] XIV, 45
   Digest of Evidence; and Appendix.
      Pt I. H.C. 1881 [C. 2778–II] XVI, 1
      Pts II–III. H.C. 1882 [C. 3309–II] XIV, 495

Return by Provinces and Counties of Evictions which have come to the knowledge of the Constabulary in Each Year, 1849 to 1882. H.C. 1881 (185) LXXVII, 725

Returns of Cases of Evictions in Ireland in Each Quarter in Each Year, showing the Number of Families and Persons Evicted in Each County, and the Number Readmitted as Tenants and as Caretakers
   for 1880. H.C. 1881 (2) LXXVII, 713
   for 1881. H.C. 1882 (9) LV, 229
   for Jan.–Mar. 1882. H.C. 1882 (145) LV, 237
   for Apr. 1882. H.C. 1882 (199) LV, 241
   for May 1882. H.C. 1882 [C. 3240] LV, 245
[Other papers on evictions are in H.C. 1880 LX and H.C. 1882 LV.]

Return of Outrages reported to the Royal Irish Constabulary from 1844 to 1880. H.C. [C. 2756] LXXVII, 887.

Numerical Returns of Outrages reported to the Constabulary Office in Ireland during 1881, with Summaries for the Preceding Years. H.C. 1882 [C. 3119] LV, 619

Return of Outrages reported to the Royal Irish Constabulary Office in Each Month
   for 1880–81 and Jan. 1882. H.C. 1882 (7) LV, 615
   for 1881–82 and Jan. 1883. H.C. 1883 (6) LVII, 1047

Report of the Special Commission, 1888 [*appointed to inquire into*

Charges and Allegations made against Certain Members of Parliament in O'Donnell v. Walter]. H.C. 1890 [C. 5891] XXVII, 477

The Special Commission Act, 1888. Reprint of the Shorthand Notes of the Speeches, Proceedings and Evidence taken before the Commissioners appointed under the above-named Act, 12 vols, London 1890

Royal Commission on Labour: Assistant Commissioners' Reports on the Agricultural Labourer; Vol. IV (Ireland), Pt IV by Mr Wilson-Fox. H.C. 1893/4 [C. 6894–XXI] XXXVII, Pt I, 341.

NEWSPAPERS AND JOURNALS

Miscellaneous
Daily Express (Dublin)
Evening Mail (Dublin)
Gaelic American (New York)
Irish Farmer's Gazette (Dublin)
Irish People (Dublin)
Irish Nation (New York)
Irish Times (Dublin)
Irish World (New York)
New York *Herald*
Spectator (London)

Provincial Papers
Ballinrobe Chronicle
Carlow Independent
Carlow Sentinel
Clare Advertiser (Kilrush)
Clare Freeman (Ennis)
Clare Independent (Ennis)
Clonmel Chronicle
Connaught Telegraph (Castlebar)
Cork Examiner
Cork Weekly Herald
Dundalk Democrat
Galway Vindicator
Leitrim Advertiser (Mohill)
Kerry Independent
Kerry Sentinel
Kildare Observer
Kilkenny Independent
Kilkenny Journal
King's County Chronicle
Leinster Express (Portlaoighise [Maryborough])
Leinster Leader (Naas)
Limerick Reporter

Longford Independent
Mayo Constitution
Mayo Examiner
Midland Tribune (Birr [Parsonstown])
Monaghan Reporter
Munster Express (Waterford)
Nenagh Guardian
People's Advocate (Monaghan)
Roscommon Herald
Roscommon Messenger
Sligo Champion
Tipperary Advocate
Tipperary Free Press
Tipperary Independent
Tipperary People
Waterford News
West Cork Eagle (Skibbereen)
Western News (Ballinasloe)
Westmeath Guardian
Wexford People

SELECT DOCUMENTS

Cooke, A. B., and J. R. Vincent, ed., 'Herbert Gladstone, Forster, and Ireland, 1881–2', 2 pts, *Irish Historical Studies* XVII, No. 68 (Sep. 1971) and XVIII, No. 69 (Mar. 1972)

Cooke, A. B., and J. R. Vincent, ed., 'Lord Spencer on the Phoenix Park Murders', *Irish Historical Studies* XVIII, No. 72 (Sep. 1973)

Hawkins, R., ed., 'An Army on Police Work, 1881–2: Ross of Bladensburg's Memorandum', *Irish Sword* XI (winter 1973)

Howard, C. H. D., ed., *Joseph Chamberlain: A Political Memoir, 1880–92,* London 1953

Moody, T. W., and L. Ó Broin, ed., 'The I.R.B. Supreme Council, 1868–78', *Irish Historical Studies* XIX, No. 75 (Mar. 1975)

CONTEMPORARY WORKS

Arnold-Forster, H. O., *The Truth about the Land League, its Leaders and its Teaching,* 3rd ed., London 1883

Bagenal, P. H., *The American Irish and their Influence on Irish Politics,* London 1882

Bagenal, P. H., *The Irish Agitator in Parliament and on the Platform: A Complete History of Irish Politics for the Year 1879,* Dublin 1880

Bagenal, P. H., *Parnellism Unveiled; or, The Land-and-Labour Agitation of 1879–80,* Dublin 1880

Barrington, R. M., *The Prices of Some Agricultural Produce and the Cost of Farm Labour for the Past Fifty Years. Paper Read before the Statistical and Social Inquiry Society of Ireland, December 14, 1886,* Dublin 1887

Becker, B. H., *Disturbed Ireland*, London 1881

Bryce, J., ed., *Handbook of Home Rule. Being Articles on the Irish Question*, 2nd ed., London 1887

Campbell, Sir G., *The Irish Land*, 2 pts, Dublin 1869

Cant-Wall, E., *Ireland under the Land Act: Letters Contributed to the* Standard *Newspaper*, London 1882

Cavendish, Lady F., *Diary*, ed., J. Bailey, 2 vols, London 1927

Cowper, K. C., Countess, *Earl Cowper, K.G., A Memoir by his Wife* (privately printed) [London?] 1913

Curran, J. A., *Reminiscences*, London 1915

Davitt, M., *The Fall of Feudalism in Ireland, or The Story of the Land League Revolution*, London and New York 1904

Davitt, M., 'The Irish Social Problem', *Today: A Journal of Scientific Socialism* I (Jun. 1884)

Davitt, M., *The Times–Parnell Commission: Speech Delivered in Defence of the Land League*, London 1890

Devoy, J., *The Land of Eire. The Irish Land League: Its Origin, Progress and Consequences*, New York [1882]

Devoy, J., *Recollections of an Irish Rebel*, New York 1929

Devoy's Post-Bag, 1871–1928, ed., W. O'Brien and D. Ryan, 2 vols, Dublin 1948–53

Dun, F., *Landlords and Tenants in Ireland*, London 1881.

Fisher, J., 'History of Land-Holding in Ireland', *Transactions of the Royal Historical Society* V (1877)

Gladstone, W. E., 'Mr Forster and Ireland', *Nineteenth Century* XXIV (1888)

Grimshaw, T. W., *Facts and Figures about Ireland*, Dublin 1893

Hamilton, Sir E. W., *Diary, 1880–1885*, ed., D. W. R. Bahlman, 2 vols, Oxford 1972

Hancock, W. N., *Report on the Supposed Progressive Decline in Irish Prosperity*, London 1870

Healy, T. M., *Letters and Leaders of My Day*, 2 vols, London [1928]

Healy, T. M., *Why There Is an Irish Land Question and an Irish Land League*, Dublin 1881

Hussey, S. M. (with H. Gordon), *The Reminiscences of an Irish Land Agent*, London 1904

The Irish Crisis of 1879–80: Proceedings of the Dublin Mansion House Relief Committee, 1880, Dublin 1881

Irish Land Committee, *The Land Question, No. 1: Notes upon the Government Valuation of Land in Ireland*, Dublin 1880

James, Sir H., *The Work of the Irish Leagues; The Speech . . . replying in the Parnell Commission Inquiry*, London [1890]

Jones, W. Bence, *The Life's Work in Ireland of a Landlord who Tried to Do his Duty*, London 1880 (see also criticisms by Rev. J. O'Leary and reply of W. Bence Jones, *Contemporary Review* XL (Jul.–Sep. 1881))

Kettle, A. J., *The Material for Victory*, ed., L. J. Kettle, Dublin 1958

Lalor, J. F., *James Fintan Lalor: Patriot and Political Essayist* [collected writings, ed. L. Fogarty], Dublin 1918

Le Caron, Henri [pseud.], *Twenty-five Years in the Secret Service: The Recollections of a Spy,* London 1892

Lloyd, C. D. C., *Ireland under the Land League: A Narrative of Personal Experiences,* Edinburgh 1892

Lucy, Sir H. W., *A Diary of Two Parliaments,* Vol. II: *The Gladstone Parliament, 1880–1885,* London 1886

McCarthy, J., *Reminiscences,* 2 vols, London 1899

McCarthy, J., *The Story of an Irishman,* London 1904

McCarthy, J., and Mrs Campbell Praed, *Our Book of Memories,* London 1912

McKnight, T., *Ulster As It Is,* 2 vols, London 1896

Mill, J. S., *England and Ireland,* London 1868

Morris, W. O'C., 'The Land System of Ireland' in *Oxford Essays, 1856,* Oxford 1856

Morris, W. O'C., *Letters on the Land Question of Ireland,* London 1870

Murphy, J. N., *Ireland, Industrial, Political, and Social,* London 1870

O'Brien, R. B., *The Irish Land Question and English Public Opinion,* London 1880

O'Brien, W., *Recollections,* London 1905

O'Connor, T. P., *Memoirs of an Old Parliamentarian,* 2 vols, London 1929

O'Connor, T. P., *The Parnell Movement,* London 1886

O'Donnell, F. H., *A History of the Irish Parliamentary Party,* 2 vols, London 1910

O'Leary, J., *Recollections of Fenians and Fenianism,* London 1896

O'Reilly, B., *John MacHale, Archbishop of Tuam: His Life, Times and Correspondence,* 2 vols, New York and Cincinnati 1890

Parnell, C. S., 'The Irish Land Question,' *North American Review* CXXX, No. 1 (Apr. 1880)

Playfair, L., 'On the Declining Production of Human Food in Ireland' in Sir A. Grant, ed., *Recess Studies,* Edinburgh 1870

Pringle, R. O., 'Illustrations of Irish Farming', *Journal of the Royal Agricultural Society of England,* 2nd ser., IX (1873)

Pringle, R. O., 'A Review of Irish Agriculture, Chiefly with Reference to the Production of Livestock', *Journal of the Royal Agricultural Society of England,* 2nd ser., VIII (1872)

Richardson, R., *The Irish Land Question,* London 1881

Russell, Sir C., *The Parnell Commission: The Opening Speech for the Defence,* London 1889

Rylett, H., 'Parnell', *Contemporary Review* CXXIX (1926)

Selborne, R. Palmer, Earl of, *Memorials,* Pt 2: *Personal and Political, 1865–95,* 2 vols, London 1898

Senior, N., *Journals, Conversations and Essays Relating to Ireland,* 2 vols, London 1868

Sullivan, T. D., *Recollections of Troubled Times in Irish Politics,* Dublin 1905

The Times *Reprint of Proceedings under the Special Commission Act, 1888,* London 1890

Trench, G. F., *The Land Question. Are the Landlords Worth Preserving? or Forty Years' Management of an Irish Estate,* Dublin 1881

Trench, W. S., *Realities of Irish Life,* London 1868

Tuke, J. H., *Irish Distress and its Remedies. The Land Question. A Visit to Donegal and Connaught in the Spring of 1880,* 3rd ed., London 1880

Tynan, P. J. P., *The Irish National Invincibles and their Times,* London 1894

Wilson, E. D. J., 'The Present Anarchy', *Nineteenth Century* IX (1881)

SECONDARY SOURCES

Alter, P., *Die Irische Nationalbewegung Zwichen Parlament und Revolution: Der Konstitutionelle Nationalismus in Irland, 1880–1918,* Munich 1971

Beales, D. E. D., 'Peel, Russell and Reform', *Historical Journal* XVII, No. 4 (Dec. 1974)

Beames, M., 'Cottiers and Conacre in Pre-Famine Ireland', *Journal of Peasant Studies* II (1975)

Bedarida, F., 'Irlande: La Participation des Classes Populaires au Mouvement National (1880–1921)' in *Mouvements Nationaux d'Indépendance et Classes Populaires aux XIXᵉ et XXᵉ Siècles en Occident et en Orient,* Paris 1971

Bell, G., *The Protestants of Ulster,* London 1975

Bew, P., 'Irish Histories', *Cambridge Review* XCIV (1973)

Bew, P., 'The Problem of Irish Unionism', *Economy and Society* VI No. 1 (Feb. 1977)

Black, R. D. C., *Economic Thought and the Irish Question, 1817–1870,* Cambridge 1960

Bourke, P. M. A., 'The Average Yield of Food Crops in Ireland on the Eve of the Great Famine', *Journal of the Department of Agriculture* LXVI (1969)

Brown, T. N., *Irish-American Nationalism, 1870–1890,* Philadelphia 1966

Clark, S., 'Agrarian Class Conflict and Collective Action in Nineteenth-Century Ireland', *British Journal of Sociology* XXIX (1978)

Clark, S., 'The Land War in Ireland' (abstract of unpublished Ph.D. thesis, Harvard University, 1974)

Clark, S., 'The Political Mobilisation of Irish Farmers', *Canadian Review of Sociology and Anthropology* XII (1975)

Clark, S., 'The Social Composition of the Land League', *Irish Historical Studies* XVII, No. 68 (Sept. 1971)

Connell, K. H., *Irish Peasant Society,* Oxford 1968

Connell, K. H., 'Peasant Marriage in Ireland after the Great Famine', *Past and Present* XII (1957)

Connell, K. H., 'The Potato in Ireland', *Past and Present* XXIII (1962)

Connolly, J., *Selected Political Writings*, ed., O. D. Edwards and B. Ransom, London 1973

Cooke, A. B., and J. R. Vincent, *The Governing Passion: Cabinet Government and Party Politics in Britain, 1885–86*, Brighton 1974

Corfe, T., *The Phoenix Park Murders*, London 1968

Cousens, S. H., 'Emigration and Demographic Changes in Ireland, 1851–1861', *Economic History Review* XIV (Dec. 1961)

Cousens, S. H. 'The Regional Variations in Population Changes in Ireland, 1861–1881', *Economic History Review* XVII (Dec. 1964)

Crotty, R., *Irish Agricultural Production: Its Volume and Structure*, Cork 1966

Cullen, L. M., *An Economic History of Ireland since 1660*, London 1972

Curtis, L. P., *Coercion and Conciliation in Ireland, 1880–1892: A Study in Conservative Unionism*, Oxford 1963

D'Arcy, W., *The Fenian Movement in the United States, 1858–1886*, Washington 1947

Devoy, J., 'Michael Davitt's Career', 17 pts, *Gaelic American*, Jun.–Nov. 1906 (copy bound in volume form in NLI, Ir. 92. d. 108)

Dewey, C. J., 'Celtic Agrarian Legislation and the Celtic Revival: Historicist Implications of Gladstone's Irish and Scottish Land Acts, 1870–1886', *Past and Present* LXIV (1974)

Donnelly, J. S., 'Cork Market: Its Role in the Nineteenth-Century Irish Butter Trade', *Studia Hibernica* XI (1971)

Donnelly, J. S., 'The Irish Agricultural Depression of 1859–64', *Irish Economic and Social History* III (1976)

Donnelly, J. S., *The Land and the People of Nineteenth-Century Cork*, London and Boston 1975

Donnelly, J. S., *Landlord and Tenant in Nineteenth-Century Ireland*, Dublin 1973

Ensor, R. C. K., 'Some Political and Economic Interactions in Late Victorian England', *Transactions of the Royal Historical Society* XXXI (1949)

Eversley, Lord [G. J. Shaw Lefevre], *Gladstone and Ireland. The Irish Policy of Parliament, 1850–1894*, London 1912

Finegan, A. B., 'The Land War in South-East Galway, 1879–90', (unpublished M.A. thesis, University College, Galway, 1974)

Foster, R. F., *Charles Stewart Parnell: The Man and his Family*, Hassocks 1976

Gardiner, A. G., *The Life of Sir William Harcourt*, London 1923

Garvin, J. L., and J. Amery, *The Life of Joseph Chamberlain*, 6 vols, London 1932–69

Gibbon, P. J., 'Arensberg and Kimball Revisited', *Economy and Society* II, No. 4 (Nov. 1973)

Gibbon, P. J., 'Colonialism and the Great Irish Famine of 1845–49', *Race and Class* XVII, No. 2 (1975)

Gibbon, P. J., *The Origins of Ulster Unionism: The Formation of Popular Protestant Politics and Ideology in Nineteenth-Century Ireland*, Manchester 1975

Hammond, J. L., *Gladstone and the Irish Nation*, London 1938

Handley, J. E., *The Irish in Modern Scotland*, Cork 1947

Harrison, H., *Parnell Vindicated. The Lifting of the Veil*, London 1931

Harvie, C., 'Ideology and Home Rule: J. Bryce, A. V. Dicey and Ireland, 1880–1887', *English Historical Review* XCI (1976)

Harvie, C., 'Ireland and the Intellectuals, 1848–1922', *New Edinburgh Review*, No. 38/39 (summer/autumn 1977)

Haslip, J., *Parnell: A Biography*, London 1936

Hawkins, R., 'Gladstone, Forster, and the Release of Parnell, 1882–8', *Irish Historical Studies* XVI, No. 64 (Sep. 1969)

Hawkins, R., 'Government versus Secret Societies: The Parnell Era' in T. D. Williams, ed., *Secret Societies in Ireland*, Dublin and New York 1973

Hawkins, R., 'Liberals, Land and Coercion in the Summer of 1880: The Influence of the Carraroe Ejectments', *Journal of the Galway Archaeological and Historical Society* XXXIV (1974–75)

Hazel, M. V., 'The Young Charles Stewart Parnell', *Eire–Ireland* VIII 1973

Hobsbawm, E. J., and G. Rudé, *Captain Swing*, 2nd ed., Harmondsworth 1973

Hoppen, K. T., 'Landlords, Society and Electoral Politics in Mid-Nineteenth-Century Ireland', *Past and Present* LXXV (1977)

Horn, P. L. R., 'The National Agricultural Labourers' Union in Ireland, 1873–9', *Irish Historical Studies* XVII, No. 67 (Mar. 1971)

Hurst, M., *Parnell and Irish Nationalism*, London 1968

Kee, R., *The Green Flag: A History of Irish Nationalism*, London 1972

Kennedy, R. E., *The Irish Emigration, Marriages and Fertility*, Berkeley and London 1973

Kolbert, C. F., and T. O'Brien, *Land Reform in Ireland: A Legal History of the Irish Land Problem and its Settlement* (Cambridge University, Department of Land Economy, Occasional Paper No. 3) Cambridge 1975

Lane, P. G., 'An Attempt at Commercial Farming in Ireland after the Famine', *Studies* LXI (spring 1972)

Larkin, E., 'Church, State and Nation in Modern Ireland', *American Historical Review* LXXX (1975)

Larkin, E., 'The Devotional Revolution in Ireland, 1850–75', *American Historical Review* LXXVII (1972)

Larkin, E., *The Roman Catholic Church and the Creation of the Modern Irish State, 1878–1886*, Philadelphia and Dublin 1975

Lee, J. J., 'Irish Agriculture', *Agricultural History Review* XVII, Pt 1 (1969)

Lee, J. J., *The Modernisation of Irish Society, 1848–1918*, Dublin 1973

Lee, J. J., 'The Ribbonmen' in T. D. Williams, ed., *Secret Societies in Ireland*, London and New York 1973

Lyons, F. S. L., *Charles Stewart Parnell*, London 1977

Lyons, F. S. L., 'Charles Stewart Parnell' in B. Farrell, ed., *The Irish Parliamentary Tradition*, Dublin and New York 1973

Lyons, F. S. L., 'The Economic Ideas of Parnell' in M. Roberts, ed., *Historical Studies* II, London 1959

Lyons, F. S. L., *Ireland since the Famine*, London 1971

Lyons, F. S. L., *John Dillon: A Biography*, London 1968

Lyons, F. S. L., *Parnell* (Dublin Historical Association, Irish History Series, No. 3) Dundalk 1963

Lyons, F. S. L., 'The Political Ideas of Parnell', *Historical Journal* XVI, No. 4 (Dec. 1973)

McCann, E., *War and an Irish Town*, Harmondsworth 1974

MacPherson, C. B., *The Life and Times of Liberal Democracy*, Oxford 1977

Mansergh, N. S., *The Irish Question, 1840–1921*, 3rd ed. (of *Ireland in the Age of Reform and Revolution*, 1940), London 1975

Marlow, J., *Captain Boycott and the Irish*, London 1973

Moody, T. W., 'Anna Parnell and the Land League', *Hermathena* CXVII (summer 1974)

Moody, T. W., ed., *The Fenian Movement*, Cork 1968

Moody, T. W., 'Fenianism, Home Rule and the Land War, 1850–91' in T. W. Moody and F. X. Martin, ed., *The Course of Irish History*, Cork 1967

Moody, T. W., 'Irish-American Nationalism', *Irish Historical Studies* XV, No. 60 (Sep. 1967)

Moody, T. W., 'The New Departure in Irish Politics, 1878–9' in H. A. Cronne, T. W. Moody and D. B. Quinn, ed., *Essays in British and Irish History in Honour of James Eadie Todd*, London 1949

Morley, J., *The Life of William Ewart Gladstone*, 3 vols, London 1903

Norman, E. R., *A History of Modern Ireland*, London 1971

O'Brien, C. C., *Parnell and his Party, 1880–1890*, Oxford 1957

O'Brien, J. B., 'The Land and the People of Nineteenth-Century Cork', *Journal of the Cork Historical and Archaeological Society* LXXX, No. 232 (1975)

O'Brien, J. V., *William O'Brien and the Course of Irish Politics, 1881–1918*, California 1976

O'Brien, M. and C. C., *A Concise History of Ireland*, London 1972

O'Brien, R. B., *The Life of Charles Stewart Parnell, 1846–1891*, 2nd ed., 2 vols, London 1899

O'Brien, W., *The Parnell of Real Life*, London 1926

Ó Broin, L., *Fenian Fever: An Anglo-American Dilemma*, London 1971

Ó Broin, L., 'The Invincibles' in T. D. Williams, ed., *Secret Societies in Ireland*, Dublin and New York 1973

Ó Broin, L., *The Prime Informer: A Suppressed Scandal*, London 1971

Ó Broin, L., *Revolutionary Underground: The Story of the Irish Republican Brotherhood, 1858–1924*, Dublin 1976

O'Connor, Sir J., *A History of Ireland, 1798–1924*, 2 vols, London 1925

O'Day, A., *The English Face of Irish Nationalism: Parnellite Involvement in British Politics, 1880–86*, Dublin 1977

O'Donovan, J., *The Economic History of Live Stock in Ireland*, Dublin and Cork 1940

O'Farrell, P., *England and Ireland since 1800*, London 1975

O'Farrell, P., *Ireland's English Question: Anglo-Irish Relations, 1534–1970*, London [1971]

O'Flaherty, L., *The Life of Tim Healy*, London 1927

Ó Gráda, C., 'Agricultural Head Rents, Pre-Famine and Post-Famine', *Economic and Social Review* V, No. 3 (Apr. 1974)

Ó Gráda, C., 'The Investment Behaviour of Irish Landlords, 1850–75: Some Preliminary Findings', *Agricultural History Review* XXXIII Pt 2 (1975)

Ó Gráda, C., 'A Note on Nineteenth-Century Irish Emigration Statistics', *Population Studies* XXXIX (1975)

Ó Gráda, C., 'Seasonal Migration and Post-Famine Adjustment in the West of Ireland', *Studia Hibernica* XIII (1973)

Ó Lúing, S., 'A Contribution to the Study of Fenianism in Bréifne' *Bréifne* III, No. 10 (1967)

O'Neill, B., *War for the Land of Ireland*, Dublin 1933

O'Shea, K. [Mrs C. S. Parnell], *Charles Stewart Parnell: His Love Story and Political Life*, 2 vols, London 1914

Ó Tuathaigh, G., *Ireland before the Famine, 1798–1848*, Dublin 1972

Ó Tuathaigh, G., 'Nineteenth-Century Irish Politics: The Case for Normalcy', *Anglo-Irish Studies* I (1975)

Palmer, N. D., 'Irish Absenteeism in the 1870s', *Journal of Modern History* XII (1940)

Palmer, N. D., *The Irish Land League Crisis*, New Haven and London 1940

Patterson, H., 'Refining the Debate on Ulster', *Political Studies* XXIV (1976)

Pollard, H. B. C., *The Secret Societies of Ireland: Their Rise and Progress*, London 1922

Pomfret, J. E., *The Struggle for Land in Ireland, 1800–1923*, Princeton 1930

Reid, Sir T. W., *Life of the Rt Hon. W. E. Forster*, 2nd ed., 2 vols, London 1888

Ryan, D., *The Fenian Chief: A Biography of James Stephens*, Dublin 1967

Ryan, D., *The Phoenix Flame: A Study of Fenianism and John Devoy*, London 1937

Sheehy-Skeffington, F., *Michael Davitt, Revolutionary Agitator and Labour Leader*, London 1908

Solow, B. L., *The Land Question and the Irish Economy, 1870–1903*, Cambridge, Mass. 1971

Staehle, H., 'Statistical Notes on the Economic History of Irish Agriculture, 1847–1913', *Journal of the Statistical and Social Inquiry Society of Ireland*, XVIII (1950–51)

Steele, E. D., 'Gladstone and Ireland', *Irish Historical Studies* XVII, No. 65 (Mar. 1970)

Steele, E. D., 'Ireland for the Irish', *History* LIV (1972)

Steele, E. D., *Irish Land and British Politics: Tenant Right and Nationality, 1865–1870,* Cambridge 1974

Strauss, E., *Irish Nationalism and British Democracy,* London 1951

Sullivan, M., *No Man's Land,* Dublin 1943

Tierney, M., *Croke of Cashel: The Life of Archbishop Thomas William Croke, 1823–1902,* Dublin 1976

Vaughan, W. E., 'Landlord and Tenant Relations in Ireland between the Famine and the Land War, 1850–78' in L. M. Cullen and T. Smout, ed., *Comparative Aspects of Scottish and Irish Economic and Social History,* Edinburgh 1977

Vaughan, W. E., 'A Study of Landlord and Tenant Relations in Ireland between the Famine and the Land War' (abstract of unpublished Ph.D. thesis, Trinity College, Dublin, 1974), *Irish Economic and Social History* I (1974)

Walsh, B. M., 'Marriage Rates and Population Pressure in Ireland, 1871 and 1911', *Economic History Review* XXIII (Apr. 1970)

Woods, C. J., 'The Catholic Church and Irish Politics, 1879–92', (unpublished Ph.D. thesis, University of Nottingham, 1968)

Woods, C. J. 'Ireland and Anglo-Papal Relations, 1880–85', *Irish Historical Studies* XVIII, No. 69 (Mar. 1972)

Woods, C. J., 'The Politics of Cardinal McCabe, Archbishop of Dublin, 1879–85', *Dublin Historical Record* XXVI, No. 3 (Jun. 1973)

Addendum

E. Foner, 'Class, Ethnicity and Radicalism in the Gilded Age: The Land League and Irish America', *Marxist Perspectives* I, No. 2 (summer 1978), which appeared too late to be noticed in the present work, is a valuable study making important claims for the significant role of the Land League in unifying Irish–American political opinion.

Index